"Well, I don't see any point in looking any farther. It was probably just one of those wild rumors."

NETIZENS

On the History and Impact of Usenet and the Internet

Michael Hauben
Ronda Hauben

IEEE Computer Society Press
Los Alamitos, California

Washington • Brussels • Tokyo

Library of Congress Cataloging-in-Publication Data

Hauben, Michael.
Netizens: on the history and impact of usenet and the internet / Michael Hauben, Ronda Hauben.
p. cm.
Includes bibliographical references (p).
ISBN 0-8186-7706-6
1. Internet (Computer network)—History. 2. Information superhighway. I. Hauben, Ronda. II. Title.
TK5105.875.I57H386 1997
004.67 ' 8—dc21

97-5920
CIP

IEEE Computer Society Press
10662 Los Vaqueros Circle
P.O. Box 3014
Los Alamitos, CA 90720-1314

IEEE Computer Society Press Order Number BP07706
Library of Congress Number 97-5920
ISBN 0-8186-7706-6

Additional copies may be ordered from:

IEEE Computer Society Press
Customer Service Center
10662 Los Vaqueros Circle
P.O. Box 3014
Los Alamitos, CA 90720-1314
Tel: +1-714-821-8380
Fax: +1-714-821-4641
Email: cs.books@computer.org

IEEE Service Center
445 Hoes Lane
P.O. Box 1331
Piscataway, NJ 08855-1331
Tel: +1-908-981-1393
Fax: +1-908-981-9667
mis.custserv@computer.org

IEEE Computer Society
13, Avenue de l'Aquilon
B-1200 Brussels
BELGIUM
Tel: +32-2-770-2198
Fax: +32-2-770-8505
euro.ofc@computer.org

IEEE Computer Society
Ooshima Building
2-19-1 Minami-Aoyama
Minato-ku, Tokyo 107
JAPAN
Tel: +81-3-3408-3118
Fax: +81-3-3408-3553
tokyo.ofc@computer.org

Publisher: Matt Loeb
Acquisitions Editor: Bill Sanders
Developmental Editor: Cheryl Smith
Advertising/Promotions: Tom Fink
Production Editor: Lisa O'Conner

Printed in the United States of America by BookCrafters

The Institute of Electrical and Electronics Engineers, Inc

To Floyd Hoke-Miller
who helped us recognize the importance of the Cybernetic Revolution
and to Norman O. Thompson and William Rohler
for their commitment to this revolution.

Foreword

Netizens: On the History and Impact of Usenet and the Internet is an ambitious look at the social aspects of computer networking. It examines the present and the turbulent future, and especially it explores the technical and social roots of the "Net". A well told history can be entertaining, and an accurately told history can provide us valuable lessons. Here follow three lessons for inventors and a fourth for social engineers. Please test them out when reading the book.

Keep projects simple at the beginning. Projects tend to fail, so the more one can squeeze into a year the better the chance of stumbling onto a success. Big projects do happen, but there is not enough time in life for very many of them, so choose carefully.

Innovate by taking something old and something new and putting them together in a new way. In this book the "something new" is invariably the use of a computer network. For example, ancient time-sharing computer systems had local "mail" services so their users could communicate. But the real power of e-mail was when mail could be distributed to distant computers and all the networked users could communicate. Similarly, Usenet is a distributed version of preexisting bulletin-board-like systems. The spectacularly successful World Wide Web is just a distributed version of a hypertext document system. It was remarkably simple, and seemingly obvious, yet it caught the world by complete surprise. Here is another way to state this lesson:

If a feature is good, then a distributed version of the feature is good. And vice-versa.

Keep on the lookout for "something new" or for something improved enough to make a qualitative difference. For example, in the future we will have home computers that are always on and connected to the Net. That is a qualitative difference that will trigger numerous innovations.

We learn valuable lessons by trying out new innovations. Neither the original ARPANET nor Usenet would have been commercially viable. Today there are great forces battling to structure and control the information superhighway, and it is invaluable that the Internet and Usenet exist as working models. Without them it would be quite easy to argue that the information superhighway should have a top-down hierarchical command and control structure. After all, there are numerous working models for that.

It seems inevitable that new innovations will continue to make the future so bright that it hurts. And it also seems inevitable that as innovations permeate society the rules for them will change. I am confident that Michael

Hauben and Ronda Hauben will be there to chronicle the rapidly receding history and the new future, as "Netizens" increasingly becomes more than a title for a book.

Thomas Truscott
Durham, North Carolina
December 1995

Preface: What is a Netizen?

The story of Netizens is an important one. In conducting research five years ago online to determine people's uses of the global computer communications network, I became aware that there was a new social institution, an electronic commons, developing. It was exciting to explore this new social institution. Others online shared this excitement. I discovered from those who wrote me that the people I was writing about were citizens of the Net, or Netizens.

I started using local bulletin board systems in Michigan in 1985. After seven years of participation on both local hobbyist-run computer bulletin-board systems and the global Usenet, I began to research Usenet and the Internet. I found these online discussions to be mentally invigorating and welcoming of thoughtful comments, questions and discussion. People were friendly and considerate of others and their questions. This was a new environment for me. Little thoughtful conversation was encouraged in my high school. Since my daily life did not provide places and people to talk with about real issues and real world topics, I wondered why the online experience encouraged such discussions and consideration of others. Where did such a culture spring from, and how did it arise? During my sophomore year of college in 1992, I was curious to explore and better understand this new online world.

As part of course work at Columbia University, I explored these questions. One professor encouraged me to use Usenet and the Internet as places to conduct research. My research was real participation in the online community, exploring how and why these communications forums functioned. I posed questions on Usenet, mailing lists, and freenets. Along with my questions, I would attach some worthwhile preliminary research. People respected my questions and found the preliminary research helpful. The entire process was one of mutual respect and sharing of research and ideas, fostering a sense of community and participation. I found that on the Net people willingly help each other and work together to define and address issues important to them. These are often important issues that the conventional media would never cover.

My initial research concerned the origins and development of the global discussion forum Usenet. For my second paper, I wanted to explore the larger Net, what it was, and its significance. This is when my research uncovered the remaining details that helped me recognize the emergence of Netizens. There are people online who actively contribute to the development of the

Net. These people understand the value of collective work and the communal aspects of public communications. These are the people who discuss and debate topics in a constructive manner, who e-mail answers to people and provide help to newcomers, who maintain FAQ files and other public information repositories, who maintain mailing lists, and so on. These are the people who discuss the nature and role of this new communications medium. These are the people who as citizens of the Net I realized were Netizens. However, these are not all people. Netizens are not just anyone who comes online. Netizens are especially not people who come online for individual gain or profit. They are not people who come to the Net thinking it is a service. Rather, they are the people who understand it takes effort and action on each and everyone's part to make the Net a regenerative and vibrant community and resource. Netizens are people who decide to devote time and effort into making the Net, this new part of our world, a better place. Lurkers are not Netizens, and vanity home pages are not the work of Netizens. While lurking or trivial home pages do not harm the Net, they do not contribute either.

The term Netizen has spread widely since it was first coined. The genesis comes from net culture based on the original newsgroup naming conventions. Network wide Usenet newsgroups included net.general for general discussion, net.auto for discussion of autos, net.bugs for discussion of unix bug reports, and so on. People who used Usenet would prefix terms related to the online world with the word net, similar to the newsgroup terminology. So there would be references to net.gods, net.cops or net.citizens. My research demonstrated that there were people active as members of the network, which the words net citizen do not precisely represent. The word citizen suggests a geographic or national definition of social membership. The word Netizen reflects the new non-geographically based social membership. So I contracted net.citizen to Netizen.

Two general uses of the term Netizen have developed. The first is a broad use to refer to anyone who uses the Net, for whatever purpose. Thus, the term netizen has been prefixed in some uses with the adjectives good or bad. The second use is closer to my understanding. This definition is used to describe people who care about Usenet and the bigger Net and work towards building the cooperative and collective nature which benefits the larger world. These are people who work towards developing the Net. In this second case, Netizen represents positive activity, and no adjective need be used. Both uses have spread from the online community, appearing in newspapers, magazines, television, books and other off-line media. As more and more people join the online community and contribute towards the nurturing of the Net and towards the development of a great shared social wealth, the ideas and values of Netizenship spread. But with the increasing commercialization and privatization of the Net, Netizenship is being challenged. During such a period, it is valuable to look back at the pioneering vision and actions that made the Net possible and examine the lessons they provide. That is what we have tried to do in these chapters.

Michael Hauben
New York and Beppu
November 1995
netizens@computer.org

Introduction: On the Development and Significance of the Participatory Global Computer Network

A new millennium is approaching. To welcome this transition to a new era, computers and people around the world are interconnecting and interacting in a manner that is unprecedented. There are modest estimates that as many as 27 million people and a million computers are connected via the Net. And the number is growing every day. Yet very few people know how the Net has evolved, and only a few have a perspective as to what its future direction should be.

This is a book about the creation and development of the participatory global computer network. It is about the history of the Net and the impact it is having on the lives of people today. The goal of this book is to provide needed perspective, to make it possible to understand what impact the Net has had on the present and can have on the future of our society.

The following questions have been helpful to this research:

1. What is the vision that has inspired or guided people at each step?
2. What was the social or technical problem or need that they were trying to solve?
3. What can be done to help to nourish the further extension and development of the Net and the social advance that the Net represents?
4. How can the Net be made available to a broader set of people?

One Net pioneer recently described how those who were involved in the early days of networking did not understand what particular changes their work would lead to, but they did understand that what they were doing would fundamentally change the world. He described how he realized that once two people across the continent could communicate via this new technology, then it would be possible for people around the world to communicate.

For those who are just becoming acquainted with Usenet and the Internet, Part I will provide an introduction to the online world and to some of the advantages of this new world. A glossary of acronyms is provided at the end of the book. Readers already familiar with the Net may want to start with

Part II, "The Past". All readers should find Part III, "And the Future?" and Part IV, "Contributions Toward Developing a Theoretical Framework," useful. Readers may choose to begin with any particular section that is of interest, since each has been written to be read independently. These articles are intended to contribute toward documenting the significance and nature of this eighth wonder of the world and the global communication it makes possible.

This collection of articles was written over a four-year period. During that period, there have been changes in the administration and means of access to the Net. Like leaves falling in a moving stream, however, to understand the direction and significance of the current moment, it is important to look at where the development is coming from. This collection of articles has been gathered to focus on the broader context and long-term development of Usenet and the Internet, to provide the reader with some of the needed background to be able to contribute to the current events as they unfold.

Today people around the world are communicating via these new technologies, and this communication is having a profound impact on their lives. Knowing the details of how this participatory global computer network was built will make it possible to build on the achievement that it represents. Knowing where these developments have come from can help one to judge what is the next step forward. The creation of time-sharing, packet switching and the Global Computer Network they have made possible are providing a powerful thrust forward for those who understand and are able to utilize these new communication technologies.

Ronda Hauben
New York City
March 1997

Contents

PART 1

The Present

What Has Been Created and How

1

The Net and Netizens

The Impact the Net Has on People's Lives

Welcome to the 21st Century. You are a Netizen (a Net Citizen), and you exist as a citizen of the world thanks to the global connectivity that the Net makes possible. You consider everyone as your compatriot. You physically live in one country but you are in contact with much of the world via the global computer network. Virtually, you live next door to every other single Netizen in the world. Geographical separation is replaced by existence in the same virtual space.

The situation I describe is only a prediction of the future, but a large part of the necessary infrastructure currently exists. The Net—or the Internet, BITNET, FIDOnet, other physical networks, Usenet, VMSnet, and other logical networks—has rapidly grown to cover all of the developed countries in the world.[1] Every day, more computers are attached to the existing networks, and every new computer adds to the user base—at least twenty-seven million people are interconnected today.

We are seeing a revitalization of society. The frameworks are being redesigned from the bottom up. A new, more democratic world is becoming possible. As one user observed, the Net has "immeasurably increased the quality of . . . life." The Net seems to open a new lease on life for people. Social connections that were never before possible, or relatively hard to achieve, are now facilitated by the Net. Geography and time are no longer boundaries. Social limitations and conventions no longer prevent potential friendships or partnerships. In this manner Netizens are meeting other Netizens from far away and close by that they might never have met without the Net.

A new world of connections between people—either privately, from individual to individual, or publicly, from individuals to the collective mass of many on the Net—is possible. The old model of distribution of information from the central Network Broadcasting Company is being questioned and challenged. The top-down model of information being distributed by a few for mass consumption is no longer the only news. Netnews brings the power of the reporter to the Netizen. People now have the ability to broadcast their observations or questions around the world and have other people respond. The computer networks form a new grassroots connection that allows excluded sections of society to have a voice. This new medium is unprecedented. Previous grassroots media have existed for much smaller groups of people. The model of the Net proves the old way does not have to be the only way of networking. The Net extends the idea of networking, of making connections with strangers that prove to be advantageous to one or both parties.

The complete connection of the body of citizens of the world that the Net makes possible does not yet exist, and it will be a struggle to make access to the Net open and available to all. However, in the future we might see the expansion of what it means to be a social animal. Practically every single individual on the Net today is available to every other person on the Net. International connection exists on the same level with local connection. Also, the computer networks allow a more advanced connection between the people who are communicating. With computer communication systems, information and thoughts are connected to people's names and electronic-mail addresses. On the Net, one can connect to others who have similar interests or whose thought processes he or she enjoys.

Netizens make it a point to be helpful and friendly—if they feel it will be worthwhile. Many Netizens feel they have an obligation to be helpful, answer queries, and follow up on discussions; to put their opinions into the pot of opinions. Over a period of time the voluntary contributions to the Net have built it into a useful connection to other people around the world. When I posted the question, "Is the Net a Source of Social/Economic Wealth?" many people responded. Several corrected my calling the Net a source of accurate information. They pointed out that it was also a source of opinions. However, readers can train themselves to figure out the accurate information from the breadth of opinions. Presented here is an example of the broad range of views and opinions that I was able to gather from my research on the Net. The Net can be a helpful medium to help one understand the world. Only by seeing many points of view can one figure out his or her position on a topic.

Net society differs from off-line society by welcoming intellectual activity. People are encouraged to be thoughtful and to present their ideas to the Net. People are allowed to be intellectually interesting and interested. This intellectual activity forms a major part of the online information that is carried by the various computer networks. Netizens can interact with other people to help add to or alter that information. Brainstorming among different types of people produces robust thinking. Information is no longer a fixed commodity or resource on the Net. It is constantly being added to and improved collectively. The Net is a grand intellectual and social commune in the spirit of the collective nature present at the origins of human society. Netizens working together continually expand the store of information worldwide. One person called the Net an untapped resource because it provides an alternative to the normal channels and ways of doing things. The Net allows for the meeting of minds to form and develop ideas. It brings people's thinking processes out of isolation and into the open. Every user of the Net gains the role of being special and useful. The fact that every user has his or her own opinions and interests adds to the general body of specialized knowledge on the Net. Each Netizen thus becomes a special resource valuable to the Net. Each user contributes to the whole intellectual and social value and possibilities of the Net.

LICKLIDER'S VISION

The world of the Netizen was envisioned more than twenty-five years ago by J. C. R. Licklider. Licklider brought to his leadership of the Department of Defense's ARPA Information Processing Techniques Office (IPTO) a vision of "the intergalactic computer network." He shared this vision with others when he spoke as a representative from ARPA. Licklider was a prophet of the Net. In the 1968 paper, "The Computer as a Communication Device," written with Robert Taylor, they established several principles from their observations on how the computer would play a helpful role in human communication.[2] They clarified their definition of communication as a creative process, differentiating between communication and the sending and receiving of information. For example, when two tape recorders send to or receive information from each other, that is not communication. They wrote:

> *We believe that communicators have to do something nontrivial with the information they send and receive. And . . . to interact with the richness of living information—not merely in the passive way that we have become accustomed to using books and libraries, but as active participants in an ongoing process, bringing something to it through our interaction with it, and not simply receiving from it by our connection to it. . . . We want to emphasize something beyond its one-way transfer: the increasing significance of the jointly constructive, the mutually reinforcing aspect of communication—the part that transcends "now we both know a fact that only one of us knew before." When minds interact, new ideas emerge. We want to talk about the creative aspect of communication.*[3]

Licklider and Taylor defined four principles for computers to make a contribution toward human communication:

1. Communication is defined as an interactive creative process.
2. Response times need to be short to make the "conversation" free and easy.
3. Larger networks form out of smaller regional networks.
4. Communities form out of affinity and common interests.

Licklider and Taylor's understandings from their 1968 paper have stood the test of time and do represent the Net today. In a later paper Licklider co-wrote with Albert Vezza, "Applications of Information Networks,"[4] they explore the possible business applications of information networks. Licklider and Vezza's survey of business applications in 1978 falls short of the possibilities Licklider and Taylor outlined in their 1968 paper and represent but a tiny fraction of the resources the Net currently embodies.

In the 1968 paper, Licklider and Taylor focused on the Net being comprised of a network of networks. While other researchers at the time focused on the sharing of computing resources, Licklider and Taylor kept an open mind:

> *The collection of people, hardware, and software—the multi-access computer together with its local community of users—will become a node in a geographically distributed computer network. Let us assume for a moment that such a network has been formed. . . . Through the network of message processors, therefore, all the large computers can communicate with one another. And through them, all the members of the supercommunity can communicate—with other people, with programs, with data, or with a selected combinations of those resources.*[5]

Their concept of the sharing of both computing and human resources matches the modern Net. The network of various human connections quickly forms, changes its goals, disbands, and reforms into new collaborations. The fluidity of such group dynamics leads to a quickening of the creation of new ideas. Groups can form to discuss an idea, focus in or broaden out, and re-form to fit the new ideas that have been worked out.

Netnews, IRC (Internet Relay Chat), mailing lists, and mud/mush/moo/m** (various of the discussion tools available on the Net) are extremely dynamic. Most can be formed immediately for either short- or long-term use. As interests form or events occur, discussion groups can be created. (for example, the mailing list 9NOV89-L was formed after the fall of the Berlin Wall in November 1989 and continued in order to discuss German unification.)

The virtual space created on noncommercial computer networks is accessible universally. The content on commercial networks, such as Compuserve or America Online, is only accessible to those who pay to belong to that particular network. The space on noncommercial networks is accessible from the connections that exist, whereas social networks in the physical world generally are connected by limited gateways. So the capability of networking on computer nets overcomes limitations inherent in noncomputer social networks. This is important because it reduces the problems of population growth. Population growth need not mean limited resources any more—rather that very growth of population now means an improvement of resources. Thus, growth of population can be seen as a positive asset. This is a new way of looking at people in our society. Every new person can mean a new set of perspectives and specialties to add to the wealth of knowledge of the world. This new view of people could help improve the view of the future. The old model looks down on population growth and people as a strain on the environment rather than seeing the intellectual contribution these individuals can make. However, access to the Net will need to be universal for the Net to fully utilize the contribution each person can make. As long as access is limited, the Net and those on the Net lose the full advantages it can offer. But also, the people on the Net need to be active in order to bring about the best possible use of the Net.

Licklider foresaw that the Net would allow for people of common interests, who are otherwise strangers, to communicate. Much of the magic of the Net is the ability to make a contribution of your ideas and then be connected to utter strangers. He saw that people would connect to others via this Net in ways that had been much harder in the past. Licklider observed as the ARPANET grew to span two continents that this physical connection allowed for wider social collaborations to form. This was the beginning of computer data networks facilitating connections of people around the world.

My research on and about the Net was very exciting for me. When posting inquiries, I usually received the first reply within a couple of hours. The feeling of receiving that very first reply from a total stranger is always exhilarating! That set of first replies from people reminds me of the magic of electronic mail (e-mail). It is nice that there can be reminders of how exciting this new form of communication really is—so that the value of this new use of computers is never forgotten.

CRITICAL MASS

The Net has grown so much since its birth in the 1960s that a critical mass of people and interests has been reached. This collection of individuals adds to the interests and specialties of the whole community. Most people can now gain something from the Net, while at the same time helping it out. There are enough people online now that most anyone new coming online will find something of interest. People are meshing intellects and knowledge to form new ideas. Larry Press made this clear by writing:

> *I now work on the Net at least 2 hours per day. I've had an account since around 1975 but it has only become super important in the last couple of years because a critical mass of membership was reached. I no longer work in LA, but in cyberspace.*

Although the original users of the Net were from technical and scientific communities, many of them found it valuable to explore the Net for more than just technical reasons. Today, many different kinds of people are connected to the Net. The original users of the Net (then several test-beds of network research) were from only a few parts of the world. Now people of all ages, from most parts of the globe, and of many professions, make up the Net. The original prototype networks (the ARPANET in the United States, the network of the National Physical Laboratory in the United Kingdom, CYCLADES in France, and other networks around the world) developed the necessary physical infrastructure for a fertile social network to develop. Einar Stefferud wrote of this social connection:

> *The ARPANET has produced several monumental results. First, it provided the physical and electrical communications backbone for development of the latent social infrastructure we now call "THE INTERNET COMMUNITY."*[6]

Many different kinds of people comprise the Net. The university community sponsors access for a broad range of people (students, professors, staff, retired professors, etc.). Many businesses are also connected. A "K–12 Net" that invites younger people to be a part of the online community exists. Special bulletin-board software exists to connect personal computer users to the Net. Various Unix bulletin-board systems exist to connect other users. It is virtually impossible to tell what kinds of people connect to public bulletin board systems (BBSs), as only a computer (or terminal) and modem are the prerequisites to connect. Many, if not all, FIDOnet BBSs (a very common BBS type) have at least e-mail, and many also participate in the larger Net through a gateway to Netnews. Prototype community network systems are forming around the world (for example, Cleveland Free-Net, Wellington Citynet, Santa Monica Public Electronic Network (PEN), Amsterdam Digital City, Hawaii FYI, National Capital Free-Net and others in Canada). Access via these community systems can be as easy as visiting the community library, and membership is open to all who live in the community.

In addition to the living body of resources this diversity of Netizens represents, there is also a continually growing body of digitized data that forms another resource. Whether it is Netizens digitizing great literature of the past (for example, the Gutenberg Project or Project Bartleby), people gathering otherwise obscure or non-mainstream material (for example, on various religions, unusual hobbies, gay lifestyle), or Netizens contributing new and original material, the Net follows in the great tradition of other public institutions, such as the public library or the principles behind public education. The Net shares with these institutions that it serves the general populace. The data available is just part of the treasure. Often, living Netizens provide pointers to this digitized store of publicly available information. Many of the network access tools have been created on the principle of being available to everyone. The best example is the method of connecting to file repositories via FTP (File Transfer Protocol) by logging in as an "anonymous" user. Most, if not all, World Wide Web sites, Wide Area Information Systems (WAIS), and gopher sites are open to all users of the Net. It is true that the Net community is smaller than it will be eventually, but the Net has reached a point of general usefulness no matter who you are.

This evidence is exactly why it is a problem for the Net to come under the control of commercial entities. Once commercial interests gain control, the Net will be much less powerful for the ordinary person than it is currently. The interests of commercial entities are different from those of the common person. Those pursuing commercial objectives are only interested in making a profit. A user of Compuserve or a similar commercial network pays for access by the hour. If this were extended to the present-day Net, the Netiquette of being helpful would have a price tag attached to it. If people had had to pay by the minute during the Net's development, very few would have been able to afford the network time needed to be helpful to others.

The Net has only developed because of the hard work and voluntary dedication of many people. It has grown because the Net is in the control and power of the people at the grassroots level, and because these people developed it. People's posts and contributions to the Net have been the developing forces.

GRASSROOTS

The Net brings people together. People connecting with other people can be powerful. There is power in numbers. The Net allows individuals to realize their power. The Net, uncontrolled by commercial entities, becomes the gathering, discussion, and planning center for many people. The combined efforts of people interested in communication has led to the development and expansion of the global communications system. What's on the Net? Usenet, Free-Net, e-mail, library catalogs, FTP sites, free software, electronic newsletters and journals, Multi-User Domain/Dungeon (mud)/mush/moo, Internet Relay Chat (IRC), the multimedia World Wide Web (WWW) and many kinds of data banks. Different servers, such as WWW, WAIS, and gophers attempt to order and to make it easier to utilize the vast variety of information. There are both public and private services and sources of information. The public and free services often have come about through the voluntary efforts of one or a few people. These technologies allow a person to help make the world a better place by making his or her unique contribution available to the rest of the world. People who have been overlooked or have felt unable to contribute to the world, now can. The networks allow much more open and public interaction over a much larger body of people than possible before. The common people have a unique voice that is now being aired in a new way.

This new communications system introduces every single person as someone special and in possession of a useful resource. Several people described how important is the ability to connect to others at a grassroots level:

> *Simple—by access to a vast amount of information and an enormous number of brains*—BRIAN MAY

> *For a geographically sparse group as it is, MU* allows people to get to know one another, the relevant newsgroup gives a sense that there's a community out there and things are happening, and an associated FTP site allows art and writing to be distributed.*—SIMON RABOCZI

> *In summary, nets have helped enormously in the dissemination of information from people knowledgeable in certain areas which would be difficult to obtain otherwise.*—BRENT EDWARDS

> *I get to communicate rapidly and cheaply with zillions of people around the world.*—ROSEMARY WARREN

The following examples show how this is possible.

People are normally unprotected from the profit desires of large companies. Steven Alexander from California uses the Net to try to prevent overcharging at gas stations, a good example of the power of connecting people to uphold what is fair and in the best interest of the common person in society.

FROM: STEVEN ALEXANDER

I have started compiling and distributing (on the newsgroup ca.driving) a list of gas prices at particular stations in California to which many people will contribute and keep up to date, and which, I hope, will allow consumers to counteract what many of us suspect is the collusive (or in any case, price-gouging) behavior of the oil companies.

A user from Germany also reported using the Net to muckrake:

A company said they were a [nonprofit organization]. . . . Someone looked them up in the [nonprofit] . . . Register . . . [and] they did not exist there. . . . Another one said, that he had contact with the person who sent the letter . . . only [under] another company-name, and that he simply ignored this person since he looked like a swindler. So they are swindlers, and people from the Net proved it to us, we then of course did not engage with them at all.

The Net has proven its importance in other contemporary critical situations. As the only available line of communication with the rest of the world, the Net helped defeat the attempted coup in the former Soviet Union in 1990. The members of the coup either did not know about or understand the role the Russian RELCOM network could play. The connections proved resilient enough for information about the coup to be communicated inside and out of the country in time to inform the world and encourage resistance.[7]

The Net has also proven its value by providing an important medium for students. Students participating in the Chinese pro-democracy movement have kept in touch with others around the world via their fragile connection to the Net. The Net provided an easy way of evading government censors to get news around the world about events in China and to receive encouraging feedback. Such feedback is vital when fighting on seems impossible or wrong. Similarly, students in France used the French Minitel system to organize a successful fight against plans by the French government to restrict admission to government-subsidized universities.

The information flow on the Net is controlled by those who use the Net. Users actively provide the information they and others want. There is much more active participation than what is provided for by other forms of mass media. Television, radio, and magazines are all driven by those who own them and who determine who will write. The Net gives people a medium they can control. This control of information is a great power not available before to the common person. For example, Declan McCreesh describes how this makes possible access to the most up-to-date information.

FROM: DECLAN MCCREESH

You get the most up to date info. that people around the world can get their hands on, which is great. For instance, the media report who wins a Grand Prix, what happened and not a great deal more. On the net, however, you can get top speeds, latest car and technology developments, latest rumors, major debates as to whether Formula 1 or Indy cars are better etc.

The Net helps to make the information available more accurate because of the many-to-many or broadcast and read and write capability. That new capability, which is not normally prevalent in our society, allows an actual participant or observer to report something. This gives the power of the reporter to the individual, allowing the source to report. This new medium allows everyone online to make a contribution. The old media instead controls who reports and what they say. The possibility of eyewitness accounts via the Net can make the information more accurate. This also opens up the possibility of a grassroots network, where information is passed from person to person around the world. Thus, German citizens learned about the Chernobyl explosion from the Net before the government decided to release the information to the public through traditional media. The connection is people to people rather than government to government. Citizen journalists can now distribute to more than those they know personally. The distribution of the writings of ordinary people is the second step after the advent of the inexpensive personal computer in the early 1980s. The personal computer and printer allowed anyone to produce mass quantities of documents. Personal publishing is now joined by wide personal distribution.

Not only is grassroots reporting possible, but the assumption that filtering is necessary has been challenged. People can learn to sort through the various opinions themselves. Steve Welch disagreed that the Net is a source of more accurate information, but agreed that people develop discriminatory reading skills.

FROM: STEVE WELCH

When you get more information from diverse sources, you don't always . . . get more accurate information. However, you do develop skills in discerning accurate information. . . . Or rather, you do if you want to come out of the info-glut jungle alive.

Governments that rule based on control of information will succumb eventually to the tides of democracy. As Dr. Sun Yat-Sen of the Chinese Democracy Movement (c. 1919) once said, "The worldwide democratic trend is mighty. Those who submit to it will prosper and those who resist it will perish." The Net reintroduces the basic idea of democracy as the grassroots people power of Netizens. Governments can no longer easily keep information from people.

Many groups that do not have an established form of communications available to them have found the Net to be a powerful tool. For example, for people far away from their homeland, the Net provides a new link.

FROM: GODFREY NOLAN

The Net has immeasurably increased the quality of my life. I am Irish, but I have been living in England for the past five years. It is a lot more difficult to get information about Ireland than you would expect. However a man called Liam Ferrie who works in Digital in Galway, compiles a newspaper on the weeks events in Ireland and so I can now easily keep abreast of most developments in Irish current affairs, which helps me feel like I'm not losing touch when I go home about twice a year. It is also transmitted to about 2000 Irish people all over the first and third worlds.

FROM: MADHUR K. LIMDI

I read your above posting and wanted to share my experience with you. I have been a frequent reader of news in usenet groups!! Such as soc.culture.indian misc.news.southasia and both of these keep me reasonably informed about the happenings in my home country india.

Also in the United States, the Net has provided stable communications for people of various religious and sexual persuasions. Many other communities have also found the Net to be a excellent medium to help increase communication.

FROM: GREGORY G. WOODBURY

We will be going to a march on Washington and are coordinating our plans and travel with a large number of other folks around the country via e-mail and conversations on Usenet.

FROM: JANN VANOVER

I'm a member of a Buddhist organization and just found a man in Berkeley who keeps a Mailing List that sends daily guidance and discussions for this group. So I get a little religious boost when I log on each day.

FROM: CAROLE E. MAH

For me and for many of my friends, the Net is our main form of communication. Almost every aspect of interpersonal communication on the network has a gay/lesbian/bi aspect to it that forms a tight and intimate acquaintanceship which sometimes even boils over into arguments and enmities.

This network of connections, friends, enemies, lovers, etc. facilitates political goals that would not otherwise be possible (organizing letter-writing campaigns about the Gays in the Military Ban via the ACT-UP list, being able to send e-mail directly to the White House, finding out about activism, bashing, etc. in other states and around the world, etc.).

FROM: ROBERT DEAN

As a member of the science fiction community, I've met quite a few people on the net, and then in person.

COMMUNICATION WITH NEW PEOPLE

In many Netizens' lives the Net has alleviated feelings of loneliness, which seem common in today's society. The Net's ability to help people network both socially and intellectually makes it valuable and irreplaceable in their lives. This is forming a group of people who want to keep the Net accessible and open to all.

The Net brings together people from diverse walks of life and makes it easier for these people to communicate. It brings them together in the same virtual space and removes the impact or influence of first impressions.

FROM: MALCOLM HUMES

I'm in awe of the power and energy linking thousands into a virtual intellectual coffee-house, where strangers can connect without the formalities of face to face rituals (hello, how are you today . . .) to allow a direct-connect style of communication that seems to transcend the "how's the weather" kind of conversation to just let us connect without the bullshit.

Strangers are no longer strange on the Net. People are free to communicate without limits, fears, or apprehension. It used to be that there was a rather generous atmosphere that thrived on the Net and that welcomed new users. People were happy to help others, often as a return for the help they had received. Things have changed, and the welcome to newcomers is not as universally friendly, but there are still many online who are helpful to new users, and goodwill still overpowers any unfriendly comments.

FROM: JEAN-FRANÇOIS MESSIER

My use of the Net is to get in touch with more people around the world. I don't know for what, when, how, but that's important for me. Not that I'm in a small town, far from everybody, but that I want to be able to establish links with others. In fact, because of those nets I use, I would !NOT! want to go to a small town, just because the phone calls would be too expensive. I have to say that I'm not an expressive person. I'm not a great talker, nor somebody who could make shows. . . . I'm more an "introvert".

Yet Jean-François wrote me. This is just one example of the social power of the Net. Another Netizen comments on how the Net helped her befriend strangers.

FROM: LAURA GOODIN

Last summer I was traveling to Denver and I used a listserv mailing list to find out whether a particular running group I run with had a branch there. They did, and I had a wonderful time meeting people with a common interest (and drinking beer with them); I was no longer a stranger.

BROADENED AND WORLDLY PERSPECTIVES

Easy connection to people and ideas from around the world has a powerful effect. Awareness that we are members of the human species, which spans the entire globe, changes a person's point of view. It is a broadening perspective. It is easy for people to assume a limited point of view if they are only exposed to certain ideas. The Net brings the isolated individual into contact with other people, experiences, and views from the rest of the world. Exposure to many opinions gives a person the chance to consider multiple views before settling on a specific opinion. Having access to the "marketplace of ideas" allows a person to make a reasoned judgment.

FROM: JEAN-FRANÇOIS MESSIER

My attitudes to other peoples, races and religions changed, since I had more chances to talk with other peoples around the world. When first exchanging mail with people from Yellowknife, Yukon, I had a real strange feeling: Getting messages and chatting with people that far from me. I noticed around me that a lot of people have opinions and positions about politics that are for themselves, without knowing others

Because I have a much broader view of the world now, I changed and am more conciliatory and peaceful with other people. Writing to someone you never saw, changes the way you write, also, the instancy of the transmission makes the conversation much more "live" than waiting for the damn slow paper mail. Telecommunications opened the world to me and changed my visions of people and countries. . . .

FROM: ANTHONY BERNO

I could not begin to tell you how different my life would be without the Net. My life would be short about a dozen people, some of them central, I would be wallowing in ignorance on several significant subjects, and my mind would be lacking many broadening and enlightening influences.

FROM: HENRY CHOY

More things to look at. Increased perspective on life. The computer network brings people closer together, and permits them to speak at will to a large audience. I recommend that the telecommunications and computer industry make large scale computer networking accessible to the general public. It's like making places accessible to the handicapped. People brought closer together will release some existing social tensions. People need to be heard, and they need to hear.

FROM: PAUL READY

You don't have to go to another country to meet people from there. It is not the same as personally knowing them, but I always pay special attention to information from people outside the States. They are likely to have a different perspective on things.

FROM: LEANDRA DEAN

I love to study people, and the Net has been the best possible resource to this end. The Net is truly a window to the world, and without it we could only hope to physically meet virtually thousands of people every day to gain the same insights. I shudder to think about how different and closed in my life would be without the Net.

MATERIAL CHANGES TO PEOPLE'S LIVES AND LIFESTYLES

The time spent online can affect the rest of a person's life. The connections, interfaces, or collaborations between times on and off line form an interesting area of study. Netizens attest to the power of the Net by explaining the effect the Net has had on their lives. Because of the information available and the new connections possible, people have changed the way they live their lives. There are examples of both changes in the material possessions and changes in lifestyle. The changes in lifestyle are probably the more profound changes, but the new connections made possible are also important. Often the material gains are not financial. Rather, worthwhile goods can be redistributed—from those to whom the goods may have lost personal value to those who would value them.

NETIZEN COMMENTS ON MATERIAL CHANGES

FROM: WILLIAM CARROLL

Primarily because of the information and support from rec.bikes, three years ago I gave up driving to work and started riding my bike. It's one of the best decisions I've ever made.

RESPONSE RECEIVED VIA E-MAIL

When I started using ForumNet (a chat program similar to irc, but smaller—[Now called icb]) back in January 1990, I was fairly shy and insecure. . . . I had a few close friends but was slow at making new ones. Within a few weeks, on ForumNet, I found myself able to be open, articulate, and well-liked in this virtual environment. Soon, this discovery began to affect my behavior in "real" face-to-face interaction. I met some of my computer friends in person and they made me feel so good about myself, like I really could be myself and converse and be liked and wanted.

Of course, computer-mediated social interaction is not properly a crutch to substitute for face-to-face encounters, but the ability to converse via keyboard and modem with real people at the other end of the line has translated into the real-life ability for me to reach out to people without the mediating use of a computer. My life has improved. I wouldn't trade my experience with the Net for anything.

FROM: JACK FRISCH

I must begin my comments on the Internet with one simple yet significant statement: the availability and use of the Internet is changing my life profoundly.

FROM: CAROLE E. MAH

I also used to facilitate a vegetarian list, which radically altered many people's lives, offering them access to mail-order foods, recipes, and friendship via net-contact with people who live in areas where non-meat alternatives are readily available.

FROM: JANN VANOVER

Well, the first thing I thought of is purchases I've made through the Net which have "changed my life". I drove my Subaru Station wagon until last fall when I acquired a VW Camper van that I saw on a local Net ad. I wasn't looking for a van, wasn't even shopping for another vehicle, but the second time this ad scrolled by me, I looked into it and eventually bought it. I will certainly say that driving a 23-year-old VW camper van has changed my life! I thought I would be ridiculed, but have found that people have a lot of respect and admiration for this car!

Through the Net, I heard that Roger Waters was going to perform "The Wall" again, an event I had promised myself not to miss, so I made a trip to Berlin (East and West) in 1990 to see this concert. This was CERTAINLY a life changing event, seeing Berlin less than one week after the roads were open with no checkpoints required. I don't think I would have known about it soon enough if not for the Net.

FROM: ROBERT DEAN

As for me, my main hobby is and was playing wargames and role-playing games. Net access has allowed me to discuss these games with players across the world, picking up new ideas, and gathering opinions on new games before spending money on them. In addition, I've been able to buy and sell games via Net connections, allowing me to adjust my collection of games to meet my current interests, and get games that I no longer wanted to people who do want them, whether they live down the road from me in Maryland, or in Canada, Austria, Finland, Germany or Israel. I have also taken an Esperanto course via e-mail, and correspond irregularly in Esperanto with interested parties world wide.

FROM: CARYN K. ROBERTS

Usenet & Internet . . . are available to me at work and by dialup connection to work from home. I have been materially enriched by the use of the Net. I have managed to sell items I no longer needed. I have been able to purchase items from others for good prices. I have saved money and am doing my part to recycle technology instead of adding burdens to the municipal waste disposal service

Using the Net I have also been enriched by discussions and information found in numerous newsgroups from sci.med to sci.skeptic to many of the comp. groups. I have offered advice to solve problems and have been able to solve problems I had by using information in these forums.*

THE NET AS A SOURCE OF ENORMOUS RESOURCES

Before the Net was widely seen as an enormous social network, some were experimenting with the sharing of computing resources. The following are some examples of ways Netizens utilize the information resources available on the Net:

FROM: TIM NORTH

I'm faculty here at . . . University and I use the Net as a major source of technical information for my lectures, up-to-date product information, and informed opinion. As such I find that I am constantly better informed than the people around me. (That sounds vain, but it's not meant to be. It's simply meant to emphasize how strongly I feel that the Net is a superb information resource.)

FROM: R. J. WHITE

I used the Net to find parts for my 1971 Opel GT. I was living in North America at the time, and going through the normal channels, like GM, are no good. The Net was like an untapped resource.

FROM: JOHN HARPER

[My] uses of the network [1] I once asked a question about an obscure point in history of maths on the sci.math newsgroup and got a useful answer from Exeter, UK. Beforehand I had no idea where anyone knowing the answer might be. I had drawn a blank in Oxford. [2] I asked a question about a slightly less obscure point on comp.lang.fortran which generated a long (and helpful) discussion on the Net for a week or two.

FROM: PAUL READY

Yes, it is a worldwide rapid distribution center of information, on topics both popular and obscure. It may not make the information more valuable, but it certainly increases the information, and the propagation of information. To those connected, it is a valuable resource. Flame wars aside, a lot of generally inaccessible information is readily available.

FROM: LEE ROTHSTEIN

Usenet and mailing lists create a group of people who are motivated and capable of talking about a specific topic. The software allows deeply contextual conversations to occur with a minimum of rehash. As experience develops with the medium, each user realizes that the other that he talks to or will talk to generally help him/her, and can do him/her no harm because of the remoteness imposed by the cable.

FROM: LU ANN JOHNSON

Hi! Usenet came to my rescue—I'm a librarian and was working with a group of students on a marketing project. They were marketing a make-believe product—a compact disc of "music hits of the 70's". They needed a source to tell them how much it cost to produce a CD—without mastering, etc. I exhausted all my print resources so I posted the question in a business newsgroup.

Within hours I learned from several companies that it cost about $1.50 to produce a CD :) The students were very grateful to get the information.

FROM: LAURA GOODIN

I teach self-defense, and in rec.martial-art someone posted information about a study on the effectiveness of Mace for self-defense that I had been looking for for years.

FROM: CLIFF ROBERTS

I have been using Internet through a program in New Jersey to bring the fields of Science and Math to grammar school children grades K-8. We have implemented a system where the class rooms are equipped with PC's and are able to dial in to a UNIX system. There they can send e-mail and post questions to a KidsQuest ID. The ID then routes the questions to volunteers with accounts on UNIX. The scientists then answer or give advice of where to find the information they want. Another well accepted feature is to list out the soc.penpals list and e-mail people in different countries that are being studied in the schools.

FROM: JOE FARRENKOPF

I think Usenet is a very interesting thing. For me, it's mostly just a way to pass . . . time when bored. However, I have gotten some very useful things from it. There is one group in particular called comp.lang.fortran, and on several occasions when I've had a problem writing a program, I was able to post to this group to get some help to find out what I was doing wrong. In these cases, it was an invaluable resource

COLLABORATIVE WORK

As new connections are made between people, more ideas travel over greater distances. This allows either like-minded people or complementary people to come in touch with each other. The varied resources of the networks allow these same people to keep in touch even if they would not have been able to be in touch before. Electronic mail allows enough detail to be contained in a message that most, if not all, communications can take place entirely electronically. This medium allows for new forms of collaborative work to form and thrive. New forms of research will probably arise from such possibilities. Here are some examples:

FROM: WAYNE HATHAWAY

One "unusual" use I made of the Net happened in 1977. . . . Along with five other "Net Folks" I wrote the following paper: "The ARPANET TELNET Proto-

col: Its Purpose, Principles, Implementation, and Impact on Host Operating System Design," with Davidson, Postel, Mimno, Thomas, and Walden: Fifth Data Communications Symposium, Snowbird, UT; September 27-29, 1977. What's so unusual about a collaborative paper, you ask? Simply that the six of us never even made a TELEPHONE call about the paper, much less had a meeting or anything. Literally EVERYTHING—from the first ideas in a "broadcast" mail to the distribution of the final "troff-ready" version—was done with e-mail. These days this might not be such a deal, but it was interesting back then.

FROM: PAUL GILLINGWATER

. . . in Vienna was an on-line computer mediated art forum . . . with video conferencing between two cities, plus an on-line discussion in a virtual MUD-type conference later that evening.

RESPONSE RECEIVED VIA E-MAIL

In response to your question about having fun on the net, and being creative, one incident comes to mind. I had met a woman on ForumNet (a system like IRC). She and I talked and talked about all sorts of things. One night, we felt especially artistic. We co-wrote a poem over the computer. I'd type a few words, she'd pick up where I left off (in the middle of sentences or wherever) and on and on. I don't think we had any idea what it was going to be in the end, thematically or structurally. In the end, we had a very good poem, one that I would try to publish if I knew her whereabouts anymore. . . .

IMPROVING THE QUALITY OF EVERYDAY LIFE

Information flow can take various shapes. The strangest and perhaps most interesting one is how emotion can be attached to information flow, although they often seem like two very different things. I received a large number of responses that reported real-life marriages arising from Net meetings. The Net facilitates the meeting of people of like interests. The newness of the Net means we cannot fully understand its impact. However, it is worth noting that people have also broken up online. So while it is a new social medium, a range of dynamics will exist.

FROM: CARYN K. ROBERTS

I have found friends on the Net. A lover. And two of the friends I met, also met online and got married. I attended the wedding (in California).

FROM: SCOTT KITCHEN

I think I can add something for your paper. I met my fiancee 4 years ago over the net. I was at Ohio State, and she was in Princeton, and we started talking about an article of hers I'd read in rec.games.frp. We got to talking, eventually met, found we liked each other, and the rest is history. We were married 31 December 1994.

FROM: GREGORY G. WOODBURY

I met the woman who became my wife when I started talking to the folks at "phs" (the third site of the original Usenet) during the development of Netnews. I would not have been wandering around that area if I hadn't been interested in the development of the net.

FROM: LAURA GOODIN

And now, the BEST story: about eight months ago I was browsing soc.culture.australia and I noticed a message from an Australian composer studying in the US about an alternative tune to "Waltzing Matilda." I was curious, so I responded in e-mail, requesting the tune and just sort of shooting the breeze. We began an e-mail correspondence that soon incorporated voice calls as well. One thing led inexorably to another and we fell in love (before we met face to face, actually). We did eventually meet face to face. Last month he proposed over the Internet (in soc.culture.australia) and I accepted. Congratulatory messages came in from all over the United States, Australia, and New Zealand. Houston (that's his name) and I keep our phone bills from resembling the national debt by sending 10 or 12 e-mails a day (we're well over 1400 for eight months now), and chatting using IRC. A long-distance relationship is hellish, but the pain is eased somewhat by the Internet.

FROM: CHUQ VON ROSPACH

oh, and in the "how the Net made my non-net life better" category, I met my wife via the net. Does that count?

WORK

The fluid connections and the rapidly changing nature of the networks make the Net a welcome medium for those who are job hunting and for those who have jobs to offer. The networks have a large number of people who are looking for jobs. Placing job announcements is easy, and they can be kept available for as long as the job is offered. Résumés can be sent quickly and easily by e-mail. Companies can respond quickly and easily to such submissions, also by e-mail.

Besides finding work, the Net helps people who are currently employed perform their job in the best manner. Many people utilize the Net to assist them with their jobs. Several examples of each follow:

FROM: LAURA GOODIN

My division successfully recruited a highly-qualified consultant (a Finn living in Tasmania) to do some work for us; the initial announcement was over Usenet; subsequent negotiations were through e-mail.

FROM: JJ

I've hired people off the net, and from meeting them in muds, when I find somebody who can THINK. People who can think are hard to find anywhere.

FROM: DIANA GREGORY

I have learned to use UNIX, and as a result may be able to keep/advance in my job due to the 'net.

FROM: NEIL GALARNEAU

It helps me do my job (MS Windows programming) and it helps me learn new things (like C++).

FROM: KIERAN CLULOW

The Internet access provided me by the university has greatly facilitated my ability to both use and program computers and this has had the direct result of improving my grades as well as gaining me a good job in the computer field. Long live the Internet (and make it possible for private citizens to get access!)

FROM: MARK GOOLEY

I got my job by answering a posting to a news-group.

FROM: ANTHONY BERNO

I develop for NEXTSTEP, and the Net is very useful in getting useful programming hints, info on product releases, rumors, etcetera.

FROM: GREGORY G. WOODBURY

Due to contacts made via Usenet and e-mail, I got a job as a consultant at BTL in 1981 after I lost my job at Duke. Part of the qualifications that got me in the door was experience with Usenet.

IMPROVED COMMUNICATIONS WITH FRIENDS

Another way of improving daily life is by making communications with friends easier. The ease of sending e-mail is bringing back letter writing. However, the immediacy of e-mail means less care need be taken in the process of writing. E-mail, IRC, and Netnews make it much easier to keep in touch with friends outside one's local area.

NETIZEN COMMENTS ON IMPROVED COMMUNICATIONS

FROM: BILL WALKER

I also have an old and dear friend (from high school) who lives in the San Francisco area. After I moved to San Diego, we didn't do very well at keeping in touch. She and I talked on the phone a couple of times a year. After we discovered we were both on the net, we started corresponding via e-mail, and we now exchange mail several times a week. So, the Net has allowed me to keep in much closer touch with a good friend. It's nothing that couldn't be done by phone, or snail mail, but somehow we never got around to doing those things. E-mail is quick, easy and fun enough that we don't put it off.

FROM: ANTHONY BERNO

Incidentally, it is also one of my primary modes of communication with my sister (who lives in N.Z.) It's more meditative than a phone call, faster than a letter, and cheaper than either of them.

FROM: CAROLE E. MAH

It also facilitates great friendships. Most of my friends, even in my own town, I met on the network. This can often alleviate feelings of loneliness and "I am the only one, I must be a pervert" feelings among queer people just coming out of the closet. They have a whole world of like-minded people to turn to on Usenet, on Bitnet lists, on IRC, in personal e-mail, on BBSs and AOL type conferences, etc..

FROM: JANN VANOVER

Apart from purchases, I have been contacted by: 1) a very good friend from college who I'd lost track of. She got married to a man she met in a singles newsgroup (they've been married 2 years+) 2) someone who went to my high school, knew a lot of the same people I did, but we didn't know each other. We are now "mail buddies" 3) an old girlfriend of my brothers. They went out for eight years, but I learned more about her from ONE e-mail letter than I had ever learned when meeting her in person.

FROM: GODFREY NOLAN

Above all it helps me keep in touch with friends who I would inevitably lose otherwise. The Net helps those that move around for economic reasons to lessen the worst aspects of leaving your friends in the series of places that you once called home. It's the best thing since sliced bread.

PROBLEMS

With all of the positive uses and advantages of the Net, it is not perfect. The blind view of people on the Net seems to shield most, but not everyone. For example, there is a relatively large male-to-female population ratio on the Net. Women online can feel the effects of this difference. Women who have easily identifiable user names or IDs are prone to be the center of much attention. While that might be good, much of that attention can be of a hostile or negative nature. This attention may be detrimental to women who try to be active on the Net. Net harassment can spread against users for other reasons as well. People with unpopular ideas need to be strong to withstand the abuse they may receive from others.

The worst non-people problem seems to be information overflow. Information adds up very quickly, and it can be hard to organize and sort through it all. Technology is now being developed to handle this problem.

FROM: SCOTT HATTON

There is a problem with this brave new world in that a lot of people don't appreciate there's another human being at the other keyboard. Flaming is a real problem—especially in comp.misc. This is all a new facet of the technology as well. People rarely trade insults in real life like they do on Internet. There's a tendency to stereotype your opponent into categories. I think this is because you're not around to witness the results. I find this more on Internet newsgroups than on CompuServe. I think this is down to maturity—a lot of folk on the Internet are students who aren't paying for their time on the system. Those on CompuServe are normally slightly older, not so hot-headed and are paying for their time. Damn. Now I'm at stereotyping now. It just goes to show. . . .

FROM: JOE FARRENKOPF

There is something else I've discovered that is really rather fascinating. People can be incredibly rude when communicating through this medium. For example, some time ago, I posted a question to lots of different newsgroups, and many people felt my question was inappropriate to their particular group. They wrote to me and told me so, using amazingly nasty words. I guess it's easier to be rude if you don't have to face a person, but can say whatever you want over a computer.

FROM: BRAD KEPLEY

I get a little irritated with people always claiming someone else is "wasting bandwidth" because they disagree with them. About half the time it turns out that the person being told to shut up was right after all. Then again, when you look at things like alt.binaries.pictures.erotica and other "non-bandwidth-wasting" activities, it seems almost comical to me when someone says this. There is nothing more wasteful than 95% of what Usenet is used for. It's a joke to say that a particular person is 'wasting' it. To say that they are off-topic makes more sense. I guess this is just a gripe rather than what you are looking for. Wasting bandwidth again. :)

CONCLUSION

For the people of the world, the Net provides a powerful means for peaceful assembly. Peaceful assembly allows people to take control of their lives, rather than that control being in the hands of others. This power deserves to be appreciated and protected. Any medium or tool that helps people hold or gain power is something special that has to be protected.

The Net has made a valuable impact on human society. My research has demonstrated that people's lives have been substantially improved via their connection to the Net. This sets the basis for providing access to all in society. Using similar reasoning, J. C. R. Licklider and Robert Taylor believed that access to the then-growing information network should be made ubiquitous. They felt that the Net's value would depend on high connectivity. In their 1968 article, "The Computer as a Communication Device," they argued that the network's impact upon society will depend on how available the network is to society as a whole.[8]

Society will improve if Net access is made available everyone. Only if access is universal will the Net itself advance. Ubiquitous connection is necessary for the Net to encompass all possible resources. One Net visionary, Steve Welch, responded to my research by calling for universal access:

If we can get to the point where anyone who gets out of high school alive has used computers to communicate on the Net or a reasonable facsimile or successor to it, then we as a society will benefit in ways not currently understandable. When access to information is as ubiquitous as access to the phone system, all Hell will break loose. Bet on it.

Steve is right. "All Hell will break loose" in the most positive of ways imaginable. The philosophers Thomas Paine and Jean Jacques Rousseau, and all other fighters for democracy would have been proud.

Similar to past communications advances such as the printing press, mail, and the telephone, the Global Computer Communications Network has already fundamentally changed our lives. Licklider predicted that the Net would fundamentally change the way people live and work. It is important to try to understand the Net's impact, so as to help extend and reinforce this achievement.

NOTES

1. See *Internet Society News* 2 (Spring 1993) inside back cover for a map showing Net penetration around the world. Larry Landweber maintains and posts updated connectivity maps and tables. See, for example, ftp://ftp.cs.wisc.edu/connectivity-table/Connectivity_Table.text
2. J. C. R. Licklider and Robert W. Taylor, "The Computer as a Communication Device," reprinted in *In Memoriam: J. C. R. Licklider 1915–1990* (Palo Alto, Calif: Digital Systems Research Center, 1990); originally published in *Science and Technology*, April 1968. Available online at http://memex.org/licklider.html
3. *Ibid.*, 21.
4. *Proceedings of IEEE* 66 (November, 1978): 43–50.
5. Licklider and Taylor, 32.
6. Stefferud, Einar *et al.*, "Quotes from Some of the Players," *ConneXions—The Interoperability Report* 3 (10): 21.
7. See article by Larry Press posted on the comp.risks newsgroup, September 6, 1991.
8. Licklider and Taylor, 40.

Much thanks is owed to the many who contributed Usenet posts and e-mail responses to requests for examples of how the Net has changed people's lives. Only a few of the many replies received could be quoted but all contributed to this work.

The following people who were quoted indicated that their e-mail addresses be included:

Jim Carroll	jcarroll@jacc.com
Kieran Clulow	u1036254@vmsuser.acsu.unsw.edu.au

Robert Dean	robdean@access.digex.net
Jack Frisch	frischj@gbms01.uwgb.edu
Scott Hatton	100114.1650@compuserve.com
Lu Ann Johnson	ai411@yfn.ysu.edu
Jean-François Messier	messier@igs.net
Larry Press	lpress@isi.edu
Clifford A. Roberts	cliffr@donuts0.bellcore.com
Chuq Von Rospach	chuqui@plaidworks.com
Gregory G. Woodbury	news@wolves.durham.nc.us

An early version of this chapter by Michael Hauben was made available online in Summer 1993. A revised version was printed in the *Amateur Computerist* 6 (Fall/Winter 1994–1995).

Appendix to Chapter 1
The Posts for the Research

1. Is the Net a Source of Social/Economic Wealth? & Other Thoughts
2. The Magic of E-Mail—Beginnings
3. Does the Net Bring Real-Life Advantages?
4. Looking for Exciting Uses of the Net
5. Connecting Others to the Net
6. Looking for Stories of Net Harassment
7. Does the Net Help You Be Creative or Have Fun?

IS THE NET A SOURCE OF SOCIAL/ECONOMIC WEALTH? & OTHER THOUGHTS

POST
Newsgroups: news.misc, alt.culture.usenet, alt.amateur-comp, sci.econ,
comp.misc, soc.misc, comp.org.eff.talk
Subject: Is the Net a Source of Social/Economic Wealth? & Other Thoughts

There are some notes I have made in trying to form a proposal for a paper I am writing for an Independent Project in College. I would appreciate any ideas or suggestions in e-mail. Please send e-mail to me at:

hauben@cs.columbia.edu

The points I would most like some feedback on are 1-6.

However, it might be useful if anyone is interested in the question of whether or not the Net (and its users) is a source of creation of economic, social, or intellectual wealth. This might make an interesting discussion via public follow-ups.

MY PROPOSAL

I want to understand this idea of Internetworking and cooperative attitude. The social connections and collaborations that the Internet and other parts of the global computer network make possible are new and very important. This more widespread communication brings the general populace of the world in better intersection/global social intercourse.

Question about Battle for use and right to utilize. And people have taken the battle up in order to keep access open and for all. Forces for restriction and censorship. Only through battle that net has stayed open. Net *inherently* allows people choice to speak.

Is it secret that Usenet did restrict corporations/private from abusing Net as it is research-oriented and developed only via because it was an experiment? (NOT A FLAME)

*****1. What does communication over the networks mean? Is it "value-added" somehow in that any response might bring something added into the amount of information or value. Does communication via the Net represent the quicker building by people on other people's work thus representing advancements (in ideas, products, production, etc..)

*****2. Does the Net represent intellectual wealth? Does the net represent the growth and increase in Gross National Product /Wealth or Wealth of Nations? (What if any theoretical background is there to this?) William Petty maybe Bacon, or Royal Society.

*****3. What does the Net make possible? Is the "Communication" on the net different than normal/before modes of communication? Does the widespread of connections and zero-time (Ability to turnaround information and/or publication or exchange of information in almost no time) of producing things prove revolutionary?

*****4. Provides a Forum that facilitates Intellectual Ferment

*****5. Net makes knowing real conditions of society possible—because you have a "direct" connection to "many" people—the masses.

*****6. Accurate Information (similar to point 5)

7. How does the network make these "connections" possible easier than before? (These connections being finding people in the world to enjoy exchanging information, debating, connecting intellectually or whimsically—helping to find people who you can or want to interact/communicate with.)

8. Who has access and can gain the advantage of this service/connection/resource/revolution? Is this only an advantaged group of people, or is it growing quickly? Or should it grow quicker? What direction is access going towards for? What is Clinton/etc.. doing? (Business?) Is there a fight against the continued openness and/or growing openness of letting the great body of people communicate accurate information that is normally controlled in normal modes of mass media.

Thanks
—Michael Hauben

THE MAGIC OF E-MAIL—BEGINNINGS

POST:
Subject: The Magic of E-Mail—Beginnings
Newsgroups: comp.mail.misc, alt.amateur-comp, alt.folklore.computers,
soc.college, alt.culture.usenet, news.misc

Do you remember the first e-mail message you sent? Do you remember the first e-mail you replied to? Do you remember the first response you received in e-mail? Do you remember the first e-mail response you received seemingly before you sent out the original message? <chuckle>—Do you remember the magic?—

Excitement is a key word, as is immense usefulness. Whether you are a scientist, a student or a casual user, person-to-person communication via the computer is *VERY* exciting. Remember your first time and write it down. Keep your memory and save it for posterity. You . . . We . . . are all part of what is a relatively early period of the computer communications revolution. Save your experience in order to help recognize and remember this period of change—this beginning.

———

And if you do write down (or type in) your first (or first couple) of real *exciting* e-mail beginnings please e-mail them to me. I will try to post a summary to usenet. And talk about e-mail from e-mail or e-mail in response to Usenet, or e-mail in connection with something before the current e-mail or what you think might come in the future.

Thanks,
—Michael

DOES THE NET BRING REAL-LIFE ADVANTAGES?

POST:
Article 891 of alt.amateur-comp:
Newsgroups: soc.singles, rec.autos, soc.college, alt.amateur-comp,
soc.culture.usa, comp.misc
From: hauben@cs.columbia.edu (Michael Hauben)
Subject: Does the Net Bring Real-Life Advantages?
Message-ID: <C5II5B.KJr@cs.columbia.edu>
Summary: Has the Net improved or broadened your off-line world?
Date: Thu, 15 Apr 1993 06:31:58 GMT

How has the Net changed your life? Has anyone who has used the Net actually been able to add to their off-line life successfully? I am doing research for a paper for college, and I am interested in the material changes that the Net helps develop through the increased communication.

Has access to the Net and your participation on it allowed you to do something that you wouldn't have done before—offline? Anything would be interesting—meeting people/new friends, marrying someone from on-line, joining groups, certain opportunities that were there because of the connection via the Net, etc.. I am interested in hearing about actions caused by use of any part of the Net (Usenet, talk, e-mail, etc.). The *KEY* point is that the cause or facilitator of the event needs to be because of the Net somehow. If you have any interesting, or useful stories, or ideas please either e-mail them to me, or post a follow-up to this message!

Thanks,
—Michael

LOOKING FOR EXCITING USES OF THE NET.

POST:
Subject: Looking for Exciting Uses of the Net

I am doing research for a paper for a college independent study about the net and communications. I would appreciate hearing about using any part of the net: Usenet News/Netnews, irc, e-mail, mailing-lists, Freenets, FTP, wais, gopher, etc..

I would like to know about people's uses of the network(s) that have been especially interesting, valuable and/or exciting. I want to hear about people's delights and also about disappointments using the Net. Please do NOT send me information about use by businesses or corporations for commercial purposes. I am NOT interested in commercial or proprietary uses. I AM interested in uses that serve the public, that are open, that serve science, research, education, and social aims and objectives. I am also interested in uses that serve to help people personally on their work (programming, et al.) or hobbies.

Either e-mail me at hauben@cs.columbia.edu or post a public follow-up. Both if possible.

Thanks,
—Michael Hauben

CONNECTING OTHERS TO THE NET

Subject: Connecting Others to the Net
Newsgroups: news.misc, alt.culture.usenet, alt.amateur-comp, comp.misc, soc.misc

Hi,

I would like to hear from people the various ways in how they have introduced others to Usenet and the Internet. What ways have been successful and relatively inexpensive in getting family, friends, and other associates connected?

I am interested because I am interested in people's attempts (consciously or unconsciously) to further the expansion of the Net.

To the further expansion of the Net! :)
—Michael Hauben

LOOKING FOR STORIES OF NET HARASSMENT

POST:
Subject: Looking for Stories of Net Harassment
Newsgroups: alt.censorship, news.misc, comp.mail.misc, alt.amateur-comp

Have you ever experienced harassment on the net? Have you tried to utilize the communicative aspects of Usenet, E-mail or other computer networking capabilities but wound up discouraged? Please let me know if you have been the victim of censorship, harassment or some kind of blocking at some point in your usage of computer-facilitated communication. If so, do you think this "discouragement" was wrong or vicious, or malicious.

Thank you,
—Michael

And lastly maybe it would be helpful to find out why you thought you were treated such.

DOES THE NET HELP YOU BE CREATIVE OR HAVE FUN?

POST:
Subject: Does the Net Help You Be Creative or Have Fun?
Newsgroups: soc.culture.usa, talk.bizarre, alt.mud, alt.irc, news.misc, alt.culture.usenet, alt.amateur-comp, rec.music.misc, rec.arts.misc

I am conducting research for an independent study about computer and communication for college. So far I have asked and received many "serious" answers and replies dealing with work, keeping in touch with friends around the world, etc. However I am also interested in what effect the Net (Netnews, the Internet, other Nets, FTP, irc, gopher, etc.) has on either creative endeavors you might have, or just plain silly or fun things. Has access to the Net helped you in any creative hobbies you might have, or just given you a chance to have fun?

For example. have your music tastes expanded, or do you know about more plays happening, have you learned about other who are musicians, or artists or writers? And if so, have you gotten a chance to jam, paint, write, or somehow help each other? Have there been any on-going creative collaborative music/art/literary experiments? How has the computer assisted communication helped you be creative or expanded your boundaries?

The other side is, have you found more ways to just have fun, or of new ways of having fun.

As I am not exactly sure where to post this message, I would appreciate any suggestions as to other groups to post the message to.

Thanks!
—Michael Hauben

2

The Evolution of Usenet
The Poor Man's ARPANET

In Fall of 1992, an undergraduate college student had a term project to do. The assignment required that the project be the result of using resources beyond research from books. His professor proposed that students consider interviewing people, sending letters, and other means of gathering data.

The student had done some reading and found a source describing how computer networks had become "the largest machine that man has ever constructed—the global telecommunications network"[1] The student decided that he would do his research on this computer network that spans the globe and that many computer users have access to. He planned to use the network as much as possible to conduct his research.

After reading some of the few books and articles that he could find to describe the global computer network, he gathered a few significant quotes and wrote a brief introduction stating that he was trying to determine the subject for a term paper. He asked if the quotes seemed accurate and if readers had any advice. Some of the quotes were from a journal article discussing how the disintegration of Eastern Europe was in part due to the lack of free speech impeding computer development.[2] The student also asked if there was any evidence that the Berlin Wall had fallen because of new developments in computer communications. He raised several other questions and included quotes from his reading. Then he took this research proposal and posted it on the computer network news system called Usenet.

Posting is sending an article to be propagated around the world. Usenet is similar to an electronic news magazine or a world town meeting. It has various newsgroups organized by different topic areas in a variety of languages and on many different subjects. And the number of newsgroups is continually growing.

Net users can post articles to many of the newsgroups, can respond to someone else's article, or can send a message in response to the author of an article via e-mail.

The student posted his questions to a number of newsgroups. In his post, he wrote:

> *The Largest Machine: Where it came from and its importance to Society*
>
> *I propose to write a paper concerning the development of "The Net." I am interested in exploring the forces behind its development and the fundamental change it represents over previous communications media. I will consult with people who have been involved with Usenet from its beginnings, and the various networks that comprise the Computer Network around the world. I wish to come to some understanding of where the Net has come from, so as to be helpful in figuring out where it is going to.* [3]

Within a few hours, responses began to arrive via electronic mail. Among the responses he received was one from a biologist in Russia who explained how pressure for the free flow of information was a force for change in Russia. "Hello," the scientist wrote, "I would also consider another side of the coin: the world is divided on people who use the possibility of computer-mediated communications and the ones who do not. But I am not a specialist in your field."

"And as one from the East," he continued, "I know well that the Internet is the first and only connection to the rest of the world for us in Russia. But unfortunately, to get it there is not too easy. . . . If you have some questions you think I could answer—please send me email. . . ."

The student sent the Russian scientist some excerpts from an article about the lack of free speech in Eastern Europe and its effects on computer development and asked some questions about the excerpts. In response to the questions, the Russian scientist answered:

> *[The] first time I saw a computer was in 1985, when our institute got one. It was [an] Apple II. At that time, I had no idea about what a network is, and it was a time when PCs just started to appear in the environment of [the] "normal Russian". . . As you can see, it was already Gorbachev's time, and communists were stopping (or already were unable) to keep a very strong control on information flow in the society. So it was easier to access the PC in our institute than to get permission to use photocopy devices. Then the number of PCs was fast growing, and now we have more then 15 PCs, but still no Internet connection. . . . Most scientific institutes now have access to the net. But usually it is restricted to the possibility of using the electronic mail system. . . .*

I would say that in the past networks had no direct effect on the life of people there, and now they become more and more important. One of the points is that it is practically the only way to communicate with the West. Telephone lines are so bad that to send a FAX message is almost impossible, conventional mail will reach the address with [a] probability of 50% and it will take at least one month, . . . [but] e-mail . . . will be received in 12-24 (!) hours. I have used it for the last year and never had any problems. I am lucky that one of my relatives has e-mail! I guess, you understand how the possibility to communicate is important for [the] scientific community. . . .

The student received many other responses. One came from a German student who described how the Berlin Wall had fallen because of the increased communication made possible by computer networks. The German student pointed out that accurate information about events such as the Chernobyl nuclear power plant explosion had become available to people who were no longer dependent upon government channels as their only source of information. There were responses from a teacher in Australia, a businessman in California, a net pioneer, and many others.

The student decided to prepare another post. He had become interested in how far and wide the network reached and in who would have access to the post he was making. He posted the following message:

Subject: I want to hear from the four corners of the Net—that means YOU!

I would like to hear from EVERYONE on the Net-Frontier. If you think you are weird or abnormal (or special) in terms of net-connections or usenet connections, please tell me about it. .

To the further expansion of the Net! :)

He received answers from more than fifty people around the world, from France to India and Africa. A response from Japan explained:

Yes, I believe I'm connected through some sort of hokey mechanism, but that's just because I'm in Japan. Connectivity doesn't register highly on the importance scale here. Takes a few hours for mail to get from one side of Tokyo to the other.

So what makes me so "special" as far as net connections go? A few things. I can not receive most newsgroups and can not post to any. Yet a friend of mine in the same building as me (on another floor) receives a mostly different set of newsgroups and can post to a few. The interesting bit about any group we both get is that we don't always get the same articles. Japan, the "leader" of technology, doesn't know a thing about actually using computers. Just my opinion, of course—my company won't listen to me anyway! Hope this adds to your research. . . .[4]

The student received a response from an employee in a large American company. The writer explained:

> *Not too strange, but I work for a big company that leeches off two small "service providers" for free mail and news feeds. Kind of funny, really. . . . Hey, Usenet broke . . . and I can't receive mail from the Internet anymore, although I can send it.*

He described how the company told him " 'Sorry . . . the problem is with our feeds. We'll try to get them to fix it.' Strange enough, these small services . . . [a medical school and a public access usenet site] wouldn't drop everything to fix our problem. How dare they! Of course MY suggestion, 'PAY THEM SOME MONEY,' was completely ignored."

He went on to explain that he had been told that his company "won't let us have a direct connection to the Internet for security concerns. I understand, but it doesn't make me happy."

A response from Krakow, Poland explained that their site in the Department of Physics at Warsaw University was one of the first four sites in Poland to have access to Usenet.

A response from a French user explained how the government charged a lot of money for an Internet connection in France and thus discouraged use: "It's cheaper to send a 'hello' to someone in the US than to someone 5 kilometers from my desk!," the French user wrote. "If you have a 'stupidity chapter' in your paper, this could fill a few lines."

From Wellington, New Zealand, the student learned that there was a "burgeoning Net Community in Wellington, as there were two Internet connections, one by a private net.enthusiast, and another run by the Wellington City Council on an old PDP-11 computer." They offered the citizens of Wellington "free ftp, telnet, IRC, archie, gopher, E-mail, and Usenet—and all the 1,935 locally carried newsgroups."

A scientist at Bell Telephone Laboratories wrote: "Some people say that many of us at Bell are on the fringe, but we're probably in the core of things in the Internet. :-)"

Other responses came from university students and hobbyists in the United States and from Net users in Germany, Italy, India, and other countries around the world.

The student also received offers of help in finding information including recommendations of books to consult. Some of the responses included offers to send him articles or reports that would be helpful with his research.

Several people wrote describing the unusual or interesting net connections they used to connect to Usenet. A user in South Africa told how he distributed news and e-mail and was trying to gain access to a satellite in order to set connections up with the interior of Africa that lacked the otherwise needed infrastructure. There were many other stories of unusual or pioneering efforts to make connections possible for people to Usenet.

Many people wrote asking for a copy of the paper when it was written. In response to requests that he post a draft of the paper before it was completed, the student wrote a draft and posted it on Usenet. He received several helpful comments. He wrote the final draft, handed it in to his teacher, and posted it on Usenet. A lively discussion ensued. The student's paper had maintained that the ability of users to post on Usenet was a sign that Usenet was democratic. A document describing Usenet to new users that was posted in the new users newsgroup maintained that Usenet was an anarchy. The discussion raised the question of whether there can be an official statement maintaining that something is an anarchy.

A number of people wrote the student asking him if they could distribute the paper more broadly, quote the paper in their upcoming book, or post the paper on their local BBS. Another student who was writing a proposal for his Master's thesis cited the paper as an important source. All this occurred within two weeks of the paper being posted.

The student's experience is but one example of the important educational possibilities represented by Usenet and the worldwide communications network it is part of. Yet there are many people who still know nothing of Usenet, and many who are on Usenet do not realize the important potential it makes possible. In a similar manner, many people do not know how Usenet developed nor the obstacles the networking pioneers were continually faced with in their efforts to create and nourish Usenet. Since the details of how Usenet was created can provide helpful insight into how to deal with the problems encountered as the Net continues to grow, an account of how Usenet was created follows.

USENET IS BORN

Usenet was born in 1979 when Tom Truscott and Jim Ellis, graduate students at Duke University, conceived of creating a computer network to link together those in the Unix community. They met and discussed their idea with other interested students, including Steve Bellovin, a graduate student at the neighboring University of North Carolina at Chapel Hill. Using homemade autodial modems and the Unix-to-Unix copy program (UUCP), the Unix shell, and the *find* command that were being distributed with the Unix operating system Version 7, Bellovin wrote some simple shell scripts to have the computers automatically call each other up and search for changes in the date stamps of the files. If there were such changes, the changed files were copied from one computer to the other.

Soon three computer sites—*duke* at Duke University, *unc* at the University of North Carolina at Chapel Hill and *phs* at the Physiology Department of the Duke Medical School—were hooked together, and a simple program made it possible to connect the three sites.

Gregory G. Woodbury, a Usenet pioneer from Duke University, describes how "News allowed all interested persons to read the discussion, and to (relatively) easily inject a comment and to make sure that all participants saw it."[5]

The program was slow so the students enlisted Stephen Daniel, also a graduate student at Duke, to rewrite the code in the C programming language. Daniel writes:

> *. . . a news program written, I believe, by Steve Bellovin as a collection of shell scripts was already working, but it was slow, taking upwards of a minute of time on an unloaded PDP 11/70 to receive an article. I got involved when I happened to drop in on a conversation between Tom Truscott and Jim Ellis, who were complaining about how slow this news program was. I suggested that if it was so slow it could easily be rewritten in C to run faster. I soon found myself volunteering to do just that.*[6]

Daniel agreed to write the program in C with help from Tom Truscott. This became the first released version of Usenet in the C programming language, which came to be known as A News.

Other people at Duke and the University of North Carolina took part in getting the network debugged. Once the program was functioning on their respective machines, Jim Ellis went to a meeting of what was then the academic Unix users group known as Usenix. In the following account, Tom Truscott describes what happened:

> *James Ellis (jte) gave a short talk and handed out a 5 page "Invitation to a General Access UNIX Network" at the January 1980 Usenix Conference in Boulder, Colorado. We made up 80 copies and they were gobbled up (not surprising, there were a record-smashing 400 attendees). . . . Afterwards, jte mentioned that the audience particularly enjoyed his description of Duke's two home-built 300 baud autodialers.*[7]

The invitation they distributed explained:

> *The initially most significant service will be to provide a rapid access newsletter. Any node can submit an article, which will in due course propagate to all nodes. A "news" program has been designed which can perform this service. The first articles will probably concern bug fixes, trouble reports, and general cries for help. Certain categories of news, such as*

"have/want" articles, may become sufficiently popular as to warrant separate newsgroups. (The news program mentioned above supports newsgroups.)[8]

The invitation urged:

This is a sloppy proposal. Let's start a committee. No thanks! Yes, there are problems. Several amateurs collaborated on this plan. But let's get started now. Once the net is in place, we can start a committee. And they will actually use the net, so they will know what the real problems are.

Several months later, the software for the A News program for Usenet was put on the conference tape for general distribution at the Summer 1980 Usenix meeting in Delaware. The handout distributed at the conference explained, "A goal of USENET has been to give every UNIX system the opportunity to join and benefit from a computer network (a poor man's ARPANET, if you will). . . ."[9]

Daniel explains why the term "poor man's ARPANET" was used:

I don't remember when the phrase was coined, but to me it expressed exactly what was going on. We (or at least I) had little idea of what was really going on on the ARPANET, but we knew we were excluded. Even if we had been allowed to join, there was no way of coming up with the money. It was commonly accepted at the time that to join the ARPANET took political connections and $100,000. I don't know if that assumption was true, but we were so far from having either connections or $$ that we didn't even try. The "Poor man's ARPANET" was our way of joining the Computer Science community and we made a deliberate attempt to extend it to other not-well-endowed members of the community. It is hard to believe in retrospect, but we were initially disappointed at how few people joined us. We attributed this lack more to the cost of autodialers than lack of desire.[10]

The ARPANET, which Daniel refers to, pioneered the networking technology that serves as the foundation of today's global Internet. The first host connected to the ARPANET was the SDS Sigma-7 on Sept. 2, 1969 at the UCLA (University of California at Los Angeles) site. It began passing bits to other sites at SRI (SDS-940 at Stanford Research Institute), UCSB (IBM 360/75 at University of California at Santa Barbara), and Utah (DEC PDP-10 at the University of Utah). There were many unexpected problems and obstacles, but through the collaborative work by the pioneers using the network they were creating, the number of sites steadily increased. By 1977, the ARPANET extended to more than fifty sites, from Hawaii to Norway. Since the project was originally funded under the US Department of Defense's (DOD) Advanced Research Projects Agency (ARPA), only those academic computer science departments with DOD funding had the possibility of access to the ARPANET.

Usenet, however, was available to all who were interested, as long as they had access to the Unix operating system (which in those days was available at a very low cost to the academic and computer research community). And posting and participating in the network was possible at no cost to the individuals who participated, except for the cost of their equipment and the telephone calls to receive or send Netnews (as Usenet was called). Therefore, the joys and challenges of participating in the creation of an ever-expanding network, an experience available to an exclusive few via the ARPANET, became available via Usenet to those without political or financial connections—to the common folk of the computer science community.

As Daniel notes, Usenet pioneers were surprised at how slowly Usenet sites expanded at first. But when the University of California at Berkeley (UCB) joined Usenet, links began to be created between Usenet and the ARPANET, as Berkeley was a site on the ARPANET. At first, it is reported, mailing lists of discussions among Arpanauts (as ARPANET users were called by those on Usenet) were poured into Usenet.[11] This first connection, however, between the ARPANET and Usenet, Daniel reports, only contributed to "the sense of being poor cousins." Daniel explains:

> *It was initially very hard to contribute to those lists, and when you did you were more likely to get a response to your return address than to the content of your letter. It definitely felt second class to be in read-only mode on human-nets and sf-lovers, which were two popular ARPANET mailing lists.*[12]

Daniel also clarifies the different philosophies guiding the development of Usenet as opposed to the ARPANET.

> *Usenet was organized around netnews, where the receiver controls what is received. The ARPANET lists were organized around mailing lists, where there is a central control for each list that potentially controls who receives the material and what material can be transmitted. I still strongly prefer the reader-centered view.*

With the increasing connections to the ARPANET from Usenet, the number of sites on Usenet grew. A map from June 1981 shows the number of different sites on Usenet during this early period (see Figure 1).

There are many stories of frustration as Usenet developed.[13] Despite such frustration, there were many who helped Usenet grow and develop. Unix enthusiasts and pioneers at some large organizations, such as AT&T's Bell Labs, did whatever they could to provide support for Usenet. At one point,

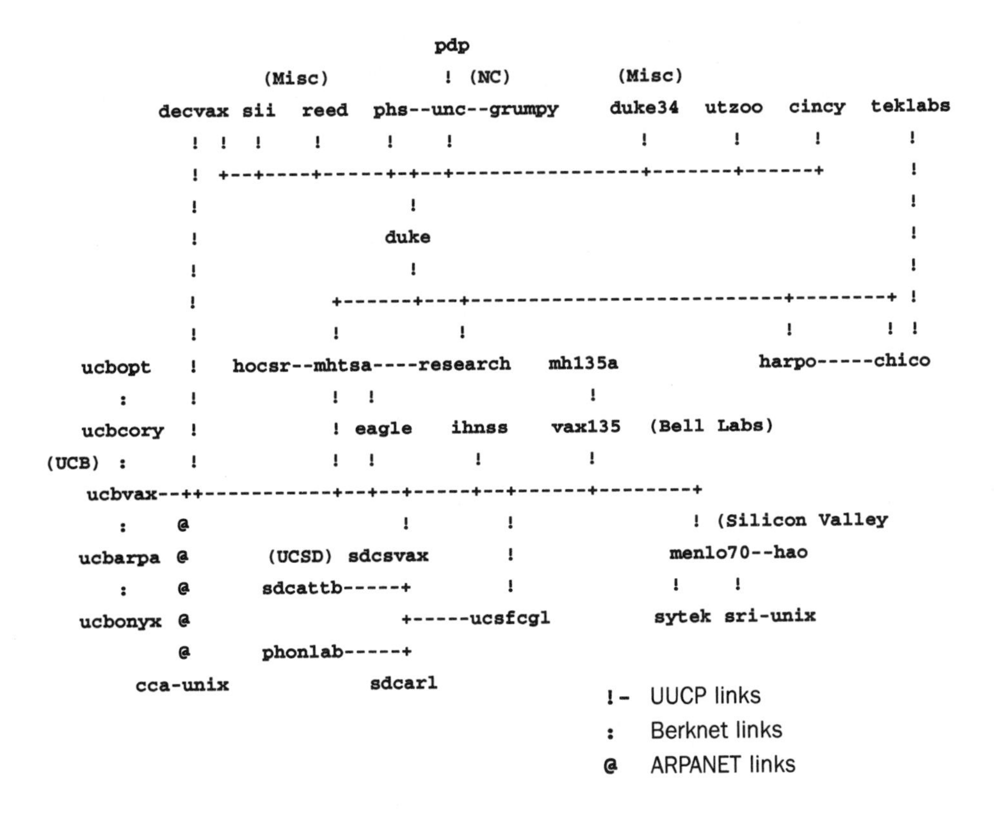

Figure 1. Map of Usenet sites June 1981 (Source: Usenet History Archive)

AT&T realized that it would save millions of dollars if it worked out the bugs to have internal e-mail. In the process it gave support to the Usenet pioneers who were trying to develop more efficient e-mail routing programs. Digital Equipment Corporation (DEC) also supported Usenet in various ways, and the spread of Usenet and Unix encouraged the sale of Unix-based computers from DEC. Usenet newsgroups provided much needed technical help for users of Unix and Unix-based computers.

By 1982, the continuing explosion of Usenet surprised even its most dedicated fans. One of those active on Usenet from its earliest days to the present, Gregory G. Woodbury, describes the shock experienced when the pioneers realized that Usenet was taking a totally unexpected course of development.

> *I do not recall that anyone was quite expecting the explosion that followed. What developed took everybody by surprise. When the direction of evolution took an unexpected turn, and a continental network emerged, spanning the continent from California to North Carolina, and Toronto to San Diego, it was sort of a shock to realize what had happened.*[14]

Statistics presented by Gene Spafford, another Usenet pioneer, at an IETF (Internet Engineering Task Force) meeting in 1988 documented the tremendous growth and development of Usenet. Usenet developed from two articles a day posted at three sites in 1979 to 1,800 articles a day posted at 11,000 sites by 1988.[15]

Year	Number of Sites	Articles/Day	Megabytes/Day
1979	3	~2	—
1980	15	~10	—
1981	150	~20	—
1982	400	~50	—
1983	600	~120	—
1984	900	~225	—
1985	1,300	~375	1+
1986	2,500	~500	2+
1987	5,000	~1000	2.5+
1988	11,000	~1800	4+

Today, Usenet continues to grow in the number of sites participating, in the number of posts it carries, and in the number of newsgroups. Usenet is transported among Unix systems by UUCP connections and via NNTP (Netnews Transfer Protocol) along the Internet, which is the child of the old ARPANET.

Often in the past, pioneers of Usenet were convinced that the load of posts or the number of sites was becoming too great and that further growth could not be sustained. That fear is now facetiously referred to by the phrase "imminent death of the Net predicted." Although each time the problems have seemed insurmountable, they have been investigated and solutions found through the hard work of many Net participants (often referred to on Usenet as netizens).

In the past few years a system of Free-Nets and community networks has begun to develop, many utilizing the Netnews software to make Usenet available to the community for free or at a very low cost. Cleveland Free-Net, sponsored by Case Western Reserve University and other community organizations in Cleveland, Ohio, was the first Free-Net. It used the Netnews software to create a set of local newsgroups reflecting the different community services in the Cleveland area such as the hospitals, public schools, public libraries, and museums. Cleveland Free-Net users also have access to the worldwide newsgroups of Usenet. The software used by such community networks makes it relatively easy to read and post on Usenet and in a variety of local discussion groups. A number of community networks have come on line around the United States and in Canada. Many others are in the planning stages. There is a Free-Net in Erlangen, Germany and in Finland. There are digital cities in the Netherlands and civic networks in Italy and New Zealand. And people with telnet access can join many of these community networks free of charge and thus have e-mail and Usenet access through them.

The ARPANET pioneered important breakthroughs in computer networking technology. It also pioneered the ability to collaborate online and to utilize dispersed resources—both people and computers. Usenet represents the continuation of this tradition by making access to these collaborative research relationships available to a broader set of people. The extension of Usenet has required a great deal of pioneering effort and technical development, but those participating in Usenet have been there to solve the problems.

Writing in 1968 before the creation of the ARPANET, J. C. R Licklider, who has been called the "Father of the ARPANET," and Robert W. Taylor predicted the challenges that would face society with the development of computer networks:

> *First, life will be happier for the on-line individual because the people with whom one interacts most strongly will be selected more by commonality of interests and goals than by accidents of proximity. Second, communication will be more effective and productive, and therefore more enjoyable. Third, much communication and interaction will be with programs and programming models, which will be . . . both challenging and rewarding. And, fourth, there will be plenty of opportunity for everyone (who can afford a console) to find his calling, for the whole world of information, with all its fields and disciplines, will be open to him—with programs ready to guide him or to help him explore. . . .*
>
> *For the society, the impact will be good or bad depending mainly on the question: Will "to be on line" be a privilege or a right? If only a favored segment of the population gets a chance to enjoy the advantage of "intelligence amplification," the network may exaggerate the discontinuity in the spectrum of intellectual opportunity.*
>
> *On the other hand, if the network idea should prove to do for education what a few have envisioned in hope, if not in concrete detailed plan, and if*

> *all minds should prove to be responsive, surely the boon to humankind would be beyond measure.*
>
> *Unemployment would disappear from the face of the earth forever, for consider the magnitude of the task of adapting the networks software to all the new generations of computer coming closer and closer upon the heels of their predecessors until the entire population of the world is caught up in an infinite crescendo of on-line interactive debugging.*[16]

Their vision of an ever-growing part of the population of the world being needed to participate in the debugging and development of the network that will make a new world possible is still a helpful vision. The Wonderful World of Usenet news is a world that needs and will reward one's participation.

NOTES

1. Ithiel de Sola Pool, *Technologies Without Boundaries*, Eli M. Noam, ed. (Cambridge, Mass.: Harvard University Press, 1990), 56.
2. See, for example, Gary L. Geipel, A. Tomasz Jarmoszko, and Seymour Goodman, "The Information Technologies and East European Societies" in *East European Politics and Societies,* 5 (Fall 1991): 394–438.
3. Michael Hauben, post, October, 1992.
4. See also Izumi Aizu, *Cultural Impact on Network Evolution in Japan: Emergence Of Netizens* (Tokyo: Institute for HyperNetwork Society, 1995) available at http://www.glocom.ac.jp/Publications/Aizu/nete&c.html.
5. See, for example, Gregory G. Woodbury, "Net Cultural Assumptions," reprinted in *Amateur Computerist* 6 (Fall/Winter 1994–1995), 6–9.
6. E-mail correspondence from Stephen Daniel.
7. Usenet History Archives, October 12, 1990, http://www.duke.edu/~mg/usenet.hist/nethist.901012.Z
8. Tom Truscott, "Invitation to a General Access Unix Network," Duke University, Durham, North Carolina.
9. Copy made available by Bruce Jones.
10. Usenet History Archives, January 26, 1993. See nethist.930126.Z. By 1979–1980, UCB was under contract to ARPA to provide a version of Unix (Berkeley Systems Distribution) for the ARPA contractors who were going to be upgraded to VAX computers.
11. E-mail correspondence from Stephen Daniel.
12. E-mail correspondence from Stephen Daniel.
13. One of the most outstanding is recounted by Amanda Walker, who remembered how it was necessary to send an e-mail message across the continent twice, using three networks, to get it from the Computer Science Department to the Computer Center on the Case Western Reserve University campus. Usenet History Archives, October 16, 1990. See nethist.901016.Z

14. Woodbury, 7.
15. Gene Spafford, Usenet History Archives, October 11, 1990, nethist.901011.Z, based on data from Adams, Spencer, Horton, Bellovin, and Reid. Updating these statistics in 1993, David Lawrence estimates that in the two-week period ending March 9, 1993, about 26,000 articles per day were posted to 4,902 groups for 65 total megabytes (52 megabytes without headers).
16. *In Memoriam: J. C. R. Licklider 1915–1990* (Digital Systems Research Center, 1990), 40. Originally published as "The Computer as a Communication Device," *in Science and Technology,* April 1968. Available online at http://memex.org/licklider.html

Special thanks to the Usenet pioneers and to Bruce Jones for the history materials they have gathered and made available.

An early version of this chapter by Ronda Hauben was presented as a talk at the MACUL (Michigan Association of Computer Users in Learning) Conference in Detroit, Michigan on March 12, 1993. The talk was also posted online.

3

The Social Forces Behind the Development of Usenet

Right at this moment, somewhere in the world, someone is being helpful (or someone is being helped). At the same time, others are participating in online discussions and debates. A new communications medium is currently in its infancy. Over the past two decades a global computer telecommunications network has been developing. One element of this network is called Usenet (also known as Netnews). The original carrier of this news was called UUCPnet (or just UUCP).

The basic element of Usenet is a post. Each individual post consists of a unique contribution from a user, placed in a subject area called a newsgroup. In Usenet's beginning (and still to some extent today), posts were transferred using the UUCP utility distributed with Unix. This utility allows the use of phone lines to transmit computer data among separate computers.

Usenet grew from the ground up in a grassroots manner. Originally, there was no official structure. What began as two or three sites on the network in 1979 expanded to 15 in 1980, to 150 in 1981, to 400 in 1982. The very nature of Usenet is communication. Usenet greatly facilitates inter-human communication among a large group of users. The rawest principle of Usenet is its importance. In its simplest form, Usenet represents democracy.

Inherent in most mass media is central control of content. Many people are influenced by the decisions of a few. Television programming, for example, is controlled by a small group of people compared to the size of the audience. The audience has very little choice over what is emphasized by most mass media. Usenet, however, is controlled by its audience. Usenet should be seen as a promising successor to other people's presses, such as broadsides at the time of the American Revolution and the penny presses in England at the turn of the nineteenth century. Most of the material written to Usenet is contributed by the same people who actively read Usenet. Thus, the audience of Usenet decides the content and subject matter to be thought about, presented, and debated. The ideas that exist on Usenet come from the mass of people who participate in it. In this way, Usenet is an uncensored forum for debate where many sides of an issue come into view. Instead of being force-fed by an uncontrollable source of information, the participants set the tone and emphasis on Usenet. People control what happens on Usenet. In this rare situation, issues and concerns that are of interest, and thus important to the participants, are brought up. In the tradition of amateur radio and Citizen's Band radio, Usenet is the product of the users' ideas and will. Amateur radio and CB, however, are more restricted than Usenet. The range of Usenet connectivity is international and quickly expanding into every nook and cranny around the world. This explosive expansion allows growing communication among people around the world.

In the 1960s, the Advanced Research Projects Agency (ARPA) of the Department of Defense funded research of fundamental importance to the development and testing of computer communications networks. ARPA-sponsored research laid the groundwork for the development of other networks such as UUCPnet. ARPA funded an experiment to attempt to connect incompatible mainframe computers.[1] This experimental connection of computers was called the ARPA Computer Network or the ARPANET. ARPA's stated objectives were:

1. *To develop techniques and obtain experience on interconnecting computers in such a way that a very broad class of interactions were possible and*
2. *To improve and increase computer research productivity through resource sharing.*[2]

ARPA was sponsoring both communications research and the study of how to conserve funds by avoiding duplication of computer resources.[3] Bolt Beranek and Newman (BBN), a Cambridge, Massachusetts company, was chosen to construct the IMP subnetwork, and AT&T was chosen to provide the communications lines. The ARPANET was needed because it was found that a data connection over existing telephone voice lines was too slow and not reliable enough to make a useful connection.[4] Packet switching was developed for use as the protocol for exchanging information over the lines. Packet switching is a communications process in which all messages are broken up into small data packets which are transmitted interspersed and reassembled. In this way, short, medium and long messages get transferred with minimum delay.[5]

The ARPANET was a success. It contributed several advances to communications research. ARPANET researchers were surprised at the enthusiastic adoption of electronic mail (e-mail) as the primary source of communication early on. E-mail was a source of increased productivity through the use of the ARPANET.[6] By 1983, the ARPANET officially shifted from using NCP (Network Control Program) to TCP/IP (Transmission Control Protocol/Internet Protocol.) A key part of TCP/IP's success lies in its simplicity. It is easy to implement over various platforms, and this simplicity has accounted for its continued existence as a *de facto* Internet standard up to the present. The ARPANET's lasting contribution was demonstrating how a backbone infrastructure can serve as a connection between gateways. A gateway is a computer or part of a computer programmed to receive messages from one network and transfer them onto another network.

The ARPANET quickly grew to more than 50 nodes between Hawaii and Norway.[7] However, it did not extend to all who could utilize it. Computer scientists at universities without Department of Defense contracts noticed the advantages and petitioned the National Science Foundation (NSF) for similar connectivity. CSnet was formed to service these computer scientists. CSnet was initially financed by the NSF. Very quickly, the desire for interconnection spread to other members of the university community. Soon CSnet grew to serve other scientists in addition to computer scientists at universities and came to mean "Computer *and* Science Network" rather than just "Computer Science Network."[8]

By the mid-1980s, the ARPANET was phased out by the Department of Defense and was replaced by various internal networks (such as MILNET). The role of connecting university communities and regional networks was taken over by the NSF-funded NSFnet, which originated as a connection for university researchers to the five National Supercomputer Centers. CSnet and NSFnet were made possible by the research on the ARPANET. The NSFnet became the U.S. backbone for the global network known as the Internet.

ARPANET research was pioneering communications research.[9] Researchers discovered the link between computer interconnection and increased productivity from human communication. The sharing of resources was proven as a way to save money and to increase computer use and productivity. The development of packet switching revolutionized the basic methodology of connecting computers.

The source of these discoveries were the people involved. The people involved in the ARPANET project were very intelligent and forward looking. They recognized that they were developing future technologies, and thus did not develop products that commercial industry could (and would) develop. Instead, they understood that the communications technologies they were developing had to come from a not-for-profit body. ARPA researchers had no proprietary products to support and no commercial deadlines to meet. Either requirement would have made developing networks of incompatible computers impossible or limited. Current users of international computer networks are in debt to the pioneers of the ARPANET.

The ARPANET was successful in its attempt to connect various spatially remote computers, and, thus, more importantly, the people who used those computers. However, these people were either professors at universities with Department of Defense research contracts or employees of a limited number of defense industry companies. There were still many people who wanted a connection but were not in a position to gain one. Duke University and the University of North Carolina at Chapel Hill were two such locations. In these underprivileged fertile grounds the grassroots computer communications breakthrough, Usenet, originated and developed.

The Unix operating system provides the basic tools needed to share information between computers. Unix[10] was developed as "a system around which a fellowship would form."[11] One of the programmers of Unix, Dennis Ritchie, wrote that the intended purpose of Unix was to "encourage close communication."[12] Unix's general principles thus conceptually foreshadowed the basic tenet of Usenet. How else should one go about designing communications programs but on an operating system designed with the basic principle of encouraging communication? The Unix utility UUCP was created at Bell Labs in 1976 by Mike Lesk. It was further developed by David Nowitz and later by Nowitz, Peter Honeyman, and Brian E. Redman. UUCP provided a simple way of passing files between any two computers running Unix and UUCP. One of AT&T's motivations in developing Unix was to make software production cheaper in order to bring down the cost of telephone service. Unix's popularity also arose from AT&T's prohibition from profiting from sources other than its main business, phone services, under the terms of the 1956 Consent Decree. Unix was thus available on a "no cost" (or very low cost) basis. The operating system was seen as an "in-house" tool on DEC and other computers and was in use throughout Bell Labs. Many universities used the same type of computer and were licensed by AT&T to utilize Unix. It thus spread widely. Schools picked it up, and computer science students used it to learn about operating systems, as Unix was a model of elegance and simplicity compared to most operating systems of the time. Unix became a widely used operating system in the academic world, paving the way for an international public communications system.

When Usenet was developed in 1979, it was created as a "Unix Users Network." The developers thought Usenet would provide a forum for people to solve problems they had in using Unix, as AT&T initially provided little external support for Unix. In an early handout, Usenet was referred to as a "poor man's ARPANET."[13] In an e-mail message, Stephen Daniel explained that people who didn't have access to the ARPANET were hungry for similar opportunities to communicate.[14]

Usenet has been full of surprises from the beginning. The originators of Usenet underestimated the hunger of people for meaningful communication. As Usenet was originally intended to provide an easy method of communicating with other users at the same site, the programmers thought people would want to have local bulletin boards.[15] However, people were attracted by the possibility of communicating with others outside the local community as well. Even today, the global communication it makes possible is part of what makes Usenet so enticing. It was also thought Netnews would be useful as a method of communication at individual locations, and between sites close to each other.[16] Usenet grew as a grassroots connection of people. The people who utilized Netnews wanted to communicate, and communicate they did! People have a fundamental need to communicate and Usenet aptly fills the bill.[17]

By early 1981, the gap between the ARPANET and Usenet was bridged. The University of California at Berkeley had connections to both the ARPANET and Usenet. This allowed Usenet pioneer Mark Horton to bring mailing-list discussions from ARPANET mailing lists into Usenet newsgroups.[18] This was a significant achievement. Communities other than ARPA sponsored researchers were finally able to see what the ARPANET had made possible. The gatewaying of ARPANET mailing lists into Usenet attracted a wave of people when two ARPANET mailing lists (SF-Lovers and Human-Nets) began to appear on Usenet. These lists provided interesting material and discussions. The size of the news feed (that is, the raw data of Usenet) thus became larger and provided more for people to read. Later, other sites would serve as gateways to even more discussion lists from the ARPANET. Netnews was also seen as a superior method of holding discussions. Gatewaying these FA (From ARPANET) newsgroups proved to be politically courageous. The ARPANET had been accessible to only a certain group of people, and these gateways challenged that notion. The effect on the ARPANET was important, as Steve Bellovin, another of the Usenet pioneers, wrote:

> *The impact of Usenet on the ARPANET was more as a (strong) catalyst to force reexamination (and benign neglect) on the strict policies against interconnection. UUCP mail into the ARPANET became a major force long before it was legit. And it was obviously known to, and ignored by, many of the Powers that Were.*[19]

Usenet, a network made possible by UUCP, expanded to connect people between two countries when the University of Toronto Zoology Department joined the Net in May 1981.[20] Two companies, AT&T and DEC, proved helpful by distributing Netnews and electronic mail long distance. Each UUCP site had to either pay the phone bill to connect to the next system, or arrange for the other system to make the phone call. System administrators at AT&T and DEC did the legwork necessary to take e-mail and news where it might not have reached. However, easy connections were not always available. In one instance, Case Western Reserve University graduate students had to route mail across the continent twice in order to send mail through UUCP to reach their professors who were connected to the ARPANET next door.[21] Usenet encouraged connectivity to the ARPANET. Gradually, the ARPANET was interconnected with other networks, eventually functioning more as a backbone to other networks than as a self-contained network.[22]

Contributed effort is the crucial foundation of UUCPnet and Usenet. There are those who donate time and energy by contributing to Usenet's content—writing messages and answering messages or participating in debate. Without the time and effort put in by its users, Usenet would not be what it is today. Also important to Usenet's success are the system administrators who make the functioning of Usenet possible. Netnews takes up disk space on computers throughout Usenet, and in some cases phone calls must be made to transfer the raw data of the news. In particular, system administrators at AT&T and DEC found it worthwhile to transport Netnews across the country. Certain sites emerged as clearing houses for Usenet and UUCP e-mail.[23] These computers served as major relay stations of both news and e-mail. A structure grew that became the "backbone" of "the Net." Backbone sites formed the trunk of the circulatory system of news and e-mail. A backbone site would connect to other central distribution computers and to numerous smaller sites. These central backbone sites provided a crucial organization to the Usenet communications skeleton, but people formed the center of these connections. For example, *ihnp4* at AT&T existed mainly because of Gary Murakami's effort and only partially because of management support. Usenet services and support were not officially part of Murakami's job description. After Murakami left the Bell Labs Indian Hill Laboratory in Naperville, Illinois, Doug Price put in the time and effort to keep things running smoothly. Certain system administrators in universities also picked up the responsibility for distributing Netnews and e-mail widely. Often these individuals would find ways of having their site pick up the phone bill. Sometimes sites would bill the recipients. Also, those who received a free connection were expected to provide the same to others.[24]

At the beginning, expansion of the number of sites receiving Usenet was slow.[25] Why was this? Initially, Usenet was only transported via UUCP connections. Soon other resources were used, such as the airmailing of magnetic-tape data to provide connectivity.[26] Today, Usenet travels over all types of connections. The evolving ARPANET (and now the Internet) provided a faster way of transporting Netnews. However, a large number of Usenet recipients still only have connectivity via UUCP. Universities and certain businesses can afford to connect to the Internet, but many individuals also want a connection. Even as late as 1992, when 60 percent of Usenet traffic was carried over the Internet via the instantaneous Network News Transport Protocol (NNTP), 40 percent of Usenet was still carried via the slower UUCP connections. There are still many examples of various types of connections using UUCP. These representatives of the "fringe" provide a clue as to what the early days of this communication were like.[27]

The number of sites receiving Usenet is continually increasing, demonstrating its popularity. People are attracted to Usenet because of what it makes possible. People want to communicate and enjoy the thrill of finding others across the country (or across the world) who share a common interest or with whom to be in contact. Besides the common thrill, it is possible to form serious relationships online. Usenet makes this discovery possible because it is a public forum. People expose their ideas broadly, making it possible to find compatriots in thought. The same physical connections which carry Usenet often also transport private electronic mail. However, the interactions and discoveries are only made possible by the public aspect of Usenet. Mailing lists have as wide a range of discussion, but are available to much smaller groups. Being on Usenet can become tiresome at times,[28] but it is rare that anyone leaves it permanently. Unless, of course, a person's life changes and this change means that time once spent online is no longer available. As more universities, schools, libraries, businesses, and individuals connect, the value of Usenet grows. Each new person can eventually add his or her unique opinion to the collection of thoughts and information that Usenet already has. Each new connection also increases the area where new connections can be made through cheap local phone calls. The potential for inexpensive expansion is limited only by the oceans, other natural barriers, or perhaps by mistaken government policies.

The ARPANET was supplemented by CSnet and eventually replaced by U.S. government funding of its successor, NSFnet. Both CSnet and NSFnet were created by the U.S. government in response to research scientists' and professors' pleas to have a network similar to the ARPANET. The NSFnet was also created to provide access to the five supercomputer computing centers around the country. The NSFnet, as the backbone of the U.S. portion of the Internet, provided another route for the distribution of Usenet. Similar to the ARPANET, NSFnet was a constant connection run over leased lines. One of the ways Netnews is distributed is using the NNTP protocol over Internet connections. This allows for Netnews and e-mail to be distributed quickly over a large area. Internet connections also assist in carrying Usenet and e-mail internationally. The Internet-class networks and connections include the established government and university sponsored connections. However individuals at home are often connected by phone lines using SLIP, PPP, and various versions of UUCP. There are also commercial services that, for a fee, provide connections for electronic mail and Usenet access, as well as access to the Internet.

Much of the development of Usenet owes a big thanks to the early restrictions on commercial uses. Where else in our society has the commercial element been so clearly separated from any entity? Forums of discussion and communication become clogged and congested when advertisements use space. Because of the voluntary actions of those who use and redistribute Netnews and e-mail, many people on Usenet feel it wrong to assist commercial ventures. When people feel someone is abusing the nature of Usenet, they let the offender know through e-mail and in public messages. In this manner, users work to keep Usenet a forum free from commercial exploitation. Usenet has not been allowed to be abused as a profit-making venture for any one individual or group. Rather, people are fighting to keep it a resource that is helpful to society as a whole.

On what was the ARPANET and afterward the NSFnet portion of the Internet, there were Acceptable Use Policies (AUP) that existed because these networks were initially founded and financed by public money. On these networks, commercial usage was prohibited, which meant it was also discouraged on other networks that gatewayed into the NSFnet. Unfortunately, the NSF encouraged privatization of the NSFnet backbone.[29] However, the discouragement of commercial usage of the global Usenet is separate and developed differently from the AUP.

The social network that Usenet represents supersedes the physical connection it rides on. The current Netnews rides on many of the physical networks that exist today. However, if ever there were the need, Usenet could reestablish itself outside of the current physically organized networks. The essence of Usenet means it will survive because of its users' determination. Usenet draws its strength from being a peer-to-peer network. People who use Usenet do so because they wish to communicate with others. This communal wish means that people on Usenet find it in their own and in the community's interest to be helpful. In this way, Usenet exists as a worldwide community of resources ready to be shared. Where else today is there so much knowledge that is freely available? Usenet represents a living library and is an important part of the worldwide computer network.

The very nature of Usenet promotes change. Usenet was born outside of established "networks" and transcends any one physical network. It exists of itself and through other networks. It makes possible the distribution of information that might otherwise not be heard through "official channels." This role makes Usenet a herald for social change. Because of the inherent will to communicate, people who do not have access to Usenet will want access when they become exposed to it, and people who currently have access will want Usenet to expand its reach so as to further even more communication. Usenet could grow to provide a forum through which people influence their governments, allowing for the discussion and debate of issues in a mode that facilitates mass participation. This discussion becomes a source of independent information. An independent source is helpful in the search for the truth.

Administrators and individuals who handle the flow of information have been predicting the "imminent death of the Net" since 1982.[30] The software that handles the distribution of Netnews has gone through several versions to handle the ever-increasing amount of information. People who receive Netnews have either had to decrease the number of days individual messages stay at the site or the number of newsgroups they receive; or they have had to allocate more disk space for the storage of Netnews. Despite all predictions and worries, the desire for communication has helped this social network develop and expand. Brad Templeton once wrote, "If there is a gigabit network with bandwidth to spare that is willing to carry Usenet, it has plenty more growth left."[31] Various research labs have been working on producing usable gigabit networks.

Usenet is a democratic and technological breakthrough. The computer networks and Usenet are still developing. People need to work towards keeping connections available and inexpensive, if not free, so as to encourage the body of users to grow. There is a growing number of cities across the world where the public has access to computer networks as a civic service. This direction should be encouraged. Exclusive arrangements for access are to be discouraged. The very nature of Usenet means people are going to be working for its expansion. Others will be working for the expansion for their own gain, and some forces will be an active force against expansion of Usenet. I can only ask that people attempt to popularize and encourage the use of and fight for Usenet.

NOTES

1. "In September 1969, the embryonic (one-node!) ARPANET came to life when the first packet-switching computer was connected to the Sigma 7 computer at UCLA. Shortly thereafter began the interconnection of many main processors (referred to as HOSTS) at various university, industrial, and government research

centers across the United States." (Leonard Kleinrock, "On Communications and Networks," *IEEE Transactions on Computers* C-25 (December 1976): 1328).

2. F. Heart, A. McKenzie, J. McQuillan, and D. Walden, *ARPANET Completion Report* (Washington, D.C.: DARPA and BBN, 1978), II-2.
3. Alexander McKenzie and David C. Walden, "ARPANET, the Defense Data Network, and Internet" in The Encyclopedia of Telecommunications, vol. 1, Fritz E. Froehlich, Allen Kent and Carolyn M. Hall.l, eds. (New York: Marcel Dekker, 1991), 346.
4. Lawrence G. Roberts, "The ARPANET and Computer Networks," in *A History of Personal Workstations*, Adele Goldberg, ed. (New York: ACM Press, 1988), 145.
5. Kleinrock, 1327.
6. McKenzie and Walden, 357.
7. Heart *et al.* II-25.
8. McKenzie and Walden, 369.
9. "For many of the people in government, at the major contractors, and in the participating universities and research centers the development of the ARPANET has been an exciting time which will rank as a high point in their professional careers. In 1969 the ARPANET project represented a high risk, potentially high impact research effort. The existence of the net in practical useful form has not only provided communications technology to meet any short term needs, but it represents a formidable communications technology and experience base on which the Defense Department as well as the entire public and private sectors will depend for advanced communications needs. The strong and diverse experience base generated by the ARPANET project has placed this country ahead of all others in advanced digital communications science and technology." (*ARPANET Completion Report*, III-109.)
10. Unix was born in 1969, the same year as the ARPANET.
11. Dennis. M. Ritchie, "The Evolution of the UNIX Time-Sharing System," *Bell Systems Technical Journal* 63 (8) Part 2 (October 1984): 1578.
12. *Ibid.*
13. Stephen Daniel, James Ellis, and Tom Truscott, "USENET—A General Access UNIX Network," unpublished leaflet, Durham, North Carolina, Summer 1980.
14. Stephen Daniel, personal communication, November 1992.
15. Steve M. Bellovin and Mark Horton, "USENET— A Distributed Decentralized News System," unpublished manuscript, 1985.
16. *Ibid.*
17. See, for example, Gregory G. Woodbury's "Net Cultural Assumptions," reprinted in *Amateur Computerist* 6 (Winter/Spring 1994–1995), 7.
18. "Correct. The original concept was that most of the traffic would be the form now known as UNIX wizards (or whatever it's called this week). Growth was slow until Mark started feeding the mailing lists in because there was nothing to offer prospective customers. Given a ready source of material, people were attracted." Comment from Steve Bellovin, October 10, 1990, Usenet History Archive (http://www.duke.edu/~mg/usenet.hist/nethist.901010.Z)

Archive (http://www.duke.edu/~mg/usenet.hist/nethist.901010.Z)

19. Steve Bellovin, October 10, 1990, Usenet History Archives, http://www.duke.edu/~mg/usenet.hist/nethist.901010.Z
20. Henry Spencer, Usenet History Archives, http://www.duke.edu/~mg/usenet.hist/history.Z
21. Amanda Walker, Oct. 16, 1990, Usenet History Archives, http://www.duke.edu/~mg/usenet.hist/nethist.901016.Z
22. "Indeed, during a typical measurement period in June 1988, over 50% of the active ARPANET hosts were gateways, and they accounted for over 80% of the traffic." McKenzie and Walden, 369.
23. At AT&T, the computers *research*, then *allegra*, then *ihnp4* served as major mail and/or news distribution sites. At DEC, *decvax* gradually increased its role (for example, *decvax* in New Hampshire would call long distance to San Diego, California.)
24. For example, Duke University fed Usenet data to Greg Woodbury who in turn gave "feeds" to others who requested them from him. See "Net Cultural Assumptions."
25. See table in Chapter 2, p. 44.
26. Andy Tannenbaum is quoted as saying something similar to "Never underestimate the bandwidth of a station wagon full of nine-track tape (or magnetic tape)."
27. Usenet began with a spirit that still exists today. On several newsgroups I posted asking how users were connected to Usenet. In return I received numerous wonderful answers. One new pioneer was going to use packet radio to send e-mail up to the CIS's orbiting Mir Space Station. Others around the world sent me information about their connection. These responses show how the world is still in the infancy of this communications interconnectivity!
28. "Flame wars" (highly emotional attacks) can become annoying. There are ebbs and flows of interesting posts. Even though Usenet is addictive, it can also be overwhelming.
29. See, for example, the U.S. Office of Inspector General's Report "Review of NSFNET" (March 1993) for documentation of the process set in motion to implement the privatization of the NSFnet.
30. Usenet History Archives, http://www.duke.edu/~mg/usenet.hist/
31. Usenet History Archives, http://www.duke.edu/~mg/usenet.hist/posthist.Z

Special thanks to Bruce Jones for establishing and archiving the Usenet History Archives at ftp://weber.ucsd.edu/pub/usenet.hist/. Also thanks to the Usenet pioneers for getting Usenet off to the right start.

An early version of this chapter by Michael Hauben was made available online in Winter 1992. A revised version was printed in the *Amateur Computerist* 5 (Spring 1993).

4

The World of Usenet

During the past several decades there have been important technological breakthroughs. The personal computer, a science-fiction dream for generations, is now available in many homes in the same way that the electric typewriter or television were just a few years ago. One of the most important developments of our time, however, is a public computer conferencing network called Usenet, transported via physical networks such as the Internet, UUCP, and others, which encourages discussion and the free exchange of ideas on a worldwide scale.

Usenet makes it possible for computer users around the world to have public discussions, raise questions or problems so they get help, or send e-mail to each other, often instantaneously. One user explains that Usenet is like a newspaper where "everyone's letter to the editor is printed."[1] Usenet has also been described as a series of electronic magazines. "These 'magazines,' called *newsgroups,* are devoted to particular topics, ranging from questions about UNIX, programming languages, and computer systems to discussions of politics, philosophy, science, and recreational activities."[2] Usenet can be compared to an electronic town meeting of the world or to a series of electronic soap boxes. Others have observed that "It's now as if everyone owns a printing press," or, even better, "a publishing house." Computer users with access to Usenet can read articles on a broad range of topics. They can contribute their responses or post articles of their own on any subject in an appropriate newsgroup. Their submissions are then copied electronically to computers around the world that are also part of the Usenet network. Usenet demonstrates what can happen when people are encouraged and allowed to develop computer technology.

An important element, according to Gregory G. Woodbury, who has written an account of the early days of Usenet, is that the Usenet software was created under the conditions of the academic Unix license, which then provided that the program be put into the public domain. Since everyone involved at the time was working in an academic environment (including Bell

Labs, which Woodbury notes was "academic, really") where information was shared, the emphasis was on communication, not on copyright or other proprietary rights. "Everyone *wanted* to be on the Net," he notes, "and it was clear they were cooperating in doing so."[3]

The phenomenal growth of Usenet during the early 1980s was an acknowledgment that it was a superior means of dealing with the growing number of mailing lists on various subjects that had developed on the early ARPANET network. The original script files had been rewritten in C by Steve Bellovin for use at *unc* and *duke*, according to Gene Spafford's history of the period. Stephen Daniel, Spafford explains, "did another implementation in C for public distribution."[4] After Tom Truscott made modifications in this program, the software became known as the A News release of Netnews.

"Under the strain of being an international network," Woodbury explains, "with several new machines being added daily, certain limitations in the basic assumptions made themselves painfully obvious." The continuing expansion led to a rewriting of the software in 1981 by Mark Horton, a graduate student at the University of California at Berkeley, and Matt Glickman, a high-school student. This version was released to the public as B News, version 2.1, in 1982. Then, in 1985, the ever-expanding nature of Usenet led Henry Spencer and Geoff Collyer at the University of Toronto to set to work on what is now known as C News, which they released in 1989. Spencer and Collyer paid careful attention to the performance aspects of C News, resulting in software that was able to handle the phenomenal expansion of Usenet.[5] A subsequent version of the Netnews software, known as INN, was written by Rich Salz and used to transport Usenet.

The administration and coordination of this worldwide network depends to a great extent on the cooperation and diligent work of the system administrators at the participating sites. In the early development of Usenet, some of these administrators knew each other and worked together to establish a series of general procedures for processes such as adding newsgroups. Known as the "backbone cabal," this group worked together to hash out ways to deal with problems that threatened the voluntary, cooperative nature of the Net.

Those who were part of this informal structure would contact new site administrators who joined the Net. The character of the Net as a voluntary association of people who posted because they wanted to communicate was conveyed. And the fact that posts were entered into the "public domain" was established as an essential principle of the Net.[6]

Some people have defined Usenet as those sites receiving what has been called the "seven sisters hierarchies," the seven main newsgroups hierarchies—comp, misc, news, rec, sci, soc, and talk, and the newsgroup news.announce.important. Others have defined Usenet as those sites that receive at least one of the newsgroups that appears on the list of Usenet newsgroups. There are also other hierarchies, which include alt, gnu, bit, and various country designations, including, among others, nl (netherlands), fj (from Japan), fr (France), and de (Germany).

Usenet is now made up of thousands of newsgroups organized around different topics. And the number of groups is continually growing. There are procedures for creating new newsgroups in the main hierarchies. When there is a proposal for a new newsgroup, those on Usenet can discuss the proposal. When the vote is called, the new group can be created if there are 100 more votes for the proposed group than against it.[7] A more informal procedure is used for creating an alt newsgroup than that used to create a newsgroup in one of the "seven sisters" hierarchies. The guidelines provide for posting a proposal or charter for the new newsgroup to the alt.config newsgroup. The proposal is discussed, then the newsgroup can be set up as an alt group when a new newsgroup control message is posted to the control newsgroup.

Many of the people using and contributing to Usenet are people who work with computer technology. Many of these people need Usenet to help them solve problems they encounter with computer technology. One of the early functions of Usenet was to help identify bugs in new technology and to share the fixes to such problems.[8]

My experience with Usenet has been inspiring. I was interested in discussions involving economics and the history of economic thought. When I first got onto Usenet, I could not figure out where such discussions took place. I managed to get access to the misc.books.technical newsgroup. I did not know what the other newsgroups were or how to find out. Not knowing how to proceed, I entered the following post:

From: au329@cleveland.Freenet.Edu (Ronda Hauben)

Newsgroups: misc.books.technical

Date: 10 Jan 92 07:48:58 GMT

Organization: Case Western Reserve University, Cleveland, Ohio, (USA)

Nntp-Posting-Host: cwns9.ins.cwru.edu

I am interested in discussing the history of economics—i.e. mercantilists, physiocrats, adam smith, ricardo, marx, marshall, keynes etc. With the world in such a turmoil it would seem that the science of economics needs to be reinvigorated. Is there anyplace on Usenet News where this kind of discussion is taking place? If not is there anyone else interested in starting a con-

> *ference.economics and how would I go about doing this. This is my first time on Usenet News.*
>
> *Ronda*
>
> *au329@cleveland.freenet.edu*

One of the many responses I received said: "Start discussing on sci.econ. We're all ears."[9]

I received several other responses via e-mail also pointing me to the sci.econ newsgroup or indicating interest in the topic. A computer user from California sent me e-mail with a list of all the existing newsgroups. Another user from Scotland wrote telling me the name of the news file which listed the names of all of the other newsgroups. It is considered good Netiquette (Network Etiquette) to help new users, and many of the experienced users are very willing to do so.

A few users suggested that I might want to try to start a newsgroup for the history of economics, but that it would probably be a wise idea to either wait until I got used to Netnews before trying to initiate a group or to get help from a user with more experience.

The list of newsgroups posted on Usenet in newsgroups such as news.misc contains descriptions of each group. For example, the newsgroup "sci.econ" is described as "the science of economics."

I have found the discussions in sci.econ very valuable. There are often debates over important economic questions. Many of the questions discussed concern broad social issues—for example, the development of different social forms of society, whether economics is a science, whether the so-called free market has ever existed to regulate production, and so on. There has been discussion of a variety of economic and political issues—social security, rent control, strikes in Germany, national health-care reform, the need for shorter hours of work, plant closures, taxes, the economic programs of presidential candidates, the role of markets in setting prices, and the economic program of Henry George.

Many newsgroups on Usenet are about computers and computer-related subjects. There are newsgroups where one can ask questions regarding access to Usenet or about books that are recommended for people who want to learn more about Unix or any other area of computer use. It is also possible to write to someone who has posted a question and ask the user to forward a copy or summary of the responses received so the post does not have to be duplicated. There are newsgroups dealing with political issues, social issues, current events, hobbies, science, education, and many other subjects.

When a critique of GM plant closures was posted after GM announced that it would lay off 70,000 people, several people sent e-mail saying that it was good to see the post. Thus when someone makes an interesting post, it is possible to send e-mail to the person and begin to correspond or just encourage him or her to continue to post.

There are also new democratic procedures being developed. For example, when a vote is in progress to determine whether or not there should be a new newsgroup in the seven sisters hierarchies, voters are asked to verify that their vote is accurately recorded, and a list is posted announcing the final totals. Thus a procedure has been worked out on Usenet that votes cannot be by secret ballot, but must be open and posted, with the people voting having the ability to verify the vote totals.[10]

Unfortunately, there are also frustrating aspects of Usenet. The great variety and number of posts can take considerable time to survey, and it is often difficult to keep up with the volume. To help deal with this problem, a variety of software readers have been created.[11] Although these readers have been copyrighted, many are freely available as long as they are for personal use. Despite difficulties in keeping up with the volume of posts and other problems that have developed in the course of building the Netnews network,[12] many on Usenet are willing to be active participants in the development and working out of the content and form of the network. Many people send e-mail or post public responses when they have something to say about a post. In this way, communication is encouraged, as one person builds on another's contribution, and all become more knowledgeable through the process of democratic discussion and debate.

Usenet has thus evolved a functioning governing structure that is democratic and open in ways that have only been dreamed of in the past. Many of the details of the copying, distribution, and propagation of Usenet are done via automated machinery and programs that require that the system administrators, who make the system function, work together to solve their common problems. This same kind of cooperative relationship has been encouraged by these system administrators among the users of Usenet, and this cooperative standard of activity is known as Netiquette.

Many on Usenet call its structure anarchy. But, Jean Jacques Rousseau, in *A Discourse on Political Economy*, explains that the best laws are those which the population implements voluntarily rather than by force. Netiquette is a system of rules or standards that users on the Net are encouraged to follow. Throughout the development of Usenet, commercial traffic and commercial uses of Netnews have been strictly limited for several reasons. Among these has been the need, since the early days of Usenet, to keep commercial traffic from both escalating phone costs and noise (that is, the proportion of useless information to useful information) on Usenet. When the Internet became one of the major transport mechanisms of Usenet traffic, prohibitions against commercial traffic arising from the public funding of the NSF backbone became a factor.[13] This restriction of commercial purposes has resulted in the open communication and cooperation which commercial agendas make difficult. Thus the governing laws (Netiquette) and structures (cooperative and helpful) demonstrate that more democratic government is now possible and can achieve significant social advances. On Usenet, participants gain from being active and from helping each other. People who post or send e-mail are contributors to the culture and all gain from each other's efforts. A vibrant and informative, bottom-up, interactive grassroots culture has been created, and a broad, worldwide, informative and functioning telecommunications network is the product of their cooperative labor.

Because those who are able to connect to Usenet are in touch with people around the globe, an exciting world of people and computers is available to a user who has access to Usenet.[14] Also, the achievement of Usenet demonstrates the importance of facilitating the development of uncensored speech and communication. There is debate and discussion. One person influences another. And people build on each other's strengths, interests, and differences.

In the past, it would have required the labor of many people, much paper, ink, and other supplies to accomplish such a massive communication network via traditional means such as newspapers and magazines. With Usenet, however, this communication among people and computers is accomplished via a high degree of automation. Usenet makes it possible for people to print their own copies of what is available online, using only the paper, ink, or other resources they need. By participating in Usenet, millions of people and their computers are connected to the global telecommunications network. So welcome to the world of Usenet. Something very special is happening, and it is one of the important achievements of the twentieth century.

NOTES

1. "Interview with a Staff Member," *Amateur Computerist* 4 (Winter/Spring 1992): 10.
2. Bart Anderson, Bryan Costales, and Harry Henderson, *UNIX Communications* (Carmel, Ind: SAMS, 1991) 213.
3. Gregory G. Woodbury, "Net Cultural Assumptions," reprinted *in Amateur Computerist,* 6 (Winter/Spring 1994-1995), 7. Woodbury also notes the concern of some people at Bell Labs that AT&T's rights in and to Unix source code and proprietary information be protected. However, he emphasizes that individual posters were concerned with the ability to communicate, not with copyright protection.

4. Gene Spafford, "USENET Software: History and Sources" (periodically posted on Usenet in the newsgroup news.misc).
5. Details are described by Geoff Collyer and Henry Spencer in "News Need Not Be Slow," *USENIX Conference Proceedings* (Winter 1987): 181–190.
6. Woodbury's article, "Net Cultural Assumptions," describes how the "public domain assumption" changed when the United States revised its copyright law and became a Berne signatory in the late 1980s. The implications of this change have been debated on Usenet.
7. But whether the new newsgroup will be carried has traditionally depended upon the system administrators of the largest systems and the new group's inclusion in the list of newsgroups.
8. Ronda Hauben, "Interview with Henry Spencer: On Usenet News and C News," *Amateur Computerist* 5 (Winter/Spring 1993): 2.
9. E-mail from Adam Grossman.
10. There are problems, however, with the online voting process. For example, sometimes those campaigning for a particular outcome recruit others to vote a certain way, rather than encouraging them to participate in the discussion to determine what principles should guide how they vote.
11. See Gene Spafford's "USENET Software: History and Sources" for a history and description of many of the software readers now available.
12. Various problems have developed that users need to deal with. Some involve efforts to impose copyright restrictions on posts which would make copying and propagation impossible. There are some users who try to intimidate people who post by attacking them ("flaming"). A more recent problem is the spread of ads on Usenet. These problems must be understood in the context of the significant advance that the Netnews network represents.
13. The National Science Foundation (NSF) had an Appropriate Use Policy (AUP) governing what was allowed to be transported across the nets that it funded with public moneys. It limited usage basically to research and education activities. As Usenet was transported across the NSFNet backbone, this NSF policy helped Usenet develop as an educational rather than commercial network. It is questionable as to whether a commercial network could have developed, given the secret and proprietary activities of commercial enterprises. However, once the AUP restriction was lifted by the NSF to accommodate and support the growing commercial use of the Internet by Advanced Networks and Services (ANS), a company founded by MCI and IBM that became part of the MERIT, NSF, ANS organizational chain, access was opened up to commercial traffic, endangering continuing development of the education and research function that the Net thus far has achieved.
14. See, for example, "Interview with a Staff Member," *Amateur Computerist* 4 (Summer 1992): 22.

A special thanks to the many people on Usenet who commented on this article in its various draft stages and for their helpful comments and criticisms. Also thanks to the pioneers of Usenet who answered questions and made historical material available.

An early version of this chapter by Ronda Hauben appeared on Usenet in Spring 1992. A revised version was published in the Usenet supplement of the *Amateur Computerist* in Fall 1994 as Part 2 of "In Defense of Technology."

PART 2

The Past

Where Has It All Come From

5

The Vision of Interactive Computing and the Future

What is the reality behind all the talk about the so-called Information Superhighway? This is an important question which U.S. government policy-makers seem to be ignoring. However, understanding the history of the current global computer networks is a crucial step toward building the network of the future. There is a vision that guided the origin and development of the Internet, Usenet, and other associated physical and logical networks. What is that vision?

While the global computer networks are basically young, their growth since the beginnings of the ARPANET in 1969 has been substantial. The ARPANET was the experimental network connecting the mainframe computers of universities and other contractors funded and encouraged by the Advanced Research Projects Agency (ARPA) of the U.S. Department of Defense. The ARPANET started out as a research test-bed for computer networking, communication protocols, and computer and data resource sharing. However, it developed into something surprising. The widest use of the ARPANET was for computer-facilitated human to human communication using electronic mail (e-mail) and discussion lists. Popular lists included Human-Nets, Wine-Tasters and SF-Lovers. The human communications achievements of ARPANET research continue to be a popular use of the Net by a growing number of people through e-mail, Usenet discussion groups, mailing lists, and Internet Relay Chat. The ARPANET was the product of previous U.S. government funded research in interactive computing and time-sharing of computers.

Until the 1960s, computers operated almost exclusively in batch mode. Programmers punched or had their programs punched onto cards. Then the stack of punched cards was provided to the local computer center. The computer operator assembled stacks of cards into batches to be fed to the computer for continuous processing. Often, a programmer had to wait more than a day in order to see the results from his or her input. In addition, if there were any mistakes in the creation of the punched cards, the stack or part of it had to be punched again and resubmitted, which would take another day. Bugs in the code could only be discovered after an attempt to compile the code. Therefore "debugging" was a slow process. This batch processing mode was a very inefficient way of utilizing the power of the computer. People began thinking of ways to alter the interface between people and computers. The idea of time-sharing developed among some in computer research communities. Time-sharing makes it possible for several people to utilize a computer (then predominately the IBM mainframe) simultaneously. Time-sharing operates by giving each user the impression that he or she is the only one using the computer. In effect, the computer provides slices of CPU time to all the users in a rapid, sequential manner.

Crucial to the development of the global computer networks was the vision of the original researchers interested in time-sharing. These researchers began to think about social issues related to time-sharing. They observed that communities formed from the people who used time-sharing systems and considered the social significance of these communities. Two of the pioneers involved in research in time-sharing at MIT, Fernando Corbató and Robert Fano, wrote:

> *The time-sharing computer system can unite a group of investigators in a cooperative search for the solution to a common problem, or it can serve as a community pool of knowledge and skill on which anyone can draw according to his needs. Projecting the concept on a large scale, one can conceive of such a facility as an extraordinarily powerful library serving an entire community—in short, an intellectual public utility.*[1]

Research in time-sharing started in the early 1960s at different research centers. Some early sites were CTSS (Compatible Time-sharing System) at MIT, DTSS (Dartmouth Time-sharing System) at Dartmouth, a system at BBN, and Project GENIE at the University of California at Berkeley. J. C. R. Licklider, the founding director of ARPA's Information Processing Techniques Office (IPTO), thought of time-sharing as interactive computing. Interactive computing meant the user could communicate and respond to the computer's responses in a way that batch processing did not allow.

Licklider was one of the early users of the new time-sharing systems, and he took the time to play around with one. Examining the uses of this new way of communicating with the computer enabled Licklider to think about future possibilities. Licklider went on to establish the priorities and direction for ARPA's IPTO research monies. Many of the interviewees in a series of interviews conducted by the Charles Babbage Institute (CBI) said that ARPA's money was given under Licklider's guidance to seed research that would be helpful to society in general and only secondarily helpful to the military.

Both Robert Taylor and Larry Roberts, successors to Licklider as director of IPTO, pinpoint Licklider as the originator of the vision which set ARPA's priorities and goals, guiding ARPA to help develop the concept and practice of networking computers.

In one of the CBI interviews, Roberts said:

> *What I concluded was that we had to do something about communications, and that really, the idea of the galactic network that Lick talked about, probably more than anybody, was something that we had to start seriously thinking about. So in a way networking grew out of Lick's talking about that, although Lick himself could not make anything happen because it was too early when he talked about it. But he did convince me it was important.* [2]

Taylor, also in a CBI conducted interview, pointed out the importance of Licklider's vision to future network development:

> *I don't think . . . anyone who's been in that DARPA position since [Licklider] has had the vision that Licklider had. His being at that place at that time is a testament to the tenuousness of it all. It was really a fortunate circumstance. I think most of the significant advances in computer technology, especially in the systems part of computer science . . . were simply extrapolations of Licklider's vision. They were not really new visions of their own. So he's really the father of it all.*[3]

Taylor, who directly succeeded Licklider as Director of the IPTO at ARPA, also described how research in time-sharing led to surprising results. A phrase that J. C. R. Licklider frequently used to express his vision was "an intergalactic network." Taylor explains that Licklider used this phrase to describe the potential community he realized would emerge from the interconnection of the local communities of Net users that developed from time-sharing. At first, Taylor notes, ARPA-supported research had as its goal achieving compatibility and resource sharing across different computer systems. However, he explains:

> *They were just talking about a network where they could have a compatibility across these systems, and at least do some load sharing, and some program sharing, data sharing—that sort of thing. Whereas, the thing that struck me about the time-sharing experience was that before there was a time-sharing system, let's say at MIT, then there were a lot of individual people who didn't know each other who were interested in computing in one way or another, and who were doing whatever they could, however they could. As soon as the time-sharing system became usable, these people began to know one another, share a lot of information, and ask of one another, "How*

> *do I use this? Where do I find that?" It was really phenomenal to see this computer become a medium that stimulated the formation of a human community. . . . And so, here ARPA had a number of sites by this time, each of which had its own sense of community and was digitally isolated from the other one. I saw a phrase in the Licklider memo. The phrase was in a totally different context—something that he referred to as an "intergalactic network." I asked him about this . . . in fact I said, "Did you have a networking of the ARPANET sort in mind when you used that phrase?" He said, "No, I was thinking about a single time-sharing system that was intergalactic. . . ."*[4]

As Taylor noted, the users of the time-sharing systems would form, usually unexpectedly, a new community. People were connected to others who were also interested in these new computing systems.

The vision driving ARPA inspired bright researchers working on computer related topics. Roberts explains that Licklider's work (and that of the IPTO directors after him) educated people who were to become the future leaders in the computer industry. Roberts describes the impact that Licklider and his vision made on ARPA and future IPTO directors:

> *Well, I think that the one influence is the production of people in the computer field that are trained, and knowledgeable, and capable, and that form the basis for the progress the United States has made in the computer field. That production of people started with Lick, when he started the IPTO program and started the big university programs. It was really due to Lick, in large part, because I think it was that early set of activities that I continued with that produced the most people with the big university contracts. That produced a base for them to expand their whole department, and produced excitement in the university.*[5]

Roberts describes how ARPA-supported university research had a significant impact on the computer industry as well.

> *So it was clear that that was a big impact on the universities and therefore, in the industry. You can almost track all those people and see what effect that has had. The people from those projects are in large part the leaders throughout the industry.*[6]

Licklider's vision was of an "intergalactic network," a time-sharing utility that would serve the entire galaxy. This early vision of time-sharing spawned the idea of interconnecting different time-sharing systems by networking them together. This network would allow those on geographically separated time-sharing systems to share data, programs, research, and, later, other ideas—anything that could be typed out. In their article, "The Computer as a Communication Device," Licklider and Taylor predicted the creation of a global computer network. They wrote:

> *We have seen the beginnings of communication through a computer—communication among people at consoles located in the same room or on the same university campus or even at distantly separated laboratories of the same research and development organization. This kind of communication—through a single multiaccess computer with the aid of telephone lines—is beginning to foster cooperation and promote coherence more effectively than do present arrangements for sharing computer programs by exchanging magnetic tape by messenger or mail.*[7]

They point out how the interconnection of computers leads to a much broader class of connections than might have been expected. A new form of community is generated:

> *The collection of people, hardware, and software—the multiaccess computer together with its local community of users—will become a node in a geographically distributed computer network. Let us assume for a moment that such a network has been formed. . . . Through the network of message processors, therefore, all the large computers can communicate with one another. And through them, all the members of the supercommunity can communicate—with other people, with programs, with data, or with selected combinations of those resources.*[8]

Licklider and Taylor consider more than just hardware and software when they write about the new social dynamics that the connections of dispersed computers and people would create.

> *[These communities] will be communities not of common location, but of* common interest. *In each field, the overall community of interest will be large enough to support a comprehensive system of field-oriented programs and data.*[9]

In exploring this community of common affinity, they describe the main advantages that come from connecting to and being part of these new computer-facilitated communities. Life will be enriched for those people who can communicate online with others who have similar goals and interests, as they will not be limited by geography. Communication will be more productive and thus more enjoyable. And the kind of programs that those online will have access to will be customized to one's interests and abilities, and thus more satisfying. They describe the advantages to society that the increased opportunities and resources made possible by the Net can provide for everyone.[10]

Since the advantages that computer networks make possible for society will only happen if these advantages are available to all who want to make use of them, Licklider and Taylor realized there is a crucial challenge put on the agenda of our times by the development of the Net. They conclude their article with a prophetic question: "Will 'to be on line' be a privilege or a right?"[11]

They argue that it must be a right. Otherwise, instead of providing all of the many benefits it makes possible, the Net would only increase the inequities of intellectual opportunity that currently exist.

The challenge they raise is one of access. The full positive effects of computer networking will only come about if the networks are made easy to use and available to all. They argue that access should be made available because of the ensuing global benefits. They conclude by describing how humankind can benefit immeasurably from the educational opportunities the Net makes possible: "[I]f the network idea should prove to do for education what a few have envisioned in hope. . . surely the boon to humankind would be beyond measure."[12]

Licklider and Taylor raise the important point that access should be made available to all who want to use the computer networks. It is important to ask if the National Information Infrastructure is being designed with the principle of equality of access. The vision of the interconnection and interaction of diverse communities guided the creation of the original ARPANET. In the design of the expansion of the Net, it is important to keep in mind the original vision and to consider whether that vision continues to be the appropriate guide. However, very little emphasis has been placed on either the study of Licklider's vision or the role and advantages of the Net up to this point. In addition, the public has not been allowed to play a role in the planning process for the U.S. government's new initiatives. This is a plea to you to demand more of a part in the development of the future of the Net!

NOTES

1. Robert Fano and Fernando Corbató, "Time-sharing on Computers", in *Information, A Scientific American Book* (San Francisco: W. H. Freeman, 1966), 76–77.
2. Lawrence G. Roberts, interview by Arthur L. Norberg, 4 April 1989, San Mateo, California. Charles Babbage Institute, The Center for the History of Information Processing, University of Minnesota, Minneapolis, Minnesota.
3. Robert W. Taylor, interview by William Aspray, 28 February 1989, Palo Alto, California. Charles Babbage Institute, The Center for the History of Information Processing, University of Minnesota. Minneapolis, Minnesota.
4. *Ibid.*
5. Lawrence G. Roberts interview.
6. *Ibid.*
7. J. C. R. Licklider and Robert Taylor, "The Computer as a Communication Device," in *In Memoriam: J. C. R. Licklider: 1915–1990,* (Palo Alto, Calif.: Digital Systems Research Center, 1990), 28–29.

8. *Ibid.*, 32.
9. *Ibid.*, 38.
10. *Ibid.*, 40.
11. *Ibid.*
12. *Ibid.*

An early version of this chapter by Michael Hauben was posted online in Spring 1993. A revised version appeared in the *Amateur Computerist* 6 (Fall/Winter 1994–1995).

6

Cybernetics, Time-sharing, Human–Computer Symbiosis and Online Communities

Creating a Supercommunity of Online Communities

FOUNDATIONS OF THE CYBERNETIC REVOLUTION

In 1961, MIT was to celebrate its centennial anniversary. Martin Greenberger, who had joined the MIT faculty in 1958, describes how a call went out for appropriate ways to celebrate:

> *I proposed a series of lectures on the computer and the future. We threw open the hatches and got together the best people we could assemble—whatever their fields. We asked these thinkers to project ahead and help us understand what was in store.* [1]

Charles Percy Snow, a British writer, was invited to be the keynote speaker. His talk, "Scientists and Decision Making," discussed the need for democratic and broad-based participation in the decisions of society. "We happen to be living at a time of a major scientific revolution," he observed, "probably more important in its consequences, than the first Industrial Revolution, a revolution which we shall see in full force in the very near future."[2]

He and the other speakers expressed their concern that the challenges represented by the computer be understood and treated seriously. They felt that there would need to be government decisions regarding the development and application of the computer. They cautioned that these decisions be entrusted to people who understood the problems the computer posed for society. Also, they were concerned that the smaller the number of people involved in important social decisions, the more likely serious errors of judgment would be made. They urged that it was necessary to open up the decision-making process to as broad a set of people as possible.

Present at this gathering were several of the pioneers who had helped to set the foundation for the developing cybernetic revolution. What was the revolution they were describing? John Pierce, a pioneer in electronics research at Bell Labs, was one of the speakers at the MIT Centennial Conference. In an article published several years later in *Scientific American*, Pierce described the foundation of the cybernetic revolution that was then unfolding.[3] Pierce noted the intellectual ferment that accompanied two publications in 1948. One was "The Mathematical Theory of Communication" by Claude Shannon, published in July and October 1948 in the *Bell Systems Technical Journal*. The other was the publication of Norbert Wiener's book *Cybernetics: Control and Communication in the Animal and the Machine.*

Summing up Shannon's contribution, Pierce described how Shannon had changed communication theory from guesswork to science. Pierce wrote:

> *Shannon has made it possible for communication engineers to distinguish between what is possible and what is not possible. Communication theory has disposed of unworkable inventions that are akin to perpetual motion machines. It has directed the attention of engineers to real and soluble problems. It has given them a quantitative measure of the effectiveness of their system.*[4]

In the 1930s, the mathematician and computer pioneer Alan Turing had determined that it was possible to design a universal or general-purpose computer. Such a computer would be able to do any calculation that could be done by a machine, provided the computer was given a program describing the calculation. Building on Turing's contribution, Shannon had demonstrated how Boolean algebra and logic could be used in the analysis and synthesis of switching and computer circuits.

Another founder of the Cybernetics Revolution was Norbert Wiener. Pierce recalled the important intellectual catalyst that Wiener's book provided when it appeared in 1948. Wiener was interested in the means by which feedback could be communicated to help correct problems that develop in an organism. Describing the contribution Wiener's work made in defining the need for feedback, Pierce gives the example of a community "where the Lords of Things as They Are protect themselves from hunger by wealth, from public opinion by privacy and anonymity, from private criticism by the laws of libel and the possession of the means of communication." It is in such a society, he explains, that "ruthlessness can reach its most sublime levels." And he points out that the creation of such a society requires "the control of the means of communication" as "the most effective and important element."[5] Such a community, he observed, is very unstable.

Wiener, in an interview in 1959, explained why such a community is unstable. Describing the importance of accurate information and feedback, Wiener used the example of driving a car:

> *. . . instead of seeing where you are going, somebody puts a picture in front of you. Clearly, it won't be very long before you hit the curb. This is true in other spheres. Facing the contingencies of life depends on adequate and true information. The more that information is conditioned by the people who are doing the controlling, the less they will be able to meet emergencies. In the long run, such a system of misinformation can only lead to catastrophe.*[6]

In *Cybernetics*, Wiener defined three central concepts as crucial to any organism or system: communication, control, and feedback. He coined the term *cybernetics* to designate the important role that feedback plays in a communication system. The word was derived from the Greek *kybernetes* meaning *governor* or *steersman*.[7] The digital computer had raised the question of the relationship between the human and the machine. Wiener proposed to explore this relationship in a scientific manner, examining which "functions should properly be assigned to these two agencies." He believed this to be the crucial question for our times.[8]

Important to Wiener's vision was the understanding that the more complex the machine, such as the developing digital computer, the more, not less, direction and intelligence were required on the part of its human partner. Wiener often pointed to the literal way in which the computer interpreted the data provided to it. He explained the necessity for increased human guidance and forethought when directing computers:

> *Here I must enter a protest against much of the popular understanding of computing machines and similar quasi-mechanical aids. Many people suppose that they are replacements for intelligence and have cut down the need for original thought . . . .This is not the case. If simple devices need simple thought to get the most out of them, complicated devices need a vastly reinforced level of thought . . . . Moreover this work cannot be put off until the machines have already processed their data. It is very rare, and to say the least, by no means normal, that data that has been thoughtlessly selected can be organized by an afterthought so as to produce significant results.*[9]

In the introduction to *Cybernetics*, Wiener described some of the important influences on his development as a scientist and on his thinking in the field of cybernetics. In the 1930s, he was invited to attend a series of private seminars on the scientific method held by Dr. Arturo Rosenblueth of the Harvard Medical School in Cambridge, Massachusetts. He and Dr. Rosenbleuth had a common interest in understanding the scientific method, and both believed that science had to be a collaborative endeavor.[10] Scientists involved in a variety of fields of study were invited to the seminars to encourage an interdisciplinary approach to the problems of communication in machine and animals. Describing the methodology of the seminars, Wiener writes:

> *In those days, Dr. Rosenblueth . . . conducted a monthly series of discussion meetings on scientific method. The participants were mostly young scientists at the Harvard Medical School, and we would gather for dinner about a round table in Vanderbilt Hall . . . . After the meal, somebody—either one of our group or an invited guest—would read a paper on some scientific topic, generally one in which questions of methodology were the first consideration, or at least a leading consideration. The speaker had to run the gauntlet of an acute criticism, good-natured but unsparing . . . . [A]mong the former habitués of these meetings there is more than one of us who feels that they were an important and permanent contribution to our scientific unfolding.*[11]

Wiener was a member of this group until the onset of World War II ended the seminars. After the war was over, Wiener began a set of seminars near MIT modeled on his earlier experience in the seminars with Dr. Rosenblueth. The post-war seminars that Wiener convened were to have an important influence on the work of several of the pioneers of the upcoming computer networking revolution.

Another MIT pioneer, Jerome Wiesner, who later became a Science Advisor to President Kennedy, described the role Wiener's seminars played in helping to develop the interdisciplinary tradition of research at MIT's Research Laboratory for Electronics (known as the RLE). Wiener's ideas about communication and feedback in man and machine, along with Shannon's work in information theory "spawned new visions of research for everyone interested in communications, including neurophysiology, speech, and linguistics investigation," wrote Wiesner. "The work was both theoretical and experimental as well as basic and applied." He described how it led to exciting new ideas and to their implementation in practice which "remains a hallmark of the present-day RLE."[12]

Wiesner provides the following account of the seminars that Wiener set up after World War II:

> *In the winter of 1947, Wiener began to speak about holding a seminar that would bring together the scientists and engineers who were doing work on*

> *what he called communications. He was launching his vision of cybernetics in which he regarded signals in any medium, living or artificial, as the same; dependent on their structure and obeying a set of universal laws set out by Shannon. In the spring of 1948, Wiener convened the first of the weekly meetings that was to continue for several years . . . The first meeting reminded me of the tower of Babel, as engineers, psychologists, philosophers, acousticians, doctors, mathematicians, neurophysiologists, philosophers, and other interested people tried to have their say. After the first meeting, one of us would take the lead each time, giving a brief summary of their research, usually accompanied by a running commentary by Wiener, to set the stage for the evening's discussion. As time went on, we came to understand each other's lingo and to understand, and even believe, in Wiener's view of the universal role of communications in the universe. For most of us, these dinners were a seminal experience which introduced us to both a world of new ideas and new friends, many of whom became collaborators in later years.*[13]

INTERACTIVE COMPUTING, TIME-SHARING, AND HUMAN–COMPUTER SYMBIOSIS

Wiener's stress on interdisciplinary and practical work in the field of communications helped to set the foundation for upcoming developments in digital computers. By the mid 1950s, several members of the MIT community had been introduced to a new form of computing—interactive computing—in their work on the Whirlwind Computer. Whirlwind research began at MIT in 1947, providing those involved with important practical experience in digital computing. Whirlwind came on line around 1950 and was used until 1957, when the MIT Computation Center began using another vacuum-tube computer, the IBM 704.[14] Only when the Computation Center was upgraded from vacuum tube computers to the first transistorized computer in the IBM family, the IBM 7090, did time-sharing become possible.[15]

IBM, which was a main provider of computers during this period, promoted batch processing and saw it as the form of computing for the future. Reseachers at MIT, however, had a different vision. Some had worked on the Whirlwind Computer and had experienced a form of interactive computing that made it possible to use the computer directly, rather than having to submit punch cards to a central computer center and await the results.[16] The experience of real-time activity at the computer had been a significant advance over the frustration of awaiting the results of one's program under the batch processing system.

Computer resources during this period were very expensive. In general, the cost prohibited a single person from using a computer in real time. A few far-sighted researchers, however, had the idea of a time-sharing system that would take advantage of the speed of the computer, allowing several users to work with it at the same time. The computer scheduled their work in a way that gave the illusion that each was using the computer independently. In June 1959, Christopher Strachey, a British researcher, presented a talk at the International Conference on Information Processing, UNESCO, proposing time-sharing.[17] Also in 1959, John McCarthy, an MIT faculty member, wrote a memo describing a new form of computing that time-sharing would make possible and proposing that MIT plan to implement this form of computing once the IBM 7090, the new transistorized computer that they were expecting to replace the IBM 704, arrived. McCarthy advocated developing a "general-purpose system where you could program in any language you wanted."[18] In a memorandum to MIT Professor P. M. Morse in January 1959, McCarthy wrote:

> *This memorandum is based on the assumption that MIT will be given a transistorized IBM 709 about July 1960. I want to propose an operating system for it that will substantially reduce the time required to get a problem solved on the machine . . . . The proposal requires a complete revision in the way the machine is used . . . . I think the proposal points to the way all computers will be operated in the future, and we have a chance to pioneer a big step forward in the way computers are used.*[19]

At the same time as McCarthy was proposing a new form of computing—time-sharing and interactive computing—another computer pioneer, J. C. R. Licklider, who would play an important role in the developing computer revolution, was working on a paper exploring the concept of human–computer interaction that Norbert Wiener had stressed was so crucial.

Licklider had done his graduate work in psychology and, after World War II, he did research at Harvard and worked as a lecturer. He attended the post-war Wiener circles. "At that time," Licklider explained in an interview, "Norbert Wiener ran a circle that was very attractive to people all over Cambridge, and Tuesday nights I went to that. I got acquainted with a lot of people at MIT."[20] He describes another important influence on his work, the Summer Projects at MIT that he attended. Beginning in the summer of 1952, an interdisciplinary series of summer projects, which Licklider found "exhilarating," were carried on at MIT for several years. He remembered how "they brought together all these people—physicians, mathematicians. You would go one day and there would be John von Neumann, and the next day there would be Jay Forrester having the diagram of a core memory in his pocket and stuff—it was fantastically exciting."[21]

Licklider became involved with MIT and Lincoln Laboratory and "computers and radar sets and communications." He was the only psychologist in this interdisciplinary group of physicists, mathematicians and engineers. "So it was a fantastic opportunity," he noted. The lab he worked at was run by the RLE and he described how it "gave me a kind of access to the most marvelous electronics there was."[22]

By 1958–1959, Licklider was working with the engineering company Bolt Beranek and Newman doing acoustical research. There he had access to digital computers, first a Royal McBee LGP-30, and then one of the earliest DEC PDP-1 computers. Licklider learned how to program on the LGP-30, and, when the PDP-1 arrived, one of the earliest time-sharing systems was created for it. Licklider notes the grand time he had exploring what it made possible:

> *Well, it turned out that these guys at MIT and BBN . . . We'd all gotten really excited about interactive computing, and we had a kind of little religion growing here about how this was going to be totally different from batch processing.*[23]

It was during this period that Licklider carried out an experiment to try to determine how the computer could aid him in his intellectual work. He explains:

> *More significantly from my point of view, a lot hinged on a little study I had made on how I would spend my time. It showed that almost all my time was spent on algorithmic things that were no fun, but they were all necessary for the few heuristic things that seemed to be important. I had this little picture in my mind of how we were going to get people and computers really thinking together.* [24]

Inspired by the Wiener seminars, Licklider tried to set up an interdisciplinary study circle to conduct a study for the Air Force. He explains:

> *Oh, yes. We had a project with the Air Force Office of Scientific Research to develop the systems concept. Now it's corny, but then it was an interesting concept. We were trying to figure out what systems meant to the engineer and scientific world. That involved some meetings in which we brought [together] good thinkers in several fields. We wanted a kind of miniature Wiener circle . . . . we put a lot of hours into trying to do that.*[25]

This study is described in the article "Man-Computer Symbiosis." Norbert Wiener had proposed that man-computer symbiosis was a subset of the man-computer relationship. Licklider took that observation seriously and wrote an article which was published in March 1960 exploring the meaning and import of man-computer interaction and interdependence. He wrote:

> *Man-computer symbiosis is an expected development in cooperative interaction between men and electronic computers. It will involve very close coupling between the human and electronic members of the partnership. The main aims are 1) to let computers facilitate formulative thinking as they now facilitate the solution of formulated problems, and 2) to enable men and computers to cooperate in making decisions and controlling complex situations without inflexible dependence on predetermined programs.* [26]

The article became an important formulation of a vision of computing for the developing computer revolution in time-sharing and networking. Licklider did not promote the computer as a replacement for humans nor see humans as servants to computers. Instead he proposed research exploring the role of humans and machines. His goal was to enhance the symbiotic relationship between the human and computer partners needed to aid intellectual activity.

CTSS AND PROJECT MAC

One of those who was to play an important role in implementing the vision of human–computer symbiosis was Robert M. Fano. Fano worked at RLE after receiving his Ph.D. from MIT in June 1947. In the preface to his book *Transmission of Information*, he described his early contact with Norbert Wiener and Claude Shannon.[27] He explained how he studied the theoretical questions raised by Wiener and Shannon and did research to explore the theories they had pioneered.

In 1960, Fano was a senior faculty member at MIT. Gordon Brown, then Dean of the Engineering School of MIT, arranged for several faculty members to take a course in computing taught by Fernando Corbató and John McCarthy. Fano, remembering his excitement in learning how to program during this course, recalled, "I wrote a program that worked."[28]

Gordon Brown, according to Fano, understood that the computer was going to be very important and encouraged his senior faculty to become familiar with it. In 1960, the MIT administration appointed a committee to make recommendations about the future needs of MIT regarding computers. Fano was one of the faculty members appointed to the committee. This committee created a technical committee made up of Fernando Corbató, John McCarthy, Marvin Minsky, Doug Ross, and Jack Dennis, with Herb Teager acting as chair. This committee became known as The Long Term Computation Study Group.

During this period, the celebration of MIT's centennial was being planned. Eight talks were scheduled. After one of the speakers canceled at the last minute, John McCarthy, who had been working on the long-range computer study, was invited to speak. In his talk, McCarthy described the rationale behind time-sharing and the important vision for the future of computing that it represented. Other participants at the conference included Norbert Wiener, Claude Shannon, John Kemeny, Robert Fano, Alan Perlis, and J. C. R. Licklider. In the course of the conference, Wiener explained that "a computing machine is a general-purpose device that can be programmed to do very specific jobs."[29] But, he warned, if you fail to give a necessary instruction to a computer, "you cannot expect the machine itself to think of this restriction."[30] Wiener explained that humans had to oversee the computer. "The unsafe act," he cautioned, "may not show its danger until it is too late to do anything about it."[31]

In his comments, Licklider described how a human being "must not have so to clutter his mind with codes and formats that he cannot think about his substantive problem."[32] Licklider described his vision of the future of the computer:

> *In due course it will be part of the formulation of problems; part of real-time thinking, problem solving, doing of research, conducting of experiments, getting into the literature and finding references . . . It will mediate and facilitate communication among human beings.*[33]

He expressed his hope that the computer "through its contribution to formulative thinking . . . will help us understand the structure of ideas, the nature of intellectual processes."[34] And he proposed that "one of the most important present functions of the digital computer in the university should be to catalyze the development of [computer] science."[35]

Another participant at the conference, the linguist Yehoshua Bar-Hillel, pointed out that no one at the conference knew what was going to happen in the future, either in the long term or short term. Because of this uncertainty, it was important to decide what type of future it would be worthwhile to encourage. There were two paths to choose from, and he posed the question as to which path should be taken. "Do we want computers that will compete with human beings and achieve intelligent behavior autonomously, or do we want what has been called man-machine symbiosis?"[36]

"I think computer people have the obligation to decide which of the two aims they are going to adopt," he proposed. Arguing that the human brain was more developed than it would be possible to make a machine brain at the current stage of technological development, he recommended that the best path was that of man-machine symbiosis:

> *I admit that these two aims do not definitely exclude each other, but there has been an enormous waste during the last few years in trying to achieve*

what I regard as the wrong aim at this stage, namely, computers that will autonomously work as well as the human brain with its billion years of evolution.

Shortly after the conference, in the summer of 1961, Fano took a sabbatical. He went to work at Lincoln Labs because he hoped to learn more about digital computers there. Describing the important change he observed in how communications systems were viewed, he explained:

You know, we used to talk about components such as modulators and detectors and all the gadgets that went into communication systems. That's the past. We have to talk about functions now, because with a computer you can implement any function you want. [37]

He proposed that one had to begin to think about communication in the general purpose way that the digital computer was making possible.

In the meantime, the Long Term Computation Study Group published its reports. There were two proposals for how to proceed; one from Herbert Teager, who had been chairman of the committee, and a second from the rest of the committee. Fernando Corbató, a member of the committee and then Associate Director of the MIT Computing Center, set out to implement an "interim" solution to the kind of computing the majority report proposed. Corbató describes the subsequent events.

I started up with just a couple of the key staff people, Marjorie Daggett . . . and Bob Daley. We hammered out a very primitive prototype. . . . We started thinking about it in spring of 1961. I remember that by the summer of 1961 we were in the heat of trying to work out the intricacies of the interrupts.[38]

He explains how he and the other programmers were acting on the vision that had been developed by the majority of the Long Term Study Group Committee:

I sketched out what we would try to do and Marjorie, Daley and I worked out the hairy details of trying to cope with this kind of poor hardware. By November, 1961 we were able to demonstrate a really crude prototype of the system. [39]

They gave a seminar and demonstration with their prototype time-sharing system in November 1961. Corbató recalls:

That's the date that's branded in my mind. It was only a four-Flexowriter system. . . . People were pleased that there were finally examples surfacing from [the work]. They did not view it as an answer to anybody's problem. . . . We made the [first] demo in November 1961 on an [IBM] 709. The

> *switch to the [IBM] 7090 occurred in the spring of 1962 at the Comp Center.*[40]

Corbató describes how CTSS (Compatible Time-Sharing System), as the time-sharing system he was working on was called, could not go into operation until the transistorized IBM 7090 hardware had arrived and could be used in early spring of 1962.[41] Only then could they begin to deal with the real problems of making a working system.

Corbató gave a talk at a conference about CTSS in May 1962, but they still did not have a working system running. By October 1962, however, J. C. R. Licklider had accepted a position with ARPA under the U.S. Department of Defense, on his condition that he would be allowed to implement the vision of interactive computing and time-sharing.

In November 1962, Licklider and Fano both attended an unclassified meeting held for the Air Force in Hot Springs, Virginia. Fano had been invited to chair a session on communications, and he and Licklider both attended some of the sessions on command and control. On the way back from the conference, on the train returning to Washington D.C., several people from the meeting were in the same car. They all chatted about what had happened and moved from seat to seat to talk to different people. "And I did spend quite a bit of time with Lick," Fano recalled, "and I understood better what he had in mind."[42]

Fano spent Thanksgiving Day 1962 thinking over the discussion he had had with Licklider. The day after Thanksgiving he had a meeting previously scheduled with the provost at MIT, Charlie Townes. When Fano told the provost what he had been thinking, Townes told him, "Go ahead." Fano wrote out his thoughts in a two-page memorandum that he distributed broadly around MIT. In the proposal, he put forward three goals: 1) time-sharing 2) a community using it and 3) education, which meant developing both undergraduate and graduate courses.

The following Tuesday, Fano met with Julius A. (Jay) Stratton, then president of MIT. Fano was surprised when Stratton asked him which building he would use for the project, encouraging him to begin to implement his proposal.

In reviewing the period, Corbató described how Licklider went to ARPA "as a 'Johnny Appleseed' with a mission" and that that was more than his superiors had expected. They tolerated it, Corbató observed, but Licklider was "the one who was driving it rather than them."[43] Licklider added that while his superiors called for command and control, he made clear he was going to be involved with "interactive computing. . . . I just wanted to make it clear," Licklider noted, "that I wasn't going to be running battle planning missions or something. I was going to be dealing with the engineering substratum that [would] make it possible to do that stuff [command and control] right."[44]

Fano developed a funding proposal for Project MAC. It was submitted to ARPA. The contract was signed on June 30, 1963, the day before the 1963 summer study to demonstrate and create enthusiasm for time-sharing and interactive computing began at MIT. "Time-sharing," Martin Greenberger recalled, "on the Computation Center machine was available on the opening day of the summer project."[45]

When asked how he felt when he learned that there would be funding to develop CTSS as part of Project MAC, Corbató recalled, "Well, it was a cooperative thing. Nobody had license to run wild—but you had license to try to make something happen."[46] Corbató clarified, "I wasn't trying to start a company or anything like that; my goal was to exhibit it." By mid-October a second time-sharing computer was available for Project MAC. And it was operating within a week.

Reviewing the reasons for the success of Project MAC, Greenberger explained, "CTSS was an open system. It challenged the user to design his own subsystem, no matter what discipline he came from, no matter what his research interest."[47]

Fano pointed out that one of the goals of Project MAC had not been achieved. This goal identified an important technical and social need that would inspire future networking developments. The ever-developing and changing computer hardware and software posed the challenge of providing a support network for users, both locally and remotely. He explained:

> *One of our goals was to make the computer truly accessible to people wherever they were. We did not succeed. For people who lived in the community that used the system, it was fine. In any system like that, you keep learning things, you keep using new things, and so you keep having troubles. If you can go next door and say, "Hey, I was doing this and something strange happened, do you know what I did wrong?" usually somebody in your neighborhood will be able to help you. If instead you are far away, you are stuck. . . .We tried to develop some way of helping the remote users . . . .Well, we never did it. So in fact, we failed to make the computer truly accessible regardless of the location of the user.* [48]

Despite the problems, Greenberger observed, "I think one of the greatest successes was that CTSS gave so many people, with such widely different backgrounds, a system and experience that they would not have gotten any other way at that point."[49] Fano explained that the importance of developing time-sharing was not just in developing something technical. Rather, he noted, "I am really talking about the interaction of users in the sharing. That's important. I feel that systems that do this as easily as time-sharing systems do not exist."[50] Remembering how Project MAC created an online community, Fano recalled "friendship being born out of using somebody else's program, people communicating through the system and then meeting by accident and saying 'Oh, that's you.' All sorts of things. It was a nonreproducible community phenomenon," he concluded.[51]

Offering his summary of the achievements, Corbató explained:

> *Two aspects strike me as being important. One is the kind of open system quality, which allowed everyone to make the system kind of be their thing rather than what somebody else imposed on them . . . . So people were tailoring it to mesh with their own interests. And the other thing is, I think, we deliberately kept the system model relatively unsophisticated (maybe that's the wrong word—uncomplicated), so we could explain it easily.*[52]

The achievements of Project MAC and the other time-sharing systems built as a result of Licklider's tenure at ARPA provided the basis for the vision that would guide the development of the ARPANET.[53] In their paper, "The Computer as a Communication Device," Licklider and Robert Taylor predicted:

> *In a few years, men will be able to communicate more effectively through a machine than face to face . . . We believe that we are entering into a technological age, in which we will be able to interact with the richness of living information—not merely in the passive way that we have become accustomed to using books and libraries, but as active participants in an ongoing process, bringing something to it through our interaction with it, and not simply receiving something from it by our connection to it.*[54]

While they acknowledged that technical uses, such as the switching function, were important in the transfer of information, such uses were not the aspect they were interested in. Instead they proposed that there was a power and responsiveness that online interaction with a computer made possible that would significantly affect the communication possible between the humans using the computer.

Though they were familiar with commercial time-sharing facilities that called themselves "multi-access," they explained that these had not succeeded in creating the kind of multi-access computer communities that the academic and research time-sharing systems spawned.

They described these time-sharing communities, of which Project MAC was an early example, as "socio-technical pioneers . . . out ahead of the rest of the computer world." They attributed this to the fact that some of the members of these online communities were computer scientists and engineers who understood both the concept of human–computer interaction and the technology of interactive, multi-access systems. Among the members of these online communities were creative people in different fields and disciplines who recognized the potential value of these multi-access communities to their work. Those in these online communities had access to large multi-access computers and knew how to use them. The collaborative efforts of those online had a regenerative effect.[55]

Elaborating on what they meant by regenerative, they wrote that in the half-dozen time-sharing online communities in existence during the 1960s, those doing research and development of computer systems and applications provided mutual support for each other. The product was a growing quantity of resources, including programs, data, and technical know-how. "But we have seen only the beginning," they predicted. "There is much more programming and data collection—and much more learning how to cooperate—to be done before the full potential of the concept can be realized." They cautioned, however, that these systems could only be developed interactively. And they explain that, "The systems being built must remain flexible and open-ended throughout the process of development, which is evolutionary."[56]

They observe that there were systems advertising themselves via the same labels as "interactive," "time-sharing" and "multi-access." But these were commercial systems, and they found that there were distinct differences between the commercial systems and academic and research time-sharing systems. The commercial systems did not offer the same "power," "flexibility" of software resources, and the general purposeness that the research and academic time-sharing systems at MIT, UCB, Stanford, and SDC had made available to over 1,000 people for a number of years.[57]

Discussing their vision of the future, they predicted that linking up the existing online communities would create a still more powerful and important development—online supercommunities made up of the existing communities created by the time-sharing systems. "The hope," they explained, "is that interconnection will make available to all the communities the programs and data resources of the entire supercommunity." They predicted that the future would bring "a mobile network of networks—ever changing in both content and configuration." And just as Licklider and Taylor realized that a time-sharing system was more than a collection of computers and software, Corbató notes that it was Fano who recognized that "a time-sharing system was more than just a set of people using a common resource; it was also a means of communicating and sharing ideas."[58]

Another time-sharing pioneer, Doug Ross, observed that Project MAC made CTSS available, rather than waiting for the ideal technical system to be developed, as others had favored. By producing a prototype and encouraging others to contribute to it, CTSS had a significant impact on those who then had the ability to build into the system what they needed and to contribute so it would serve their needs. "I always say," Ross concluded, "you can't design an interface from just one side."[59] This quality of putting an open system out and encouraging people to contribute to it to make it what they needed, made it possible to build a human-centered rather than technology-centered system.[60]

Summing up the achievement of the Project MAC pioneers, John A. N. Lee, editor of two special issues of *The IEEE Annals of the History of Computing* which document the development of time-sharing and Project MAC at MIT, writes:

> *With the development of computer networking, which almost naturally followed on the development of time-sharing and interactive computing, it is as if the whole world now time-shares myriad computers, providing facilities which were beyond the dreams of even the MIT researchers of 1960 . . . But this is where it started—with the ideas of John McCarthy, the implementation skills of Fernando Corbató, the vision of J. C. R. Licklider, and the organizational skills of Robert Fano.*[61]

THE IMPLICATIONS

The pioneers of cybernetics and multi-access computing who gathered at the MIT centennial in the Spring of 1961 to discuss the future of computing proposed that the crucial issue in trying to solve a problem is how to formulate the question. They expressed concern that the computer would bring great changes into our world and recommended that people who understood the issues involved be part of setting government policy regarding these developments.

The pioneers also observed that there were opposing visions of what the future should be. One road was that of human–computer symbiosis, of a close interaction between the human and the computer so each could function more effectively. "The hope is that, in not too many years," J. C. R. Licklider wrote, "human brains and computing machines will be coupled together very tightly, and that the resulting partnership will think as no human brain has ever thought and process data in a way not approached by the information-handling machines we know today."[62] The other road was that of creating computers that would be able to do the thinking or problem solving without human assistance. Pioneers such as Licklider explained that "man-computer symbiosis is probably not the ultimate paradigm for complex technological systems" and that at some point in the future "electronic or chemical 'machines' will outdo the human brain in most of the functions we now consider exclusively within its province." He maintained, however, that, "there will nevertheless be a fairly long interim during which the main intellectual advances will be made by men and computers working together in intimate association."[63] Though Licklider was willing to concede "dominance in the distant future to celebration of machines alone," he recognized the creative and important developments that the partnership between the human and computer would make possible. He predicted that the years of human–computer symbiosis, "should be intellectually the most creative and exciting in the history of mankind."[64]

In the years following the development of CTSS and Project MAC and the linking of different time-sharing systems to create a supercommunity of online communities which became known as the ARPANET, the firm foundation set by CTSS and Project MAC and the helpful vision and direction set by Licklider, Fano, and other pioneers of the period gave birth to the sprawling and impressive networking communities that today we call the Internet and Usenet.

The pioneers of time-sharing and interactive computing provided a vision of human–computer symbiosis as an intellectual advance for humans. Online human–computer and computer-facilitated human-to-human communication were seen as the embodiment of this symbiosis. The vision of the computer pioneers of the 1960s, of human–computer symbiosis and of a multi-access, interactive, network of networks, or a supercommunity of online communities, is a vision that can still fruitfully guide work to build and extend the global computer network in the United States and around the world today.

NOTES

1. "The Project MAC Interviews," *IEEE Annals of the History of Computing* 14 (2) (1992): 15 (hereafter, *Annals*). The interviews were conducted on October 18, 1988, in two group interviews/recollection exchanges. The interviewers were John A. N. Lee and Robert Rosin. The participants were Fernando J. Corbató, Robert M. Fano, Martin Greenberger, J. C. R. Licklider, Douglas T. Ross, and Allan L. Scherr.
2. Martin Greenberger, ed. *Management and Computers of the Future* (Cambridge, Mass.: The MIT Press, 1962) 8. This book was later published in hard cover and paperback under the title *Computers and the World of the Future.*
3. John R. Pierce, "Communication," *Scientific American* 227 (September 1972), 31–41. The September 1972 issue of *Scientific American* also appeared as a book, *Communications: A Scientific American Book* (San Francisco: W. H. Freeman, 1972).
4. *Ibid.*, 33.
5. *Ibid.*, 41.

6. "Challenge Interview: Norbert Wiener: Man and the Machine," June 1959, in *Collected Works of Norbert Wiener with Commentaries*, vol. 4 (Cambridge, Mass.: The MIT Press, 1985) 717.
7. Norbert Wiener, *Cybernetics: or Control and Communication in the Animal and the Machine* (Cambridge, Mass.: The MIT Press, 1948), 11–12. Wiener wrote, "In choosing this term, we wish to recognize that the first significant paper on feedback mechanisms is an article on governors, which was published by Clerk Maxwell in 1868. . . . We also wish to refer to the fact that the steering engines of a ship are indeed one of the earliest and best-developed forms of feedback mechanisms."
8. Norbert Wiener, *God and Golem, Inc.* (Cambridge, Mass.: The MIT Press, 1964), 71.
9. Norbert Wiener, "A Scientist's Dilemma in a Materialist World," in *Collected Works,* vol. 4, 709.
10. Norbert Wiener, *I Am A Mathematician* (Cambridge, Mass.: The MIT Press, 1956), 171.
11. Wiener, *Cybernetics*, 1.
12. From "The Legacy of Norbert Wiener: A Centennial Symposium," Cambridge, Massachusetts, 1994, 19. Licklider, Fano, Minsky, and other MIT pioneers refer to the important influence that being part of the RLE had on their subsequent work.
13. *Ibid.*
14. One of the reasons that a computer using vacuum tubes was not appropriate for a time-sharing system, according to Robert Fano, was that the "mean time between failures was seven or nine [hours]." See *Annals* 14 (2) (1992): 25.
15. Chronology from *Annals* 14 (1) (1992): 18.
16. See *Annals* 14 (1) (1992): 38 for a description of the frustrations of batch processing.
17. See C. Strachey, "Time-sharing in large fast computers," *Proc Int. Conf. on Info Processing,* UNESCO, June, 1959, 336–341. See also Frederick Brooks Jr., *The Mythical Man-Month: Essays on Software Engineering* (Reading, Mass.: Addison-Wesley, 1972), 146.
18. See "John McCarthy's 1959 Memorandum," *Annals* 14 (1) (1992): 20–21. See also J .A. N. Lee, "Claims to the Term Time-Sharing, *Annals* 14 (1) (1992): 16–17.
19. "John McCarthy's 1959 Memorandum," 20.
20. *Annals* 14 (2) (1992): 16.
21. *Ibid.*
22. *Ibid.*
23. *Ibid.*
24. "An Interview with J. C. R. Licklider" conducted by William Aspray and Arthur L. Norberg, tape recording, Cambridge, Massachusetts, 28 October 1988, OH 150, Charles Babbage Institute, University of Minnesota, Minneapolis, Minnesota. See also J. C. R. Licklider, "Man–Computer Symbiosis," *IRE*

Transactions on Human Factors in Electronics, vol. HFE-1 (March 1960): 4–11. Reprinted in *In Memoriam: J. C. R. Licklider 1915–1990* (Palo Alto, CA.: Digital Systems Research Center, 1990), 1–19.

25. "Interview with Licklider."
26. Licklider, *Man–Computer Symbiosis,* 1.
27. Robert Fano, *Transmission of Information* (Cambridge, Mass.: The MIT Press, 1961) vii.
28. "An Interview with Robert M. Fano" conducted by Arthur L. Norberg on 20–21 April 1989, Cambridge, Massachusetts, tape recording, Charles Babbage Institute, Center for the History of Information Processing, University of Minnesota, Minneapolis.
29. *Management and the Future of the Computer*, 22
30. *Ibid.*, 24.
31. *Ibid.*, 32.
32. *Ibid.*, 205.
33. *Ibid.*, 206.
34. *Ibid.*, 207.
35. *Ibid.*.
36. *Ibid.*, 324.
37. *Annals* 14 (2) (1992): 20.
38. *Annals* 14 (1) (1992): 44. Teager's recommendations are described on pages 24–27. Excerpts from the Long Range Computation Study Group's recommendation for a time-sharing systems which resulted in Corbató's work on CTSS are in the same issue on pages 28–30.
39. *Ibid.*, 45. "What we had done was [that] we had wedged out 5K words of the user address space and inserted a little operating system that was going to manage the four typewriters. We did not have any disk storage, so we took advantage of the fact that it was a large machine and we had a lot of tape drives. We assigned one tape drive per typewriter."
40. *Ibid.*, 45–46. Corbató describes how he thought CTSS would be running on the IBM 7090 by the time he was to give a talk on it at the AFIPS Spring Joint Computer Conference in May 1962, but they were not able to get it running by the time the paper was presented. Despite his disappointment, the paper is an important historical document. See Fernando J. Corbató, Marjorie Merwin-Daggett, and Robert C. Daley, "An Experimental Time-Sharing System," *Proceedings-Spring Joint Computer Conference, AFIPS* 21, 335-344.
41. It was called the Compatible Time-Sharing System, as it was developed in the Computation Center and so had to be compatible with the batch system running there.
42. *Annals* 14 (2) (1992): 22.
43. *Ibid.*, 24
44. *Ibid.*
45. *Ibid.*, 26. Fano explained that Licklider wanted interactive computing with time-

sharing. He notes that "one was the 'tool' the other the 'goal'. This is where the name MAC came from. There was a goal and there was a tool—the tool that was most appropriate at that time." He goes on to explain that there had been the vision on the part of people like John McCarthy and later Licklider "of what could come out of it when you started building a computer utility. It didn't exist then. It didn't exist until the time of Project MAC because it was just that year that Corby finished the model that really could serve a community. It didn't exist before." *Ibid.*, 23.

46. *Ibid.* 26.
47. *Ibid.* Greenberger describes how he designed a subsystem for CTSS where students created a set of commands to simulate the stock market, accounting, production scheduling, online modeling, and so on. They put these commands together into a system under CTSS that they called OPS (On-line Programming and Simulation). *Ibid.*, 27.
48. *Ibid.*, 31.
49. *Ibid.*, 32.
50. *Ibid.*, 35.
51. *Ibid.*, 33.
52. *Ibid.*
53. By Fall 1967, according to the "Time-Sharing System Scorecard," there were 35 time-sharing systems, either operational or planned, at research and academic sites, mainly in the United States. The scorecard also lists 15 commercial time-sharing installations being planned or in existence. "Prolog to the Future," *Annals* 14 (2) (1992): 42-47.
54. "The Computer as a Communication Device," *Science and Technology* 76 (April 1968): 21–31, as reprinted in *In Memoriam: J. C. R. Licklider: 1915-1990,*" 21.
55. *Ibid.*, 30–31.
56. *Ibid.*, 31.
57. The time-sharing systems they are describing are listed in the "Time-Sharing System Scorecard" as having been begun in the following years: MIT (Project MAC at MIT, begun in May 1963), UCB (Project GENIE at the University of California, Berkeley, begun in April 1965), Stanford University (Stanford, California, begun in August 1964), and SDC (Systems Development Corporation, Santa Monica, California, begun in August 1964).
58. *Annals* 14 (1) (1992): 48.
59. *Ibid.*, 51.
60. *Annals* 14 (2) (1992). One of the interviewers, Robert Rosin, noted, "You see, if what you're trying to do is optimize technical resources (physical resources), Herb's point of view was exactly right. If you try to optimize the use of human resources, then the point of view you were taking was a lot closer to reality."
61. *Annals* 14 (1) (1992): 3–4.
62. Licklider, "Man–Computer Symbiosis," 3. Licklider proposed the role that each partner will play in the symbiotic relationship. The human partner will "set the

goals, formulate the hypotheses, determine the criteria, and perform the evaluations." The computers "will do the routinizable work that must be done to prepare the way for insights and decisions in technical and scientific thinking." *Ibid.*, 1.

63. *Ibid.*, 2–3.
64. *Ibid.*

Thanks to Tom Van Vleck, Alex McKenzie, and Fernando Corbató for pointing out sources that were helpful in doing the research for this paper. Also, thanks to Scott Dorsey who suggested I try to find out about Project MAC. Robert Fano provided helpful corrections. Marilyn Potes and Sumner Rosen provided essential reference material. Various people on Usenet provided valuable comments and corrections. Another reference which covers this material is "The Evolution of Interactive Computing Through Time-Sharing and Networking" by Judy Elizabeth O'Neill, June 1992. The interviews in the *IEEE Annals of the History of Computing* special issues (vol. 14, nos. 1 and 2) are an important source of information about the period. They are supplemented by interviews that are available from the Charles Babbage Institute.

An earlier version of this chapter by Ronda Hauben was posted on Usenet in Winter 1994.

7

Behind the Net
The Untold Story of the ARPANET and Computer Science

The global Internet's progenitor was the Advanced Research Projects Agency Network (ARPANET), financed and encouraged by the U.S. Department of Defense. This is important to remember, because the support and style of management by ARPA of its contractors was crucial to the success of the ARPANET. As the Internet develops and the struggle over the role it plays unfolds, it will be important to remember how the network developed and the culture with which it was connected. The culture of the Net as a facilitator of communication is an important feature to understand.

The *ARPANET Completion Report*, published jointly in 1978 by BBN of Cambridge, Massachusetts, and ARPA, concludes by stating:

> *. . . it is somewhat fitting to end on the note that the ARPANET program has had a strong and direct feedback into the support and strength of computer science, from which the network itself sprung.*[1]

In order to understand the wonder that the Internet and various other components of the Net represent, we need to understand why the *ARPANET Completion Report* ends with the suggestion that the ARPANET is fundamentally connected to and born of computer science rather than of the military.

THE HISTORY OF ARPA LEADING UP TO THE ARPANET

A climate of scientific research surrounded the entire history of the ARPANET. ARPA was formed to fund basic research, and thus was not oriented toward military products. The formation of this agency was part of the U.S. government's response to the then Soviet Union's launch of Sputnik in 1957.[2] One area of ARPA-supported research concerned the question of how to utilize the military's investment in computers to do Command and Control Research (CCR). J. C. R. Licklider was chosen to head this effort. Licklider came to ARPA from BBN in October 1962.[3] His educational background was a combination of engineering studies and physiological psychology. His multi-disciplinary experiences provided Licklider with a perspective uncommon among engineers.

As a result of Licklider's arrival, the Agency's contracts were shifted from nonacademic contractors toward "the best academic computer centers."[4] The then-current method of computing was batch processing. Licklider saw that improvements could be made in CCR only from work that would advance the current state of computing technology. He particularly wanted to move forward into the age of interactive computing, and Defense Department contractors were not moving in that direction. In an interview, Licklider described how at one of the contractors, System Development Corporation (SDC), the computing research being done "was based on batch processing, and while I was interested in a new way of doing things, they [SDC] were studying how to make improvements in the ways things were done already."[5] To reflect the changed direction Licklider was bringing to ARPA-supported research, his division of ARPA was renamed the Information Processing Techniques Office (IPT or IPTO). The office "developed into a far-reaching basic research program in advanced technology."[6]

The *Completion Report Draft* states that "Prophetically, Licklider nicknamed the group of computer specialists he gathered the 'Intergalactic Network'."[7] Before work on the ARPANET began, the foundation had been established by the creation of the Information Processing Techniques Office of ARPA. Robert Taylor, Licklider's successor at the IPTO, reflects on how this foundation was based on Licklider's interest in interconnecting communities:

> *Lick was among the first to perceive the spirit of community created among the users of the first time-sharing systems. . . . In pointing out the community phenomena created, in part, by the sharing of resources in one time-sharing system, Lick made it easy to think about interconnecting the communities[,] the interconnection of interactive, on-line communities of people . . .*[8]

The "spirit of community" was related to Licklider's interest in having computers help people communicate with other people.[9] Licklider's vision of an "intergalactic network" connecting people represented an important conceptual shift in computer science. This vision guided the researchers who created the ARPANET. After the ARPANET was functioning, the computer scientists using it realized that assisting human communication was a major fundamental advance that the ARPANET made possible.

As early as 1963, a commonly asked question of the IPTO directors by the ARPA directors about IPTO projects was "'Why don't we rely on the computer industry to do that?', or occasionally more strongly, 'We should not support that effort because ABC (read, 'computer industry') will do it—if it's worth doing!'"[10] This question leads to an important distinction: ARPA research was different from what the computer industry had in mind to do, or was likely to undertake. Since Licklider's creation of the IPTO, the work supported by ARPA/IPTO continued his explicit emphasis on communications. The *Completion Report Draft* explains:

> *The ARPA/IPTO theme . . . is that the promise offered by the computer . . . as a communication medium between people, dwarfs into relative insignificance the historical beginnings of the computer as an arithmetic engine.*[11]

The *Completion Report Draft* goes on to differentiate the research ARPA supported from the research done by the computer industry:

> *The computer industry, in the main, still thinks of the computer as an arithmetic engine. Their heritage is reflected even in current designs of "their communication systems." They have an economic and psychological commitment to the arithmetic engine model, and it can die only slowly. . . .*[12]

The *Completion Report Draft* further analyzes this problem by tracing it back to the nation's universities:

> *. . . furthermore, it is a view that is still reinforced by most of the nation's computer science programs. Even universities, or at least parts of them, are held in the grasp of the arithmetic engine concept. . . .*[13]

ARPA's IPTO was responsible for the research and development which led to the success of first the ARPANET, and later the Internet. Without this support and commitment, such a development might never have happened. One of ARPA's criterion for supporting research was that the research had to offer an order of magnitude of advance over the current state of development. Such research is never immediately profitable. In society, therefore, there is the need for organizations that do not pursue profit as their goal, but rather work on furthering the state of the art. Computer networking was developed and spread widely in an environment outside of commercial and profit considerations, an environment that supported such research.

Others understood the communications promise of computers. For example, in RFC-1336, David Clark, a senior research scientist at MIT's

Laboratory for Computer Science, describes the impact of the Internet in making possible new means of human-to-human communication:

> *It is not proper to think of networks as connecting computers. Rather, they connect people using computers to mediate. The great success of the Internet is not technical, but in human impact. Electronic mail may not be a wonderful advance in Computer Science, but it is a whole new way for people to communicate. The continued growth of the Internet is a technical challenge to all of us, but we must never lose sight of where we came from, the great change we have worked on the larger computer community, and the great potential we have for future change.*[14]

Research predating the ARPANET had been done by Paul Baran, Thomas Marill and others.[15] This led Lawrence Roberts and other IPTO staff to formally introduce the topic of networking computers of differing types (that is, incompatible hardware and software) together in order to make it possible for ARPA's Principal Investigators (PI) to share resources. The ARPA Principal Investigators meeting was held annually for university and other contractors to summarize results of the previous year and discuss future research. In the Spring of 1967 it was held at the University of Michigan in Ann Arbor. Networking was one of the topics brought up at this meeting. As a result of discussion at this meeting, it was decided that there had to be agreement on conventions for character and block transmission, error checking and retransmission, and computer and user identification. These specifications became the contents of the inter-host communication's "protocol." Frank Westervelt was chosen to write about this protocol, and a communication group was formed to study the questions.[16]

In order to develop a network of varied computers, two main problems had to be solved:

> 1. *To construct a "subnetwork" consisting of telephone circuits and switching nodes whose reliability, delay characteristics, capacity, and cost would facilitate resource sharing among the computers on the network.*
> 2. *To understand, design, and implement the protocols and procedures within the operating systems of each connected computer, in order to allow the use of the new subnetwork by those computers in sharing resources.*[17]

After one draft and additional work on this communications position paper were completed, a meeting was scheduled in early October 1967 by ARPA at which the protocol paper and specifications for the Interface Message Processor (IMP) were discussed. A subnetwork of IMPs, dedicated minicomputers connected to each of the participant's computers, was the method chosen to connect the computers (hosts) to each other via phone lines. This standardized the subnet to which the hosts connected. Researchers at each site would have to write the software necessary to connect their local host computer to the IMP at their site. ARPA picked 19 possible participants in what was now known as the "ARPA Network."

From the time of the 1967 PI meeting, various computer scientists who were ARPA contractors were busy thinking about the planning and development of the ARPANET. Part of that work was a document outlining a beginning design for the IMP subnetwork. This specification led to a competitive procurement for the design of the IMP subnetwork.

By late 1967 ARPA had given a contract to the Stanford Research Institute (SRI) to write specifications for the communications network they were developing. In December of 1968, SRI issued the report, "A Study of Computer Network Design Parameters." Elmer Shapiro played an important role in the research for this report. Based on this work, Lawrence Roberts and Barry Wessler of ARPA wrote the final ARPA version of the IMP specification.[18] This specification was ready to be discussed at the June 1968 PI meeting.

The Program Plan, "Resource Sharing Computer Networks," was submitted June 3, 1968 by the IPTO to the ARPA Director, who, with unusual speed, approved it on June 21, 1968. It outlined the objectives of the research and how the objectives would be fulfilled. The proposed network was impressive, as it would prove useful to both the computing research centers that connected to the network and to the military. The proposed research requirements would provide immediate benefits to the computer centers the network would connect. ARPA's stated objectives were to experiment with varied interconnections of computers and the sharing of resources in an attempt to improve productivity of computer research. Justification was drawn from technical needs in both the scientific and military environments. The Program Plan developed into a set of specifications. These specifications were connected to a competitive Request for Quotation (RFQ) to find an organization that would design and build the IMP subnetwork.[19]

Following the approval of the Program Plan, 140 potential bidders were mailed the Request for Quotation. After a bidders conference, 12 proposals were received and from them ARPA narrowed the field to four bidders. BBN was the eventual recipient of the contract.[20]

The second technical problem, as defined by the *ad hoc* Communications Group, still remained to be solved. The set of agreed upon communications settings (known as a protocol), which would allow the hosts to communicate with each other over the subnetwork, had to be developed. This work was left "for host sites to work out among themselves."[21] This meant that the software necessary to connect the hosts to the IMP subnetwork had to be developed. ARPA assigned this duty to the initially designated ARPANET sites. Each of the first sites had a different type of computer to connect. ARPA trusted that the programmers at each site would be capable of modifying their operating systems in order to connect their systems to the subnetwork. In addition, the sites needed to develop the software necessary to utilize the other hosts on the network. By assigning them responsibilities, ARPA made the academic computer science community an active part of the ARPANET development team.[22]

Stephen Crocker, one of graduate students involved with the development of the earliest ARPANET protocols, associates the placement of the initial ARPANET sites at research institutions with the fact that the ARPANET was ground-breaking research. He wrote in a message responding to questions on the COM-PRIV mailing list:

> *During the initial development of the Arpanet, there was simply a limit as to how far ahead anyone could see and manage. The IMPs were placed in cooperative ARPA R&D sites with the hope that these research sites would figure out how to exploit this new communication medium.*[23]

The first sites of the ARPANET were picked to provide either network support services or unique resources. The key services the first four sites provided were:[24]

UCLA	Network Measurement Center
SRI	Network Information Center
UCSB	Culler-Fried interactive mathematics
UTAH	graphics (hidden line removal)

Crocker recounts that these four sites were selected because they were "existing ARPA computer science research contractors." This was important because "the research community could be counted on to take some initiative."[25]

The very first site to receive an IMP was UCLA. Professor Leonard Kleinrock of UCLA was involved with much of the early development of the ARPANET. His work in queuing theory gave him a basis to develop measurement techniques used to monitor the ARPANET's performance. This made it natural that UCLA received one of the first nodes, as it would be important to measure the network's activity from early on—one of the first two or three sites had to be the measurement site in order for the statistics to be based on correct data for analysis purposes and UCLA accordingly came to be the Network Measurement Center (NMC).[26]

THE NETWORK WORKING GROUP

Once the initial sites were chosen, representatives from each site gathered together to talk about how to solve the technical problem of getting the hosts to communicate with each other. The *Completion Report Draft* tells us about this beginning:

> *To provide the hosts with a little impetus to work on the host-to-host problems, ARPA assigned Elmer Shapiro of SRI "to make something happen," a typically vague ARPA assignment. Shapiro called a meeting in the summer of 1968 which was attended by programmers from several of the first hosts to be connected to the network. Individuals who were present have said that it was clear from the meeting at that time, no one had even any clear notions of what the fundamental host-to-host issues might be.*[27]

This group, which came to be known as the Network Working Group (NWG), was exploring new territory. The first meeting took place several months before the first IMP was configured. The group had to begin with a blank slate. In Crocker's recollections of the important developments produced by the NWG which were provided as the introduction to RFC-1000, the reader is reminded that the thinking involved was groundbreaking and thus exciting. Crocker remembers that the first meeting was chaired by Elmer Shapiro of SRI, who initiated the conversation with a list of questions.[28] Also present at this first meeting were Steve Carr from the University of Utah, Crocker from UCLA, Jeff Rulifson from SRI, and Ron Stoughton from UCSB. These attendees, most of them graduate students, were the programmers described in the *Completion Report Draft*.

According to Crocker, this was a seminal meeting. The attendees could only be theoretical, as none of the lowest levels of communication had been developed yet. They needed a transport layer or low-level communications platform to build upon. BBN would not deliver the first IMP until August 30, 1969. It was important to meet before this date, as the NWG "imagined all sorts of possibilities."[29] Only once they started thinking together could this working group actually develop anything. These fresh thoughts from fresh minds helped to incubate new ideas. The *Completion Report Draft* properly acknowledges what this early group helped accomplish. "Their early thinking was at a very high level."[30] A concrete decision made at the first meeting was to continue holding meetings similar to the first one. This set the precedent of holding exchange meetings at each of their sites.

Crocker, describing the problems facing these networking pioneers, writes:

With no specific service definition in place for what the IMPs were providing to the hosts, there wasn't any clear idea of what work the hosts had to do. Only later did we articulate the notion of building a layered set of protocols with general transport services on the bottom and multiple application-specific protocols on the top. More precisely, we understood quite early that we wanted quite a bit of generality, but we didn't have a clear idea how to achieve it. We struggled between a grand design and getting something working quickly.[31]

The initial protocol development led to DEL (Decode-Encode Language) and NIL (Network Interchange Language). These languages were more advanced than what was needed and could not be implemented at the time. The basic purpose was to form an on-the-fly description that would tell the receiving end how to understand the information that would be sent. The discussion at this first set of meetings was extremely abstract as neither ARPA nor the universities had conceived of an official charter. However, the lack of a specific charter allowed the group to think broadly and openly.

BBN had provided details about the host-IMP interface specifications from the IMP side. This information gave the group some definite starting points to build from. Soon after BBN provided more information, members of the NWG, of BBN, and of the Network Analysis Corporation (NAC) met for the first time on Valentine's Day, 1969. The NAC had been invited because it had been contracted by ARPA to specify the topological design of the ARPANET and to analyze its cost, performance, and reliability characteristics.[32] As all the parties had different priorities, the meeting was a difficult one. BBN was interested in the lowest level of making a reliable connection. The programmers from the host sites were interested in getting the hosts to communicate with each other either via various higher-level programs. Even when the crew from BBN did not turn out to be the "experts from the East," members of the NWG still expected that "a professional crew would show up eventually to take over the problems we were dealing with."

A step of great importance that began the open documentation process occurred as a result of a "particularly delightful" meeting a month later in Utah. The participants decided it was time to start recording their meetings in a consistent fashion. What resulted was a set of informal notes titled "Request for Comments" (RFC). Crocker writes about their formation:

I remember having great fear that we would offend whomever the official protocol designers were, and I spent a sleepless night composing humble words for our notes. The basic ground rules were that anyone could say anything and that nothing was official. And to emphasize the point, I labeled the notes "Request for Comments." I never dreamed these notes would be distributed through the very medium we were discussing in these notes. Talk about Sorcerer's Apprentice![33]

Crocker replaced Shapiro as the Chairman of the NWG soon after the initial meeting. He describes how they wrestled with the creation of the host–host protocols:

Over the spring and summer of 1969 we grappled with the detailed problems of protocol design. Although we had a vision of the vast potential for inter-computer communication, designing usable protocols was another matter. A custom hardware interface and custom intrusion into the operating system was going to be required for anything we designed, and we anticipated serious difficulty at each of the sites. We looked for existing abstractions to use. It would have been convenient if we could have made the network simply look like a tape drive to each host, but we knew that wouldn't do.[34]

The first IMP was delivered to UCLA in late August, 1969. The next was delivered to SRI a month later in October.[35] As soon as more than one IMP existed, the NWG had to implement a working communications protocol. The first set of pairwise host protocols included remote login for interactive use (telnet), and a way to copy files between remote hosts (FTP). Crocker writes:

In particular, only asymmetric, user-server relationships were supported. In December 1969, we met with Larry Roberts in Utah, [and he] made it abundantly clear that our first step was not big enough, and we went back to the drawing board. Over the next few months we designed a symmetric host-host protocol, and we defined an abstract implementation of the protocol known as the Network Control Program. ("NCP" later came to be used as the name for the protocol, but it originally meant the program within the operating system that managed connections. The protocol itself was known blandly only as the host-host protocol.) Along with the basic host-host protocol, we also envisioned a hierarchy of protocols, with Telnet, FTP and some splinter protocols as the first examples. If we had only consulted the ancient mystics, we would have seen immediately that seven layers were required.[36]

The NWG went on to develop the protocols necessary to make the network viable. The group grew as more and more sites connected to the ARPANET. The group became large enough (around 100 people) that one meeting was held in conjunction with the 1971 Spring Joint Computer Conference in Atlantic City. A major test of the NWG's work came in October 1971, when a meeting was held at MIT. Crocker continues the story:

[A] major protocol "fly-off"—Representatives from each site were on hand, and everyone tried to log in to everyone else's site. With the exception of

one site that was completely down, the matrix was almost completely filled in, and we had reached a major milestone in connectivity. [37]

The NWG was creating what was called the "host to host protocol." Explaining why this was important, the authors of the *Completion Report Draft* wrote:

. . . [T]he problem is to design a host protocol which is sufficiently powerful for the kinds of communication that will occur and yet can be implemented in all of the various different host computer systems. The initial approach taken involved an entity called a "Network Control Program" which would typically reside in the executive of a host, such that processes within a host would communicate with the network through this Network Control Program. The primary function of the NCP is to establish connections, break connections, switch connections, and control flow. A layered approach was taken such that more complex procedures (such as File Transfer Procedures) were built on top of similar procedures in the host Network Control Program.[38]

As the ARPANET grew, the number of users bypassed the number of developers, signaling the success of these networking pioneers. Crocker appointed Alex McKenzie and Jon Postel to replace him as chairmen of the Network Working Group. The *Completion Report Draft* details how this role changed:

McKenzie and Postel interpreted their task to be one of codification and coordination primarily, and after a few more spurts of activity the protocol definition process settled for the most part into a status of a maintenance effort.[39]

ARPA was a management body which funded academic computer scientists. ARPA's funding paved the way for these scientists to create the ARPANET. BBN helped by developing the packet switching techniques which served as the bottom level of transmitting information between sites. The NWG provided an important development in its "Request for Comments" documentation which made possible developing the new protocols.

RFCS AS "OPEN" DOCUMENTATION

The open exchange of ideas initiated from the very first meeting of the Network Working Group was continued in the Request For Comments. As meeting notes, the RFCs were meant to keep members updated on the status of various developments and ideas. They were also meant to gather responses from people. RFC-3, "Documentation Conventions," documents the "rules" governing the production of these notes beginning with the open distribution rule:

> *Documentation of the NWG's effort is through notes such as this. Notes may be produced at any site by anybody and included in this series.*[40]

These opening sentences invite anyone willing to be helpful into the protocol definition process. This is important because all restrictions are lifted by these words, allowing for the open process aimed for. (RFC-3 is reproduced in the appendix at the end of this chapter.) The guide goes on to describe the rules concerning the content of the RFCs:

> *The content of a NWG note may be any thought, suggestion, etc. related to the HOST software or other aspect of the network. Notes are encouraged to be timely rather than polished. Philosophical positions without examples or other specifics, specific suggestions or implementation techniques without introductory or background explication, and explicit questions without any attempted answers are all acceptable. The minimum length for a NWG note is one sentence.*[41]

In RFC-3, Crocker continues to explain the philosophy behind the perhaps unprecedented openness represented:

> *These standards (or lack of them) are stated explicitly for two reasons. First, there is a tendency to view a written statement as ipso facto authoritative, and we hope to promote the exchange and discussion of considerably less than authoritative ideas. Second, there is a natural hesitancy to publish something unpolished, and we hope to ease this inhibition.* [42]

This open process encouraged and led to the exchange of information. Technical development is only successful when information is allowed to flow freely and easily between the parties involved. Encouraging participation is the main principle that made the development of the Net possible.

Statements like the ones contained in RFC-3 are democratic in their support of a process of openness. They were written during the late 1960s, a time of popular protest for freedom of speech. People were demanding more of a say in how their countries were run. The open environment needed to develop new technologies is consistent with the cry for more democracy that students and others raised throughout the world during the 1960s. What is amazing is the collaboration of the NWG (mostly graduate students) and ARPA (a component of the military) during the 1960s and 1970s. This seems unusual given the active student anti-war movement. Robert Braden of the Internet Activities Board reflects on this collaboration:

> *For me, participation in the development of the ARPAnet and the Internet protocols has been very exciting. One important reason it worked, I believe, is*

> *that there were a lot of very bright people all working more or less in the same direction, led by some very wise people in the funding agency. The result was to create a community of network researchers who believed strongly that collaboration is more powerful than competition among researchers. I don't think any other model would have gotten us where we are today.*[43]

Such collaboration is why the work of these computer scientists led to such amazing and democratic achievements, the Net and the cooperative culture of the Net.[44]

Calling their notes a "Request for Comment" established a significant tradition. It predates the Usenet post, which in a fashion could also be called a "request for comment." Both are the presentation of a particular person's ideas, questions, or comments to the general public for comments, criticism, or suggestions. Early RFCs established this tradition. Many RFCs are in fact comments on previous RFCs.[45]

CONCLUSION

How were the developments of the ARPANET made possible? None of the participants had previous solutions to any of the problems they faced in establishing a working packet-switched testbed with host–to–host connectivity. They had to put much thought and work into their research. As the resulting ARPANET was tremendously successful and fulfilled ARPA's project objectives, it is important to see what can be learned from the research and research methods from which it emerged. Bernie Cosell, who worked at BBN during this early period, describes the importance of an open process in a developmental situation:

> **no*one* had the necessary expertise [and vision] to figure any of this out on their own. The cultures among the early groups were VERY different [—] multics, sigma-7, IBM . . . at Rand, . . . PDP-10s at BBN and SRI. . . [and possibly] UCSB and Utah had pdp-10's, too. The pie-in-the-sky applications ranged over a WIDE landscape, with no one knowing quite where it would lead. Some kind of free, cross-cultural info/idea exchange *had* to happen.*[46]

The computer scientists and others involved were encouraged in their work by ARPA's philosophy of gathering the best computer scientists working in the field and supporting them.

> *IPT usually does little day-to-day management of its contractors. Especially with its research contracts, IPT would not be producing faster results with such management—research must progress at its own pace. IPT has gen-*

> *erally adopted a mode of management which entails finding highly motivated, highly skilled contractors, giving them a task, and allowing them to proceed by themselves.*[47]

The work of the Network Working Group was vital to the development of the ARPANET. Vinton Cerf, another of the graduate students involved with the early protocol development and still closely connected to the Internet, echoed this sentiment in his paper "An Assessment of ARPANET Protocols":

> *The history of the Advanced Research Project Agency resource sharing computer network (ARPANET) is in many ways a history of the study, development, and implementation of protocols.*[48]

Cerf supports Cosell's opinion about the uncertainty and newness of the entire project:

> *The tasks facing the ARPANET design teams were often unclear, and frequently required agreements which had never been contemplated before (e.g., common protocols to permit different operating systems and hardware to communicate). The success of the effort, seen in retrospect, is astonishing, and much credit is due to those who were willing to commit themselves to the job of putting the ARPANET together.*[49]

The NWG's work blazed the trail which the developers of the TCP/IP suite of protocols (Transport Control Protocol/ Internet Protocol) successfully followed when the need to expand and include other networks based on technologies other than NCP arose. The principles embodied in RFC-3 and the open RFC documentation process provided a strong foundation which began with NCP and was continued by the work on TCP/IP. NCP was developed in the field, and versions of it were released early in its development so various programmers could work on implementing and improving the protocol. In addition, all specifications were free and easily available for people to examine and comment on. Through this principle of early release, problems and kinks were found and worked out in a timely manner. The future developers of TCP/IP learned from the developers of NCP a practice of developing from the bottom up. The bottom-up model allows for a wide range of people and experiences to join in and perfect the protocol and make it the best possible.

The public funding of the ARPANET project meant that the documentation could be made public and freely available. The documentation was neither restricted nor classified. This open process encouraging communication was necessary for these pioneers to succeed. Research in new fields of study requires that researchers cooperate and communicate in order to share their expertise. Such openness is especially critical when no one person has the answers in advance. In his article, "The Evolution of Packet Switching," Larry Roberts described the public nature of the process:

> *Since the ARPANET was a public project connecting many major universities and research institutions, the implementation and performance details were widely published.*[50]

The people at the forefront of development of these protocols were the members of the Network Working Group, many of whom came from academic institutions, and who therefore had the support and time needed for the research. In summing up the achievements of the process that developed the ARPANET, the *Completion Report Draft* explains:

> *The ARPANET development was an extremely intense activity in which contributions were made by many of the best computer scientists in the United States. Thus, almost all of the "major technical problems" already mentioned received continuing attention and the detailed approach to those problems changed several times during the early years of the ARPANET effort.*[51]

Fundamental to the ARPANET, as explained by the *Completion Report*, was the discovery of a new way of looking at computers. The developers of the ARPANET viewed the computer as a communications device rather than only as an arithmetic device.[52] This new view, which came from research conducted by those in academic computer science, made the building of the ARPANET possible. Such a shift in understanding the role of the computer was fundamental in advancing computer science. The ARPANET research has provided a rich legacy for the further advancement of computer science, and it is important that the significant lessons learned be studied and used to further advance the study of computer science.

NOTES

1. F. Heart, A. McKenzie, J. McQuillan, and D. Walden, *ARPANET Completion Report* (Washington, D.C.:DARPA and BBN, 1978) III-132 (hereafter, *Completion Report*).
2. *ARPANET Completion Report Draft, September 9, 1977*, unpublished manuscript, III-6. (Hereafter, *Completion Report Draft)*
3. *Ibid.*
4. *Ibid.*, III-7.
5. "Interview with J. C. R. Licklider" conducted by William Aspray and Arthur L. Norberg, tape recording, Cambridge, Massachusetts, 28 October 1988, OH 150, Charles Babbage Institute, University of Minnesota, Minneapolis, Minnesota.

6. *Completion Report Draft*, III-7.
7. *Ibid.*
8. *Ibid.*, III-21.
9. See, for example, J. C. R. Licklider and Robert Taylor, "The Computer as a Communication Device," in *In Memoriam: J. C. R. Licklider 1915–1990* (Palo Alto, CA.: Digital Systems Research Center, 1990), originally published in *Science and Technology*, April 1968.
10. *Completion Report Draft*, III-23
11. *Ibid.*, III-24.
12. *Ibid.*
13. *Ibid.*
14. RFC-1336, "Who's Who in the Internet," G. Malkin, May 1992, 15.
15. See Chapter 8 of this volume, "The Birth and Development of the ARPANET" and *Completion Report*, section 1.1.2, starting on III-9.
16. *Completion Report Draft,* III-25, III-26.
17. *Completion Report*, II-7–II-8.
18. *Completion Report Draft,* III-31–III-33.
19. *Ibid.*, III-35 and *Completion Report*, II-2.
20. *Completion Report Draft*, III-35, III-36.
21. *Ibid.*, III-67.
22. *Ibid.*, III-39 and personal discussion with Alex McKenzie, November 1, 1993.
23. E-mail message to Com-Priv mailing list (com-priv@psi.com). Subject "Re: RFC1000 (Partial response to part 1)." Date: Nov. 27, 1993.
24. Vinton G. Cerf, private e-mail correspondence, dated Nov. 27, 1993. Subject: "Re: Early Days of the ARPANET and the NWG".
25. "The Origins of RFCs" by Stephen D. Crocker is contained in J. Reynolds and J. Postel, RFC-1000, 1.
26. The following quotes show some of the reasoning that went into the choice of the initial ARPANET sites:

    > *CCN's [The Campus Computing Network of UCLA] chance to obtain a connection to the ARPANET was a result of the presence at UCLA of Professor L. Kleinrock and his students, including S. Crocker, J. Postel, and V. Cerf. This group was not only involved in the original design of the network and the Host protocols, but also was to operate the Network Measurement Center (NMC). For these reasons the first delivered IMP was installed at UCLA, and ARPA was thus able to easily offer CCN the opportunity for connection* (Completion Report Draft, *III-689).*

    > *UCLA was specifically asked to take on the task of a "Network Measurement Center" with the objective of studying the performance of the network as it was built, grown, and modified; SRI was specifically asked to take on the task of a "Network Information Center" with the objective of collecting information about the network, about host resources, and at the same time generating computer based tools for storing and accessing that collected information* (Completion Report Draft, *II-16).*

> *The accessibility of distributed resources carries with it the need for an information service (either centralized or distributed) that enables users to learn about those resources. This was recognized at the PI meeting in Michigan in the spring of 1967. At the time, Doug Engelbart and his group at the Stanford Research Institute were already involved in research and development to provide a computer-based facility to augment human interaction. Thus, it was decided that Stanford Research Institute would be a suitable place for a "Network Information Center" (NIC) to be established for the ARPANET. With the beginning of implementation of the network in 1969, construction also began on the NIC at SRI* (Completion Report Draft, *III-60).*

27. *Completion Report Draft,* III-67.
28. E-mail message to Com-Priv mailing list. Subject: "Re: RFC1000 (End of response to part 1)," Date: Nov. 27, 1993.
29. RFC-1000.
30. *Completion Report Draft,* III-67.
31. E-mail message to Com-Priv mailing list. Subject "Re: RFC1000 (Response to part 2)", Date: Nov. 27, 1993.
32. *Completion Report,* III-30.
33. RFC-1000, 3.
34. *Ibid.*
35. In RFC-1000, Stephen Crocker reports on the process of the installation of the first IMP:

> *[T]ime was pressing: The first IMP was due to be delivered to UCLA September 1, 1969, and the rest were scheduled at monthly intervals.*
>
> *At UCLA we scrambled to build a host-IMP interface. SDS, the builder of the Sigma 7, wanted many months and many dollars to do the job.*
>
> *Mike Wingfield, another grad student at UCLA, stepped in and offered to get the interface built in six weeks for a few thousand dollars. He had a gorgeous, fully instrumented interface working in five and one half weeks. I was in charge of the software, and we were naturally running a bit late. September 1 was Labor Day, so I knew I had a couple of extra days to debug the software. Moreover, I had heard BBN was having some timing troubles with the software, so I had some hope they'd miss the ship date. And I figured that first some Honeywell people would install the hardware—IMPs were built out of Honeywell 516s in those days—and then BBN people would come in a few days later to shake down the software. An easy couple of weeks of grace.*
>
> *BBN fixed their timing trouble, air shipped the IMP, and it arrived on our loading dock on Saturday, August 30. They arrived with the IMP, wheeled it into our computer room, plugged it in and the software restarted from where it had been when the plug was pulled in Cambridge. Still Saturday, August 30. Panic time at UCLA.*
>
> *The second IMP was delivered to SRI at the beginning of October, and ARPA's interest was intense. Larry Roberts and Barry Wessler came by for a visit on November 21, and we actually managed to demonstrate a Telnet-like connection to SRI.*

36. RFC-1000, 4.
37. *Ibid.*
38. *Completion Report Draft*, II-24.
39. *Ibid.*, III-69.
40. RFC-3, "Documentation Conventions," Stephen Crocker, April 1969, 1.
41. *Ibid.*
42. *Ibid.*
43. RFC-1336, 5.
44. This democratic community is in danger of being fundamentally altered. This study of the history of the development of the ARPANET, in conjunction with Chapter 3, "The Social Forces Behind the Development of Usenet," is meant to help people understand where the Net has come from, in order to defend it, and try to fight to keep it open and democratic—"the eighth wonder of the world," as some call the Internet.
45. Some examples of comments upon comments include:
    RFC-1 Crocker, S. Host software, 1969 April 7
    RFC-65 Walden, D. Comments on Host/Host Protocol document #1
    RFC-36 Crocker, S. Protocol notes, 1970 March 16
    RFC-38 Wolfe, S. Comments on network protocol from NWG/RFC #36
    RFC-39 Harslem, E.; Heafner, J. Comments on protocol re: NWG/RFC#36
    RFC-33 Crocker, S. New Host-Host Protocol, 1970 February 12
    RFC-47 Crowther, W. BBN's comments on NWG/RFC #33 1970 April 20
46. Bernie Cosell, "Re: RFC1000—Questions about the Origins of ARPANET Protocols 2/2," alt.folklore.computers, Nov. 23, 1993.
47. *Completion Report Draft*, III-47.
48. Vinton Cerf, "An Assessment of ARPANET Protocols," Infotech Education Ltd., Stanford University, California, (n.d.), 1.
49. *Ibid.*
50. Lawrence Roberts, "The Evolution of Packet Switching," *Proceedings of the IEEE* 66 (November 1978): 267.
51. *Completion Report Draft*, II-24–II-25.
52. *Ibid.*, III-24.

Special thanks to Alexander McKenzie of BBN, Stephen Crocker of TIS, and Vinton Cerf of CNRI for making research materials available.

An early version of this chapter by Michael Hauben was posted on Usenet in January 1994.

Appendix

Network Working Group 4689
RFC-3 April 1969
Steve Crocker
UCLA

DOCUMENTATION CONVENTIONS

The Network Working Group seems to consist of Steve Carr of Utah, Jeff Rulifson and Bill Duvall at SRI, and Steve Crocker and Gerard Deloche at UCLA. Membership is not closed.

The Network Working Group (NWG) is concerned with the HOST software, the strategies for using the network, and initial experiments with the network.

Documentation of the NWG's effort is through notes such as this. Notes may be produced at any site by anybody and included in this series.

CONTENT

The content of a NWG note may be any thought, suggestion, etc. related to the HOST software or other aspect of the network. Notes are encouraged to be timely rather than polished. Philosophical positions without examples or other specifics, specific suggestions or implementation techniques without introductory or background explication, and explicit questions without any attempted answers are all acceptable. The minimum length for a NWG note is one sentence.

These standards (or lack of them) are stated explicitly for two reasons. First, there is a tendency to view a written statement as *ipso facto* authoritative, and we hope to promote the exchange and discussion of considerably less than authoritative ideas. Second, there is a natural hesitancy to publish something unpolished, and we hope to ease this inhibition.

FORM

Every NWG note should bear the following information:

1. "Network Working Group"
   "Request for Comments:" x
   where x is a serial number.
   Serial numbers are assigned by Bill Duvall at SRI

2. Author and affiliation
3. Date
4. Title. The title need not be unique.

DISTRIBUTION

One copy only will be sent from the author's site to

1. Bob Kahn, BB&N
2. Larry Roberts, ARPA
3. Steve Carr, UCLA
4. Jeff Rulifson, UTAH
5. Ron Stoughton, UCSB
6. Steve Crocker, UCLA

Reproduction if desired may be handled locally.

OTHER NOTES

Two notes (1 & 2) have been written so far. These are both titled HOST Software and are by Steve Crocker and Bill Duvall, separately.

Other notes planned are on

1. Network Timetable
2. The Philosophy of NIL
3. Specifications for NIL
4. Deeper Documentation of HOST Software.

[Note: This document is available at ftp://ftp.internic.net/rfc/]

8

The Birth and Development of the ARPANET

The Nutrition of a Commonwealth consisteth, in the Plenty, and the Distribution of Materials, Condusive to Life.

THOMAS HOBBES, *THE LEVIATHAN*

The method I take. . . is not yet very usual; for instead of using only comparative and superlative words, and intellectual arguments, I have taken the course (as a Specimen of the Political Arithmetic I have long aimed at) to express myself in terms of Number, Weight, or Measure; to use only arguments of Sense, and to consider only such Causes, as have visible Foundations in Nature; leaving those that depend upon the mutable Minds, Opinions, Appetites, and Passions of particular Men, to the Conservation of others."

SIR WILLIAM PETTY, *POLITICAL ARITHMETICK*

The creation of a global computer network is one of the surprising developments of our times. This achievement raises the questions: What are the factors that nourished the growth and development of this network? What are the impediments to its continued development and expansion?[1]

INTRODUCTION

J. C. R. Licklider was one of the early computer pioneers who helped to make the global computer network a reality. His vision of an "intergalactic computer network" helped to inspire these developments. He and Albert Vezza, describing an earlier networking advance, wrote, "Shakespeare could have been foreseeing the present situation in information networking when he said, . . . What's past is prologue; what's to come, in yours and my discharge."[2] The story of the network's growth and development contains important lessons for its continued expansion. The development of this international network, linking millions of people around the world, now stands at a turning point. Will it continue to go forward or will it be detoured? An understanding of the environment and policies that nourished the development of the global computer network provides a foundation on which to base its further expansion. Such an understanding will also make it possible to contribute to the cooperative networking culture that has evolved and flourished through these policies.

THE DEVELOPMENT OF THE ARPANET

In 1962, the report "On Distributed Communications Networks," by Paul Baran, was published by the Rand Corporation.[3] Baran's research, funded under a standing contract from the U.S. Air Force, discussed how the U.S. military could protect its communications systems from serious attack. Baran outlined the principle of "redundancy of connectivity" and explored various models of forming communications systems and evaluating their vulnerability. The report proposed a communications system where there would be no obvious central command and control point, so that all surviving points would be able to reestablish contact in the event of an attack on any one point. Thus damage to a part would not destroy the whole, and its effect on the whole would be minimized.

One of his recommendations was for a national public utility to transport computer data, much in the way the telephone system transports voice data. "Is it time now to start thinking about a new and possibly non-existent public utility," Baran asked, "a common user digital data communication plant designed specifically for the transmission of digital data among a large set of subscribers?"[4] He cautioned against limiting the choice of technology to create such a network to that which was currently in use. He proposed that a packet switching, store and forward technology be developed for a data network. The eleven-report series he wrote with others was the first published description of what we now call packet switching.[5] Another networking pioneer, Donald W. Davies, of the United Kingdom, also did important work in this field and has been credited with introducing the term packet switching.

Other researchers were interested in computers and communications, particularly in the computer as a communication device. J. C. R. Licklider was one of the most influential. He was particularly interested in the man-computer communication relationship. "Lick," as he asked people to call him, wondered how the computer could help humans to think and to solve problems. In the article "Man–Computer Symbiosis" he explored how the computer could help humans to do intellectual work.[6] Licklider was also interested in the question of how the computer could help humans to communicate better. In another article, "The Computer as a Communication Device," Licklider and Robert Taylor wrote, "In a few years men will be able to communicate more effectively through a machine than face to face. . . . When minds interact, new ideas emerge."[7]

What pioneers such as Paul Baran and J. C. R. Licklider were proposing was the development of computer technology in a direction that had not been developed before. Larry Roberts, also a pioneer during these important early days of networking, points out that Baran's work was either classified or otherwise "unfortunately . . . very sparsely published in the scientific press."[8] Thus according to Roberts, the impact of Baran's work on the actual development of packet switching networks "was mainly supportive, not sparking its development." Licklider, however, had access to military research and writing, but he was also involved in the academic computer science research and education community.[9] Roberts describes how he was influenced by Licklider's vision of an intergalactic computer network to change his life and career. Licklider's concept of an intergalactic computer network, Roberts explains, represented the effort to "define the problems and benefits resulting from computer networking."[10]

After informal conversations with three important computer science pioneers, J. C. R. Licklider, Fernando Corbató and Alan Perlis, at the Second Congress on Information System Sciences in Hot Springs, Virginia, in November 1964, Larry Roberts "concluded that the most important problem in the computer field before us at the time was computer networking; the ability to access one computer from another easily and economically to permit resource sharing." Roberts recalled, "That was a topic in which Licklider was very interested and his enthusiasm infected me."[11]

During the early 1960s, the DOD under ARPA established two new funding offices, the IPTO and another for behavioral science. From

1962–1964, Licklider took a leave from BBN in Cambridge, Massachusetts to give guidance to these two newly created offices. In reviewing this seminal period, Alan Perlis recalled how Licklider's philosophy guided ARPA's funding of computer science research. Perlis explained:

> *I think that we all should be grateful to ARPA for not focusing on very specific projects such as workstations. There was no order issued that said, "We want a proposal on a workstation." Goodness knows, they would have gotten many of them. Instead, I think that ARPA, through Lick, realized that if you get "n" good people together to do research on computing, you're going to illuminate some reasonable fraction of the ways of proceeding because the computer is such a general instrument. We owe a great deal to ARPA for not circumscribing directions that people took in those days. I like to believe that the purpose of the military is to support ARPA, and the purpose of ARPA is to support research.*[12]

Licklider was guided in his philosophy by the rationale that a broad investigation of a problem was necessary to solve the problem. "There's a lot of reasons for adopting a broad delimitation rather than a narrow one," he explained, "because if you're trying to find out where ideas come from, you don't want to isolate yourself from the areas that they came from."[13] And he succeeded in attracting others involved in computer research to his vision that computer networking was the most important challenge of the time.

In 1966–1967, MIT's Lincoln Laboratory in Lexington, Massachusetts and System Development Corp. (SDC), in Santa Monica, California received a grant from the U.S. Department of Defense to begin research on linking computers across the continent. Describing this work, Roberts explained, "Convinced that it was a worthwhile goal, the first task was to set up a test environment to see where the problems would be."[14] Since computer time-sharing experiments at MIT [CTSS] and at Dartmouth [DTSS] had demonstrated that it was possible to link different computer users to a single computer, the cross country experiment built on this advance, that is, once time-sharing was possible, the linking of remote computers became feasible.

Roberts reported that there was no trouble linking dissimilar computers (the TX-2 computer at Lincoln Laboratory in Massachusetts and the Q-32 computer at SDC in California). The problem, he claimed, was with using telephone circuit switching technology because the throughput was inadequate to accomplish their goals. Thus their experiment set the basis for the research needed to set up a nationwide store and forward, packet switching data network.

During this period, ARPA was funding computer research at several U.S. universities and research laboratories. The decision was made to include these research contractors in an experimental network, eventually called the ARPANET. A plan was created for a working network to link 16 research groups together. This plan was made available at the October 1967 ACM Symposium on Operating Principles in Gatlinburg, Tennessee.[15] The planned research was to be encouraged and funded by the IPTO. Roberts was recruited to head the IPTO and guide the research. A Request for Proposal (RFP) set out specifications for the project and asked for bids, inviting proposals to create an operational network at four sites and to provide a design for a network that could include 16 sites.

The award for the contract went to BBN in January 1969. The planned network would make use of minicomputers to serve as switching nodes for the host computers at four sites that were to be connected to the network. The Honeywell DDP-516 minicomputers were chosen for the network of interface message processors (IMPs) that would be linked to each other. At first, each of the IMPs (or nodes) would be linked to one host computer. These IMPs, configured with 12,000 16-bit words of memory, were among the most powerful minicomputers available at the time.

The opening stanzas of a poem by Vinton Cerf, an ARPANET pioneer, describe computer science research before and after the ARPANET.

Like distant islands sundered by the sea,
We had no sense of one community.
We lived and worked apart and rarely knew
That others searched with us for knowledge, too.

Distant ARPA spurred us in our quest
And for our part we worked and put to test
New thoughts and theories of computing art;
We deemed it science not, but made a start.

Each time a new machine was built and sold,
We'd add it to our list of needs and told
Our source of funds "Alas! Our knowledge loom
Will halt 'til it's in our computer room."

. . . .

But, could these new resources not be shared?
Let links be built; machines and men be paired!
Let distance be no barrier! They set
That goal: design and build the ARPANET![16]

On August 30, 1969, the first IMP arrived at the University of California, Los Angeles (UCLA), which was to be the first site of the new network. It was connected to the SDS Sigma 7 computer at UCLA using the SEX operating system. Shortly thereafter IMPs were delivered to the other three sites in this initial test-bed network. At Stanford Research Institute (SRI), the IMP was connected to an SDS-940 computer using the GENIE operating system. At the University of California, Santa Barbara (UCSB), the IMP was connected to an IBM 360/75 using OS/MVT. And at the University of Utah (Utah), the fourth site, the IMP was connected to a DEC PDP-10 using the TENEX operating system.

By the end of 1969, the first four IMPs had been connected to the host computers at their individual sites and the network connections between the IMPs were operational. The researchers and scientists involved could begin to identify the problems they had to solve to develop a working network where there would be communication from host to host.

There were programming and other technical problems to be solved so that the different computers would be able to communicate with each other. Also, there was a need for an agreed-upon set of signals that would open up communication channels, allow data to pass through, and then close the channels. These agreed-upon standards were called protocols. The initial proposal for the ARPANET required that the sites work together to establish the necessary protocols. In 1968, the first meetings of a group to discuss establishing these protocols took place.[17] In 1969, the group, which called itself the Network Working Group (NWG), began to put together a set of documents that would be available to everyone involved for consideration and discussion. They called these documents Requests For Comment (RFC), and RFC 1, dated April 1969, was mailed to each participant.[18]

As the problems of setting up the four computer network were identified and solved, the network was expanded to several more sites.[19] By April 1971, there were 15 nodes and 23 hosts in the network. The earliest sites attached to the network were connected to Honeywell DDP-516 IMPs.[20] These sites were:

1. UCLA
2. SRI
3. UCSB
4. U. of Utah
5. BBN
6. MIT
7. Rand Corp.
8. SDC
9. Harvard
10. Lincoln Lab
11. Stanford
12. U. of Illinois, Urbana
13. Case Western Reserve U.
14. Carnegie Mellon U. (CMU)
15. NASA-AMES

Later, a smaller minicomputer, the Honeywell 316, was utilized. It was compatible with the DDP-516 IMP but was available at half the cost. Some nodes were configured using these smaller minicomputers as TIPs (Terminal IMPs) beginning with NASA-AMES TIP and MITRE TIP.

By January 1973, there were 35 nodes, of which 14 were TIPs, including a satellite link which connected California with a TIP in Hawaii. With the rapid increase in network traffic, problems were discovered with the reliability of the subnet, and there was a need to determine how to make the needed changes. In mid-1973, Norway and England were added to the Net by a low-speed line, creating new problems to be solved. By September 1973, there were 40 nodes and 45 hosts on the network. And the traffic had expanded from 1 million packets per day in 1972 to 2.9 million packets per day. By 1977, there were 111 host computers connected via the ARPANET. By 1983 there were 4,000.[21]

As the network was put into operation, the researchers learned which of their original assumptions and models were sound and which were inaccurate. For example, BBN describes how they had initially failed to understand that the IMPs would need to do error checking of the IMP/host interface. They explain:

> *The first four IMPs were developed and installed on schedule by the end of 1969. No sooner were these IMPs in the field than it became clear that some provision was needed to connect hosts relatively distant from an IMP (i.e., up to 2,000 feet instead of the expected 50 feet). Thus, in early 1970 a "distant" IMP/host interface was developed. Augmented simply by heftier line drivers, these distant interfaces made clear, for the first time, the fallacy in the assumption that had been made that no error control was needed on the host/IMP interface because there would be no errors on such a local connection.*[22]

The expanding operational network made it possible to uncover the actual bugs and make the needed corrections. In describing the importance of an operational network to the research efforts, as opposed to being limited to a laboratory model, Alex McKenzie and David Walden, in their article "ARPANET, the Defense Data Network, and Internet," write:

> *Errors in coding control were another problem. However carefully one designs, codes, and performs quality control, errors can still slip through. Fortunately, with a large number of IMPs in the network, most of these errors are found quickly because they occur so frequently. For instance, a bug in an IMP code that occurs once a day in one IMP, occurs every 15 min in a 100-IMP network. Unfortunately, some bugs still will remain. If a symptom of a bug is detected somewhere in a 100-IMP network once a week (often enough to be a problem), then it will happen only once every 2 years in a single IMP in a development lab for a programmer trying to find the source of the symptom. Thus, achieving a totally bug-free network is very difficult.*[23]

In October 1972, the First International Conference on Computer Communications was held in Washington, D.C. A public demonstration of the ARPANET was given, setting up an actual node with 40 terminals. Representatives from projects around the world including Canada, France, Japan, Norway, Sweden, Great Britain, and the United States discussed the need to begin work establishing agreed upon protocols. The International Network Working Group (INWG) was created to begin discussions for a common protocol, and Vinton Cerf, who was involved with UCLA ARPANET, was chosen as the first chairman. The vision proposed for the international interconnection of networks was "a mesh of independent, autonomous networks interconnected by *gateways*, just as independent circuits of ARPANET are interconnected by IMPs."[24]

The network continued to grow and expand.

In 1975, the ARPANET was transferred to the control of the Defense Communications Agency (DCA).

Evaluating the success of ARPANET research, Licklider recalled that he felt ARPA had been run by an enlightened set of military men while he was involved with it.

> *I don't want to brag about ARPA. It is in my view, however, a very enlightened place. It was fun to work there. I think I've never encountered brighter, more creative people, than the inhabitants of the third floor E-ring of the pentagon. But that, I'll say, was a long time ago, and I simply don't know how bright and likeable they are now. But ARPA didn't constrain me much.*[25]

The following description of his experience on the early ARPANET was posted on Usenet by Eugene Miya, who had been a student at one of the early ARPA sites:

> *It was an effort to connect different kinds of computers back when a school or company had only one (that's 1) computer. The first configuration of the ARPANET had only 4 computers, I had luckily selected a school at one of those 4 sites: UCLA/Rand Corp, UCSB (us), SRI, and the U of Utah.*
>
> *Who? The U.S. DOD: Defense Department's Advanced Research Projects Agency. ARPA was the sugar daddy of computer science. Some very bright people were given some money, freedom, and had a lot of vision. It not only started computer networks, but also computer graphics, computer flight simulation, head mounted displays, parallel processing, queuing models, VLSI, and a host of other ideas. Far from being evil warmongers, some neat work was done.*
>
> *Why? Lots of reasons: intellectual curiosity, the need to have different machines communicate, study fault tolerance of communications systems in the event of nuclear war, share and connect expensive resources, very soft ideas to very hard ideas. . . .*

> *I first saw the term "internetwork" in a paper from Xerox PARC (another ARPANET host). The issue was one of interconnecting Ethernets (which had the 256 [slightly less] host limitation). . . . I learned much of this with the help of the NIC (Network Information Center). This does not mean the Internet is like this today. I think the early ARPANET was kind of a wondrous neat place, sort of a golden era. You could get into other people's machines with a minimum of hassle (someone else paid the bills). No more. . . .*
>
> *Where did I fit in? I was a frosh nuclear engineering major, spending odd hours (2 a.m.–4 a.m., sometimes on Fridays and weekends) doing hackerish things rather than doing student things: studying or dating, etc. I put together an interactive SPSS and learned a lot playing chess on an MIT[-MC] DEC-10 from an IBM-360. Think of the problems: 32-bit versus 36-bit, different character set [remember I started with EBCDIC], FTP then is largely FTP now, has changed very little. We didn't have text editors available to students on the IBM (yes you could use the ARPANET via punched card decks). Learned a lot. I wish I had hacked more.*[26]

Miya's account, describing the stimulating research environment created via the ARPANET, documents how this environment not only helped to create a global computer network, but also led to the creation of new networking applications. For example, one of the surprising developments was the great popularity of electronic mail. Analyzing the reasons for this unanticipated benefit from their ARPANET research, Licklider and Vezza wrote:

> *By the Fall of 1973, the great effectiveness and convenience of such fast, informed message services . . . had been discovered by almost everyone who had worked on the development of the ARPANET—and especially by the then Director of ARPA, S. J. Lukasik, who soon had most of his office directors and program managers communicating with him and with their colleagues and their contractors via the network. Thereafter, both the number of (intercommunicating) electronic mail systems and the number of users of them on the ARPANET increased rapidly.*[27]

Licklider and Vezza describe the advantages of e-mail, explaining "that, in an ARPANET message, one could write tersely and type imperfectly, even to an older person in a superior position and even to a person one did not know very well, and the recipient took no offense." There was none of the formality and perfection that were required in a typed letter. They reasoned that perhaps this was

> *because the network was so much faster, so much more like the telephone. . . . Among the advantages of the network message services over the telephone were the fact that one could proceed immediately to the point without having to engage in small talk first, that the message services produced a preservable record, and that the sender and receiver did not have to be available at the same time.*[28]

Agreeing about the importance of the development of e-mail, the authors of the *ARPANET Completion Report* (1978) wrote:

> *The largest single surprise of the ARPANET program has been the incredible popularity and success of network mail. There is little doubt that the techniques of network mail developed in connection with the ARPANET program are going to sweep the country and drastically change the techniques used for intercommunication in the public and private sectors.*[29]

Not only did the ARPANET make it possible to learn what the actual problems of networking would be, the communication it made possible gave the researchers the ability to collaborate to solve the problems. Summarizing the important breakthrough this technology represented, the authors of the *ARPANET Completion Report* wrote:

> *This ARPA program has created no less than a revolution in computer technology and has been one of the most successful projects ever undertaken by ARPA. The program has initiated extensive changes in the Defense Department's use of computers as well as in the use of computers by the entire public and private sectors, both in the United States and around the world. Just as the telephone, the telegraph, and the printing press had far-reaching effects on human intercommunication, the widespread utilization of computer networks which has been catalyzed by the ARPANET project represents a similarly far-reaching change in the use of computers by mankind.* [30]

"The full impact of the technical changes set in motion by this project may not be understood for many years," they appropriately concluded.[31]

NOTES

1. See, for example, the methodology proposed by Sir William Petty in "Political Arithmetick" in *The Writings of Sir William Petty,* Charles Hull, ed. originally published in London, 1899 (New York: Augustus Kelley Publishers, reprint, 1986), 244–313.
2. "Applications of Information Networks," *Proceedings of the IEEE* 66 (November 1978): 1344.
3. Paul Baran, "On Distributed Communications Networks" (Rand Corporation, 1962), 2.
4. *Ibid.*, 40. See also Baran *et al.*, "On Distributed Communications," Vols. I through XI, Memorandum, Rand Corporation, August 1964, and description by Larry Roberts, "The ARPANET and Computer Networks" in *A History of Personal Workstations*, Adele Goldberg, ed. (New York: ACM Press, 1988), 147.

5. L. Roberts, "The Evolution of Packet Switching," *Proceedings of the IEEE* 66 (November 1978): 1307–1313; and "The ARPANET and Computer Networks," in *A History of Personal Workstations*, 143–144 (hereafter, *Workstations*).
6. J. C. R. Licklider, "Man–Computer Symbiosis," in *In Memoriam: J. C. R. Licklider 1915–1990* (Palo Alto, CA.: Digital Systems Research Center, 1990), 1–19.
7. J. C. R. Licklider and Robert Taylor, "The Computer as a Communication Device," in *In Memoriam: J. C. R. Licklider 1915–1990* (Palo Alto, CA.: Digital Systems Research Center, 1990), 21.
8. "The ARPANET and Computer Networks," *Workstations,* 144.
9. *Ibid.*
10. *Ibid.*
11. *Ibid.*
12. "Participants Discussion," *Workstations*, 129.
13. "Some Reflections on Early History," *Workstations,* 118. Licklider also commented on how people who were opposed to defense research during the 1960s wrote research proposals for ARPA to spend money on something other than airplane carriers (p. 130).
14. "The ARPANET and Computer Networks," *Workstations,* 145. See also Thomas Marill and Lawrence G. Roberts, "Toward a Cooperative Network of Time-Shared Computers," *Proceedings—Fall Joint Computer Conference* (1966): 425–431.
15. *Workstations,* 146. Describing ARPA's decision to build a network to connect the computer science and research contractors as the initial plan for the ARPANET, Roberts writes:

    > *These projects and their computers provided an ideal environment for an experimental network project; consequently the ARPANET was planned during 1967 with the aid of these researchers to link these projects' computers together. One task was to develop a computer interface protocol acceptable to all 16 research groups. A second task was to design a new communications technology to support 35 computers at 16 sites with 500,000 packets/day traffic. The initial plan for the ARPANET was published in October 1967 at the ACM Symposium on Operating System Principles in Gatlinburg Tennessee (pp. 145-146).*

    Also, Roberts describes the network design for the ARPANET. He writes:

    > *The communications network design was that of the now conventional packet network; interface message processors (IMPs) at each node interconnected by leased telecommunication lines providing a store and forward service on very short messages (p. 146).*

16. From Vinton G. Cerf, "Requiem for the ARPANET," in *Users' Dictionary of Computer Networks* (Bedford, Mass.: Digital Press, 1989). Copyright ©Vint Cerf; reprinted with permission.
17. A description of the beginning of the Network Working Group, "The Origins of RFCs" by Stephen D. Crocker, is contained in J. Reynolds and J. Postel, RFC 1000.

18. F. Heart, A. McKenzie, J. McQuillian, and D. Walden, *The ARPANET Completion Report* (Cambridge, Mass.: DARPA and BBN, 1978), III-46–III-48 (hereafter, *Completion Report*).
19. *Ibid.*
20. List of sites based on a posting on Usenet by Joel Levin on October 17, 1990. *The ARPANET Completion Report* confirms these sites, but names Burroughs as one of the first 15 sites. The first three sites were:
    1. UCLA (University of California at Los Angeles)
    2. SRI (Stanford Research Institute)
    3. UCSB (University of California at Santa Barbara)
21. See *Completion Report* and Alexander A. McKenzie and David C. Walden, "ARPANET, the Defense Data Network, and Internet" in *the Encyclopedia of Telecommunications*, vol. 1, Fritz E. Froelich, Allen Kent, and Carolyn M. Hall, eds. (New York: Marcel Dekker, 1991), 341–376.
22. *Completion Report*, III-55.
23. See *Completion Report* and McKenzie and Walden, 361.
24. McKenzie and Walden, 361–362.
25. *Workstations,* 126.
26. Eugene Miya, "Re: Internet: The Origins," October 16, 1990, in alt.folklore.computers, comp.misc.
27. "Applications of Information Network," *Proceedings of the IEEE* 66 (November 1978): 1331.
28. *Ibid.*
29. *Completion Report*, III-113–III-116.
30. *Ibid.*, I-2.
31. *Ibid.*

Thanks to Harvey Lynn of Rand Corporation and Alex McKenzie of BBN for making important materials available and to Bernard Galler, John A. N. Lee, and Judy O'Neill for commenting on earlier versions of this article.

An early version of this chapter by Ronda Hauben was presented at the IAMCR conference "Europe in Turmoil: Global Perspective," Dublin, Ireland, June 1993 and was printed in the *Amateur Computerist* 5 (Summer/Fall 1993).

9

On the Early History and Impact of Unix

Tools to Build the Tools for a New Millennium

When the barbarian, advancing step by step, had discovered the native metals, and learned to melt them in the crucible and to cast them in moulds; when he had alloyed native copper with tin and produced bronze; and, finally, when by a still greater effort of thought he had invented the furnace, and produced iron from the ore, nine tenths of the battle for civilization was gained. Furnished, with iron tools capable of holding both an edge and a point, mankind were certain of attaining to civilization.

LEWIS HENRY MORGAN, *ANCIENT SOCIETY*

[T]he spread and success of Unix, first in the Bell organizations and then in the rest of the world, was due to the fact that it was used, modified, and tinkered up in a whole variety of organizations within Bell Laboratories

VICTOR VYSSOTSKY, *PUTTING UNIX IN PERSPECTIVE*

IRON TOOLS AND SOFTWARE TOOLS

Our era is witnessing the birth of an important new technology, different from any in the past. This new technology is the technology of software production. The new tools of our era are tools that make it possible to produce software. Unlike the tools forged in the past, software tools are not something you can grab or hold. Similarly, the processes required to develop this new technology are new. Knowing the details of how such tools have been created will make it possible to realize the promise they represent for our time and for the future.

Describing a previous technological leap, the American anthropologist Lewis Henry Morgan called the production of iron "the event of events in human experience. . . .Out of it," he wrote, "came the metallic hammer and anvil, the axe and the chisel, the plow with an iron point, the iron sword; in fine, the basis of civilization which may be said to rest upon this metal." Morgan maintained that until the human species had mastered the skills and methods necessary for forging iron, social development had been paused awaiting the achievement of this next necessary technological advance. "The want of tools," he wrote, "arrested the progress of mankind in barbarism. There they would have remained to the present hour, had they failed to bridge the chasm." Frustrated by the lack of knowledge about how iron was invented, Morgan lamented, "It would be a singular satisfaction could it be known to what tribe and family we are indebted for this knowledge and with it for civilization."[1]

We are more fortunate than our ancestors. We can know some of the details of whom to credit for the technological achievements of the computer communications revolution. Documenting their contributions while many of the pioneers are still alive will provide future generations with knowledge of who they are indebted to for this stunning advance. Like the invention of iron, the technology of software production promises to make possible an important new level of civilization. Such knowledge will also help those who want to build on what has already been achieved.

CREATING A TECHNOLOGY OF SOFTWARE DEVELOPMENT

In *Introduction to Computer Science*, Alan Perlis, one of the early pioneers of computer science, observed that the nature of computer programming is too often misunderstood. "Although computer programming is often inaccurately considered an art," he wrote, "it is actually an infant technology."[2]

Like Morgan, Perlis believed that the progressive and accelerating ability to use and produce tools represents a defining element in the advance of human society. He observed that the rapid increase in the ability of the human species to use and mold new tools was guided by two laws. The first law describes the rapid increase in the number of people who can wield the tools and in the number of tools available. The second describes how the rapid development of tools to create tools guarantees the continuing expansion of the ability to use the tools. Perlis wrote:

> *First, the increase in the population trained to use tools and in the number of tools available for their use implies that the potential for tool utility grows as a product rather than as a sum. Second, the amount of composition—that is the number and uses of tools to produce new tools—grows as a part of the product and assures an even greater overall growth in tool use.*[3]

Among the tools Perlis saw coming into common use "are those which perform automatically at great speed, and whose management must perform in the same way. Here," he explained, "the computer is essential because of the need for quick response."[4]

THE CREATION OF TIME-SHARING

The development of the modern computer raised the question of how to manage its operation more efficiently. An important solution to the problem of computer management, proposed in 1959, was the sequential and automatic interspersing of many tasks known as time-sharing.[5] Among the earliest time-sharing systems were those developed at MIT. By 1963, there were two versions of the Compatible Time Sharing System (CTSS) operating at MIT on two IBM 7094 computers, one at the Computation Center, and another at MIT's Project MAC.

Those using the early time-sharing systems at MIT and elsewhere soon discovered the delights of interactive computing made possible by time-sharing.[6] Describing the advantages of interactive computing, time-sharing pioneers Robert Fano and Fernando Corbató wrote:

> *For professional programmers the time-sharing system has come to mean a great deal more than mere ease of access to the computer. Provided with the opportunity to run a program in continuous dialogue with the machine, editing, "debugging" and modifying the program as they proceed, they have gained immeasurably in the ability to experiment. They can readily investigate new programming techniques and new approaches to problems.*[7]

The results of this programming flexibility led both to a bolder and more flexible approach to problem solving and to undertaking new areas of research.

Fano and Corbató reported that users not only built on each other's work, but also that they came to depend more and more on the computer to facilitate their work. The most surprising development they encountered, however, was the fact that the users themselves created many of the programming commands used in the system, instead of needing professional programmers. While at a conventional computer installation, they noted, "one hardly ever makes use of a program developed by another user, because of the difficulty of exchanging programs and data," in the Project MAC time-sharing environment, "the ease of exchange has encouraged investigators to design their programs with an eye to possible use by other people. They have acted essentially as if they were writing papers to be published in technical journals."[8]

Fano and Corbató envisioned that time-sharing systems would have a profound impact on the future.

> *Communities will design systems to perform various functions—intellectual, economic and social—and the systems in turn undoubtedly will have profound effects in shaping the patterns of human life. The coupling between such a utility and the community it serves is so strong that the community is actually a part of the system itself.*[9]

They foresaw the development of a symbiotic relationship between the computer system and its human users which "will create new services, new institutions, a new environment and new problems." Among these, they proposed, would be the question of access. "How will access to the utility be controlled?" they asked, "To what ends will the system be devoted, and what safeguards can be devised for its misuses? It is easy to see," they concluded, "that the progress of this new technique will raise many social questions as well as technical ones."[10]

Others during this period were concerned with the impact the computer would have on society. For example, one of the inventors of time-sharing, computer pioneer John McCarthy, predicted that, "The computer gives signs of becoming the contemporary counterpart of the steam engine that brought on the industrial revolution."[11] Unlike the steam engine, however, the utility of the computer was dependent on the successful development of software programs written to direct it. Therefore, along with the increasing speed and capacity of computer hardware, came an increase in the demand for and in the cost of software. By the mid 1960s, the U.S. government was spending increasing amounts of money to create programs to utilize computer resources. "The U.S. government," wrote McCarthy, "with a dozen or so big systems serving its military and space establishments, is spending more than half of its 1966 outlay of $844 million on software."[12]

Pointing out the need for studying the process of programming, McCarthy observed, "What computers can do, depends on the state of the art and the science of programming as well as on speed and memory capacity."[13] McCarthy recognized that the computer was more than an efficient bookkeeping machine. There was a need to discover what new applications were possible, and to create those new applications. Therefore, there would be a need for breakthroughs in the process of programming. McCarthy believed that it was important for the user to be able to program in order to realize the potential of the computer. He pointed out that programming was a skill that was not difficult to learn, and that it was more important to understand the task being automated than to master programming languages. "To program the trajectory of a rocket," McCarthy offers as an example, "requires a few weeks' study of programming and a few years' study of physics."[14]

Early explorations in time-sharing prepared the foundation for an important leap in the process of creating software. The discovery was made that simple programming tools could be created to aid in software development. These tools could help those who understood the tasks to be automated to write programs. Such a program was carried out by research programmers and developers at Bell Labs in the 1970s and early 1980s, building on the principles developed by the pioneers of time-sharing and Project MAC.

THE MULTICS COLLABORATION

In 1964, MIT joined with GE and AT&T in a project designed to implement time-sharing by developing a new computer and a new operating system. The joint research project among GE, MIT, and AT&T was created to extend time-sharing techniques from a pilot program into a useful prototype for a future information utility. The researchers realized that there was no existing computer that would meet the demands of time-sharing. Therefore, part of the goal of their collaboration was to make it possible to develop both a new computer and a new operating system.

The collaborative project was called Multics (Multiplexed Information and Computing Service) and was to be implemented on the GE 645 computer.[15] Technical leadership of the project included F. J. Corbató from MIT and V. A. Vyssotsky from Bell Labs.[16] "One of the overall design goals is to create a computing system," they wrote, "which is capable of meeting almost all of the present and near-future requirements of a large computer utility. Such systems must run continuously and reliably 7 days a week, 24 hours a day in a way similar to telephone or power systems, and must be capable of meeting wide service demands: from multiple man–machine interaction to the sequential processing of absentee-user jobs. . . ."[17]

The goal of the research was to produce a prototype time-sharing system. Berkley Tague, one of the Bell Labs researchers involved in the Multics project writes, "The Multics Project was a joint project of Bell Labs, the GE Computer Systems Division, and MIT's Project MAC to develop a new computer and operating system that would replace MIT's CTSS system, Bell Labs BESYS, and support the new GE machine."[18] Although AT&T withdrew from the project in 1969, the joint work achieved significant results. Summarizing these achievements, Tague writes, "Multics was one of the seminal efforts in computing science and operating system design. It established principles and features of operating system design that are taken for granted today in any modern operating system."[19]

THE NEED FOR OPERATING SYSTEM RESEARCH AT BELL LABS

Even though AT&T withdrew from the research collaboration on Multics, computer scientists at Bell Labs wanted some way of continuing the advanced form of programming research that their work with CTSS and Multics had made possible. As early as 1957, Bell Labs had found they needed an operating system for their in-house computer center which was then running many short batch jobs. Describing the situation then facing the Labs, Vyssotsky explains, "We just couldn't take the time to get them on and off the machine manually. We needed an operating system to sequence jobs through and control machine resources."[20] The BESYS operating system was created at Bell Labs to deal with their in-house needs. When asked by others outside Bell Labs to make a copy available, they did so but with no obligation to provide support. "There was no support when we shipped a BESYS tape to somebody," Vyssotsky recalls, "we would answer reasonable questions over the telephone. If they found troubles or we found troubles, we would provide fixes."[21]

By 1964, however, Bell Labs was adopting third-generation computer equipment and had to decide whether they would build their own operating system or go with one that was built outside. Vyssotsky recounts the process of deliberation at the time: "Through a rather murky process of internal deliberation we decided to join forces with General Electric and MIT to create Multics." He explains that Bell Labs "planned to use the Multics operating system as a mainstay for Bell Laboratories' internal service computing in precisely the same way that we had used the BESYS operating system."[22]

UNIX IS BORN AND THE INTRODUCTION OF PIPES

When AT&T decided to pull out of the Multics collaboration, they took the research operating system off their GE 645 computer and put up the GECOS operating system. Although GECOS was adequate for applications, explained Vyssotsky, "It was nowhere near as satisfactory if you were trying to do things that were technically difficult and imperfectly defined which is the main task of research."[23]

For the pioneering work of Bell Labs research programmers like Ken Thompson and the research purposes of the Labs, an operating system more like what Multics had promised was needed. Along with the advantages of immediate feedback which time-sharing provided, the Bell Labs researchers wanted to continue to be able to work collaboratively in the way that time-sharing had made possible.

"What we wanted to preserve," one of the creators of Unix, Dennis Ritchie writes,

> *was not just a good programming environment in which to do programming, but a system around which a fellowship could form. We knew from experience that the essence of communal computing, as supplied by remote-access, time-shared machines, is not just to type programs into a terminal instead of a keypunch, but to encourage close communication.*[24]

Ritchie describes how an informal group led by Thompson had begun investigating alternatives to Multics before the GE-645 Multics machine had been removed from their lab.[25] Thompson and Ritchie presented Bell Labs with proposals to buy them a computer so they could build their own interactive, time-sharing operating system, but their proposals weren't acted on. Eventually, Thompson found a little-used PDP-7 computer. According to Vyssotsky, the orphaned PDP-7 computer "was a machine more nearly in the class of a Commodore 64 than the class of a PC-AT."[26]

Ritchie, Thompson, and Rudd Canady, who had been part of the Multics project, applied the lessons they had learned from working on Multics to the design of a file system for an experimental operating system. Writing on a chalkboard, they created a file system design based on the "particularly simple way of viewing files that was suggested by the Multics I/O system."[27]

"Soon," Ritchie recounts, "Thompson began implementing the paper file system (perhaps 'chalk file system' would be more accurate) that had been designed earlier."[28] Thompson was eager to get a working model so he could test it out. He proceeded to create the other aspects of an operating system.

"A file system without a way to exercise it is a sterile proposition," notes Ritchie, "so he [Thompson] proceeded to flesh it out with the other requirements for a working operating system, in particular the notion of processes."[29]

Describing the primitive conditions that Thompson faced, Ritchie writes, "At the start, Thompson did not even program on the PDP itself, but instead used a set of macros for the GEMAP assembler on a GE-635 machine."[30] A paper tape was generated on the GE 635 and then tested on the PDP-7 until, according to Ritchie, "a primitive Unix kernel, an editor, an assembler, a simple shell (command interpreter), and a few utilities (like the Unix **rm, cat, cp** commands) were completed. At this point, the operating system was self-supporting, programs could be written and tested without resort to paper tape, and development continued on the PDP-7 itself."[31]

Ritchie describes how Thompson's PDP-7 assembler was a model of simplicity. "There were no libraries, no loader or link editor," he writes, "the entire source of a program was presented to the assembler, and the output file—with a fixed name—that emerged was directly executable."[32] Ritchie notes that once the assembler was completed, "the system was able to support itself."[33] And thus the operating system we now call Unix was born.

Among the other active contributors during this period were Bell Labs researchers Rudd Canady and Joe Ossanna. The researchers were anxious to continue their work on a more advanced computer than the PDP-7. However, their efforts to get AT&T to buy them a more advanced computer for their time-sharing research hadn't succeeded. With the help of Ossanna and another Bell Labs researcher, Lee McMahon, they were finally able to convince management to buy them a new PDP-11 computer. To obtain this agreement, however, the researchers promised to create a text processing system. Doug McIlroy explains that "typists everywhere were seen as potential customers of the promised document-preparation program. Only later did Ossanna spot the patent department as a ripe candidate. By then there had already been clients in the telephone-operations business."[34] By Spring 1971, the Bell Labs Unix pioneers had created a text formatter, fulfilling their promise. They had translated one they had created for the PDP-7 from a program McIlroy had written in the BCPL language while working on Multics. The text formatter was an assembler program for the PDP-11.[35]

One of the important developments in Unix was the introduction of pipes.* Pipes had been suggested by McIlroy during the early days of creat-

*Pipes made it possible to take simple programs and combine them so as to create a customized program. According to McIlroy, "A pipe connects the output of one program to the input of another running simultaneously." (See the appendix to this chapter for an example of a powerful use of pipes referred to by Ken Thompson as a thunderclap.)

ing Unix. Ritchie explains how "the idea, explained one afternoon on a blackboard, intrigued us but failed to ignite any immediate action. There were several objections to the idea as put. . . .What a failure of imagination," he admits.[36] McIlroy concurs, describing how the initial effort to add pipes to Unix occurred about the same time in 1969 that Ritchie, Thompson, and Canaday were outlining ideas for a file system. "That was when," he writes, "the simple pipeline as a way to combine programs, with data notationally propagating along a chain of (not necessarily concurrent) filters was articulated."[37] However, pipes weren't implemented in Unix until 1972. "Thanks to McIlroy's persistence," Ritchie writes, "pipes were finally installed in the operating system (a relatively simple job), and a new notation was introduced."[38] Several of the old commands had to be changed to make them usable with pipes, notes Ritchie. Summarizing how pipes found their way into Unix, Vyssotsky notes that Thompson put them in, but that "it was McIlroy who said, 'look, you ought to do it.' Pipes, like most things in Unix, were not a radically new idea."[39] He describes how similar ideas had appeared in other languages such as SIMULA as early as 1967.

Dick Haight, a Unix pioneer who helped develop the Programmer's Workbench of Unix tools, was present the day that pipes were introduced into Unix. He describes what happened:

> *I happened to have been visiting the research crew the day they implemented pipes. It was clear to everyone practically minutes after the system came up with pipes working, that it was a wonderful thing. Nobody would ever go back and give that up if they could help it.*[40]

Also describing the day pipes were introduced, McIlroy writes:

> *Open Systems! Our Systems! How well those who were there remember the pipe-festooned garret where Unix took form. The excitement of creation drew people to work there amidst the whine of the computer's cooling fans, even though almost the same computer access could be had from one's office or from home. Those raw quarters saw a procession of memorable events. The advent of software pipes precipitated a day-long orgy of one-liners. . . . As people reveled in the power of functional composition in the large, which is even today unavailable to users of other systems.* [41]

THE SOFTWARE TOOL

Pipes had been created by the time the Version 3 Unix Manual appeared in February 1973. The date listed for the creation of pipes is January 15, 1973.[42] Not only were pipes a significant addition to Unix, but according to McIlroy, pipes made possible a subsequent important discovery. "In another memorable event," he writes, "the unarticulated notion of software tools, which had been bolstered by pipes, was finally brought home by the liberation of the pattern matching program **grep** from within the editor."

McIlroy describes how he asked Thompson to create a program to help him with some work that he was trying to do. This program resulted in the invention of the software tool **grep.** Following is McIlroy's account of how **grep** was taken out from the editor, leading to a clearer understanding of the notion of a software tool. He writes:

> *Grep was invented for me. I was making a program to read text aloud through a voice synthesizer. As I invented phonetic rules I would check Webster's dictionary for words on which they might fail. For example, how do you cope with the digraph 'ui', which is pronounced many different ways: 'fruit', 'guile', 'guilty', 'anguish', 'intuit', 'beguine'? I would break the dictionary up into pieces that fit in ed's limited buffer and use a global command to select a list. I would whittle this list down by repeated scannings with ed to see how each proposed rule worked.*
>
> *The process was tedious, and terribly wasteful, since the dictionary had to be split (one couldn't afford to leave a split copy on line). Then ed copied each part into /tmp, scanned it twice to accomplish the g command, and finally threw it away, which takes time too.*
>
> *One afternoon I asked Ken Thompson if he could lift the regular expression recognizer out of the editor and make a one-pass program to do it. He said yes. The next morning I found a note in my mail announcing a program named grep. It worked like a charm. When asked what that funny name meant, Ken said it was obvious. It stood for the editor command that it simulated, g/re/p (global regular expression print).*
>
> *Progress on my talking program accelerated dramatically. From that special-purpose beginning, grep soon became a household word. (Something I had to stop myself from writing in the first paragraph above shows how firmly naturalized the idea now is: "I used ed to grep out words from the dictionary.") More than any other single program, grep focused the viewpoint that Kernighan and Plauger christened and formalized in* Software Tools: *make programs that do one thing and do it well, with as few preconceptions about input syntax as possible.*[43]

Grep is listed in the manual for Version 4 Unix which is dated November 1973. The date given for the creation of **grep** is March 3, 1973, following the creation of pipes.[44] The creation of **grep,** McIlroy explains, was followed by the invention of other special-purpose software programs that could be used as tools. He writes:

> *A while later a demand arose for another special-purpose program, gres, for substitution: g/re/s. Lee McMahon undertook to write it, and soon foresaw*

> *that there would be no end to the family: g/re/d, g/re/a, etc. As his concept developed it became sed, a tool of remarkable utility that is largely unappreciated today, because it capitalizes on the perfect familiarity with ed that was universal ten years ago, but no more. Sed covers a lot of needs. For example, we have never seen fit to adopt the widespread "head" utility because "sed 10q" does just as well.*[45]

What McIlroy refers to as "the unarticulated notion of software tools . . . brought home by the liberation of . . . grep from within the editor" has become one of the significant achievements of the Bell Labs research work on Unix. By making it possible to use **grep** to search for a data pattern in a file, without having to use an editor to go inside the file, the Bell Labs researchers discovered that they could create a plethora of software tools to be used in varying combinations, thus facilitating the customized application by a user, a goal sought by those doing research in programming.[46]

McIlroy explains that the notion of "software tool" only became articulated among the Bell Labs researchers with the publication of the book *Software Tools* by Kernighan and Plaugher. "Still unnamed in our circles," McIlroy notes, "until Kernighan and Plauger wrote their book, the idea nevertheless became a guiding principle."[47] McIlroy adds that "We were definitely building tools before K&P, though we lacked the suggestive word."[48]

Describing how the notion of software tools helps to create an effective programming environment, Brian W. Kernighan and Rob Pike, authors of *The Unix Programming Environment,* explain that each tool is designed to be used with other tools and achieving this end is more important than how each is designed internally.[49] The most important aspect considered with each tool is the function that the tool is to have. New tools are designed once a new function is intended. In "Program Design in the UNIX Environment" they write:

> *The guiding principle for making the choice should be that each program does one thing. Options are appropriately added to a program that already has the right functionality. If there is no such program then a new program is called for. In that case the usual criteria for program design should be used: the program should be as general as possible, its default behavior should match the most common usage and it should cooperate with other programs.*[50]

Thus Unix, according to Kernighan and Pike, created "a new style of computing, a new way of thinking of how to attack a problem with a computer. This style," they explain, "was based on the use of tools: using programs separately or in combination to get a job done, rather than doing it by hand, by monolithic self-sufficient subsystems, or by special-purpose, one-time programs."[51]

The philosophy of using software tools that developed from research in Unix is outlined in the "Foreword" to the special issue of *The Bell System Technical Journal* published in 1978, on "The Unix Time-Sharing System." Describing the principles they found to be important components of the Unix philosophy of software design, the researchers write:

> *UNIX utilities are usually thought of as tools—sharply honed programs that help with generic data processing tasks. Tools were often invented to help with the development of UNIX programs and were continually improved by much trial, error, discussion, and redesign, as was the operating system itself. Tools may be used in combination to perform or construct specific applications.*[52]

They explain that a distinctive style evolved as part of Unix research. "UNIX software works smoothly together; elaborate computing tasks are typically composed from loosely coupled small parts, often software tools taken off the shelf."[53]

"Sophisticated tools to make tools have evolved," they observe.[54] Software development tools such as **nroff** and **troff** were created. Not only was it important to create tools, but soon tools to create tools, like **yacc** and **lex,** were developed. **Yacc** and **lex** were used to create numerous little languages and applications like **eqn** and **awk** that greatly enhanced the popularity of Unix.

The evolution of the tool **diff** created by McIlroy, a commonly used software tool, is an example of how tools were continually improved, based on the experience gained using them. McIlroy reports how he based his work on algorithms created by others and then he tried three different algorithms before settling on the one finally used.[55] Other Unix tools were created through a similar process. Each program was created to fulfill some simple capability and was called a tool. The programs were designed to be fun to use and helpful to programmers. Among the principles guiding the tool-builders were:

> *(i.) Make each program do one thing well. To do a new job, build afresh rather than complicate old programs by adding new "features."*
>
> *(ii) Expect the output of every program to become the input to another, as yet unknown, program. Don't clutter output with extraneous information. Avoid stringently columnar or binary input formats. Don't insist on interactive input.*
>
> *(iii) Design and build software, even operating systems, to be tried early, ideally within weeks. Don't hesitate to throw away the clumsy parts and rebuild them.*
>
> *(iv) Use tools in preference to unskilled help to lighten a programming task, even if you have to detour to build the tools and expect to throw some of them out after you've finished using them.*[56]

"Our goals throughout the effort," write Ritchie and Thompson, in describing the research objectives of their work on Unix, "when articulated at all, have always been to build a comfortable relationship with the machine and to explain ideas and inventions in operating systems and other software."[57]

Frederick P. Brooks, Jr. is another computer pioneer who recognized the importance of pipes and combining single-function programs into what he calls a "unified programming environment" to make the work of programmers more productive. Brooks describes Unix as one of "the first integrated environments to come into widespread use," which "improved productivity by integral factors."[58]

In explaining how such an environment functions, he writes:

> *They attack the accidental difficulties that result from using individual programs* together, *by providing integrated libraries, unified file formats, and pipes and filters. As a result, conceptual structures that in principle could always call, feed, and use one another can indeed easily do so in practice.*[59]

Following the development of single-function software tools that could be used together via pipes to create a better programming environment came the development of whole toolchests and workbenches of tools to make the work of programmers into a more rational process.

OPEN SOURCE CODE AND THE EARLY DEVELOPMENT OF UNIX

Since the Unix programming environment was used by the researchers themselves, they came to learn its weaknesses and problems and were encouraged to make needed improvements. Contributing to the value of Unix during its early development was the fact that the source code was open and available. It could be examined, improved, and customized. In an article "Can UNIX Survive Secret Source Code?", Mike Lesk, a Bell Labs researcher, observed that only when computer source code is open and can be modified will it be developed and vibrant. He gives the example of COMIT, the string processing language. At one point, its owners decided there would no longer be any modifications in the code, and so only distributed it in binary form. "You haven't heard of COMIT since," he notes. He describes how the same fate befell TRAC, a language close to FORTH. "Software is more attractive to hackers," Lesk maintains, "if it can be changed. As more and more UNIX suppliers restrict access to source code, fewer and fewer advanced research shops will be attracted to UNIX."[60]

Commenting on the importance of open source code in the early years of Unix development at Bell Labs, Thompson and Ritchie write, "Because all source programs were always available and easily modified on-line we were willing to revise and rewrite the system and its software when new ideas were invented, discovered, or suggested by others."[61] Not only was the source code open and available to the Bell Labs researchers developing the system, but the Labs also made the sources available on tape at the request of academic colleagues. Robert Fabry, a professor at the University of California at Berkeley, was able to get a tape of Version 4 Unix, and that began the long and important role played by faculty and students at the University of California at Berkeley in the development of Unix.[62]

Source code tapes were made available to interested researchers in the academic and computer science community for a nominal fee. For example, when John Lions, a professor of computer science at the University of New South Wales in Australia, read a paper published by Thompson and Ritchie in mid-1974, he wrote them for a copy of the Unix tape. After signing a license agreement with the Labs, and a token payment of $110 Australian ($150 U.S.), the Unix Edition 5 tape and manuals arrived, "as a late Christmas present," in December 1974.[63]

Although Bell Labs made the tape and manuals available, they did so with no support. Berkley Tague explains the release was "*caveat emptor*—i.e. dollars on the table up front and no support promised."

Henry Spencer, a Unix pioneer from the University of Toronto in Canada, and one of the programmers of C News, describes how early users of Unix in the academic community had to provide their own support. He explains:

> *It was very common at the time. This was in the days when UNIX was still treated by the Bell System as, "Oh, just something we happen to do for our own internal use. You can have a copy if you want, but if you got problems, don't bother us." And the result was if you wanted UNIX support you did it yourself or it didn't happen.*[64]

Lions agrees. "We needed help," he notes, "but we couldn't get any from outside sources so we ended up generating our own expertise."[65] Not only did those working on Unix implementation at the University of New South Wales have access to the code, but Lions explains how Ian Johnstone, the tutor working with him in his Operating Systems class, suggested making some of the code for the Unix kernel available to the students in his class. "I think it was in 1975," remembers Lions, that Ian Johnstone asked, "'Why don't we run off a few of the source files for the kernel and ask the students to take a look at them? Then we can ask them some questions; maybe it will be interesting'."[66] Lions took Johnstone's suggestion and made some of the Unix source code available to his class, but his students complained. They felt they needed to see the source code for the whole kernel in order to make sense out of any part.

Taking their suggestion, Lions decided to make a large part of the source code available to his class. "The following year," he recounts, "I prepared a booklet containing the source files for a version of Edition 6 UNIX that could then run on a PDP-11/40 system." Lions followed the book of source code with a book of "explanatory notes that was intended to introduce students to the code."[67] Lions explains that working on his book, *A Commentary on the UNIX Operating System,* was a real learning experience. By slowly and methodically surveying the whole kernel he notes, "I came to understand things that others had overlooked."[68]

When he read the manual and wasn't quite certain about his interpretation, Lions would read the code. Through this process, he was able to determine that the manual was "really quite accurate in its description of what a program actually does. In the Thompson/Ritchie era," he observes, "words were carefully chosen."[69] Lions writes, "In our opinion, it is highly beneficial for students to have the opportunity to study a working operating system in all its aspects."[70]

"Moreover," he adds, "it is undoubtedly good for students majoring in computer science to be confronted at least once in their careers with the task of reading and understanding a program of major dimensions."[71] Lions found that, "On the whole the authors of UNIX, Ken Thompson and Dennis Ritchie, have created a program of great strength, integrity and effectiveness," which he urged his students to "admire and seek to emulate."[72] Not only did students in Lions' class read and study the Unix source code and Lions' *Commentary*, but Lions sent more than 200 copies of his book to Bell Laboratories. Eventually, Bell Labs took over distribution of the book.

Tague relates how Lions' book of commentary and the Unix source code were used at AT&T "as part of the documentation package for those who wanted to understand or modify the UNIX(r) source code that the USG [Unix Support Group] shipped."[73] Even after Unix V6 had been replaced by Unix V7, Tague explains that Lions' *Commentary* continued to be useful as an introduction to Unix. Tague writes:

> *It outlined the conceptual architecture, very clearly in the short form of the system before it had accreted all the minor changes and feature additions that disguised the original clarity of its structure. All new people were given a copy when they joined the USG. And I suspect most development groups did the same.*[74]

Pioneers such as Henry Spencer agree on how important it was to those in the Unix community to have the source code. He notes how having the sources made it possible to identify and fix the bugs that they discovered, "There is something the UNIX community has always been fairly strong on," he explained during an interview, "admitting things you know don't work about the software." Even in the late 1970s and early 1980s, remembers Spencer, "practically every UNIX site had complete sources."[75]

One of the early functions of Usenet, the early online community of Unix systems begun in 1979, according to Spencer, was to provide cooperative software support for the Unix community. He elaborates:

> *Well, for one thing, Usenet predated a lot of company bbs's and the like. It was basically a cheap way to hear about things fast and this was at a time when practically every UNIX site had complete sources and so a bug report often came with a fix. It was a way of finding out what people had discovered and what fixes they'd worked out for it. Quickly and easily. And for that matter, if you ran into something that you couldn't solve yourself, putting out an inquiry to a bunch of fairly bright people who were fairly familiar with the code, often got a response, "O Yeah. We solved that one" or "You're right. There's a bug. Here's how to fix it" or sympathy even if no one had a fix for it.*[76]

Another Unix pioneer, Dick Haight, corroborates the important role open source code played for those in the Unix community:

> *That, by the way, was one of the great things about UNIX in the early days: people actually shared each other's stuff. It's too bad that so many sites now have purposefully turned off the read privileges in order to keep their ideas from being stolen. Not only did we learn a lot in the old days from sharing material, but we also never had to worry about how things really worked because we always could go read the source. That's still the only thing that matters when the going gets tough.*[77]

Unix was continually used and improved by its creators. A growing community of programmers, system administrators, and users, both at Bell Labs and at academic and research sites outside the Labs, also used, developed, and debugged the code. The fact that the source code was open and available made this possible. The result was the creation of Unix as a powerful and flexible programming environment.

Though Unix was primarily designed to "help build research software," Bell Labs software developers soon found that, "what worked well in a programming laboratory also worked well on modest projects to develop minicomputer-based systems in support of telephone company operations."[78]

AT&T AUTOMATES INTERNAL OPERATIONS

In the late 1960s, there had been an upsurge in demand for telephone company service which taxed all AT&T's resources.

The 1970 annual report of AT&T described the crisis:

> *The company concluded that the convergence of a number of adverse factors contributed to the crisis, including an unforecasted rapid upsurge of demand for business traffic on a poor switching system, faulty trunk maintenance and administration, inadequate training of maintenance personnel and poor main distributing frames administration.*[79]

Section 1 of the U.S. Communications Act of 1934 charges the Federal Communications Commission (FCC) with promoting a "rapid, efficient, nationwide and worldwide wire and radio communications service with adequate facilities at reasonable charge."[80] This legislative obligation put pressure on AT&T to create and support Bell Labs' efforts to push forward the forefronts of computer science, since the most advanced technology and science were needed for AT&T to meet its obligations as a regulated communications utility.

Under pressure from both the New York Public Service Commission (NYPSC) and the FCC, AT&T had to find a way to upgrade their service.[81] In response to these requirements, a push began within AT&T to "use the computer to support the operation of the Bell System Network."[82] Berkley Tague, who would be instrumental in implementing this change at AT&T, describes the broad scope of the effort that AT&T instituted to deal with the service crisis. He lists "[m]onitoring and alarms, maintenance and staff management, inventory and order control, revenue data collection and billing, traffic measurement and control, circuit provisioning, etc."[83] and he provides the following illustration:

> *The data that has to be collected to bill for calls was being stored on a variety of media—e.g. paper AMA tape, a punched paper tape a few inches wide, IBM compatible mag tape, and probably a few others. These tapes had to be mounted, saved, trucked to DP centers for processing, etc. They could be lost or damaged in handling. An obvious solution was to send the data over datalinks—our own network—to the DP [data processing] centers. Minicomputer-based systems were designed to collect, preprocess and transmit this data in some cases; in others, the electronic switches themselves were programmed to do the job. The goal was to eliminate the need for people handling physical media—a process that is both expensive and error-prone.*[84]

Software was needed to facilitate these changes. Tague explains how the Unix system, originally created for computer research, also served the needs of program developers. "The difference," he explains, distinguishing between the needs of researchers and the concerns of developers, involved "support, stability, and reliability." He describes how developers have to meet deadlines and so only tolerate absolutely necessary changes to the system. A researcher, on the other hand, according to Tague, will "tolerate a fair amount of upset and change and revision if it improves your toolkit significantly,"[85] even if it makes it necessary to recode the work.

The use of Unix by developers for support operations began in the 1972 period. Tague describes how "a number of developers were planning to build their own operating systems—typically their first system and often their first major programs."[86] Having experience with Unix, he advocated Unix for the job. It was an uphill battle to convince developers to adopt Unix when there was no support offered, and it was made up of 12,000 lines of undocumented code.

In 1973, Tague pointed out the need for a central support group and volunteered to form the group. He was given the job. The goal of the Unix Support Group (USG), which Tague created in September 1973, was to "provide the stability and support that would buffer developers from the experiments that researchers were daily imposing on the evolving UNIX system." He describes how Dennis Ritchie promised him a portable version of Unix, which was delivered as promised by October 1973.[87] Recoding the Unix kernel from assembler language, which was specific to each computer, into the C programming language was an important feat. Once the Unix kernel was coded in C, it would become possible to implement Unix on different computers without having to rewrite the majority of the code.

The effort to make Unix machine independent was desirable, so that AT&T wouldn't be dependent on any one vendor for its computer hardware, software, or service. Tague explains, "A goal of my effort was to gain vendor independence so we could get competitive bids on volume buys when we deployed these mini-based systems across the Bell System."[88]

Every project adopting Unix, Tague reports, added their own features and function to it, and it became the responsibility of the USG to choose among or merge the variations. The University of California at Berkeley, according to Tague, performed a similar job with the variations of Unix developed by academic computer scientists outside of AT&T.

CREATING A PROGRAMMER'S WORKBENCH

While Tague was working on Unix Support Operations, other Bell Labs researchers were planning another major project that would impact on software development and on the use of a new form of tool.

Rudd Canaday (who had designed the original Unix file system with Thompson and Ritchie), Dick Haight, Ted Dolotta, John Mashey, and others formed the Programmer's Workbench Group (PWB) within the Business Information Systems (BIS) project.[89] Tague explains that

> *BIS problem was to get a common "workbench" that would drive code onto any of the three or four commercial vendor's mainframes that were used by BIS. By putting a UNIX(r) system in front of the large mainframe systems, developers got the advantages of UNIX(r) in developing code and a place they could store debugged standard command sequences that drove development and testing on the target mainframes.*[90]

David Nowitz, a Unix pioneer who helped with the development of UUCP, and then went on to collaborate in the creation of honeydanber UUCP,[91] explains that when he was hired by Bell Labs in 1969, there were programmers working on many different computers with many different languages. The problem these different computers represented for those at AT&T, is described by Haight:

> *We had a real problem to solve at the time. For one thing, we had a fairly large group of software developers at the Labs working on several different main frames. The biggest group, of course, consisted of people working on either IBM 360s or 370s.*[92]

The programmers working on the IBM 360 or 370 had to contend with batch processing and IBM's Job Control Language (JCL) problems. Other programmers were working with the UNIVAC and another group with Xerox computers. A few were using early but expensive time-sharing systems like TSO (IBM's time-sharing) and Univacs Remand Service.

"These systems," Haight relates, "not only offered very different programming environments, but proved to be very expensive to use and *very* unfriendly." Describing the task they were charged with, Haight continues, "Basically, we ended up trying to give all these people a cheap text-editing front end that they could use for interactive program entry. For that to happen, we needed to develop a programming environment that was consistent with what they already were using."[93]

They developed a software subsystem that included five components which all of the programmers working on the different computers could use. The subsystem which they created was called the Programmer's Workbench (PWB). It included RJE (Remote Job Entry), an editor, a program for tracking version changes, a word processor, and software to simulate test input.[94] Haight believed that Unix was "the best program development system around" and that this "'development environment' notion was the very concept that got PWB going back in '73."[95]

The vision of the PWB/Unix was conceived of in mid April 1973 and installed on the first workbench machine, a PDP 11/45, in October 1973. By 1977 the PWB was serving 1,000 users.[96] The programmers working on the PWB rejected the top-down software design philosophy, that is, of creating a fully integrated facility, implementing it, and then making it available to users. Instead, they adopted a bottom-up philosophy. They designed independent single-function tools and made them available to users as early as possible. Users were encouraged to provide feedback. The PWB programmers had actual feedback to help them determine what modifications were needed to improve the tools. Evan Ivie, a Bell Labs researcher who was one of the creators of the PWB, describes why the PWB/Unix group adopted the bottom-up philosophy of software design:

> *The idea of designing and building a complete and fully integrated Workbench system was rejected for a number of reasons, not the least of which is the fact that no one in the programming field knows what that system should look like at this point in time. Instead, every effort was made to identify some of the immediate needs of potential users and to develop pieces of the Workbench that could satisfy those needs quickly. This approach provided the Workbench designers with much valuable user feedback quickly, and it allowed the projects to start picking up pieces of the Workbench to satisfy their most critical needs immediately and thus to start a phased transition to the complete Workbench.*[97]

The design for implementing Unix on the IBM System/370 was done in 1979, coding was done in 1980, and, by early 1981, the first production system IBM 3033AP was installed at Bell Labs at Indian Hill. Unix had been suggested as the development system for programmers for the switching system software for the 5ESS switch because the Programmer's Workbench provided "editors, source code control, and software generation systems."[98]

In 1981, after a production Unix system was running on an IBM 3033AP in Indian Hill, the application software tools were ported from the PDP-11/70 computer to the 3033AP. Shell scripts were carried over and then users were transferred.[99]

By 1984 the largest user of the Unix system for the IBM System/370 was the development project for the 5ESS switch. The creation at Bell Labs of software for the 5ESS switch required more than a million lines of code.[100] Unix with the Programmer's Workbench software was chosen for the 5ESS switch software development project because the researchers felt that Unix "provided a better development environment than any other operating system available. In addition, the developers were all trained in using this system and all the software tools had been developed."[101]

The elaborate process of porting Unix to the IBM 3033AP is described by the researchers:

> *Over 300 tools, written in both C and shell command language, were identified and examined. After careful study, almost half of the tools were found to be little-used and were eliminated for porting to the 3033AP. The C programs required recompiling to generate objects that would run on a 3033AP; in general, they compiled without problems. The shell scripts were carried over with almost no problems. Regression tests were used . . . and other programs were unit tested. System testing, which consisted primarily of generating the system software for the 5ESS switch, was then done. . . . The effort to port the application tools was small and again proved the strength and computer independence of the UNIX operating system and the associated application programs.*[102]

The rationale leading to the creation of the Programmer's Workbench is outlined by Ivie. He wrote:

> *Although the computer industry now has some 30 years of experience, the programming of computer-based systems persists in being a very difficult and costly job. This is particularly true of large and complex systems where scheduled slips, cost overruns, high bug rates, insufficient throughput, maintenance difficulties, etc., all seem to be the rule instead of the exception. Part of the problem stems from the fact that programming is as yet very much a trial and error process.*[103]

"There are at this point," he observed, "only the beginnings of a methodology or discipline for designing, building and testing software. The situation is further aggravated by the rapidly changing hardware industry and by the continuing evolution of operating systems which continues to nullify much of the progress that is made in the development of programming tools. What can be done," he asked, "to move the programming industry toward a more professional and stable approach to software development?"[104]

After enumerating several of the alternatives, he explained that his proposal involved "a very different approach to improving the development process." His recommendation was "... that the programming community develop a program development 'facility' (or facilities) much like those that have been developed for other professions (e.g. carpenter's workbench, dentist's office, engineer's laboratory)." Such an approach, he explained, "would help focus attention on the need for adequate tools and procedures; it would serve as a mechanism for integrating tools into a coordinated set; and it would tend to add stability to the programming environment by separating the tools from the product (the current approach is equivalent to carpenter's leaving their tools in each house they build)."[105]

The Business Information Systems Programs (BISP) area of Bell Labs that was to use the Workbench program had among the computers it used an IBM 370/158 and 168, a UNIVAC 1108 and 1110, two Xerox Sigma 5s, and several minicomputers.[106] The Workbench encouraged the development of machine independent programming tools.

> *Each tool must now function for programmers developing code for a number of different vendor machines. There is no room for shortcuts which are dependent on the idiosyncrasies of a given machine (or a given project.) One is thus forced into a more stable and generalized software development approach which should be more applicable to new machines.*[107]

Summing up the Programmer's Workbench philosophy, Ivie wrote that "the programming profession has yet to produce a software development methodology that is sufficiently general so that it can be transferred from one project to another and from one machine to another." With the development of the Programmer's Workbench, he hoped, "a machine dedicated to the software development and maintenance function can serve as a vehicle for the development of such a methodology."[108]

RATIONALIZING THE PROCESS OF SOFTWARE PRODUCTION

In their article published in *Scientific American* in 1966, Fano and Corbató noted that the creation of a working computer in 1944 was followed by a series of quantum leaps in both the speed of the electronics and the development of special languages which facilitated human–computer communication. In another article in the same special issue of *Scientific American*, John McCarthy identified the importance of being able to program for making use of the computer. He also noted that spending time mastering a programming language was less important than understanding the functions the software is to serve. Their descriptions demonstrate that the computer is an all-purpose machine that can be directed to do whatever tasks humans can conceive of programs to describe. This poses a dilemma. Since humans are still needed to create directives for the computer, the challenge raised is how the process of programming can be made more rational and productive.

Perlis had observed that the technical progress of a society was marked by the development of tools and the ever-developing set of people capable of wielding those tools. He noted the continuing evolution of the process of producing tools. In the evolution of Unix, the need for software tools became evident and a series of tools was developed to meet these needs. The creation of time-sharing and the development of Unix as a time-sharing system has helped to create a community of people who not only use Unix, but who also continue its development. The contributions to the evolution of Unix by researchers at Bell Labs, by those at the University of California at Berkeley, and by other users and programmers around the world, are an important achievement in the development of the process of software creation.

Writing in 1975, one of the team of researchers creating the PWB, P. J. Plauger observed that "building on the work of others is the only way to make substantial progress in any field."[109] Describing the process of creating software tools, Plauger explained that each tool is a small programming project requiring anywhere from a few man-months to a few hours to complete. He proposed that these tools need to be designed in a standard way so that they can interface with and be combined in a useful way with other tools for a variety of different purposes. "The programmer working this way becomes a tool builder, and his impact extends far beyond the task he may originally have set out to solve," he concluded.[110]

Placing the creation of software tools into the broader context of tool production provides a basis for evaluating the achievements and problems of this new stage. Sigvard Strandh, in *History of the Machine*, describes how mechanical hand tools had acquired a stable form at an early stage. "From the Middle Ages until the era of industrialism," he writes, "the tools of the carpenter, joiner, and smith remained more or less the same." With the publication of the great French encyclopedia between 1751 and 1780 by Diderot and D'Alembert, however, Strandh observes that the development of these tools was given a substantial boost. Publication of the descriptions of the tools used in all the trades extant at the time, in great detail, in the great French encyclopedia, made it possible for anyone interested to learn how to build the tools, "so as to be able to establish himself in one of the trades described."[111]

The publication in the great French encyclopedia made possible the constant improvement of the old hand tools, and thus made it possible to manufacture the new tools needed for new technical developments. "Industrialization," Strandh writes, "means the manual methods of manufacture are mechanized, that is, taken over by machines. The machine tool is the local outcome of the process. Mass manufacture of machine tools," which, he writes, "has been called 'the industry of industries', didn't become widespread until the 1870s."[112]

The conditions described by Strandh made possible the advances in the technology of tool production in the nineteenth century. Strandh's description provides a helpful perspective when examining the achievements of the Unix community in developing the software tool creation process. Bell Labs researchers early on recognized that software production required text editing in place of soldering, and that this substitution represented a significant challenge. The creation by Bell Labs programmers of software tools, making it possible to produce better software more efficiently, is an important development. This development is similar to the ability to improve hand tools that Morgan documents as the technological advance represented by the invention of iron. The success of writing the code for the 5ESS switch at AT&T demonstrates the achievement these software tools have made possible.[113]

Generating software is different from creating hardware and it presents a particular challenge. You can't see software tools or touch them or handle them as you can mechanical tools. "Software is invisible and unvisualizable," Brooks points out, since "the reality of software is not inherently embedded in space." He observes:

> *In spite of the progress made in restricting and simplifying the structures of software, these structures remain inherently unvisualizable and thus do not permit the mind to use some of its most powerful conceptual tools. This lack not only impedes the process of design with one mind, it also severely hinders communication among minds.*[114]

There is a particular problem posed when creating, describing, or representing software tools. Diderot was able to catalog the tools and industrial processes of his times, but such a task is much more difficult when it comes to creating such an encyclopedia or presentation of software tools, or in creating the software component catalog that McIlroy once proposed. The development of UUCP and then of Usenet, as a means of cheap communication among those of the Unix community, made it possible to surmount some of the difficulties inherent in the process of software production.[115]

The Usenet community was able to pioneer the creation of a cooperative network that helped facilitate communications among the Unix software community. "Though large institutions have been able to avail themselves of communications networks such as ARPANET, the UNIX community has made inexpensive electronic communication available to all its members via Usenet," remarked John Stoneback, a faculty member at Moravian College, in an article describing the important role that Unix played for members of the academic community.[116]

Describing the importance of the creation of the Unix communication program UUCP, McIlroy writes that

> *Before uucp, remote login was the only kind of electronic connection between Unix systems. With uucp, every PDP 11 with dial-up (not even dial-out) access became connected. E-mail and file transfer previously available only among the fortunate few sites on ARPANET, were democratized overnight. This was the brainchild of Mike Lesk.*[117]

Lesk's original plan in creating UUCP was to create an automatic software updating system.[118] That, however, was fraught with difficulties, and instead, with modifications to UUCP by David Nowitz, it became the basis for a broad ranging online computer network that came to be called Usenet. McIlroy, describing how UUCP was used by Tom Truscott and other Usenet pioneers to create an online community, writes, "Soon Truscott saw that the new medium could be used for automatic dissemination of information, and netnews was born."[119]

The Unix system is based on a methodology that helps the user to learn the new language. The methodology is similar to the way children learn to talk. As Unix pioneers Brian Kernighan and John Mashey write, "The code that people see, adapt, and imitate is usually well structured. People learn to code well in the same way that they learn to speak their native language well, by imitation and immediate feedback."[120]

"People often look at each other's code," they explain, "comment on it in person and through interuser communication facilities, and take pieces of it for their own use. The ideas of programming teams and egoless programming fit into the Unix environment well, since they encourage sharing rather than isolation."[121] There is frequent sharing and building on each other's code. While "some programs have always been 'owned' by one or two people, many others have been passed around so much that it is difficult to tell exactly who wrote them."[122] Also, they point out that "Tools have been built to automate many common programming tasks."[123]

Kernighan and Mashey explain how in its early days, up through 1974, "Unix best supported a single, cooperative, tightly coupled group of people on each machine."[124] By 1975, PWB/Unix made possible support for a larger number of users. There were large groups of over 200 users working on different machines, but the users preferred to share a machine so they could share procedures and data bases.[125] They describe how the concept of software tools spread from the Unix programming environment and PWB/Unix to the more generalized applications described by Kernighan and Plauger in their book *Software Tools*, to further applications that were ported to other machines, and then to the more generalized applications of the Lawrence Berkeley Laboratory (LBL).[126]

DOCUMENTING TECHNOLOGICAL PROGRESS

In writing about the role that technology plays in the development of society, Morgan observed that oral or written documentation helps to facilitate technological progress. Morgan described how the Greek poet Homer, by documenting the civilization that existed prior to his times, provided future generations with a yardstick by which they could measure their own accomplishments.[127]

So, too, documentation of the achievements of the Unix pioneers, and of the tools they created, is an important step to be taken by those who want to understand the progress made in our times. When amateur scientists created the Royal Society in Great Britain in the 1660s, one of their early efforts was to invite Reverend Thomas Sprat into the Society and to support him in writing a history of the documentation of technology from Homer to their own times. Diderot's work on the great French encyclopedia in the years leading up to the French Revolution played such a role summarizing the knowledge, including, most importantly, the summary of all the trades and industries with their tools existing up to his time in France.

Unix pioneers often emphasize that scientific progress can only be made by building on what has already been achieved. It is important, therefore, to recognize the Unix legacy. Unix made it possible to achieve programming projects involving millions of lines of code by creating a workbench of software development tools. The creation of a new form of tool requires a new form of tool production process and though such technology is only in its infancy, there are examples to be studied so that we know what we are building on. As Henry Spencer and Geoff Collyer recognized when they were working on increasing the performance of Netnews software, it is necessary to systematically record what is happening to be able to see what progress is being made. "To know how to get somewhere, you must know where you are starting from."[128] Similarly, it is important to systematically document the history of the significant developments of the software tool revolution, so that there will be a yardstick by which to measure the accomplishments and to determine what new questions need to be explored.[129]

NOTES

1. Lewis Henry Morgan, *Ancient Society* (Chicago: Charles H. Kerr, 1877), 42.
2. Alan Perlis, *Introduction to Computer Science* (New York: Harper and Row, 1972), 4.
3. *Ibid.*, 3.
4. *Ibid.*
5. See F. J. Fano and R. M. Corbató, "Time Sharing on Computers" in *Information: A Scientific American Book* (San Francisco: W. H. Freeman, 1966), 77; C. Strachey, "Time Sharing in Large Fast Computers," *Proc Int Conf on Info Processing*, UNESCO, June 1959, 336–341; and Frederick P. Brooks, Jr., *The Mythical Man-*

Month (Reading, Mass.: Addison-Wesley, 1972), 146. Brooks describes how both E. F. Codd and C. Strachey reported work aimed at time-sharing debugging in 1959. According to Brooks, Codd's system, which emphasized more efficient input–output and interactive debugging was not actually implemented, while Strachey's work was built on by Corbató and others at MIT.

6. Early time-sharing systems were developed at Bolt Beranek and Newman (BBN), a company then specializing in acoustical research; at MIT's Research Laboratory of Electronics (RLE); and at System Development Corporation (SDC). See Fano and Corbató, 78.
7. Fano and Corbató, 78.
8. *Ibid.*, 94. They go on to explain: "Indeed, the analogy is not farfetched: an editorial board representing the community of users acts as a referee to pass on all new commands that are to be introduced into the system and on all information that is to be stored in the public files."
9. *Ibid.*, 95.
10. *Ibid.*
11. John McCarthy, "Information," in *Information: A Scientific American Book* (San Francisco: W. H. Freeman, 1966), 1.
12. *Ibid.*, 4.
13. *Ibid.*, 8.
14. *Ibid.*, 16.
15. Doug McIlroy notes that "The Multics planners already had seen remote access prototyped at several places, including CTSS and some commercial vendors. Their bigger vision was of an 'information utility,' not just a remote-access system that allowed economies of scale in computer cycles." From e-mail correspondence July 30, 1995. Documenting the need for new hardware as well as software, E. L. Glaser, J. F. Couleur, and G. A. Oliver, in "System Design of a Computer for Time Sharing Applications," explain: "Investigation proved computers that were immediately available could not be adapted readily to meet the difficult set of requirements time-sharing places on any machine. However, there was one system that appeared to be extendible into what was desired. This machine was the General Electric 635." (*Proc-FJCC* 27, pt. 1 (November 1965): 197)
16. In their article, "Introduction and Overview of the Multics System," F. J. Corbató and V. A. Vyssotsky explain: "For several years a solution has been proposed to the access problem. This solution, usually called time-sharing, is basically the rapid time-division multiplexing of a central processor unit among the jobs of several users, each of which is on-line at a typewriter-like console." (*Proc-FJCC* 27, pt. 1 (November 1965): 186)
17. *Ibid.*, 185.
18. Ronda Hauben, "Automating Telephone Support Operations: An Interview with Berkley Tague," *Amateur Computerist* 6 (Winter/Spring 1994): 8.
19. *Ibid.*
20. N. Peirce, "Putting Unix in Perspective: An Interview with Victor Vyssotsky," *Unix Review* (January 1985): 59.

21. *Ibid.*
22. *Ibid.*
23. *Ibid.*, 60.
24. Dennis M. Ritchie, "The Evolution of the UNIX Time-Sharing System," *AT&T Bell Labs Technical Journal* 63 (8) pt. 2 (October 1984) 1578 (hereafter, "Evolution").
25. Dennis Ritchie, "The Development of the C Language," presented at the Second History of Programming Languages Conference (Cambridge, Mass.: ACM, April 1993), 1.
26. "Interview with Victor Vyssotsky," 60.
27. D. M. Ritchie, "UNIX: A Retrospective," *The Bell System Technical Journal* 57 (6) pt. 2 (July-August 1978): 1950. Ritchie refers to the article by R. J. Feirtag and E. I. Organick, "The Multics input-output system," *Proc. Third Symposium on Operating Systems Principles* (1971): 35-41.
28. "Evolution," 1580.
29. *Ibid.*
30. "The Development of the C Language," 2.
31. *Ibid.*
32. *Ibid.*
33. "Evolution," 1580. Also, there is an interesting account by Ritchie of the difference between the work at Bell Labs with Unix as opposed to their work on Multics (see "Evolution," 1587).
34. E-mail correspondence from Doug McIlroy, July 30, 1995.
35. The BCPL text formatter had been inspired by J. Saltzer's runoff program for CTSS.
36. "Evolution," 1589–90. In the lobby of the main building at Bell Labs in Murray Hill, N. J., there was an exhibit of communication breakthroughs which credits Doug McIlroy and Rudd Canaday with the invention of pipes.
37. E-mail exchange with Doug McIlroy. When asked why he had proposed that pipes be introduced into Unix, McIlroy responded:

    Data streams were a particularly clean notion of program composition that I'd talked about for a long time. I proposed them in an unclarified way for Multics in 1964. And Joe Ossanna actually wrote some elaborate IO switching for Multics, though I don't think it ever caught on. I had been much taken by Conway's idea of coroutines, which was published (in CACM?) around 1963, and was brought to high development by Dahl in Simula. I thought a lot about stream representations of algorithms. Indeed, the algorithm I am proudest of is the coroutine sieve of Eratosthenes that I described at Cambridge in 1968, and which is now one of the chestnuts of parallel computing.

38. "Evolution," 1590.
39. "Interview with Victor Vyssotsky," 60. "Co-routines had after all shown up in SIMULA by the end of 1967."
40. August Mohr, "The Genesis Story," *Unix Review* (January 1985): 5. Mohr explains, "Haight believes that the pipe facility has had a major effect on the evo-

lution of UNIX. Because of the shell and the piping facility, programs running under UNIX can be conversational without being explicitly programmed that way. This is because piping adds to the shell's ability to accomplish this purpose for the system as a whole."

41. M. D. McIlroy, "Unix on My Mind," *Proc. Virginia Computer Users Conference (Blacksburgh)* 21 (September 1991): 1–6. See also "A Research UNIX Reader: Annotated Excerpts from the Programmer's Manual 1971–1986," *Computing Science Technical Report No. 139* (Murray Hill, N.J.: AT&T Bell Laboratories, 1987), 9, describing how Thompson wrote and installed pipes.
42. M. D. McIlroy, "A Research UNIX Reader: Annotated Excerpts from the Programmer's Manual, 1971–1986," *Computing Science Technical Report No. 139* (Murray Hill, N.J.: AT&T Bell Laboratories, 1987), 9, 43.
43. Account provided by Doug McIlroy.
44. McIlroy, "A Research UNIX Reader," 24.
45. Account provided by Doug McIlroy.
46. See, for example, Frederick P. Brooks, Jr., "No Silver Bullets," *Unix Review* (November 1987): 41 and also Brooks, Jr., *The Mythical Man-Month* (Reading, Mass.: Addison-Wesley, 1972) for a helpful statement of the problem in programming research that needed to be solved.
47. "Unix on My Mind."
48. E-mail correspondence from Doug McIlroy.
49. Brian Kernighan and Rob Pike, *The Unix Programming Environment* (Englewood Cliffs, N. J.: Prentice-Hall, 1984).
50. R. Pike and B.W. Kernighan, "Program Design in the UNIX Environment," *AT&T Bell Labs Technical Journal* (October 1984): 1601.
51. *Ibid.*, 1596.
52. M. D. McIlroy, E. N. Pinson, and B. A. Tague, "Foreword," *Bell System Technical Journal* 57 (6) pt. 2 (July–August 1978): 1901.
53. *Ibid.*, 1899. See, for example, the thunderclap in the Appendix.
54. *Ibid.*, 1902. See also Stephen C. Johnson, "UNIX: The Language Forms," *USENIX Association Winter Conference Proceedings* (1987), 18.
55. Kernighan and Pike, *The Unix Programming Environment*, 200. "**idiff** is loosely based on a program originally written by Joe Maranzano. **diff** itself is by Doug McIlroy, and is based on an algorithm invented independently by Harold Stone and by Wayne Hunt and Tom Szymanski." (See J. W. Hunt and T. G. Szymanski, "A fast algorithm for computing longest common subsequences," *CACM*, May 1977.) The **diff** algorithm is described in M. D. McIlroy and J.W. Hunt, *Technical Report 41*, 1976. To quote McIlroy, "I had tried at least three completely different algorithms before the final one. diff is a quintessential case of not settling for mere competency in a program but revising until it was right."
56. "Foreword," 1902–1903.
57. Ritchie and Thompson, "The UNIX Time-Sharing System," 1926.
58. Fred Brooks, Jr., "No Silver Bullets," 42.
59. *Ibid.*

60. Michael Lesk, "Can UNIX Survive Secret Source Code?," *Computing Systems* 1 (Spring 1988): 189.
61. Ritchie and Thompson, "The UNIX Time-Sharing System," 1927.
62. Marshall Kirk McKusick, "A Berkeley Odyssey," *Unix Review* (January 1985): 30.
63. Peter Ivanov, "Interview with John Lions," *Unix Review* (October 1985): 51.
64. Ronda Hauben, "Interview with Henry Spencer: On Usenet News and C News," *The Amateur Computerist* 5 (Winter/Spring 1993): 5.
65. "Interview with John Lions," 51.
66. *Ibid.*, 52.
67. *Ibid.*
68. *Ibid.*
69. *Ibid.*, 53.
70. John Lions, *A Commentary on the UNIX Operating System* (Australia: The University of New South Wales, n.d.), 5.
71. *Ibid.*
72. *Ibid.*, 9. A short time later, in "Unix Implementation," *The Bell System Technical Journal* 57 (6) pt. 2 (July-August 1978): 1931–1932, Ken Thompson described how a goal in writing the Unix kernel was to write exemplary source code that others would emulate. Thompson writes:

    What is or is not implemented in the kernel represents both a great responsibility and a great power. It is a soap-box platform on "the way things should be done." Even so, if "the way" is too radical, no one will follow it. Every important decision was weighed carefully. Throughout, simplicity has been substituted for efficiency. Complex algorithms are used only if their complexity can be localized.

73. "Interview with Berkley Tague," 10.
74. *Ibid.* Also, Mike Blake-Knox describes how he did development work for Bell-Northern Research (BNR), which was the Bell Labs equivalent for Northern Electric (which is now Northern Telecom). He reports that he had a copy of Lions' book and used it to do Unix kernel modifications (from e-mail correspondence Feb. 13, 1994).
75. "Interview with Henry Spencer," 4.
76. *Ibid.*
77. Marc Rochkind, "Interview with Dick Haight," *Unix Review* (May 1986): 65.
78. McIlroy, Pinson, and Tague, "Foreword," 1902.
79. Alan Stone, *Wrong Number* (New York: Basic Books, 1989), 17.
80. *Ibid.*, 145. "For example, since 1893, Bell maintenance employees had left unneeded jumper wires attached to main distributing frames [which connect each customer wire pair to the line terminal in a switching center] with no ill effect, but the growth in traffic caused the weight of dead jumpers to impede the operation of the main distributing frames."
81. During this period the NYPSC imposed standards requiring regular reporting from AT&T so that progress in upgrading its service could be monitored. Also, in

1970 the FCC required monthly reports on the quality of AT&T service in 20 major cities and by 1972 in 72 administrative areas.

82. Tague situates this push as beginning around 1969.
83. "Interview with Berkley Tague," 7–8.
84. *Ibid.*, 8.
85. *Ibid.*, 9.
86. *Ibid.*
87. *Ibid.* McIlroy in e-mail correspondence clarifies, "The conversion of Unix to C in 1973 was a step toward portability, but was certainly far from achieving it. It took more work to port Unix to the 360 than to make Unix in the first place. Not until 1978 did Richard Miller in Australia and Ritchie and Johnson at AT&T demonstrate effective portability."
88. "Interview with Berkley Tague," 9. See also S. C. Johnson and D. M. Ritchie, "Portability of C Programs and the UNIX System," *The Bell System Technical Journal* 57 (6) part 2 (July-August 1978): 2021–2048.
89. The Programmer's Workbench was first suggested by Evan L. Ivie in E. L. Ivie, "The Programmer's Workbench—A Machine for Software Development," unpublished report, Bell Laboratories, May 19, 1975.
90. "Interview with Berkley Tague," 10.
91. UUCP was first designed and implemented by Mike Lesk of Bell Labs in 1976. It has undergone many revisions and improvements. It was further developed by Lesk and David Nowitz and made available outside of the Labs as part of the V7 distribution. A new revision and improvement known as the Honeydanber UUCP was written in 1983 by Peter Honeyman, Nowitz, and Brian E. Redman.
92. "Interview with Dick Haight," 55.
93. *Ibid.*
94. The subsystems that became the PWB included: 1. the ed line editor, 2. a modified RJE, 3. a piece to simulate test input to applications for the IBM and UNIVAC and Xerox computers, 4. SCCS software tool for tracking program changes, and 5. the mm macros so that people could use the system for word processing. RJE involved "transmitting jobs to target systems and returning output to appropriate users." T. A. Dolatta, R.C. Haight, and J. R. Mashey, "The Programmer's Workbench," *Bell System Technical Journal* 57(6) part 2 (July–August 1978): 2185–2186.
95. "Interview with Dick Haight," 63.
96. T. A. Dolotta, R. C. Haight, and J. R. Masey, "The Programmer's Workbench," in *Proc. Second Int. Conf. on Software Engineering* (1976), 2180–2181.
97. Evan L. Ivie, "The Programmers Workbench—A Machine for Software Development" *CACM* 20 (October 1977): 750–751. Ivie's paper described the implementation of five basic components of the workbench: job submission, module control, change management, document production, and test drivers.
98. W. A. Felton, G. L. Miller and J. M. Milner, "A Unix System Implementation for System/370," *AT&T Bell Labs Technical Journal (*October 1984): 1752.

99. *Ibid.*, 1763–1764. Ian Johnstone, who had been the tutor at University of New South Wales working with Professor John Lions, was one of the researchers invited to Bell Labs. He managed the completion at Bell Labs of the port of Unix to the IBM 370 computer. See Ian Johnstone and Steve Rosenthal, "Unix on Big Iron," *UNIX Review* (October 1984): 26. Johnstone also led the group that did the port to the AT&T 2B20A multiprocessor system.
100. E-mail correspondence from Doug McIlroy.
101. "A Unix System Implementation," 1753.
102. *Ibid.*, 1763–1764.
103. Ivie, "The Programmer's Workbench," 746.
104. *Ibid.*
105. *Ibid.*
106. *Ibid.*, 747.
107. *Ibid.*, 749.
108. *Ibid,* 753.
109. P. J. Plauger, *AFIPS Conf Proceedings* 44 (1975), 281.
110. *Ibid.*
111. Sigvard Strandh, *The History of the Machine* (New York: Dorset Press, 1989), 79.
112. *Ibid.*, 81.
113. See, for example, articles in the *AT&T Bell Labs Technical Journal* 64 (6) part 2 (July–August 1985) on "The 5ESS Switching System" and W. A. Felton, G. L. Miller, and J. M. Milner, "A UNIX System Implementation for System/370," *Bell Laboratories Technical Journal* 63 (8) part 2 (October 1984): 1751.
114. Brooks, Jr., "No Silver Bullets," 41.
115. See, for example "On the Early days of Usenet," Chapter 10 of this volume.
116. John Stoneback, "The Collegiate Community," *Unix Review (*October 1985) 26.
117. Doug McIlroy, e-mail correspondence.
118. Mike Lesk, "A Proposal for Operating System Support," copy provided by author.
119. McIlroy e-mail correspondence.
120. Brian W. Kernighan and John R. Mashey, "The Unix Programming Environment," *Computer*, April 1981, 20.
121. *Ibid.*
122. *Ibid.*
123. *Ibid.*
124. *Ibid.*
125. *Ibid.*
126. Such as Burroughs B1726. See C. R. Snow, "The Software Tools Project," *Software—Practice and Experience* 8 (September–October 1978): 585–599; and Dennis E. Hall, Deborah K. Scherrer, and Joseph S. Sventek, "A Virtual Operating System," *CACM* 23 (September 1980): 495–502.

127. Morgan writes:

> *The use of writing or its equivalent in hieroglyphics upon stone, affords a fair test of the commencement of civilization. Without literary records neither history nor civilization can properly be said the exist. The production of the Homeric poems, whether transmitted orally or committed to writing at the time, fixes with sufficient nearness the introduction of civilization among the Greeks. These poems, ever fresh and ever marvelous, possess an ethnological value which enhances immensely their other excellences. This is especially true of the Iliad, which contains the oldest as well as the most circumstantial account now existing of the progress of mankind up to the time of its composition* (Ancient Society, *31).*

128. "Collyer kept detailed records of his work on 'rnews', so he could see how much progress he was making." Geoff Collyer and Henry Spencer, "News Need Not Be Slow," *Winter 1987 USENIX Technical Conference Proceedings*, 183.
129. Although there is a rich technical literature documenting Unix development in various technical journals, historical accounts are harder to find, and it is often hard to acquire extant copies. Some of the helpful sources include the "Unix Time-Sharing System" special issue of *The Bell System Technical Journal* 57 (6) pt. 2 (July–August 1978) and "The Unix System" special issue of *AT&T Bell Laboratories Technical Journal* 63 (8) part 2 (October 1984). See also Don Libes and Sandy Ressler, *Life with Unix* (Englewood Cliffs, N.J.: Prentice-Hall, 1989). Numerous interviews and articles with or about Unix pioneers appeared during the 1980s in early issues of *Unix Review*. The issue of the *Amateur Computerist* (vol. 6, no. 1, Winter–Spring 1994) celebrating the twenty-fifth anniversary of Unix, is available online at http://www.columbia.edu/~hauben/acn/. It contains interviews with Unix pioneers John Lions and Berkley Tague, as well as an article on the development of Unix. The book *A Quarter Century of UNIX* by Peter Salus (Addison-Wesley, 1994), which appeared after this article was written, contains references to a set of interviews by Mike Mahoney from "The Unix Oral History Project: Release.0, The Beginning," edited and transcribed by Michael Mahoney, as well as other interviews.

Thanks to Doug McIlroy, David Nowitz, John Lions, and Berkley Tague for making available information that was helpful in doing the research for this article, and thanks to Doug McIlroy, Eric Allman, Tom Van Vleck, Alfred Aho, Mark Horton, Deborah Scherrer, and Tom Truscott for commenting on an earlier version.

An early version of this chapter was posted on Usenet in Summer 1993. An early draft appeared in the *Amateur Computerist* 6 (Winter/Spring 1994).

Appendix

"Like a thunderclap from the sky,
the pipeline slays the problem."

Following is a script provided by Tom Truscott. Such particularly powerful pipelines have been referred to by Ken Thompson as "thunderclaps."

To find how often each word appears in files named book.1, book.2, . . . :

```
cat book* | tr -cs '[A-Z][a-z]' '\012' | sort | uniq -c | sort -nr | more
```

Truscott notes "Alas, thanks to so many *IX variants this pipeline doesn't always work, on some the underlined text needs to be '[\012*]'."

10

On the Early Days of Usenet
The Roots of the Cooperative Online Culture

Without a historical perspective, it's quite easy to get the wrong impression of how all this came to pass. It is the result of the work of a large number of individuals, some of whom have been at it for the last 20 years.

LAUREN WEINSTEIN

Even if we have shifted away from discussing human networks, we are getting a first hand EXPERIENCE of what they are through this mailing list. No amount of "a priori" theorizing of their nature, has as much explanatory power as personal experience. By observing what happens when connectivity is provided to a large mass of people in which they can FREELY voice their ideas, doubts, and opinions, a lot of insight is obtained into very important issues of mass intercommunication.

JORGE PHILLIPS,HUMAN-NETS MAILING LIST
SUBJECT: ADMINISTRIVIA, 03 JUNE 1981

Usenet was born in 1979. It has grown from a design conceived of by graduate students Tom Truscott and Jim Ellis at Duke University in North Carolina, to a logical network linking millions of people and computers to over 20,000 different newsgroups and millions of bytes of articles available at any given time at hundreds of thousands of sites around the world. Yet little is generally known about how Usenet began and how it developed.

COMPUTER CHESS —THE MINI SLAYS THE MAINFRAME

Tom Truscott had a dream. As a kid he had read the book *Danny Dunn and the Homework Machine.* He decided that it would be neat to have a homework machine. Some things caught his imagination, and this particular goal set him on a course that would affect his future. It also would have an unexpected impact on the rest of the world. By the summer of 1970, before his senior year in high school, Truscott had enrolled in a summer computer program that gave him his first chance to use a computer, and he learned to program in BASIC. "My first large program played checkers," he remembers of that summer.[1] "It didn't play all that well," he admits, but it introduced him to some of the power of computers. As a college freshman at Duke University the next year, Truscott met another student in his chemistry lab who was an excellent chess player. Truscott describes how he told his chemistry lab partner Bruce Wright that "we could write a computer chess program that would beat Bobby Fischer." Wright "didn't think so, but we started writing the program anyway." Truscott continues, "I was interested because of the computing challenge and no doubt the fame we would garner by defeating Fischer, and I guess Bruce was interested because he wanted to learn computing." Truscott describes how the two undergraduates spent "a LOT of time" writing their chess program, and in the process they learned a lot about how *not* to write programs.

Truscott was interested in how game programs were like robots, since they functioned as autonomous creatures. "At tournaments," he points out, "the program tells me what moves to make for it, [and] asks me how much time it has left on the clock." And writing a software robot, Truscott observes, "is a lot easier than building a real one."

Once Truscott and Wright had set their sights on creating a championship chess program, Truscott set out to research what work had been done on the problem. He found that Claude Shannon had written "a very early paper on how to construct a chess playing machine."[2] "It was remarkably farsighted given the state of computing then," Truscott remembers. The next oldest paper he found was from 1958 by someone who implemented a program similar to Shannon's proposal. "It played terribly," he recalls.[3]

By Spring of 1974, Truscott had joined the Association for Computing Machinery (ACM) to receive notification of the computer chess tournaments. Reading through the journal *Communications of the ACM* in 1974, he came across an article about a new operating system created by research programmers at Bell Labs.[4] In the article, he noticed that a program created by a Bell

Labs team ran in the background sopping up idle CPU time and solving simple chess endgames (for example, King and Rook versus King). Truscott explains that there was no chance he and Wright could do something like that on the mainframe computer they were using, since it cost 20 cents per second. But he notes that their mainframe was about the fastest there was and could compute rings around the DEC PDP-11 that the Unix operating system ran on.

He and Wright created their program for an IBM System 370 Model 165 MVT/TSO mainframe computer system at Duke. It had three megabytes of main memory, which Truscott notes was later upgraded to "4 megabytes for a mere $100,000." That was, according to Truscott, "Pretty much the top of the line at the time. We did our development in batch mode," he remembers. "The source code was on punched cards and the compiled code was stored on disk." And in tournaments, he and Wright used the IBM time-sharing mode TSO.

The first computer chess tournament Truscott and Wright competed in was the North American Chess Championships held at the ACM Annual Conference in San Diego, California, in November 1974. By then, Truscott was in his senior year at Duke. He and Wright named their chess program Duchess.

Following is Truscott's description of his first tournament and how he met one of the most respected programmers in the Unix community during that tournament. Truscott writes:

> *There were twelve teams competing in the tournament. We were on a stage in a large room with seating for spectators. Each team had a computer terminal (something like a dot-matrix printer with a keyboard in front and an acoustic modem on the back). And a telephone. Boy were those phone calls expensive. But the ACM was picking up the tab, and Duke was giving us the computer time.*
>
> *At the 1974 tournament, we knocked off MIT's TECH-II in the first round. They had come in second the previous year, and we were a newcomer, so that was something of an upset. In the second round we got clobbered by the perennial champ, CHESS 4.0 from Northwestern University.*
>
> *In the third round we played Bell Labs' Belle. It was called T. Belle at that point. I had met the author earlier, before the second round, when he showed me how good his program was at solving mating problems. I wasn't that interested in chess, but humored him while he pulled a chess position out of a library and had the program find a mate in 5 (or some such). I guess if I actually played chess I would have been impressed.*
>
> *So when the third round began, Bruce Wright and I were on one side of a table, and Ken Thompson and someone else from Bell Labs (who years later I realized was Brian Kernighan), were on the other. I noticed that when Ken Thompson logged on, the Bell Labs computer printed:*

Chess tonight, please don't compute.
%

I mentioned that that was really neat to be able to get the comp center to put out a notice like that. He said something non-committal in response. So the game began. A few hours and a few thousand dollars later we really had Belle on the ropes. All it had left was a lone king and we were about to queen a pawn! But then our program ABENDed (core dumped) in a way that caused the phone line to drop. We dialed back in and set things up, same thing. Every so often it would actually make a move. But making the phone call was slow (we had to ask for an outside line from the hotel operator) and painful (rotary dial you know) and eventually our program lost on time.

After the tournament was over, Truscott and Wright examined what had happened and observed that the problem was not with their program, but rather with a bug in the TSO operating system on their mainframe. "Thus was our mighty mainframe slain by a minicomputer," he admitted. "But I didn't realize it was UNIX," Truscott recalls, noting that the victory went to the Bell Labs team and their minicomputer because of the power of the Unix operating system.

Truscott and Wright competed in every ACM Computer Chess Competition [CCC] from 1974 to 1980. The next time he met Ken Thompson was at the 1976 Unix Users Group meeting at Harvard. "That was great fun," he remembers. There were about 80 attendees. "Somewhere along the way I made the connection between Belle and Thompson and UNIX." By this time Truscott was a graduate student at Duke, where he and others had just installed Unix Version 6 on the Computer Science Department computer.

"I was also at the 1978 UNIX Users Group meeting at Columbia University, and both Ken Thompson and Dennis Ritchie were there," Truscott continues, "Thompson also competed in the 1978 ACM CCC. He had some special chess hardware but it was no match for the much-improved mainframe programs."

"Because of our mutual interests," Truscott recalls, "Thompson would even call up our computer at Duke from time to time, and 'write' me. That was pretty intense, my trying to pick perfect sentences to send along to the genius at the other end. I think it was during one of those 'write' sessions in early 1979, that he asked if I would be interested in a summer job."

Truscott accepted Thompson's offer and spent the summer of 1979 at Bell Labs in Murray Hill, New Jersey, the birthplace of Unix. That summer, a distribution of Unix Version 7 was made available to sites with licenses from AT&T to use Unix. Included in the Unix V7 distribution were a number of Unix tools such as **sed, awk, uucp,** and the Bourne Shell. These tools were very helpful and would prove invaluable in the creation of Usenet.

Truscott found that Bell Labs provided an exciting and supportive environment. Following is an excerpt from his account of the important summer of 1979 that he spent playing volleyball, eating pizza, and working on a daily basis with many of the pioneers of the Unix community. He writes:

> *Woke up at 11 a.m. Got to Bell Labs at noon so I could play volleyball out on the front lawn with Mike Lesk and Steve Bourne and other folks. After a few weeks, the security folks told us they couldn't have a regulated monopoly running around loose like that. Lunch at 1 p.m. in the Bell Labs restaurant. Ken Thompson and Dennis Ritchie and Greg Chesson were regulars. They had lunch at 1 p.m. because sometimes they didn't get to work until then. Sometimes Dennis Ritchie would entertain us with some horror story about a non-UNIX system he dealt with recently. . . .*
>
> *At 2 p.m. the day began, which involved doing pretty much whatever we wanted. Ritchie was working on "streams." I think Ken Thompson was working on typesetting software but mostly working on a chess machine. . . . Often at 7 p.m. a group would go out for dinner (they liked pizza). Occasionally someone would host dinner at their home. Afterwards I would go back to the Labs and work until midnight. And the next day I would get up "at the crack of noon" as Thompson put it.*

As the summer ended, Truscott left Bell Labs and returned to Duke.

USING UNIX TO CREATE AN ONLINE COMMUNITY

By Fall, Truscott was back at Duke and no longer in the exciting environment of the birthplace of Unix. After having worked at Bell Labs for Ken Thompson where, as in Truscott's words, "I was in UNIX heaven the whole time, returning to Duke in the Fall meant the end of that." Also, that summer he had attended the Unix User's (Usenix) Group meeting in Toronto, Canada. Once back at Duke his primary connection with the Unix community was through the Usenix newsletter *;Login:*. This newsletter, however, hadn't appeared in a while. That Fall, another Duke graduate student, Jim Ellis, installed the latest Unix (V7) edition on a Duke Computer Science computer. It broke many old programs, including a public domain *items* program that had provided a local bulletin board. Truscott recalls how the *items* program allowed items to be entered into one of several categories. "It had a number of problems," he explains, "including a 512-byte limit per item, so we were thinking about writing a completely new program. Then we could contribute it to the next user group tape and hopefully achieve some minor level of fame."

Truscott, describing his return to Duke, writes, "Of course when the summer was over and I was back at Duke, one of the first things I did was arrange a uucp connection to research. They called us nightly, which was great." Truscott and Dennis Ritchie set up a UUCP connection between *duke*, a CS Department computer site at Duke in Durham, North Carolina, and *research*, a computer site at Bell Labs in Murray Hill, New Jersey.

The UUCP program that was part of the V7 distribution of Unix made it possible to send e-mail and files to other Unix sites using telephone lines, as long as the sending computer had an autodialing modem and the receiving computer had an auto answering modem.

Truscott attributes the creation of Usenet to the confluence of these events in the Fall of 1979. The idea for Usenet developed during a long rambling conversation he and Ellis had one night to discuss these circumstances. Soon afterward, Truscott and Ellis met with two other local Unix enthusiasts, Dennis Rockwell, a graduate student who worked in the Physiology Department at Duke, and Steve Bellovin, a graduate student at the neighboring University of North Carolina (UNC) at Chapel Hill. They decided on the transfer format, i.e., on what an article would look like to make it possible to ship files via computers using UUCP, and they agreed on the basic functionality of the software they would need to create an online network.

Bellovin wrote a shell script using Unix to test the design concept. Describing the early work to create Usenet, Bellovin writes:

> *The release of the uucp program with V7 UNIX provided the initial impetus. So did the Bourne shell. So the very first version of net news was a 3-page shell script. It supported multiple newsgroups, cross-postings, and subscription lists implemented as environmental variables. As best as I can tell, this script has not survived.*[5]

Bellovin emphasizes how the ease of testing software design facilitated by Unix made it possible to create Usenet. "It's worth noting now that given the speed (or lack thereof) of the machines we had, we utterly relied on the ease of writing shell scripts to experiment with protocol variants. Compilation would have taken much too long."

Commenting about the early plan for Usenet, Bellovin notes:

> *We estimated a maximum size of 100 sites, and 1–2 articles a day, net-wide . . . you couldn't read things out of order. The goal there (and in many other spots) was to have software free of databases. Instead, we chose to let the file system do the work.*

Bellovin recalls why a news program to replace the one they had used with Unix V6 was needed.

> *Another motivation was some sort of local news system. On V6, Duke and UNC had a local news system that came from somewhere. But articles were limited to 512 bytes, and we didn't carry it forward to V7. A prime requirement was that there be an efficient way to test for the presence of news (hence the checknews program).*

The Duke and University of North Carolina graduate students hoped to contribute their news program to the Unix community to be used with Unix V7. According to Truscott, the shell script was slow, but worked. They also decided on terminology, such as 'newsgroups', to describe the subject areas they would have as part of their network. "That was probably due to the newsletter analogy," he explains since "this was . . . before the PC and bulletin boards."[6]

Stephen Daniel, another Duke graduate student, soon became involved and made a substantial contribution to the work. Truscott writes that Daniel "created the dotted newsgroup structure that we know today," for the news-naming scheme (i.e. NET.xxxx and dept.xxxx) Also, Steve Daniel wrote one of the earliest versions of the netnews software in the C programming language. This came to be known as "A-News."

Truscott and Wright continued to participate in chess tournaments. In 1980 they competed in the Third World Computer Chess Championship held in Linz, Austria. Thompson and Joe Condon, who was a technician at Bell Labs, were also in the competition. Truscott notes that Thompson and Condon

> *had completed their hardware chess machine and snagged first place. Duchess came in third. And Claude Shannon was in attendance, and even handed out the trophies at the awards ceremony. Afterwards we all went over to a TV studio to watch a West German TV special on computer chess and the championship. Claude Shannon and his wife were very engaging people. Someone took a photo of all of us, I have a copy buried somewhere.*

It is not surprising, therefore, that when Usenet was created, NET.chess was created as one of the early newsgroups.

By developing Usenet, the Unix community became the force behind the creation of an online community to welcome participants into the cooperative culture so important in creating Unix. Graduate students at Duke and the University of North Carolina were able to use Unix to create an online community to provide needed technical and social support. They named this users' network Usenet. The earliest Usenet map was made up of the first two computers that were sites for Usenet:

duke — unc

The sites were:

1. duke Duke University
2. unc University of North Carolina at Chapel Hill

Another computer at Duke, in the Physiology Department at the Medical School joined the network. The site was *phs*. The map of Usenet then became:

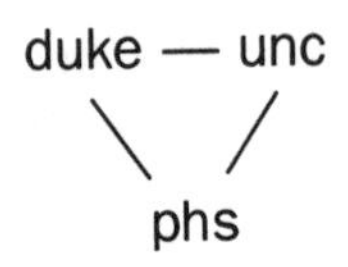

The third site was:

3. phs Physiology Department of the Duke Medical School

Soon, connections were set up with computers at Bell Labs. The computer sites *research* and then *vax135* at the Labs were added to Usenet. In the summer of 1980, Mark Horton, a graduate student at the University of California at Berkeley, brought *ucbvax* onto Usenet.[7]

A map of Usenet during the Summer 1980 shows the sites then connected:

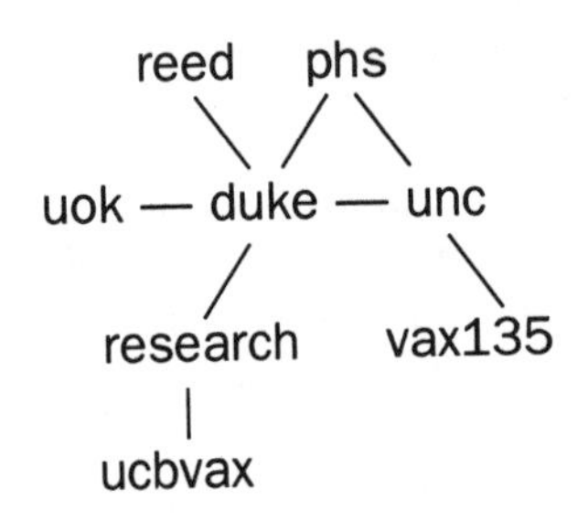

The additional sites were:

4. reed Reed College
5. uok University of Oklahoma
6. research Bell Labs Murray Hill
7. vax135 Bell Labs Murray Hill
8. ucbvax University of California at Berkeley

Horton notes that Bell Telephone Labs in Murray Hill, New Jersey, operating *research,* was the first site to pick up the phone bills for calls between *ucbvax* at the University of California at Berkeley and *duke* at Duke University via *research*. He writes: "The first cross-country link was from duke to research, then from research to ucbvax, all on research's nickel."[8]

Horton recalls how amazed he was to get e-mail messages from Usenet pioneers at Duke and the University of North Carolina just a few hours after he had sent them messages, thanks to the connectivity provided by the Bell Labs computer. "I remember," he writes, "while at Berkeley, exchanging email with the original A-News developers and being amazed that I could get a reply back a few hours later, even though research was polling both duke and ucbvax to pick up waiting mail."

The first newsgroups on Usenet, according to Truscott, were known as NET.xxxx and dept.xxxx. After Horton joined Usenet, he began feeding mailing lists from the ARPANET into Usenet. These mailing lists were identified as FA.xxxx newsgroups. Truscott notes that, "Only when ucbvax joined the net, did 'fa' appear." He explains that he didn't know about the ARPANET mailing lists until Horton joined Usenet.

At first the Usenet community could only read these ARPANET mailing lists, and could not contribute to them. "It was a one-way gateway—ARPANET into Usenet only, done with recnews, as I recall," writes Horton.[9] But at least it was possible for the Usenet community to follow the interesting discussions carried on via the ARPANET mailing lists during this early period of Usenet.

Bellovin explains why feeding the ARPANET mailing lists into Usenet was so important for the development both of Usenet and of the ARPANET. "Actually, in my opinion," Bellovin writes, "one of the key elements in the early growth of Usenet was when Mark Horton started feeding the SF lovers and human-nets mailing lists into newsgroups. Those provided a critical mass of traffic and served as a lure to attract new sites." He describes how "The ARPANET was supposed to be a self-contained entity, and only approved sites were allowed to connect." Therefore, the connection between Usenet and the ARPANET broke important new ground. Bellovin writes, "Mail to and from Usenet-only sites was an interesting test case that *wasn't* stamped out, though I think it skated on some very thin ice for a while."[10]

The *ucbvax* site at the University of California at Berkeley provided a crucial gateway between Usenet and the ARPANET. The University of California at Berkeley could provide the gateway because it was also a site on the ARPANET. The Computer Science Department vax computer (*csvax*) became the site *ucbvax* on the UUCP network. An internal network was set up to connect *ucbvax* on the UUCP network to *Berkeley* on the ARPANET. Horton explains that Professor Michael Stonebraker and Professor Domenico Ferrari, who were doing research to develop the Ingres data base, had a pair of machines (ing70) and (ingvax) which were sites on the ARPANET. They allowed Horton to use these machines for Usenet. Ing70 was the site known as *Berkeley* on the ARPANET. Horton and two other graduate students, Eric Allman and Eric Schmidt, set up the gateway between Usenet and the ARPANET and made it work. Schmidt created the local net, Berknet, to connect the ARPANET and the UUCPnet. The ARPANET and UUCPnet computers were tied together by Schmidt's Berknet. The path, Horton explains, went:

> *Any ARPA machine to Berkeley via ARPANET mail*
> *Ing70 (aka Berkeley) to csvax via Berknet*
> *ucbvax (aka csvax) to any UUCP machine via UUCP.*[11]

HUMAN-NETS AND WORLDNET

The Human-Nets mailing list (known on Usenet as the newsgroup FA.Human-nets) provided a mass of interesting posts to attract readership at a crucial period in Usenet's development. The mailing list Human-Nets, Truscott remembers, was a mailing list from the ARPANET for discussing the implications of worldwide ubiquitous networking. "This network of the future," he recalls, was referred to as WorldNet. "It was a very interesting mailing list and possible only due to the ability of the network itself to permit those interested in this obscure topic to communicate."[12]

A directory of the ARPANET mailing lists maintained at MIT during this period lists each of the mailing lists. Describing Human-Nets, it notes that this mailing list "has discussed many topics, all of them related in some way to the theme of a worldwide computer and communications network usually called WorldNet. The topics have ranged very widely from something like tutorials, to state of the art discussions, to rampant speculations about technology and its impact."[13]

An article on Usenet in October 1982 about Human-Nets explained that "one reader expressed a wish for a 'World Net' to tie all sorts of computers worldwide together."[14]

Another article in October 1982 described how WorldNet "was a nice idea to dream about," but the writer was pessimistic that it could ever be implemented, at least within the next ten years. He acknowledged, however, "Still, it's a fun idea to think about," and advised, "Maybe it should be tried on a smaller scale first (a distributed network of students with PCs at a university, perhaps a small city, or large community.) Who knows," the poster observed, "with a PC in almost every home in a few years, maybe it'll be possible and desirable."[15]

One of the moderators of Human-Nets emphasized that is was important that those interested in developing ubiquitous worldwide networking participate in such online discussions. Responding to a departing moderator's complaint that the discussion on the list had diverged to a variety of topics, the new moderator disagreed. He retorted:

> *Even if we have shifted away from discussing human networks, we are getting a first hand EXPERIENCE of what they are through this mailing list. No amount of "a priori" theorizing of their nature, has as much explanatory power as personal experience. By observing what happens when connectivity is provided to a large mass of people in which they can FREELY voice their ideas, doubts, and opinions, a lot of insight is obtained into very important issues of mass intercommunication.*
>
> *The fact that such dissimilar . . . topics have been discussed in our own instance of a human network says a lot about its nature and the interests and nature of its members and should not be considered as detracting from the quality of the discussion. . . .*
>
> *A human network is a springboard for human interaction and thus for human action. Let's view it as such and keep repression and censorship at a minimum.*[16]

UUCPNET AND THE "IRON CURTAIN" OF THE ARPANET

In contrast to the vision of ubiquitous human networking via computers discussed on the Human-Nets mailing list, the Usenet community faced a difficult battle when trying to communicate with those on the ARPANET. Posts on Usenet during the 1981 period reflect the constant efforts and the frustration experienced by those on Usenet who wanted to contribute to the ARPANET mailing lists.

Another popular ARPANET mailing list during this early period of Usenet was the Unix-wizards mailing list. It provided for discussion; the sharing of experiences, problems, and software; and for debate over various issues facing the Unix community. The mailing list was gatewayed from the ARPANET to Usenet and was available on Usenet as the newsgroup FA.unix-wizards.

Recognizing the early difficulty that those on Usenet had in posting to the ARPANET mailing lists, one user asked:

> *You mean saying -n fa.unix.wizards doesn't get back to the arpanet? Does it just get to USENET? Or does it go anywhere?*[17]

Another post reported the frustration experienced by those on Usenet who were trying to send messages to mailing lists carried on the ARPANET. The person wrote:

> *With regard to the ARPA/UUCP gateway problem, it appears that arpanet sites refuse to process mail from UUCP machines, while UUCP machines typically don't bother checking who stuff comes from before passing it on. In most cases this costs real money in terms of phone rates, use of spool space, etc. . . .*[18]

He proposed that UUCP sites retaliate so that transporting messages to Usenet from the ARPANET would be equally difficult:

> *We could have messages of the type:*
>
> *"Gateway to UUCPnet Closed . . . Service Unavailable." . . .any ideas what kind of response would result if this was implemented?"*

Responding to this proposal, another Usenet user offered his objection:

> *I'd rather see messages of this form going back to ARPA:*
>
> *"Gateway to UUCPnet open . . . No Iron Curtain here." Or some such self-righteous garbage. Seriously, the interchange of information is too useful to get embroiled in hurt feelings. I get mad when Arpa blindly refuses stuff but would rather try to shame them (good luck!) than play the same game.*[19]

There were those on the ARPANET who sympathized with the problems experienced by the Usenet community in trying to contribute to the ARPANET mailing lists. Commenting on the frustration, a user at a U.S. government site that was both on the ARPANET and on Usenet wrote: "I am also concerned about USENET participants. We really need to be able to interact with them in a better way, yet UUCP gateways to the ArpaNet are VERBOTEN."[20]

Often, Usenet users would try to send messages to the ARPANET gateway only to get back notification that their message had bounced. Common messages notifying Usenet users that their efforts to send messages to the ARPANET mailing lists had failed included:

> *Sorry not an ARPANET gateway: Unable to deliver Mail*
>
> *unix-wizards@sri-unix . . . Mail has been disallowed between the Arpanet and Uucp net*
>
> *unix-wizards@sri-unix . . . Service unavailable*

Other messages on Usenet during this period describe similar problems. For example, one user describes how he sent out five e-mail messages to the mailing list FA.unix-wizards and each came back to him undelivered. He then tried to send the messages to the mailing list again, or in frustration gave up and posted them on Usenet in the newsgroup "net.general" so others could see the problems he was having. He reported:

> *It doesn't always work, folks! Last week . . . I submitted 5 letters to ucbvax!unix-wizards; and got each one of them back the very next day, saying "service unavailable." Depending on the message I either shipped it back right away, or just put it in net.general, in disgust.*[21]

THE ARPANET↔UUCPNET GATEWAY

The path set up to make it possible for UUCP users of Usenet to contribute to the ARPANET mailing list Unix-wizards was via uucp to *ucbvax*, from *ucbvax* along Berknet to *Berkeley*, the University of California Berkeley site on the ARPANET, and from that site along the ARPANET via email to *sri-unix*, a site on the ARPANET that would distribute the mailing list back to *Berkeley* or send it out on the ARPANET. The site *sri-unix* was a computer at the Stanford Research Institute (SRI). SRI was one of the earliest sites on the ARPANET. Describing how this gateway worked, a user from the University of California at Berkeley wrote:

> *Ucbvax is currently set up such that if you, as a UUCPnet (Usenet) user, send mail to ". . . ucbvax!unix-wizards" the message will be *automatically* forwarded to unix-wizards@sri-unix (via our internal network and then via the ARPAnet).*[22]

He describes how *sri-unix* transported the message back to other sites:

> *The message is then redistributed by sri-unix to all sites on their "master" list, which should include "CSVAX.post-unix-wizards@Berkeley".*

In this way, the message was sent out on Usenet. "When we at Berkeley," he explained, "receive something addressed to this rather baroque-looking recipient, it is handed over to our network news program. From there, the message is redistributed via UUCPnet to the rest of the world."

"ARPAnet access," he noted, "is not available (at least through Berkeley) for 'private communications', which would include someone on the UUCP-net attempting to respond to an INDIVIDUAL who submitted something via the ARPAnet, or vice versa."

A user at the Ballistics Research Labs (BRL) noted the burden the gateway imposed on both the University of California at Berkeley and SRI and offered to help if necessary. He wrote:

> *BRL has a strong commitment to UNIX, and we encourage discussions about UNIX. If SRI gets overwhelmed by the burden of distributing the list, or if we "clone" several lists, we will be glad to take the task of mailing the stuff.*[23]

By September 1981, a post indicated that the *ucb* <=> *sri-unix* gateway for the Unix-wizards mailing list was being changed. "This is the last message you'll be receiving on Unix-wizards through SRI-UNIX," the writer reported. "Now the list will be mailed out of SRI-WARF(host 1/73)."[24] Posts could still be sent to *sri-unix*, but they would then be forwarded for transporting to *sri.warf*.

Numerous other users commented on the precariousness of this UUCPnet–ARPANET gateway used by the Usenet community during this period. For example, Dave Farber at the University of Delaware warned, "As to relaying to the ARPAnet, communications could be stopped easily by some agency stating to the sites doing the relaying under the table—to stop it."[25] Farber was part of the effort to have the National Science Foundation set up CSnet as a way to extend access to the ARPANET to NSF-supported academic and industrial researchers. He expressed his hope that CSnet would become a force to change the frustrating situation.

Usenet users had to use some kind of gateway to post to any ARPANET mailing list. "Certain newsgroups (fa.all)," a user on Usenet explained, "are not supposed to be posted to by people. Rather, you are supposed to mail to ucbvax!<newsgroup> to get it to the arpanet people too . . . Another reason was the gateway restriction—direct replies didn't work!"[26]

ARPANET users also encountered difficulties with communication using the ARPANET. Describing the problem MIT experienced as a result of its efforts to support the ARPANET mailing lists, a user at MIT wrote:

> *There is always the threat of official or public accusations of misuse of the networks for certain mailing lists. This actually happened with a list called WINE-LOVERS and Datamation [a technical journal] . . . The fiasco nearly resulted in MIT being removed from the network, and cost us several months of research time while we fought legal battles to show why our machines should not be removed from the ARPAnet. . . . In short, we are all in the hands of our neighbors. The best thing to do is to ensure that we are all educated as to how to take care of each other and ourselves.*[27]

USENET AS A PUBLIC COMPUTER-USERS' NETWORK

While the ARPANET during this period was subject to the regulations and policies set by the U.S. Defense Communications Agency (DCA), Usenet was considered a public computer users' network. Policies were proposed, and then were subject to discussion by the Usenet community. For example, in October 1981, Horton proposed the following statement of policy for Usenet:

> *USENET is a public access network. Any User is allowed to post to any newsgroup (unless abuses start to be a problem). All users are to be given access to all newsgroups except that private newsgroups can be created which are protected. In particular, all users must have access to the net and fa newsgroups, and to local public newsgroups such as general [net.general].*
>
> *The USENET map is also public at all times, and so any site which is on USENET is expected to make public the fact that they are on USENET, their USENET connections (e.g. their sys file), and the name, address, phone number and electronic address of the contact for that site for the USENET directory.*[28]

In another post, a writer describing the wide range of topic areas on Usenet explained:

> *The net represents a wide spectrum of interest (everything from the latest kill-the-millions-hardware to the latest sci-fi movies).*

Noting the broad range of sites on Usenet, he wrote:

> *The participants of the net, include major (and not so major) universities, corporations, think tanks, research centers, and the like.*
>
> *All these people seem to have one thing in common—the willingness to discuss any idea, whether it is related to war, peace, politics, science, technology, philosophy (ethics!), science fiction, literature, etc. While there is a lot of flame, the discussion usually consists of well thought out replies to meaningful questions. [He gave examples such as "Should the Postal Service be allowed to control electronic mail?"]*
>
> *. . . I am told that a lot of traffic on the net is not discussion, but real honest-to-goodness work. (Code, applications, ideas, and such.)*[29]

Those posting to Usenet included Unix users, ARPANET users, Usenet users working at Bell Labs, at other industrial sites, at University sites, at government sites, and so on. For example, both Thompson and Ritchie, creators of Unix, sometimes responded to Usenet discussions. Thompson contributed to the NET.chess discussions and Ritchie contributed occasionally to FA.unix-wizards, among other newsgroups.

Following is a description of Usenet posted in March 1982.

> *USENET is an international network of UNIX sites, with hookups into the ARPA network, too. It is basically a fancy electronic Bulletin Board System. Numerous BTL [Bell Telephone Labs] machines are connected at HO, IH, MH, with a few elsewhere, too.*

> *In addition, there are major sites at universities:*
> *U C Berkeley, Duke, U Waterloo, and so on . . .*
> *and at industry nationwide:*
> *DEC, Tektronics, Microsoft, Intel, etc.*
> *There are numerous bulletin board categories, set up in a hierarchy.*[30]

The article describes how the FA.xxx newsgroups on Usenet "can reach a very large user community, including USENET, sites on UUCP, Berknet, BLN, and the ARPANET, as well as sites on the ARPANET which are not on Usenet who get the news via direct electronic mailing." It explains that "Net.all newsgroups are available to all people on the entire network who read netnews." Though not all sites got every newsgroup, "Usenet is defined as all sites that net.all reaches."

A post by Horton characterizes Usenet as a logical network, as opposed to a physical network. Horton explains that Usenet is a network of sites running Netnews software:

> *For those of you who don't know, USENET is a logical network of sites running netnews. Netnews is a network oriented bulletin board, making it very easy to broadcast a query to a large base of people. USENET currently has around 50 sites and is growing rapidly.*[31]

Horton emphasizes that Usenet is a users' network. He explains: "USENET exists for and by the users, and should respond to the needs of those users."[32]

He also notes that "USENET is a cashless network." This meant that "No person or organization may charge another organization for news, except that by prearrangement." He explains that a site could charge only for the extra expenses incurred in sending Usenet to another site. And almost every site that received news had to be willing to forward it to at least two additional sites.

Horton's policy proposal suggested that articles should be of high quality, signed, and that offensive articles shouldn't be posted. "Peer pressure via direct electronic mail will, hopefully, prevent any further distasteful or offensive articles. Repeated violations of this policy," he noted, "can be grounds for removing a user or site from the network."

Common to many of the posts in these early years is the encouragement that users participate and voice their concerns and opinions, both in the ongoing discussion in various newsgroups and in determining the practices and policies guiding how Usenet functions. For example, Adam Buchsbaum, a high-school student who played an important role in early Usenet, started the NET.columbia newsgroups, a newsgroup about space issues. He posted the opening message inviting participation:

Greetings fellow space enthusiasts! This newsgroup was designed to inform people on developments in our space program. Although named "columbia," it will contain articles about the entire space program, including the shuttle for which it is named. Please feel free to reply, comment, criticize, and submit your articles. Also, I hope this will serve as an open ground for discussion about events in the space program. Comments, etc. can be mailed to myself (research!sjb) or submitted directly into the newsgroup. In all, I hope that this will provide an atmosphere for people who are interested in the space program to discuss it and be informed of new events.[33]

Such articles on Usenet, welcoming contributions from all participants, helped to set a firm foundation for interesting and lively discussion on early Usenet newsgroups.

CHANGING TO B NEWS

The continuing expansion and popularity of Usenet created a need for changes in the software. Explaining some of the problems that the ever-larger number of posts were creating for those using Netnews, Horton describes how A-News recorded subscriptions as a one-line pattern, and a time stamp recorded which messages were read, so that users were expected to read all new Netnews at once. Horton writes:

In the Spring of 1981, Usenet had grown to the point where it was awkward to use A-News. It was important to read news in newsgroup order (not by time of arrival) and to quit in the middle leaving some news unread. Also, the user interface of A-News resembled V7 /bin/mail, and users were expressing a preference for other e-mail styles (Mail, MH, etc.) and for the Berkeley msgs program. [34]

By then Horton was finishing his dissertation, so he did not have the time to do the needed work. Fortunately, however, as Horton recounts, "One day, into my office walked Matt Glickman. He was a local high-school student on spring break, looking for a computer project. We teamed up to design B news, and he did most of the coding that week. (The actual production release of B news was announced by Matt at the Winter 1982 Usenix.) I'll never forget the smile on Matt's face when he told me, 'You know, you've made my spring break!' "

Horton explains:

B News was patterned after the Rand MH e-mail program, and designed to be compatible enough that MH could be used to read the news. It put each newsgroup in a separate directory (causing a 14 byte limit on newsgroup names that lasted until years later when subgroups made subdirectories) and used a .newsrc file to record newsgroup subscriptions and which messages were read. . . . It defaulted to a msgs-style user interface and provided a read-it-all-now escape to a mail program like Mail. In those days it was also reasonable to dump it all to a printer and read it like a newspaper.[35]

In a post announcing B News, Glickman described the features of the new version of Netnews software:

I'm working on a new netnews. It is not ready. It is taking a lot longer [then] . . . it should. I hope to have a rough version running locally this week. Initially, the major new features will be: 1) No more .bitfile, .uindex, or .nindex. Everyone has a .newsrc file in their home directory which contains a list of the articles they've already read. This will allow skipping articles and coming back to them later: random-access. The same interfaces are around: /bin/mail, msgs, and print. The -c option still works in the same way, but I'm beginning work on an improved interface with the Berkeley Mail program so that netnews will know which articles were looked at during Mail.

Among the features Glickman describes are a new article format and an expire feature so articles could be read out of order, but would be canceled at a predetermined date. The netnews command was to be split into two commands, *inews,* to insert news, and *readnews*, to read news. B News also would provide directories for each newsgroup in a spool directory, and all the articles would have sequentially numbered filenames in their directories.

"I'll try to keep you posted on late-breaking developments," Glickman promised.[36]

AUTOMATING AT&T AND USENET

In the summer of 1981, Horton received his Ph.D. from the University of California at Berkeley and went to work in Columbus, Ohio, at a Bell Labs facility there.

During this period, AT&T was automating much of its operations. Usenet users who worked at AT&T recognized that helping to develop and participate in Usenet and the UUCPnet that was being developed along with Usenet could help AT&T solve some of the problems of developing large-scale software systems.

In a post on Usenet, Bob Rosin described the difficulties that those working on large-scale software projects encountered and the important technological problem this represented:

There is no cheap, easy way to accumulate the years of experience necessary to deal with complex software based systems. One need only examine the ugly reinventions of assembly language generated by ignorant non-converts and to watch thousands of neophytes wallow in the pits of personal computer assemblers to realize that, while software is in its infancy, people who have studied and built software are way ahead of the great unwashed.[37]

Recognizing the difficulties inherent in large-scale software projects, some at Bell Labs labored to encourage management to improve the software development environment. This included adopting and spreading Usenet and e-mail among programmers. An article posted on Usenet described these efforts:

There is a lot of effort going on now to try to convince management in Bell Labs to improve the software work environment. Good electronic mail and bulletin boards are an important part of that environment. There is a lot of interest in netnews here, with lots of people from management and even the legal department looking at it.[38]

During this period, Bell Labs was doing work to develop and implement the 5 ESS (Electronic Switching System) switch. Describing how the 5 ESS was an all-purpose electronic switch that would replace the other switches that had been developed for particular purposes, John Hobson wrote in Human-Nets:

Yes, there is such a thing as a #5 ESS. This is a bigger and better ESS, designed to be a replacement for all others. That is, there is one basic configuration, and different versions depending on the capacity needed. This is an improvement over the #1/1A, #2, #3 and #4 ESSes, which are fundamentally different machines, each designed to cover one range of line/trunk numbers. (#1/1A is used in large metropolitan switching offices, #4 in small, rural ones.) The #5 ESS is expected to be out in the field sometime next year.[39]

The 5 ESS project was a large-scale programming effort, involving many programmers and millions of lines of computer code. Describing the 5 ESS project in a post that appeared on Usenet, the writer explains:

Our project (#5 ESS) uses a lot of remote command execution to support our multi-machine development scenario (13 11/70's + 2 VAXes + 1 IBM 3033-AP). This environment is treated as though it is what it isn't, a single machine. That is we have developers spread across 7–9 PDP-11's + a 370 and they all work on the same project (We produce "load modules" for 3 processor types . . . that way.)[40]

Even though Usenet provided needed support for programmers involved in such pioneering efforts as the 5 ESS, articles on Usenet describe how difficult it often was for system administrators to convince their management that it was worthwhile to support Usenet at a work site. For example, describing the situation at Bell Labs, one poster wrote:

> *Much of the netnews distribution within bell labs is done without any explicit approval. I would be surprised to learn that many other of the corporate participants in Usenet had explicit approval from management. This makes us all very vulnerable.* [41]

Another poster from *cincy,* a site at the University of Cincinnati, in the Department of Computer Science and Engineering, verified that this was the situation elsewhere. He wrote: "When I was at cincy, we had a HARD fight to get the administration to pay the bill."[42]

Because of the difficulties that those at commercial sites had maintaining their participation in Usenet, a debate developed between those who felt that Usenet should be uncensored and those who felt that an uncensored Usenet might lead their management to cut off access to Usenet. One poster explained the dilemma:

> *I am beginning to wonder about USENET. I thought it was supposed to represent electronic mail and bulletins among a group of professionals with a common interest, thus representing fast communications about important technical topics. Instead it appears to be mutating into electronic graffiti. If the system did not cost anything, that would be fine, but for us here at Tektronix, at least, it is costing us better than $200 a month for 300-baud long distance to copy lists of people's favorite movies, and recipes for goulash, and arguments about metaphysics and so on. Is this really appropriate to this type of system?*[43]

There were also those at university and government sites who were fearful that certain types of posts might jeopardize grants their sites received. Others maintained that Usenet should be uncensored, but that sites could decide what newsgroups they would carry or what posts they might read. For example, one Usenet user wrote:

> *What I would really like is to work out methods that would allow as free a flow of information as possible. Some of the problem with the lack of control we have now (i.e. either too many newsgroups/lists or too many messages on one list) may be solvable by implementing new tools and conventions without resorting to brute force.*
>
> *I believe that there are limits to how much the group of users on one machine can store and comprehend, and that we ought to try to have this be what moderates groups (along with a certain amount of peer-pressure to keep the quality up). Something more along the lines of democracy or physical law than dictatorship, anarchy or even socialism.*[44]

Some felt that the content of Usenet should be restricted to topics that management or funding agencies would approve of. Others argued that a site could choose which newsgroups to carry, but that that should not limit the broad range of newsgroups available. In summarizing a discussion on this issue that took place at Usenix, Horton noted that newsgroups that seem trivial to one site might be important to another and he reported that those discussing the problem at the Usenix meeting felt that sites could determine what they would carry, but shouldn't impose their tastes on all of Usenet.

A similar debate occurred on the Unix-wizards mailing list. A post reports that some Unix-wizards had dropped off the list complaining about trivia. Others responded that they didn't want anyone deciding what they could read or not read, so they wanted the list to remain uncensored.

CROSS ATLANTIC AND INTERCONTINENTAL LINKS

Not only were links within North America difficult to establish, but Dik Winter, from the Netherlands, describes how the first cross Atlantic Usenet link was delayed until 1982–1983 because of the difficulty of acquiring an autodialer modem that conformed to European standards. "In Europe," he writes, "the two people responsible for the link were Teus Hagen and Piet Beertema," both at the Mathematisch Centrum, a research site in Amsterdam (now called CWI). The mail link was between *decvax* and *mcvax*. It connected the site *decvax* at Digital Equipment Corporation (DEC) in the U.S. with *mcvax* at Mathematisch Centrum (MC) in the Netherlands.

Beertema recounts how the early transport of News into Amsterdam was from *philabs*, a site at Philips Laboratories (a North American research laboratory for the Dutch company Philips).

Hagen writes that European Unix users who met in European DEC meetings began to do networking in the late 1970s. He describes how relationships were established between Peter Collinson from the University of Kent in England, Keld Simonsen from the University of Copenhagen in Denmark, and his site at the Mathematisch Centrum in Amsterdam.

Timothy Murphy from Trinity College in Dublin, Ireland, explains that a relationship was established between Peter Collinson at the University of Kent and the site *tcdmath* at Trinity, to connect Ireland and England. He was one of the founding members of the EUUG (European Unix Users Group) when it was set up at University College in London, England. Describing how the link at Trinity was set up by Brendon Lynch, the first system administrator of the

Maths Department Unix system, Murphy notes that this link "worked remarkably well—it was far more reliable than its successors, which used to be out of action for weeks at a time." Murphy remembers that Lynch, at Trinity, "set up an incredibly complicated link from our machine to Kent, which ran on X.25 via the University Dec-20. Our Unix box communicated with the Dec-20, which then communicated with Kent." He writes that the *tcdmath* was the Irish backbone site for about 4 to 5 years, "maybe from 1980–1984."[45]

Hagen recounts how links were established with others, including Yves Devilles from INRIA in Paris, Johan Helsingius of the University of Helsinki in Finland, Daniel Karrenberg of the University of Dortmund in Germany and with other university and technical sites such as the Technical University in Vienna, the University of Stockholm in Sweden, Siemens in Germany and Olivetti in Italy. Eventually e-mail via UUCP was established with support from Armando Stettner at DEC laboratories. Those involved wanted also to have "a regular exchange of news articles (USENET) as well," Hagen adds. Usenet in Europe, he explains, "was born from a tape I took with me from [the] San Francisco USENIX conference . . . back to Amsterdam." He tells how he met Dan Lorenzeni at a USENIX conference. Since Lorenzeni worked for Philips, whose mother firm was from the Netherlands, and Hagen was from the Netherlands, an agreement was made to have Lorenzeni send Hagen tapes of news articles. Hagen describes how a 1200-baud UUCP intercontinental link was set up between *philabs* in the United States and *mcvax* in the Netherlands. He explains that they couldn't use 2400-baud modems as that "equipment was unreliable, expensive, and modems from different manufacturers could not talk to each other." On one occasion, Hagen remembers he came into the office "rather early (9:30 am) and noticed that the 1200 baud modem [was] still running. UUCP US and UUCP Holland were sending each other resync messages. It was running from 7 pm the previous night to the [next] morning. And phone charges were six dollars a minute." Within 5 minutes, Hagen remembers, he was in the Director's Office "trying to explain the high phone bill" which they had run up using "equipment which was not even allowed," as the law in the Netherlands didn't allow use of a 1200-baud modem. "After that," Hagen continues, "we made an arrangement with Dan to share more of the costs."[46]

Lorenzeni, who helped to set up the news link between *philabs* and *mcvax*, concurs. He describes how he worked with Hagen and Beertema to set up the link. "From the beginning," he writes, "they only wanted certain newsgroups. So they supplied me with the list." Lorenzeni notes, "From the start, I thought USENET was a great thing and promoted it as much as possible. Over time the S/N [signal/noise] ratio got worse and worse, but it was always fun."[47]

Hagen describes some of the frustration that European participants in Usenet experienced. "I can remember a fight in net.general," he writes, "when someone in the U.S. . . . complained about posts from Europe. The person," Hagen recounts, said "we were dummies as we introduced errors in the date/time stamp" on the posts from Europe. "He was complaining," Hagen continues, about "the fact that he was reading news articles which were replies" to posts though they were dated "a day earlier [than] the original post." He forgot, Hagen notes, that the United States was in a different time zone.

The European Usenet pioneers faced several other problems. High phone charges led them to work out a way that all would share in the costs. This led to a well-organized network of "backbones" connecting Unix user groups in different countries. Also, language differences were a problem. One of the results, Hagen remembers, was a message to all Usenet news readers noting that international meant "not everyone is speaking their own national language." He also describes how he presented the potential of a European net at a conference of EUUG in Paris in April 1982 where he showed e-mail and news and made available some modems which were subsequently spread throughout Europe.[48]

In the following post from 1983, Jim McKie at Mathematisch Centrum discusses some of the difficulties confronting these early European Usenet users. He writes:

> *Well, the net isn't collapsing over here, and is already run on a pay-as-you-read basis. I can't speak for the UK, and I am sure, as in all things, the UK would not like somewhere else in Europe to speak for her (the UK is only GEOGRAPHICALLY close to Europe), but the UK gets its news free from vax135; I don't know how much they get. And we get a small number of groups through philabs, ones which people asked us to get, not a blanket coverage anymore. Hopefully we will soon be getting some more news groups from decvax, and to those sites which ask for them, we will redistribute. Another major manufacturer has offered some free satellite time, which we are investigating. . . . We are in the fortunate position of starting up late and having someone (Teus Hagen) who put things on a nice footing. . . . But it means we have to keep trying to find cheaper ways to obtain the groups, so we can afford to make some mistakes and chuck them later. However, the real problem is that the (soon to be) 3 news feeds supply different groups, and there is no net.anything passed between the UK and Europe, so we would perhaps not get a fair and unbiased choice. . . .*[49]

Several of the European Usenet pioneers report that Armando Stettner of DEC soon became involved in helping to get Usenet to Europe. DEC was willing to pay the intercontinental phone bills, so email and news traffic were shifted to it.

Winter also describes the difficulties that those working to provide a Usenet link to Australia faced to provide Australian–North American connectivity. Robert Elz, at the University of Melbourne in Australia, describes how, working with Piers Lauder, news distribution was set up in Australia. The earliest international link was created when Ian Johnstone from the University of New South Wales (UNSW) was invited to Bell Labs in Murray Hill, New Jersey, in 1980 or 1981. "In any case," Elz writes, Johnstone

> *arranged a link from Bell Labs . . . to an IBM mainframe . . . at the University of Waterloo. The University of Sydney (or UNSW) connected to there using X.25 (which was why Waterloo was chosen . . .) This link was basically pathetic—messages lost, and lots of manual work involved in transferring what did get transferred, yet it did allow messages through, and was kind of linked to the UUCP net in the U.S. (and Canada).*[50]

Elz explains that

> *It was probably '83 when the first usenet news reached here (well, actually, before then I had dialed into Berkeley (ucbvax etc.), saved news from time to time in my directory there—anything that looked interesting, and then had it added to the next tape coming back this way, either one I brought after a visit there, or one they were mailing me for some reason). I doubt that counts as a real usenet connection, but it is probably responsible for a rumour that occasionally makes the rounds about Australia getting news via mag tape, which never really occurred in any meaningful fashion.*

Piers Lauder writes that "All news arrived via Robert's machine in Melbourne University called 'munnari' which still exists in name, if not in original form. . . . munnari acted as the gateway to the rest of Australia."[51]

During this period, Elz attended Usenix conferences in the United States, usually the summer meetings. While in the United States he would usually also spend some time at the Computer Science Research Group (CSRG) at the University of California at Berkeley. During one of the Usenix meetings, Elz writes that he and several UCB related people were hanging around the DEC stand at the conference with Armando Stettner, trying to get BSD Unix to work on the (then) new Vax 11/730. "While doing that," Elz writes, "Armando heard of our tenuous net link to the world, and offered to have decvax call us for e-mail transfer. . . . I wasn't about to say 'no' to that offer."

"Having this free link (to us) available greatly increased use of the net in Australia," Elz notes, crediting DEC, and Stettner, for "helping spread the network into the world outside North America." And he points out that "the free links available to Australia, and Europe, without question encourage[d] use that would never have happened had there not been this sort of access available—justifying paying for traffic without seeing how useful it can be is very hard to do. On the other hand," he adds, "having this period of uncharged use allowed people to see the benefits, and get accustomed to it, which then allowed people to be able to justify meeting the bills when that eventually was required."

Elz explains why it was fortunate that it was possible to have Usenet along with e-mail:

> *Usenet was just a "free optional extra" (more or less) that came with the e-mail links. If it had ever been much in the way of particular effort, it might never have survived. Still, it did allow us to keep in touch much more actively with what the rest of the world was doing. Being a communal medium it allows one to notice things by accident, which person to person e-mail might never reveal.*[52]

SETTING A FOUNDATION FOR THE FUTURE

Many of the academic, industrial and government sites participating in the early days of Usenet were involved with computer software or hardware research. The developing network of Usenet sites helped provide the Unix community with the technical and social support they needed to keep computers functioning and to deal with the perennial upgrades as computer development advanced. Often people online would ask for advice or offer information or programs to others so that users could build on each other's experiences, rather than "reinventing the wheel."

In addition to such technical cooperation, newsgroups were developed or gated to mailing lists to discuss a wide range of topics, including worldwide ubiquitous networking in the future (FA.human-nets), science fiction (FA.sf-lovers), and computer games (NET.games). Socializing was encouraged in NET.singles (or NET.social), recipes were exchanged in NET.cooks. Music was discussed and recommended in NET.music. The developments and problems of the space program were discussed in NET.columbia (on Usenet) and NET.space (an ARPANET mailing list).[53]

As the interests of people were reflected in their suggestions for new newsgroups, online discussions developed over how to create a process that would make the desired groups possible. The early development of a newsgroup creation process and the discussion of how to structure that process help to demonstrate that a great deal of effort by many people was expended to create functional and democratic procedures for the early Usenet. The earliest newsgroups were all unmoderated. Everyone had the right to participate and contribute their views. A rich and interesting content emerged that surprised even the participants.

The development and spread of computers require new means of communication. A great deal of effort and discussion went into creating Usenet. This has provided Usenet with the strong foundation needed to support the technical and educational needs that result from the increasing use of computers in our times. Usenet has grown and flourished and in turn serves the needs of those using and developing computer technology.

The Unix community gave the world software tools that could perform wondrous feats with simple programs.[54] The Usenet community took these tools and used them to open up and create channels for communication so that those in the online Unix community could help each other wield the tools. In a society that hopes to progress in this era of rapidly developing computer hardware and growing demands for computer software, more and more of the population needs to have access both to the tools and to the means of communication needed to wield these tools. This is the foundation of the cooperative and democratic culture that Usenet has pioneered and made possible. It is important to understand and build on these roots and to nourish and expand this cooperative culture. It is important to make this cooperative networking culture, this marriage of an ever larger network of computers and people, available to ever broader sectors of the population if the promise of computer technology to provide a better and more productive world is to be realized. We are much closer to the dream of a WorldNet today than we were in 1979, thanks to the hard work of the Usenet pioneers. We will need to build on the foundation they established if we hope to make the dream of a WorldNet, of ubiquitous computer networking, a reality.

NOTES

1. The following account is from e-mail correspondence from Tom Truscott that has been compiled into an unpublished interview, "Interview with Tom Truscott: On the Environment and Early Days of Usenet News."
2. Claude E. Shannon, "A Chess-Playing Machine," *Scientific American* (February 1950):48.
3. The next oldest paper Truscott found was by Alex Bernstein and M. de V. Roberts, "Computer versus Chess-Player," *Scientific American* (June 1958).
4. This was the July, 1974 paper by Dennis M. Ritchie and Ken Thompson, "The Unix Time-Sharing System," *CACM* 17 (7): 365–375. A reference to chess is on page 375.
5. Usenet Archives, Steve Bellovin, Wed Oct 10 19:48 PDT 1990: Available via ftp: weber.ucsd.edu <usenet.hist>.
6. E-mail correspondence from Tom Truscott. Although Ward Christensen and Randy Seuss had set their bulletin board up in Chicago on February 16, 1978, predating Usenet, Truscott explains that he and others who created Usenet did

not know about the Chicago BBS. The Christensen Ward BBS operated on a North Star Horizon 4 MHz Z-80 CP/M machine with a 5 Mb drive for posting and reading of messages. (See Bernard Aboba, *The Online User's Encyclopedia* (Reading, Mass.: Addison-Wesley, 1993), 59)

7. E-mail correspondence from Mark Horton, August 1995. Horton, like Truscott, was introduced to programming as a high-school student in 1970. He writes that he learned to program in BASIC, "first on the GE system, but that was expensive. First Portland and then San Dieguito HS's [high schools] got access to HP 2000 BASIC systems with unlimited usage."
8. Mark Horton, Mon Oct 15 19:49 PDT 1990, Usenet History Archives. Available online at http://www.duke.edu/~mg/usenet/usenet.hist/.
9. Mark Horton, Tue Nov 24 04:51 PST 1992, Usenet History Archives.
10. Steve Bellovin, Oct. 10, 1990, Usenet History Archives, nethist.901010.z
11. E-mail communication from Mark Horton.
12. E-mail communication from Truscott.
13. Rich Zellich, 16 Feb. 1982, posted on Usenet in post by btempleton, watmath.2114, Subject: Arpanet mailing list directory.
14. 17 Oct 1982, Zaleski at Ru-Gren, Subject: Why not AT&T for World Net by Michael Zaleski.
15. 19 Oct 1982, Greg Skinner, <uc.bds at MIT-EECS at MIT-MC>, Subject: Worldnet responses.
16. 03 June 1981, Jorge Phillips, <JP at SU-AI>, Subject: administrivia in Human-Nets Digest v 3 #112.
17. cincy.151, fa.unix-wizards, cincy!chris, Tue Apr 7 13:16:12 1981, Subject: to unix-wizards.
18. A. Feather, pur-ee.123, net.general, pur-ee!aef, Mon Aug 24 15:13:14 1981, Subject: UUCP gateway.
19. esquire.127, net.general, Wed Aug 26 09:48:51, UUCP gateway, Re: A Feather's suggestion.
20. ucbvax.2946, fa.unix-wizards, Re: PROPER FORUM, mike@bmd70@BRL, Fri Sep 4 14:55:10 1981.
21. ucbvax.2858, Sat Aug 29 10:17:34 1981, purdue!cak, Subject: Automatic forwarding of unix-wizards.
22. Geoff Peck, ucbvax.2842, Thu Aug 27 23:02:42 1981, fa.unix-wizards, ARPAnet access.
23. ucbvax.2946, fa.unix-wizards, Re: PROPER FORUM, mike@bmd70@BRL, Fri Sep 4 14:55:10 1981.
24. FA.unix-wizards, ucbvax.3198, GEOFF@SRI-CSL, Thu Sep 17 21:01:25 1981.
25. ucbvax.2955, fa.unix-wizards, Sat Sep 5 07:34:34 1981, from farber@udel. See description of CSNET in Appendix IV.
26. Net.news, cbosgd.113, Sat Oct 3 19:51:41 1981, cbosgd!mark, Re news.
27. ucbvax.5782, fa.digest-p, Thu Ja 14 05:46:13 1982, from CStacey@MIT-AI.
28. NET.news, cbosgd.120, Tue Oct 13 20:56:30 1981, cbosgd!mark, Subject: Whether the sys and uuname files are public.

29. NET.news, wolfvax.53, net.news, wolfvax!jcz, Mon Nov 2 21:47:32 1981, Net Names, In Real Life: Carl Zeigler, Location NCSU, Raleigh.
30. ucbarpa.1182, net.sources, Subject: ARPAVAX: Usenet, Tues., Apr. 20, 19:50:48 1982, misc/newsinfo, from eiss!ladm, Fri Mar 19 16:20:27.
31. Mark Horton, fa.unix-wizards, ucbvax.4080, Sun Sept. 27 22:04:41 1981, Usenet membership.
32. NET.news, cbosgd.794, Wed Dec 23 21:28:32 1981, Subject: Proposed Usenet policies.
33. net.columbia, research!sjb, Thu Sept. 17 07:28:50 1981, Adam Buchsbaum kept the official list of newsgroups and published it regularly to the net for several years in the mid 1980s.
34. Email correspondence from Mark Horton, Mon. July 24 1995. MH (Mail Handler) was developed by Bruce Borden of the Rand Corp., with help from Stockton Gaines and Norman Shapiro, to be used on the ARPANET. (See Bart Anderson, Byran Costales, and Harry Henderson, *UNIX Communications* (Carmel, Ind.: SAMS, 1991),198.)
35. Email correspondence from Mark Horton, Mon. July 24 1995.
36. Aucbonyx.118 NET.news utzoo!duke!decvax!ucbvax!Onyx:glickman Fri May 16 10:29:40 1980 New Netnews.
37. Bob Rosin, Bell Labs, Linroft, N.J., houxf.148, NET.general, houxf!rosin, Fri. May 7 09:26:53 1982, Re: debugging microcode in writable control store.
38. NET.news, ihnss.995, net.news, ihnss!warren, Subject: Misconceptions about Bell Labs Netnews Content.
39. May 26, 1981, 17:20:32 PDT, ihnss!@BERKELEY (John Hobson), Subject: #5 ESS in Human-Nets Digest v3 #108, 28 May 1981.
40. NET.blfp, alanr, Subject: Remote Command Execution, File Installation, Tue Jul 21 10:42:15.
41. ihnss!warren, ihnss.995, Subj: Misconceptions about Bell Labs, Netnews Content.
42. purdue.139, net.general, net.news, cak, Sat Dec 17 19:27:08 1981, Subj: Freedom of the dataways.
43. NET.misc, dadlaA.98, net.misc, dadlaA!steve, Mon Mar 15 21:56:49 1982, Subject: Trivia on the Net.
44. Asri-unix.429, net.news, utzoo!decvax!ucbvax!menlo70!sri-unix!knutsen Tue Jan 5 17:46:42 1982, USENET policy, reposted from Date: 15 Dec 1981 at 1522-PST, From: Andrew Knutsen <knutsen@SRI-UNIX>, Subject: Re: read-only newsgroups (net.news cbosg.193)
45. E-mail from Timothy Murphy at the Trinity College. Murphy did the technical work to split UUCP into two processes, which was necessary "as it was too large to run in the 64k data + text allowed on our pdp-11 under Unix edition 6," he explains. Hagen describes a presentation by Peter Collinson at a EUUG conference on September 7, 1983 at Trinity College. In this presentation, Collinson described how the University of Kent was working to spread networking and to become a major node for European Usenet.
46. E-mail correspondence from Teus Hagen, August 1995.

47. E-mail correspondence from Dan Lorenzeni, August 1995.
48. Jim McKie, in a draft paper he has made available, describes the importance of the Spring 1982 EUUG meeting in Paris.

    At the EUUG Paris meeting in Spring 1982, the Mathematisch Centrum in Amsterdam announced that they had connected up to USENET and were willing to call or be called by any EUUG sites in Europe. This was the beginning of a transformation of the UNIX community in Europe.

    His paper, "Where Is Europe," was presented at the 1983 Usenix Conference in Toronto.
49. Dec. 15 1981 at 1522, Andrew Knutsen <knutsen@SRI-UNIX>. From: rti!mcnc!unc!duke!decvax!linus!philabs!mcvax!jim Wed 3-Aug-83 01:12:41 EDT Jim McKie Mathematisch Centrum, Amsterdam . . . {decvax|philabs} !mcvax!jim (mcvax.5322) net.news: Re: cost of sending netnews to aliens. McKie, in overheads for a talk he gave at the 1984 Usenix Conference in Salt Lake City describing the growth of Usenet in Europe, notes that *mcvax* connected to Usenet in the Spring of 1982. By December 1982 there were 25 sites in six countries. By July 1983 there were 52 sites in ten countries.
50. E-mail from Robert Elz, October, 1995. Elz remembers that "Johnstone arranged a link from Bell Labs. This one worked by Bell Labs using cu [call unix, i.e. an application to allow dialing out from one host to connect to another—telnet over phone lines, and had some primitive capture and send mechanisms, with no correctness checking]—with a back-end process filtering the output so as not to overrun the IBM after end of line and such."
51. E-mail from Piers Lauder.
52. E-mail from Robert Elz, October 1995.
53. A listing of all the newsgroups available by March 1982 appears in appendix II.
54. See for example the thunderclap in the appendix to Chapter 9.

Thanks to Tom Truscott, Mark Horton, Rob Scott, Dik Winter, Russell Lowell and others on Usenet for their comments on an earlier draft and their helpful suggestions. In addition, thanks to Teus Hagen and Dan Lorenzeni for their helpful information about setting up the cross-Atlantic link, Timothy Murphy for background on the link to Ireland, and to Robert Elz and Piers Lauder for information about the link from North America to Australia. Also, thanks to Henry Spencer and others at the University of Toronto for archiving early Usenet posts so folks can understand the early days of Usenet when it was possible to read every post and to Jim McKie for providing helpful background material. Finally, thanks to the Usenet pioneers and to Bruce Jones for setting up the Usenet History Archives at weber.ucsd.edu <usenet.hist> and for making material available online.

An early version of this chapter by Ronda Hauben was posted to Usenet in Spring 1995. An early draft was printed in the *Amateur Computerist* 7 (Winter/Spring 1995–1996).

Appendix I

One of the Usenet pioneers, Henry Spencer, at the Zoology Department at the University of Toronto in Canada, archived Usenet from the date his site *zoo* joined Usenet in May 1981 to recent times. The earliest posts he archived are contained in the A-News archive, which covers posts that appeared on Usenet from May 1981 to 1982.

Another important source of early Usenet history has been created by a graduate student at the University of San Diego (UCSD) in California. Bruce Jones, who began work to document the sociology of Usenet for his dissertation, collected recollections and background from several of the Usenet pioneers and made them available online via anonymous ftp from weber.ucsd.edu in the directory <usenet.hist>. These are now available at http://www.duke.edu/~mg/usenet/usenet.hist.

Appendix II

Two Early Lists of Newsgroups Appearing in Usenet in 1982

net.news.group
utcsrgv!utzoo!decvax!duke!chico!harpo!mhtsa!ihnss!cbosg!teklabs!t
ekmdp!azure!curts
Tues. Jan 26 13:50:13 1982
grouplist

FA groups are "from the arpanet" and are mostly copies of mailing lists or "digests" distributed on that network. (A digest is a collection of mail put together by an editor and sent out every so often. It is much like a newsletter.)

A special convention applies to submissions to FA newsgroups. As previously described, you should not post directly to the newsgroup, since this will be seen by people on USENET but not by the people on the ARPANET who get the list directly mailed to them. Instead, send mail to the name of the group on site.

For example, to post an article to fa.human-nets, you might mail to chico!ucbvax!human-nets (if chico is the proper route to get to ucbvax—this route varies depending on your system). FA groups and their corresponding mailing lists can reach a very large user community, including USENET sites on UUCP, Berknet, BLN, and the ARPANET, as well as sites on the ARPANET that are not on USENET, which get the news via direct electronic mailing.

The following is a list of digests:

NEWSGROUP	Description
fa.arms-d	Discussion and info on strategic weapons.
fa.arpa-bboard	Announcements that are posted to all arpanet bboards are also fed into this newsgroup.
fa.digest-p	People who deal with digests. Mostly the people who moderate them.
fa.editor-p	Interest group in computer editors, both text and program.

fa.energy	Topics relating to alternate energy production, conservation, etc.
fa.human-nets	A daily moderated digest with discussions of computer-aided human-to-human communications. Probably the most widely read ARPANET publication.
fa.info-cpm	CP/M and other operating systems for micro computers.
fa.info-micro	Microprocessor and microcomputer discussions.
fa.info-terms	Opinions/queries about what's a good/bad computer terminal.
fa.info-vax	VAX interest group. Seems to be mostly VMS issues, but some hardware discussions too.
fa.poli-sci	Political Science discussions digest.
fa.sf-lovers	Science Fiction book/movie reviews, etc.
fa.space	Digest containing comments on the space program and outer space in general.
fa.tcp-ip	Digest relating to the TCP and IP network protocols.
fa.telecom	Technical topics relating to telecommunications, especially the telephone system. A digest recently spun off from fa.human-nets.
fa.teletext	Teletext discusses all aspects of "esoteric" data systems. This includes teletext, viewdata, closed-captioning, and digicasting.
fa.unix-cpm	CPM/UNIX discussions.
fa.works	Interest group on personal workstations (e.g. Apollo, Perq, Xerox Star, etc).

Newsgroups are intended to be available to all people on the entire network who read netnews. This does not mean they go to every machine, since some machines restrict the volume of news that comes in. It is assumed that users of such restricted machines can read news on another machine on which they have a login. Newsgroups reach all of USENET (including USENET sites on the ARPANET) but do not reach any sites that are not on USENET. That is, USENET is defined as all sites that net.all reaches.

NEWSGROUP	Description
net.general	General information.
net.applic	Applications programs for UNIX. Discussions seem to center around functional programming languages.
net.auto	General Information for automobile owners.
net.auto.vw	Subgroup net.auto—for owners of Volkswagon Rabbits.

net.aviation	General information about aviation.
net.bugs	General information about bug reports and fixes.
net.bugs.2bsd	Subgroup net.bugs—2nd Berkley Software distribution
net.bugs.4bsd	Subgroup net.bugs—4th Berkley software distribution
net.bugs.v7	Subgroup net.bugs—Version 7 or UNIX System III
net.chess	General information about computer chess. Gatewayed to ARPANET mailing list but appears as newsgroup rather than a digest.
net.columbia	General information on space shuttle and space programs
net.cycle	General information about motorcycles.
net.eunice	General information for sites running SRI Eunice system which simulates UNIX on VMS.
net.games	Information and discussion on computer games.
net.games.rogue	Subgroup net.games—rogue
net.games.frp	Subgroup net.games—fantasy role playing games
net.games.trivia	Trivia contests and results.
net.ham-radio	Topics of interest to amateur radio operators.
net.jokes	The latest "good" joke you've heard?
net.lan	Local area network interest group.
net.lsi	Large Scale Integrated Circuit discussions.
net.misc	Miscellaneous discussions that start in net.general but are not permanent enough for their own newsgroup.
net.movies	Movie reviews by members of USENET.
net.music	Computer generated music.
net.news	Discussion of netnews itself.
net.news.b	Subgroup net.news—specific to bnews.
net.news.directory	to post all or part of the USENET directory,
net.news.group	for discussions about proposed new newsgroups,
net.news.map	for discussions about maps of newsites.
net.news.newsite	to announce a new site.
net.news	for discussion of USENET policies.
net.oa	Office Automation/Word Processing interest group.
net.periphs	Queries and discussions about particular peripherals. ("Does anyone have a driver for a framus-11?")
net.rec	General info on recreational (participation) sports.
net.rec.bridge	Subgroup of net.rec—contract bridge.
net.rec.scuba	Subgroup of net.rec—scuba diving.
net.rec.ski	Subgroup of net.rec—skiing.
net.records	Info and opinions about records (and tapes ?).

net.rumor	For posting of rumors.
net.sources	A place for sources and the distribution of material in large volume. More for software distribution that for general info.
net.sport	General info about spectator sports.
net.sport.baseball	Subgroup of net.sport—for baseball.
net.sport.football	Subgroup of net.sport—for football.
net.sport.hockey	Subgroup of net.sport—for hockey.
net.taxes	Tax advice and queries.
net.test	Test messages are posted here.
net.travel	Requests, suggestions, and opinions about traveling
net.ucds	Circuit drawing system.
net.unix-wizards	ARPANET mailing list for UNIX Wizards. Anything and everything relating to UNIX is discussed here. This list is gatewayed to the ARPANET mailing list but appears like a regular newsgroup to USENET.

This is the first pass at establishing a list of newsgroups. My intent is to update the list every week or so. Although this list is incomplete, it seemed that a partial list at the right time might be better that a complete list that arrives too late. If you have additions, corrections, or suggestions, please send them to me at:

ucbvax!teklabs!tekmdp!curts

Curt

>From cbosg!harpo!npois!eiss!ladm Fri March 19 16:20:27 1982

Subject: newsinfo.shell

Newsgroups: net.sources

Newsgroup naming conventions:

NO prefix= LOCAL ONLY

btl. = Bell Labs

net. = USENET wide categories

fa. = from ARPA-Net (no return feed, except via mail)

____.all= everything in category "____".

The netnews newsgroups of most interest are:

general: local general information

btl.all : BTL Everything.

net.general: general net-wide announcements

net.bugs.v7: reports of bugs and/or solutions to UNIX V7

net.news.b: news about our version of netnews

FA groups are "From the Arpanet" and are mostly copies of mailing lists or "digests" distributed on that network. (A digest is a collection of mail put together by an editor and sent out every so often. It is much like a newsletter.)

NEWSGROUP	Description last update 3/19/82
fa.arms-d	Discussion and info on strategic weapons.
fa.arpa-bboard	Announcements that are posted to all arpanet bboards are also fed into this newsgroup.
fa.digest-p	People who deal with digests. Mostly the people who moderate them.
fa.editor-p	Interest group in computer editors, both text and program.
fa.energy	Topics relating to alternate energy production, conservation, etc.
fa.human-nets	A daily moderated digest with discussions of computer-aided human-to-human communications. Probably the most widely read ARPANET publication. AVAILABLE PRINTED ONLY.
fa.info-cpm	CP/M and other operating systems for micro computers.
fa.info-micro	Microprocessor and microcomputer discussions.
fa.info-terms	Opinions/queries about what's a good/bad computer terminal.
fa.info-vax	VAX interest group. Seems to be mostly VMS issues, but some hardware discussions too.
fa.poli-sci	Political Science discussions digest. TURNED OFF.
fa.sf-lovers	Science Fiction book/movie reviews, etc. PRINTED ONLY.
fa.space	Digest containing comments on the space program and outer space in general. This is fed to net.space, ALSO PRINTED.
fa.tcp-ip	Digest relating to the TCP and IP network protocols. TURNED OFF.
fa.telecom	Technical topics relating to telecommunications, especially the telephone system. A digest recently spun off from fa.human-nets. PRINTED ONLY.
fa.teletext	Teletext discusses all aspects of ``esoteric" data systems. This includes teletext, viewdata, closed-captioning, and digicasting.
fa.unix-cpm	CPM/UNIX discussions.

fa.works	Interest group on personal workstations (e.g. Apollo, Perq, Xerox Star, etc).
NEWSGROUP	Description last update: 3/19/82
net.general	General information.
net.followup	follow-up articles to those posted in net.general
net.applic	Info—applicative language and related architecture.
net.auto	General Information for automobile owners.
net.auto.vw	Subgroup net.auto—for owners of Volkswagon Rabbits.
net.aviation	General information about aviation.
net.bugs	Genreral information about bug reports and fixes.
net.bugs.2bsd	Subgroup net.bugs—2nd Berkley Software distribution
net.bugs.4bsd	Subgroup net.bugs—4th Berkley software distribution
net.bugs.v7	Subgroup net.bugs—Version 7 or UNIX System III
net.columbia	General information on space shuttle and space programs
net.cooks	Interest group—food, cooking, cookbooks, and recipes.
net.cse	Computer Science Education
net.cycle	General information about motorcycles.
net.dcom	data communication—modems,multiplexers,port selectors etc.
net.eunice	Info on sites using SRI Eunice—simulates UNIX on VMS
net.games	Information and discussion on computer games.
net.games.rog	(net.games.rogue) Subgroup net.games—rogue
net.games.frp	Fantasy Role Playing games
net.games.triv	(net.games.trivia) Trivia contests and results.
net.ham-radio	Topics of interest to amateur radio operators.
net.jokes	The latest "good" joke you've heard?
net.lan	Local area network interest group.
net.lsi	Large Scale Integrated Circuit discussions.
net.math	mathematical discussions (eg. what is lim x->0 log(x)-log(x))
net.micro	micro-computers, see also fa.info-micro.
net.misc	Discussions not permanent enough for a newsgroup.
net.movies	Movie reviews by members of USENET.
net.music	Computer generated music.
net.news	Discussion of netnews itself, and its policies

net.news.b	Subgroup net.news—specific to bnews.
net.news.direc	(net.news.directory) all or part of the USENET directory
net.news.group	for discussions about proposed new newsgroups.
net.news.map	for discussions about maps of newsites.
net.news.newsi	(net.news.newsite) to announce a new site.
net.oa	Office Automation/Word Processing interest group.
net.periphs	Queries and discussions about particular peripherals.
net.rec	Gereral info on recreational (participation) sports.
net.rec.boat	boating (sail and motor???)
net.rec.bridge	contract bridge.
net.rec.scuba	scuba diving.
net.rec.ski	skiing.
net.rec.skydiv	(net.rec.skydive) sky diving
net.records	Info and opinions about records (and tapes ?).
net.rumor	For posting of rumors.
net.sf-lovers	Science Fiction Lovers—undigested from fa.sf-lovers
net.sources	For large volume material, source program distribution
net.space	Space programs and research—undigested from fa.space
net.sport	General info about spectator sports.
net.sport.base	(net.sport.baseball) Subgroup of net.sport—for baseball.
net.sport.foot	(net.sport.football) Subgroup of net.sport—for football.
net.sport.hock	(net.sport.hockey) Subgroup of net.sport—for hockey.
net.taxes	Tax advice and queries.
net.test	Test messages are posted here.
net.travel	Requests, suggestions, and opinions about traveling
net.ucds	Circuit drawing system.
net.unix-wiza	(net.unix-wizards) Discussion of UNIX—gatewayed to ARPANET
net.wines	Info and reccomendations about wines and alcoholic beverages

Appendix III

1983 Post on CSNET

Relay-Version: version B 2.10 5/3/83; site utzoo.UUCP
Posting-Version: version B 2.10 5/3/83; site utcsrgv.UUCP
Path: utzoo!utcsrgv!peterr
From: peterr@utcsrgv.UUCP (Peter Rowley)
Newsgroups: net.news
Subject: Usenet Inc == CSNET ?
Message-ID: <1857@utcsrgv.UUCP>
Date: Sun, 31-July-83 05:48:11 EDT
Article-I.D.: utcsrgv.1857
Posted: Sun July 31 05:48:11 1983
Date-Received: Sun, 31-July-83 08:27:27 EDT
Organization: CSRG, University of Toronto
Lines: 65

>From literature and a presentation given at the Toronto USENIX, my impression is that CSNET is. . . a form with as little bureaucracy as possible, and with non-profit status. Some excerpts from "csnet news," no. 1 (may 83): "CSNET was established in 1981 with a 5 year grant from the National Science Foundation. From the beginning, the goal of the project has been to create an independent network, fully supported by membership dues and service fees.

With this in mind, NSF has adopted a schedule of dues and fees for 1983, and the Coordination and Information Centre (CIC) has developed models of expected service charges. . . .

CSNET dues support software maintenance and development, hardware, tech. staff, and other expenses associated with shared resources such as the PhoneNet relays, the Name Server facility, and the CIC. Dues also defray the costs of documentation, network management, and network governance activities. Each member of CSNET is required to pay yearly dues to support CSNET operation."

Here are the current dues:
Industrial: $30K/yr
Government: $10K/yr
Univ: $5K/yr

The two relays mentioned are at Rand Corp. in Santa Monica and U. Delaware.

A PhoneNet site dials into the closest relay, except where a site has been moved to the other relay for load balancing. An X25Net (Telenet) site accesses CSNet by buying special hardware from Telenet, getting X.25/TCP-IP sw from Purdue (runs only on BSD) and paying Telenet $1000/mo. for a 4800 baud line, packet charges not included. The break-even point for phone/telenet is about $22K/yr.

PhoneNet sites pay service fees too:

Day	Evening/Night	
Dial-out	.80	.40
Dial-in	.10	.10

These are on top of any telco charges and are in terms of $/connect-minute.

The CSNet model predicts service fees of between $125 and $625 a year for light-heavy PhoneNet mail users (note that there is no news). X25 service fees have not been established yet.

All the details can't be gone into in the space of a news article, but it appears that CSNET provides the reliable mail and name server services desired, and could handle news.

The bureaucracy involved is the 6 member management committee, which appears to be responsible to the NSF, and the >=4 member staff of the CIC, located at BBN in Cambridge Mass.

Comment:
It appears that a lot of work has gone into setting CSNET up, together with a good deal of money from the NSF. For this to happen again with USENet would probably require private, for-profit funding (public funders would say "Use CSNET"), resulting in a for-profit organization probably more expensive than CSNET.

The obvious statement to make is that sites who want a "USENet Inc." should cough up the CSNET dues and join that network, then help/urge them to get news going. Note that this would not satisfy the user-pay advocates, as univ's (and government sites) get a break on dues. I would suggest, however, that USENet as it is, with no bureaucracy at all, is a valuable thing to preserve. It has an active, informed community capable of contributing software and manpower to the net. If a new news/mail pkg is created, no bureaucracy need be convinced of its worth... all that must be done is to post it to net.sources. Those who feel it can be used, in the given environment

(with all requisite compatability problems), may use it. This seems as democratic as one could hope for.
peter rowley, U. Toronto CSRG
{cornell,watmath,ihnp4,floyd,allegra,utzoo,uw-beaver}!utcsrgv!peterr
or {cwruecmp,duke,linus,lsuc,research}!utzoo!utcsrgv!peterr
Relay-Version: version B 2.10 5/3/83; site utzoo.UUCP
Posting-Version: version B 2.10 5/3/83; site umcp-cs.UUCP
Path: utzoo!linus!decvax!harpo!seismo!rlgvax!cvl!umcp-cs!chris

From: chris@umcp-cs.UUCP
Newsgroups: net.news
Subject: CSNet
Message-ID: <1341@umcp-cs.UUCP>
Date: Mon, 1-Aug-83 18:09:10 EDT
Article-I.D.: umcp-cs.1341
Posted: Mon Aug 1 18:09:10 1983
Date-Received: Mon, 1-Aug-83 22:49:50 EDT
Organization: Univ. of Maryland, Computer Science Dept.
Lines: 18

CSNet, as it stands now, would collapse instantly under the weight of netnews. Without some way of distributing the load, the two relays would not be able to handle all the traffic. That's the basic trouble with a centralized system, and is the reason for all the research into distributed computing. You can only squeeze so much into a single system.

—Chris

PS Don't get me wrong, I think CSNet is actually doing quite well. It hasn't been around long enough to solve the initial problems (like slow software). Supposedly MMDF II is a big step in increasing speed. - ACT

—
In-Real-Life: Chris Torek, Univ of MD Comp Sci
UUCP: {seismo,allegra,brl-bmd}!umcp-cs!chris
CSNet: chris@umcp-cs

PART 3

And the Future?

11

The NTIA Conference on the Future of the Net

Creating a Prototype for a Democratic Decision-Making Process

A special issue of *Scientific American* appeared in Spring 1995, exploring the social impact that the computer and communications revolution is having on our society.[1] In the introduction to the issue was a cartoon. The cartoon shows several paleontologists on the trail of a major new discovery. The caption reads: "Well, I don't see any point in looking any further. It was probably just one of those wild rumors." They are standing in the midst of a huge footprint; however, because it is so large, they do not see it.

This cartoon is a helpful analogy to our situation today. There have been significant computer networking developments in the past 30 years, but these advances are so grand that it is easy to miss them, and to begin to turn back, just like the paleontologists. It is important to understand what these advances are, so we can recognize them, and learn what direction the footprints are pointing in.

We are at a turning point in terms of what the future direction of the global computer network will be. Changes are being made in U.S. policy and in the policy of countries around the world regarding the Net and Net access and thus there are important issues being raised about what the new policy will and should be.

In response to criticism in the United States that the online community was not being involved enough in setting the new policy, an online conference was held November 14–23, 1994, by the U.S. National Telecommunications Information Administration (NTIA). The NTIA virtual conference was co-sponsored by the National Telecommunications Information

Administration and the Information Infrastructure Task Force (IITF), as part of the U.S. government's National Information Infrastructure Initiative. The conference gave people both in the United States and around the world a chance to discuss their concerns about how to expand access to the Net.

To take part, people needed a computer, either their own or one available at one of the 80 public access sites that were set up around the United States in libraries and other public places. The online conference was available via a mailing list, where all the posts were sent to the e-mail mailboxes of those who subscribed, or as a Usenet newsgroup available at a limited number of sites. A World Wide Web site was also set up, so a netuser with access to a browser could read the posts, but could not participate. There were several forums on different topics, two of which discussed increasing access to the Net for a broader sector of the population. At the end of the conference an archive of the proceedings was to be available via the World Wide Web.*

One of the participants in the online conferences described the social and technical advance available to those who participate in the Global Computer Commmunications Network. He wrote:

> *Welcome to the 21st century. You are a Netizen, or a Net Citizen, and you exist as a citizen of the world thanks to the global connectivity that the Net makes possible. You consider everyone as your compatriot. You physically live in one country but you are in contact with much of the world via the global computer network. . . .*
>
> *The situation I describe is only a prediction of the future, but a large part of the necessary infrastructure currently exists . . . Every day more computers attach to the existing network and every new computer adds to the user base—at least twenty five million people are interconnected today. . . .*
>
> *We are seeing a revitalization of society. The frameworks are being redesigned from the bottom up. A new more democratic world is becoming possible.*[2]

This was one of the many contributions in response to the NTIA online conference. The NTIA statement welcoming participants to the online conference listed several purposes for the conference. Among those purposes were:

1. Garner opinions and views on universal telecommunications service that may shape the legislative and regulatory debate.

---

*The NTIA Virtual Archives are available on the World Wide Web at:

http://ntiaunix2.ntia.doc.gov:70/11s/virtual/ or
http://www.ntia.doc.gov/opadhome/virtual/

2. Demonstrate how networking technology can broaden participation in the development of government policies, specifically, universal service telecommunications policy.
3. Illustrate the potential for using the NII to create an electronic commons.
4. Create a network of individuals and institutions that will continue the dialog started by the conference, once the formal sponsorship is over.

"This conference," the NTIA explained, "is an experiment in a new form of dialog among citizens and with their government. The conference is not a one-way, top down approach, it is a conversation. It holds the promise of reworking the compact between citizens and their government."[3]

What was the response to the call?

In the process of the week-long discussions, a number of voices complained about the commercial entities that were slated to take over the United States portion of the backbone of the Internet. Many expressed concern that government intervention was needed to make access to the Net broadly available. They gave experiences and examples to demonstrate that leaving the problem of expanded access to commercial entities would not solve the problems that expanded access required be solved. For example, one participant wrote:

> *I want to add my voice to those favoring greater, not less, government intervention . . . to protect the interest of the people against the narrow sectarian interests of large telecommunications industries. Why the federal government gave up its part ownership in the Internet backbone is a mystery to me. An active interventionist government is essential to assure universal access at affordable prices (for) . . . people living in (the) heart of cities or in the Upper Peninsula of Michigan.*[4]

A number of people from rural and remote areas participated and explained their concern that they not be left out of the online future because connecting them to the Net would not be profitable. In response to a post from someone in Oregon, a librarian from a remote area of Michigan wrote:

> *I'd like to hear more from the Oregon edge of the world. Being from a small, rural library in the Upper Peninsula of Michigan, with a very small tax base . . . faced with geographical isolation and no clout . . . how do we get our voices heard and assure our patrons equal and universal access to these new and wonderful services . . . we have no local nodes . . . every hook up is a long distance call. What are you doing over there?*[5]

A participant working with a scientific foundation echoed this concern. He wrote:

When faced with the resources and persuasive power (legal and otherwise) of enormous multinational corporations with annual incomes that are orders of magnitude greater than some of the territories they serve, only a capable and committed national guarantee of access, and a national cost pool can provide access to these new technology resources.

And THE INTERNET IS SPECIALLY IMPORTANT to areas with limited access to technical and scientific resources. As one of the leading non-profit educational foundations devoted to the environmental problems of small tropical islands, we (Islands Resources Foundation) are amazed at the richness of the Internet resource, and terribly concerned that our constituents throughout all of the world's oceans are going to (be) closed out from access to this resource because of monopoly pricing policies.

Speaking to the NTIA, he urged, "We ask careful attention to the equity issues of access, and a federal guarantee of access and availability."[6]

Recognizing that people without computers or Net access would not be able to participate in this conference, a limited number of public access sites had been set up. One participant from San Francisco explained why making such access to the Net available was so important:

I am sitting in the corner of the card catalogue room at the San Francisco main library. . . . doing what I hope I will be able to do for the rest of my years: use computers freely. Internet, on-line discourse, rather, is invaluable; the role of the computer-friendly mind is becoming ever greater and the need to communicate within this medium needs to remain open to all. If not, we will fall into the abyss of the isolated world. . . . We could become isolated humans in a cubicle existing only through our computer. . . . I would choose otherwise. Keep computers part of the schools and libraries, and definitely make (the) Internet free to any who wish to use it. Otherwise we are doomed.[7]

Another user expressed support for library access and participation. He cautioned:

*If things go as it looks they are going now, libraries will lose out to business in the war for the net. Yes, this means that we will be drowning in a deluge of what big business tells us we want to hear and the magic of the net will vanish in a poof of monied interests. Some estimates that I have read say that it should cost no more than $10 a year per user for universal access to the national network, including library sites so that those without phones or home computers have access. The NSF has decided against funding the internet anymore and all the talk of . . . (late) is about the privatizing of the net. No one seems to get the point involved (or, worse: They *do* get the point). The backbone of the net should be retained by the government. The cost is relatively inexpensive and the benefits are grand. Paying large fees*

> *(some plans call for charges based on the amount of data consumed and others by time spent net-surfing) defeats the nature of the net. We have possibilities for direct democracy. At the very least, for representation of mentally distinct groups as opposed to physical. That is, now we are represented in Congress by geographical area, not what our opinions support.*[8]

Several people complained that Net access was not only difficult because of the cost of modem connections, but that for many people it was a financial hardship to even own a computer. As one user from Virginia explained:

> *As a newcomer to the net, I don't feel I have much relevant to say. All this chatter about Info Superhiways strikes me as so much political doubletalk. The hiway exists. But to drive on the damn thing you need a car. Computers (macs or pcs, etc.) are not items that someone making 6 or 7 dollars an hour can easily obtain.*[9]

Others described the efforts in their areas to provide public access to the Net. In Seattle, the Seattle Public Library and Computer Professions for Social Responsibility set up a system to make e-mail access and an e-mail mailbox available to all those eligible for a library card.

In Blacksburg, Virginia, U.S. government funds have helped set up the Blacksburg Electronic Village by subsidizing the installation of fiber-optic cable to all new apartments being built so that people could have direct access to the Internet.[10]

Canadian participants described how the Blue Sky Freenet in Manitoba was providing access to all of Manitoba with no extra long distance phone charges to small rural areas. "They have basically a hub, in each of the different calling areas. . . . Some places will be piggy backing on CBC radio waves, others on satellite connections, some on fiber optics."[11]

Also proposals were made to provide access to other forgotten segments of the society such as the homeless. A participant from San Francisco proposed that terminals with network access be installed in homeless shelters. The person explained:

> *Provide homeless shelters with online systems frozen into Netnews and email, or email and gopher. A 386 terminal running Linux, Xwindows and Netscape, and locked into a user group such as email and gopher, etc., would permit defining the lowest level of involvement. People need communication to represent themselves, and email for that reason, as well as Netnews.*[12]

People from other countries also contributed, providing a broader perspective than might normally be available in a national policy discussion. For example, from the Netherlands came the following observation:

> *After attending the Virtual Conference for two days now, I would like to give my first (contribution) to the discussion. Since I work for the government of The Netherlands, at the Central Bureau of Statistics, which is part of the Department of Economic Affairs, the question of availability of statistical figures intrigues me. As a result of safety precautions there is no on-line connection possible with our network. There should, however, be a source for the public to get our data from, we get paid by community money so the community should benefit (from) the results of our efforts. I am wondering how these matters are regulated in the other countries who participate in the Virtual Conference.*

"With kind greetings," he ended.[13]

And a psychology professor from Moscow State University in Russia wrote:

> *Hi, netters:*
>
> *[He explained how he had subscribed to only two mailing lists dealing with network access because he would only have time to read the few messages he expected there.] I'm glad I'm wrong. I can't follow the massive traffic of discussions. Sometimes my English is too poor to grasp the essence, sometimes I don't know the realities, legislation etc. Some themes I'm greatly pleased with . . . I agree gladly with Larry Irving—[of the NTIA, who had said he was] thrilled with the volume of traffic & quality of discussion. I am, too. Perhaps I'll find more time later to read the messages more attentively. I shall not unsubscribe, though.*
>
> *The people in the 2nd & 3rd worlds are just now trying to find our own ways to use the Internet facilities & pleasures. I am interested in [the] investigation of these ways, in teaching & helping them in this kind of activity. Besides, my group is working on bibliographic database construction and letting . . . remote access to it. For several days only we got an IP access to the WWW, we are not experienced yet to access. So I use ordinary e-mail. Good luck to all subscribers. I wish you success.*[14]

Also, as part of the discussion several participants described how they felt the ability to communicate was the real achievement represented by the Global Computer Network, rather than just a means to provide information.

In her message, "NOT JUST INFORMATION - - -> COMMUNICATION," a participant from Palo Alto, California wrote, ". . . the NTIA is building a one-way highway to a dead end when they take the word 'Telecommunications' out of their rhetoric." She listed several points for people to consider, among which were:

> 1. *Information is always old already.*

Photo taken in office of Robert M. Fano (center left) with Fernando Corbató (left). (Photo: The MIT Museum).

Claude E. Shannon at MIT. 1968.
(Photo: The MIT Museum).

Walter Lawrence, Martin W. Essigmann, and Joseph C.R. Licklider at symposium. 1953. (Photo: The MIT Museum).

(left) R.M. Fano with L.G. Kraft and W.B. Davenport, Jr., staff members of MIT Research Laboratory of Electronics. (Photo: The MIT Museum).

Norbert Wiener (left) looking at tape from autocorrolator at MIT along with Jerome B. Wiesner (middle), and Dr. Yuk W. Lee (right). 1949. (Photo: The MIT Museum).

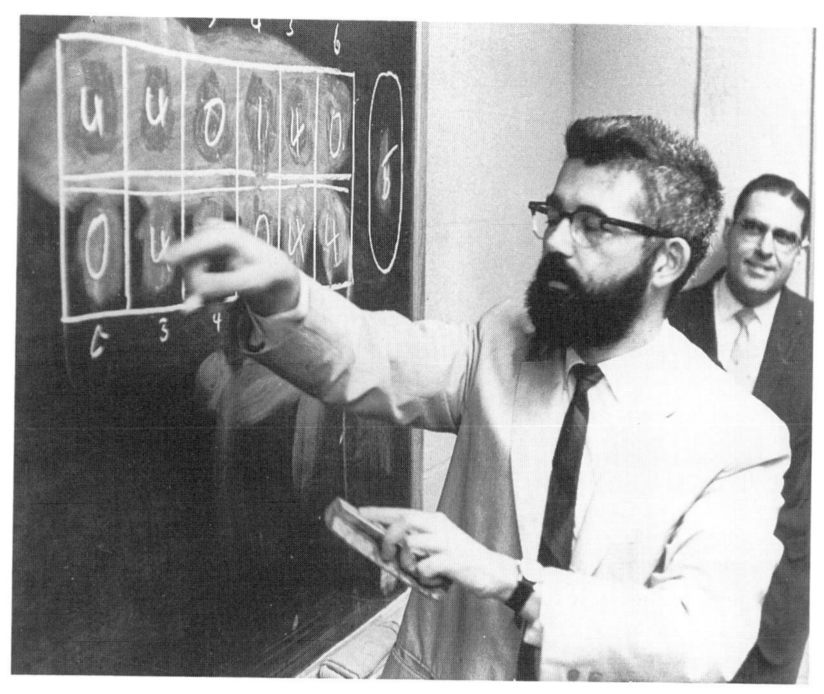

John McCarthy at MIT. 1962. (Photo: The MIT Museum).

Y.W. Lee, Amar G. Bose, and Norbert Wiener. 1954. (Photo: The MIT Museum).

MIT Computation Center IBM 704 Computer. 1957. (Photo: The MIT Museum).

Y.W. Lee, Amar G. Bose, and Norbert Wiener. 1954. (Photo: The MIT Museum).

MIT Computation Center IBM 704 Computer. 1957. (Photo: The MIT Museum).

Original ARPANET IMP installation team from BBN. Back row: Ben Barker; Front row: (left to right) Bill Bartell, Dave Walden, Jim Geisman, Bob Kahn, Frank Heart, Martin Thrope, Will Crowther, and Servo Ornstein; Seated: Truett Thach; Not pictured: Bernie Cosell. (Photo: Will Crowther).

(Left to right) J.A. Stratton, Norbert Wiener, and Claude Shannon. (Photo: The MIT Museum).

Robert M. Fano and Marvin L. Minsky examine a graphical display on the PDP-1. Early 1960s. (Photo: The MIT Museum).

Ken Thompson (left) and Brian Kernighan (right) at ACM chess tournament. 1974. (Photo: Tom Truscott).

(Right to left): Betty Shannon (seated), Tom Truscott (standing), Ken Thompson, Claude Shannon, and others after the World Computer Chess Championship in Linz. 1980. (Photo courtesy: Tom Truscott).

Stephen Daniel hacking at a terminal. 1979. (Photo: Tom Truscott).

Jim Ellis installing Unix version 7 on the Duke PDP 11/70. (Photo: Tom Truscott).

Steve Johnson, President of Usenix, presenting 1996 Usenix Lifetime Achievement Award (The Flame) to (left to right) Joseph S. Sventek, Deborah Scherrer, and Dennis Hall, on behalf of the Software Tools Users Group. (Photo: Usenix).

Ken Thompson at teletypewriter running a Unix based system. 1972. (Photo: Bell Labs).

Rudd Canaday. (Photo: Bell Labs).

Lee E. McMahon. (Photo: Bell Labs).

Doug McIlroy. 1981. (Photo: Bell Labs).

Jaap Akkerhuis playing Deborah Scherrer's Bechstein. 1988. (Photo: Deborah Scherrer).

Deborah Scherrer presenting gift from Usenix to EUUG on its 10th anniversary at the Dublin EUUG Conference. Behind Deborah Scherrer is Teus Hagen. 1987. (Photo courtesy: Deborah Scherrer).

Lorinda Cherry of Bell Labs. (Photo: Courtesy Lorinda Cherry).

Dennis Ritchie and Evi Nemeth. Usenix Conference, Anaheim. 1990. (Photo: Kirk McKusick).

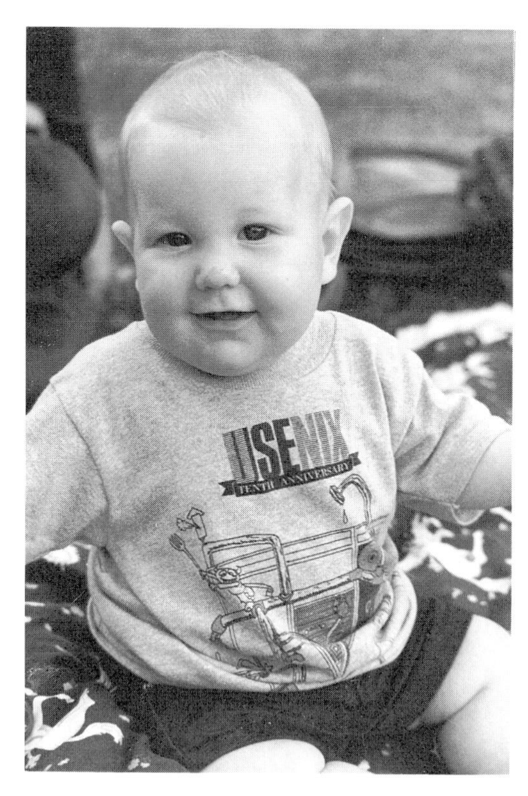

Ben Scherrer at Usenix 10th Anniversary Portland Conference. June 1985. (Photo: Teus Hagen).

Program Committee for Winter 1987 Usenix Conference in Washington, DC. Left to right around table: David Tilbrook, Peter Collison, Mike O'Dell, Neil Groundwater, John Mullen, Dennis Ritchie, Steve Johnson, John Mashey, Jim McKie, Jaap Akkerhuis, Norman Wilson, Deborah Scherrer, and Nigel Martin. (Photo: Kirk McKusick).

Computer lab at INET '96 held by the Internet Society in Montreal, Canada. June 1996. (Photo: Nicolas Luco).

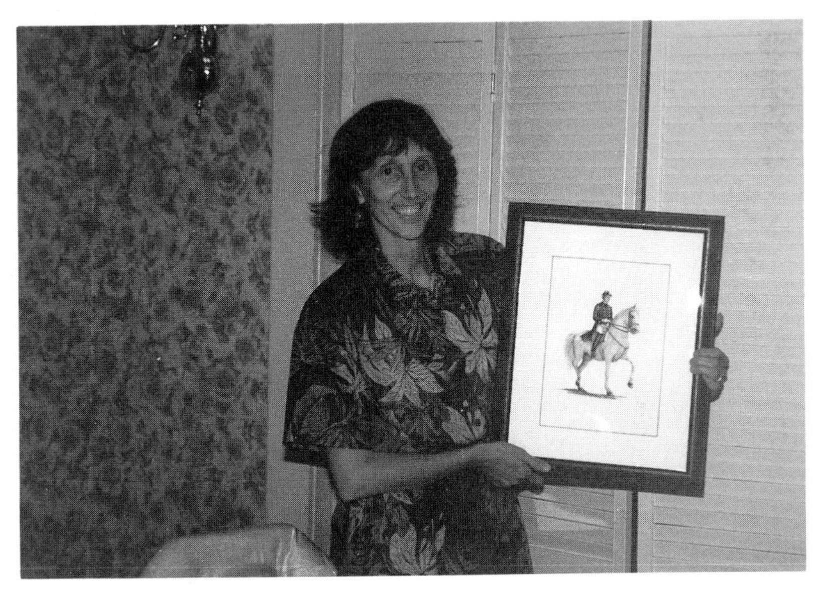

Deborah Scherrer, with gift from Usenix upon retirement from serving as Usenix President and on Board of Directors for 10 years. Usenix Conference, Anaheim. 1990. (Photo Courtesy: Deborah Scherrer).

THE USENIX ASSOCIATION PRESENTS THE 1996

Lifetime Achievement Award

to The Founders & Major Participants in the Software Tools Users Group

This award is presented to honor profound intellectual achievement and unparalleled service to the community.

Before the general availability of Unix, the Software Tools project popularized a new vision of operating system software, offering a bridge to portability and power for those beleaguered by limited, proprietary operating systems.

With its extraordinary focus on building clean, portable, reusable code shared amongst multiple applications and runnable on virtually any system, the Software Tools movement established the tradition of empowering users to define, develop, control, and freely distribute their computing environment.

We hereby recognize the following Software Tools Users Group founders and major participants:

PRINCIPAL RECIPIENTS & KEEPERS OF THE FLAME

Dennis Hall *Deborah Scherrer* *Joseph S. Sventek*

ORIGINATORS AND KEY INSPIRATION

Brian Kernighan *P. J. Plauger*

MAJOR CONTRIBUTORS

Allen Akin
Brian Anderson
Gene Autrey-Hunley
Wil Baden
Theresa Breckon Bixby
Michael Bourke
Walter E. Brown
Tonia Cantrell
Shirley Cassinelli
Tom Chappell
Barbara Chase
Tom Clarkson
Douglas Comer
Phil Davidson
Bruce Dawson
Charlie Dolan
Ben Domenico
Walt Donovan
Larry Dwyer
H. W. Egdorf
Philip Enslow
Desmond FitzGerald
Perry B. Flinn
Dan Forsyth
Chris Fraser
Major Vinton Goff
Mars Gralia
Neil Groundwater
Teus Hagen
Todd Hammond
David Hanson
Paul Howson
Margaret Hug
Van Jacobson
Steven Jones
George Kapus
Rick Kiessig
Todd Kushner
Craig Leres
Clyde Lightfoot
Dave Martin
William Meine
Robert Munn
Greg O'Brien
Michael D. O'Dell
George Pajari
Vern Paxson
Christian M. Petersen
David Phillips
Jim Poole
Jeffrey A. Poskanzer
Ken Poulton
Philip H.Scherrer
Toshiaki Saisho
Jerome Silbert
C. R. Snow
David Stoffel
Nancy Deerinck Travis
Gary Trujillo
Dave Turner
Bob Upshaw
James Ward & Colleagues at Apollo Computers
Jack Waugh
Wally Wedel
Dale Wolfe
Joseph Yao

Lifetime Achievement Award (1996) presented to The Founders and Major Participants in the Software Tools Users Group.

1974 ACM North American Chess Championship Tournament. Seated near Big Chessboards are Ken Thompson (left) and Brian Kernighan. (Photo: Tom Truscott).

Richard Haight. 1982. (Photo: Bell Labs).

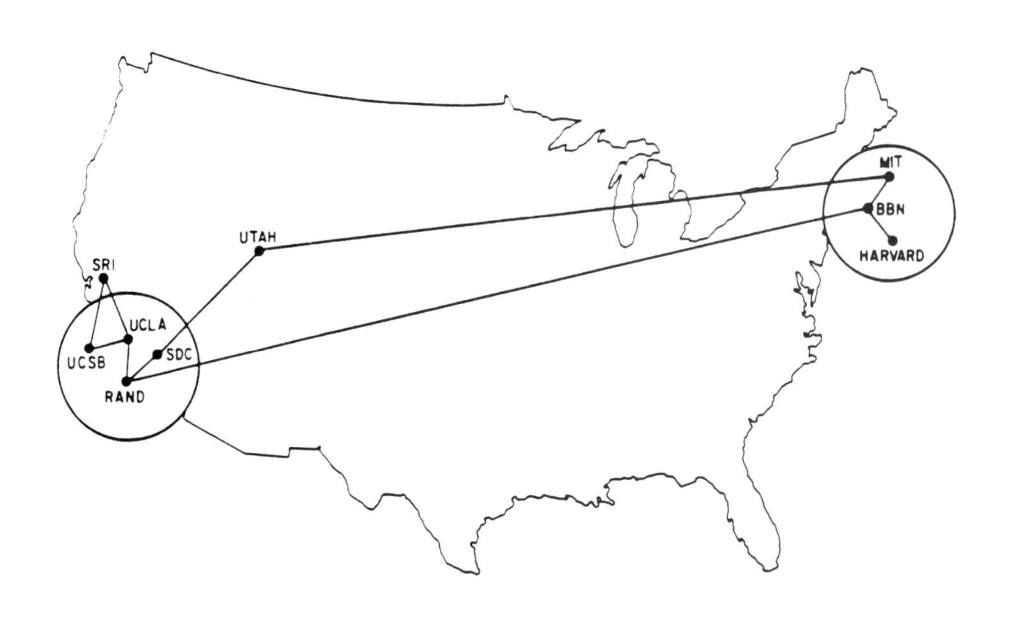

ARPANET map of June 1970. (ARPANET Completion Report).

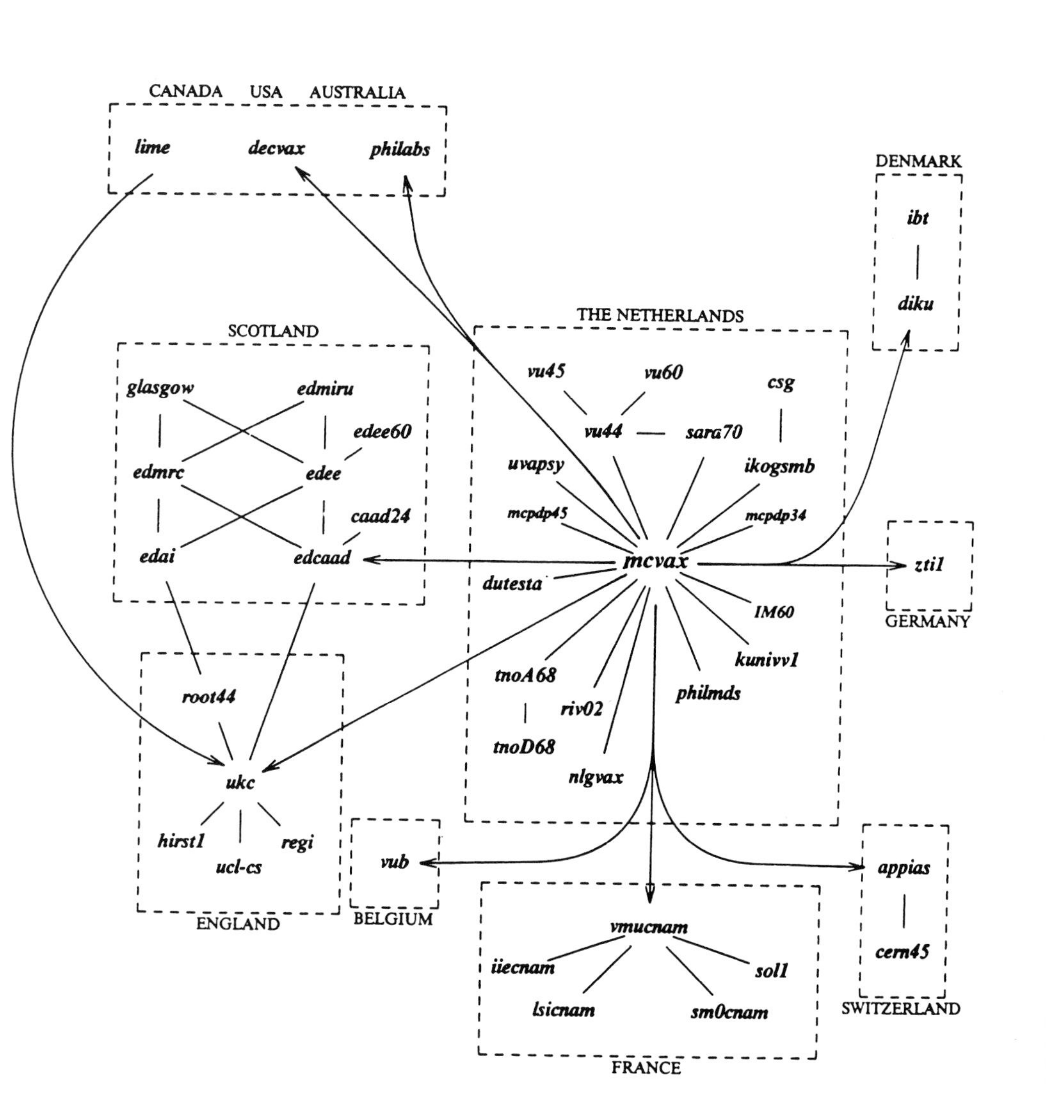

European UUCP Network map March 31st, 1983. (Map Courtesy: Jim McKie).

Map of International Connectivity. (Copyright © 1996 Larry Landweber).

2. *Telecommunications, properly algorithmed, provides dynamic information about who we are as the human race. . . .*
3. *Telecommunications is the road to direct democracy and a future for this planet.*
4. *Downstream bandwidth is just another broadcast medium. Upstream bandwidth is power for the people.*[15]

In a similar vein, another participant wrote:

> *To start off, I take issue with the term "service." As I have stated . . . the terminology being used is being adopted from an out-dated model of a Top-Down communications system. The new era of interconnection and many-to-many communication afforded by Netnews and Mailing lists (. . .) brings to the forefront a model of bottom-up rather than top-down communication and information. It is time to reexamine society and welcome the democratizing trends of many-to-many communication over the one-to-many models as represented by broadcast television, radio, newspapers and other media. Rather than service, I would propose that we examine what "forms of communication" should be available. So instead of talking about "Universal Service," we should consider "Universal Interconnection to forms of communication.*[16]

These were just some of the many concerns raised in this week-long online conference supported and sponsored by a branch of the U.S. government. The people participating raised serious questions as to whether the real issues needed to make access available for the many rather than limiting it to a multimedia plaything for the few, would be considered and examined. Many were concerned for those who did not have access to the Net, either because they did not have a modem or, even more fundamentally, because they could not afford a computer. Thus, there was a significant sentiment that computers with network access be made available in public places such as libraries so people could have access.

One participant noted that current policy favored the few having video connections rather than the many having e-mail capability. He proposed to the U.S. government:

> *Let's redirect some of the funding for high end technology into getting the mainstream public onto the net. Instead of funding an hour of video between two users, we should use the money to let 100,000 users send an email message!*[17]

Summing up the sentiment expressed during the conference, a participant wrote:

> *I find it hard to believe a state can function in the 21st century without a solid information infrastructure and citizens with enough technological savvy to use it.*[18]

The conference was a very significant event. From cities to rural and remote areas, people made the hard effort to express their concern and commitment to making access available to all. They protested the United States government's policy of giving commercial entities the Net as a policy that is in conflict with the public and social goal of universal low cost or free network access.

The hardships that participants experienced included mailboxes clogged with such a volume of e-mail that people could not keep up with it, newsgroups appearing late on Usenet and at very few sites so it was hard to get access to them, and a lack of publicity so that many did not learn of the conference until it was almost over. Yet the participants did what they could to contribute to and speak up for the right of everyone to be able to be part of the Net as a contributor, not just as a listener.

A new government form was created which is different from what has existed thus far. This online conference made clear that the hard problems of our time can be solved if the most advanced technology is used to involve the largest possible number of people in the decisions that will affect their lives.

The NTIA conference, using mailing lists and Usenet newsgroups to have broad-reaching online discussion, created a prototype for how ubiquitous networking access can be achieved within the United States and elsewhere. The NTIA conference demonstrated that by the involvement of the many the important problems of the times can be analyzed so they can be solved. The Internet and Usenet are providing important new means for people to contribute to the needed discussion to determine the principles to guide public policy decisions.

Even though the NTIA conference meant a much broader sector of the population than ever before was able to participate in the policy discussion about the future of the Net, one of the participants explained why this process was only a prototype of what was needed.

> *I think this conference was accessible to more than just "elite technocrats." I, for instance, am a graduate student at the U of MN. I have access because everyone who attends the University has access, and can apply their access via numerous computer labs that are open to all students. I think a lot of people don't realize that we're at a very critical point with determining the future of resources such as the Internet. I join you in hoping that no irreversible decisions are made on the basis of this conference—there needs to be a much wider opportunity for public comment.*[19]

EPILOGUE

What was the significance of the NTIA conference in helping to determine what direction government policy should take regarding the future of the Net?

When the NTIA conference was held in November 1994, serious questions were raised about the proposed policy of the United States government for the future development of the Internet. Although the stated goal of the conference was to broaden citizen participation in policy development, the government ignored the concerns and voices raised during the online conference and went ahead with the plans to privatize the United States portion of the backbone of the Internet by May 1, 1995.[20] One of the most difficult dilemmas of our times is how to deal with the discrepancy between the need for more public input into policy development and the actions of government officials who ignore that input.

Although the public's input was not acted upon, the NTIA conference achieved two important results. It clarified that when a broader sector of people have online access and are invited to participate in a public policy discussion on an important issue, the discussion will identify the principles to shape that public policy. And it demonstrated that the policy of privatizing the United States portion of the Internet was at odds with the principles that emerged when a broader set of the population was able to participate in the development of policy objectives.

Looking back to a comparable period in the development of the computer provides some helpful perspective for our times. At a conference at MIT in 1961 on the future of the computer, one of those present pointed out that no one knew what that future would be in the short term or the long term. Therefore, he proposed, it was important to decide what type of future to encourage and to work to make that future a reality. The 1994 NTIA online conference demonstrated that there is a need once again to determine what type of future is desired and to work toward making that future a reality. The online conference identified the goal for the future, that is, the public policy objective of promoting broad and ubiqutous access to the Internet. There is a need now to find ways for that goal to become reality.

NOTES

1. "The Computer in the 21st Century," *Scientific American* special issue (1995) 4. (Cartoon by Charles Addams, The New Yorker Magazine, 1952, 1980.)
2. From: Michael Hauben <hauben@columbia.edu>
   Date: Wed 23 Nov 1994 00:49:16 -0500
   To: redefus@virtconf.ntia.doc.gov Cc: avail@virtconf.ntia.doc.gov

Subject: Netizen Speech
Message-ID: <199411230549.AA14335@aloha.cc.columbia.edu>
(See Chapter 1 of this volume.)

3. From: NTIA Virtual Conference <ntia>
   Date: Mon 14 Nov 1994 09:07:56 -0800
   Message-Id: <199411141707.JAA06933@virtconf.digex.net>
   To: avail, intellec, opnacces, privacy, redefus, standard
   Subject: NTIA Virtual Conference KeyNote Address
4. From: James McDonough <epin@access.digex.net>
   Subject: Re: [AVAIL:42] Re: my question
   Message-Id: <Pine.SUN.3.91.941116094225.11331A
   100000@access2.digex.net>
5. From: Cynthia S. Terwilliger <twigs@umich.edu>
   Date: Nov 15 20:42:07 1994
   Subject: Re: [AVAIL:32] Re: Key Issues of Affordability and Availability
   Message-ID: <Pine.3.89.9411152007.B7150-0100000@sils.umich.edu>
6. From: Bruce Potter <ab368@virgin.uvi.edu>
   Date: Tue 15 Nov 1994 00:27:42 GMT
   Message-ID: <1994Nov15.002742.7646@virgin.uvi.edu>
   To: avail@virtconf.ntia.doc.gov
   Subject: Need for Federal Oversight of Access and Availability (For Island Resources Foundation, iresource@aol.com)
7. San Francisco Public Library "SFPL::NTIA_PUB"@DRANET.DRA.COM
   Message-Id: <941116184335.20212906@DRANET.DRA.COM>
8. From: Sean <sconnell@silver.ucs.indiana.edu>
   Subject: Re: [AVAIL:41] my question
   Date: Wed 16 Nov 1994 00:33:24 -0500 (EST)
   Message-Id: <199411160841.AAA27213@virtconf.digex.net>
9. From: Jamie Dyer <jdyer@Hopper.ITC.Virginia.EDU>
   Subject: Internet Broadcasting Corp
   Message-ID: <CzIIDo.96q@murdoch.acc.Virginia.EDU>
   Organization: University of Virginia
   Date: Sat 19 Nov 1994 11:25:00GMT
10. From: Bob Summers <bsummers@vt.edu>
    Date: Wed Nov 16 19:59:39 1994
    Message-Id: <199411170359.TAA09478@virtconf.digex.net>
    Re: [Avail:76] The Super-Highway: Where To?
11. From: az908@freenet.carleton.ca (Paul Holden)
    Date: Wed 23 Nov 1994 18:52:36 - 0500
    Message-Id: <199411232352.SAA08269@freenet.carleton.ca>
    Subject: Universal Access and the Feds. . .
12. From: San Francisco Public Library "SFPL::NTIA_PUB"@DRANET.DRA.COM
    Date: Fri 18 Nov 1994 18:24:27 -0600 (CST)
    Message-Id: <94118182427.20216603@DRANET.DRA.COM>
    Subject: NTIA Public Comment

13. From: Frank D. Bastiaans, Statistical Analyst, Division Trade and Transport
    Date: 16 Nov 1994 16:35:56 MET
    Subject: Availability of statistics
    Reply-To: FBSS@cbs.nl
    Message-Id: <81430000.00000000006A.FBSS.Z9H374IJ>
14. From: Alexander Voiskounsky <vae@motiv.cogsci.msu.su> (Psychology Department, Moscow State University)
    Newsgroups: alt.ntia.redefus
    Subject: Re: [AVAIL & REDEFUS]
    Date: Sat 19 Nov 1994 09:24:42
15. From: Marilyn Davis <evote@netcom.com>
    Date: Mon 14 Nov 1994 17:11:07 -0800 (PST)
    Message-Id: <199411150111.RAA27335@netcom12.netcom.com>
    Subject: Not Information - - -> COMMUNICATION
    To: redefus@virtconf.ntia.doc.gov
16. From: Michael Hauben <hauben@columbia.edu>
    Date: Tue 22 Nov 1994 05:03:13
    Newsgroups: alt.ntia.avail
    Subject: Need to stress concept of active communication and interconnection
    Reply-To: avail@virtconf.ntia.doc.gov
17. From: chage@rahul.net (Carl Hage)
    Date: Tue 22 Nov 94 01:27:35 (PST)
    Message-Id: <9411220927.AA20655@slick.chage.com>
    Subject: Nonprofits and the Internet
18. From: Lew McDaniel <MCDANIEL@wvuadmin3.csc.wvu.edu>
    Organization: WVU Computing Services
    Date: Mon 14 Nov 1994 14:55:34 EST
    Subject: Re: [REDEFUS:15] Pilot Projects
    Message-Id: <3A45E1049AE@wvuadmin3.csc.wvu.edu>
19. From: "Chris Silker" <silke001@maroon.tc.umn.edu>
    Date: Thu 17 Nov 1994 08:58:19
    Message-Id: <46075.silke001@maroon.tc.umn.ecu>
    Subject: Re: [AVAIL:83] AVAIL digest 11
20. Also, on May 1, 1995, there was a program at a branch of the New York Public Library. The program focused on the importance of what the Net represents to people around the world and the future potential of this new means of communication. At that meeting, people expressed their concern that the U.S. government would try to impede access to this important resource, rather than help to make it more broadly available. People at the meeting insisted that another meeting be set up to discuss how to make this important new resource available to a broader sector of the population.

An earlier version of this chapter by Ronda Hauben was presented at Telecommunities '95 in Victoria, British Columbia, in August 1995. It appeared in the conference proceedings and was later published in the *Amateur Computerist* 7 (Winter/Spring 1995–1996).

12

"Imminent Death of the Net Predicted!"

The organization of the agricultural industry could not at that period make any marked progress, for the direction of its operations was still in the hands of the feudal class, which could not in general really learn the habits of industrial life, or place itself in sufficient harmony with the workers on its domains. The industry of the towns had to proceed that of the country, and the latter had to be developed mainly through the indirect action of the former.

JOHN KELLY INGRAM, *A HISTORY OF POLITICAL ECONOMY*

In the past three decades a computer users' network has grown up and expanded, connecting computer users around the world. How has this been achieved? What are the lessons that can be learned from these developments? What is the public interest in the current debate over the future direction of the Net?

The creation of time-sharing and interactive computing was supported by United States government funding of Project MAC at MIT, and other time-sharing projects such as Project GENIE at the University of California at Berkeley. Similarly, the development and growth of the ARPANET and then the NSFnet, which made the Internet possible, were funded by public monies. Usenet, on the other hand, was developed by graduate students and researchers at universities, government, and industrial research sites. Some of these sites were supported by government grants. All sites, however, were obligated to make Usenet available to others free of charge in exchange for their news feed.

Usenet and the Internet have thus grown and flourished in a research environment. The development of the Net was the result of the work of many computer pioneers from the academic, government, and research sectors working cooperatively to produce a significant public resource. The creation and expansion of the global network shows under what conditions network development occurs. They demonstrate that an open, cooperative, experimental environment where participants support and help each other, and an environment free from market pressures, commercial time constraints, and "bottom line" considerations, can produce an invaluable public and social communications resource.

On September 15, 1993, the United States government announced a plan to privatize the NSFnet backbone to its portion of the Internet. The plan, the National Information Infrastructure (NII) Agenda for Action, proposed to privatize the public NSF backbone and put network development into the hands of the private sector subject to "market forces." The NII plan contained no examination of the great achievements represented by three decades of networking developments. Nor did it analyze the factors that made this achievement possible.

The plan to privatize the Internet was agreed upon several years earlier at a meeting held March 1–3, 1990, at Harvard University in Cambridge, Massachusetts by the Science, Technology, and Public Policy Program of the John F. Kennedy School of Government. This meeting was described in the document "Commercialization of the Internet: Summary Report" (hereafter, Summary Report).[1]

Attendance at the workshop was by invitation only. Listed participants included representatives from the Congressional Office of Technology Assessment, the Rand Corporation, Brookings Institute, DARPA, MERIT, AT&T, MCI, AMERITECH, EDUCOM, Sprint International, Research Libraries Group, the Department of Commerce's National Telecommunications and Information Administration, the State of Ohio, IBM, Litel Telecommunications, Corporation for National Research Initiatives, Performance Systems International, UUNET, Digital Equipment Corporation, and the National Science Foundation.

The workshop took as its mandate to change the role of the United States government in network development. The Summary Report quotes the Program Plan of the National Research and Education Network (NREN), proposing that "the networks of Stages 2 and 3 will be implemented and operated so that they can become commercialized. . . ."[2] It also proposes that "a specific, structured process" be set in place "resulting in transition of the network from a government operation to a commercial service."

The Summary Report describes how Stephen Wolff of the NSF outlined the acceptable use policy (AUP) that had been governing the NSFnet:

> *Under the draft acceptable use policy in effect from 1988 to mid-1990, use of the NSFNET backbone had to support the purpose of "scientific research and other scholarly activities." The interim policy promulgated in June 1990 is the same, except that the purpose of the NSFNET is now "to support research and education in and among academic institutions in the U.S. by access to unique resources and the opportunity for collaborative work."*

Wolff made the distinction between commercialization and privatization of the NSFnet: "commercialization" is "permitting commercial users and providers to access and use Internet facilities and services," while "privatization" is "the elimination of the federal role in providing or subsidizing network services."

The Summary Report claimed that despite the restrictions on commercial usage of the NSFnet, commercial use was increasing 15–20 percent each month. The problem, Wolff explained, was that such commercial use of the NSF backbone might be creating unfair competition between the U.S. government and "private providers of network services (notably the public X.25 packet-switched networks, such as SprintNet and Tymnet)."

Wolff gave no legal basis for his concern to avoid such so-called "government competition with commercial providers." Such an argument, if accepted, would effectively eliminate all government services to the public, since each might be judged as providing competition with its commercial counterparts (for example, no social security insurance, as that might compete with commercial insurance; no public schools, as they compete with private schools; no post office, as it competes with commercial mail or package delivery). Such an argument eliminates the constitutional obligation of government to provide for the health and welfare of its people.

There is no other documented or reasoned argument offered in the report for abolishing the government role in sponsoring and supporting the NSFnet backbone to the Internet.[3] To the contrary, the participants recognized that it was cheaper and more efficient for government to fund the United States portion of the backbone than to devise other means of funding government supported users. Steve Wolff explained that "it is easier for NSF to simply provide one free backbone to all comers rather than deal with 25 mid-level networks, 500 universities, or perhaps tens or hundreds of thousands of individual researchers."

The report noted that privately-owned and -funded TCP/IP companies would not be concerned with network development but with their bottom-line profits. The Summary Report explains:

> *The market-driven suppliers of TCP/IP-based Internet connectivity are naturally going after those markets that can be wired at a low cost per institution,*

> *i.e., large metropolitan areas, especially those with a high concentration of R&D facilities, such as Boston, San Francisco, and Washington, D.C. . . . This kind of targeted marketing by unregulated companies is widely recognized as cream-skimming.*

These comments demonstrate why market-driven development is contrary to the development of a network infrastructure where all areas need to be connected or the whole network is harmed.

The report also noted that unmetered access to the NSFnet encouraged academic institutions to make access available across disciplines. If, however, the network was metered, access would be limited, impeding increased utilization by broader sectors of the university community.

The report explained that in an academic network, all benefit from each other's contributions as "all networks benefit from access to each other's users and resources," while commercial entities often use the network's resources, but contribute much less to the network. "For example, because of the mailing lists available without charge on the Internet, three times as much traffic runs over the mail gateway from the Internet to MCI MAIL than to the Internet. This pattern is reinforced by the send-pays fee structure of MCI MAIL, which discourages mailing list distribution from within MCI MAIL," explained Wolff.

The Summary Report described the role of the Michigan Educational Research Information Triad (MERIT), part of Michigan's public higher-education system, and the State of Michigan Strategic Fund that provided $5 million to the NSFnet. The Report called MERIT and the State of Michigan "private entrepreneurs in the national operation of a backbone service." The problem with such an analysis is that MERIT and the State of Michigan Strategic Fund are public entities whose mandates are to use public funds to further public education in Michigan. To call them private entrepreneurs is to misrepresent the source and purpose of their funding so as to create an argument for privatization.

The Summary Report did not include dissenting opinions. Instead, the Harvard meeting encouraged the participants, many of whom subsequently became active participants on the com-priv@psi.com mailing list, to vigorously promote this significant change of direction of the NSFnet, without public debate or examination of the virtues or harm to come from such a major change of public policy. On the com-priv@psi.com mailing list, ridicule and personal attacks were used against those who expressed opposition to commercialization and privatization of the NSFnet.

Shortly after the March 1990 Harvard workshop, there were abrupt changes in the contracts between MERIT and the NSF. Reviewing these changes, the Office of the Inspector General (OIG) for the NSF, in a report issued on March 23, 1993, explained: "In April 1990 MERIT submitted a revised statement of work based on the input received from the National Science Foundation, in particular the need for adding nodes to and expanding the switching and transmission capacity for the NSFNET backbone."[4] The report also noted that on May 29, 1990 an amendment to the cooperative proposal that MERIT had with the NSF provided MERIT with funding for the revised proposal.

A significant change in the nature and oversight of the NSFnet then followed, as documented by the Inspector General's report, carrying out steps toward the transition to commercialization and privatization of the NSFnet. The NSF transferred MERIT's responsibilities to Advanced Network & Services, Inc., (ANS was made up of a public entity, MERIT, and private entities, IBM and MCI) and agreed that ANS should seek commercial users for what was previously a network restricted to academic, government, and industry research and scientific use as defined by the Acceptable Use Policy of the NSF.

After several articles by reporter Brock Meeks were published in *Communications Daily* (on February 4, 1992, February 6, 1992, and February 21, 1992), Representative Rick Boucher (D-Va.) held a Congressional hearing of the House Subcommittee on Science, Research, and Technology on March 12, 1992 to examine serious irregularities in the administration and oversight of the NSFnet by the National Science Foundation. After the hearing, the U. S. Inspector General for the NSF was asked to conduct an investigation into the unresolved questions. While the investigation was going on, Congressman Boucher's committee sponsored a change in the law regulating the obligations of the NSF. Rather than waiting for the recommendations of the Inspector General's Office, the United States Congress undermined the very oversight process it had set in motion.

When the OIG Report examined how such a substantial change in policy had come about, it noted that there was a lack of a "reasoned" documentation in NSF files providing for such a significant change of policy.[5] Although the OIG admitted that the United States government had an obligation to hear discussion on such significant changes in policy, the OIG claimed that it was within the NSF's discretion as to whether it does so or not. The Acceptable Use Policy governing the use of the NSFnet continued to be in effect for a period after the Inspector General's Report, but government officials no longer enforced it.

The Acceptable Use Policy was derived from the authority vested in the NSF under the "National Science Foundation Act of 1950, as amended." According to the OIG Report, under this act, the NSF was given the authority "to foster and support the development and use of computer and other scientific and engineering methods and technologies, primarily for research and education in the sciences and engineering."(42 U.S.C. S 1862(a)(4).)

The report explained that in 1989, the NSF drafted an "Acceptable Use Policy (AUP) to define research and education traffic that may properly be conveyed under Section 4(a) of the NSF Act." And "in March 1992, NSF's Office of General Council concluded that 'some form of acceptable use policy' will continue to be necessary to ensure that NSF funds are used to further the objectives of section 3(a)(4) of the Act."

Following is the Acceptable Use Policy (AUP) that governed NSF networking developments. These principles provide helpful guidelines for building and expanding a public computer network. The AUP states:

> *General Principle:*
>
> *(1) NSFNET Backbone services are provided to support open research and education in and among U.S. research and instructional institutions, plus research arms of for-profit firms when engaged in open scholarly communication and research. Use for other purposes is not acceptable.*
>
> *SPECIFICALLY ACCEPTABLE USES:*
>
> *(2) Communication with foreign researchers and educators in connection with research or instruction, as long as any network that the foreign user employs for such communication provides reciprocal access to U.S. researchers and educators.*
>
> *(3) Communication and exchange for professional development, to maintain currency, or to debate issues in a field or subfield of knowledge.*
>
> *(4) Use for disciplinary-society, university-association, government advisory, or standards activities related to the user's research and instructional activities.*
>
> *(5) Use in applying for or administering grants or contracts for research or instruction, but not for other fundraising or public relations activities.*
>
> *(6) Any other administrative communications or activities in direct support of research and instruction.*
>
> *(7) Announcements of new products or activities in direct support of research and instruction, but not advertising of any kind.*
>
> *(8) Any traffic originating from a network of another member agency of the Federal Networking Council if the traffic meets the acceptable use policy of that agency.*
>
> *(9) Communication incidental to otherwise acceptable use, except for illegal or specifically unacceptable use.*

UNACCEPTABLE USES:

(10) Use for for-profit activities unless covered by the General Principle or as a specifically acceptable use.

(11) Extensive use for private or personal business.

This statement applies to use of the NSFNET Backbone only. NSF expects that connecting networks will formulate their own use policies. The NSF Division of the Networking and Communications Research and Infrastructure will resolve any questions about this Policy or its interpretation.[6]

The development and growth of the ARPANET and then the NSF backbone of the United States portion of the Internet were public projects. They were financed by public funds, and the development of the network was guided and nourished by the AUP governing the funding. The AUP required that the research carried out via the Net be open and available to others. Public, educational, and scientific sectors of society need communication and are able to work openly and cooperatively to create public resources. The opposite is true of commercial sectors of society.

"The Review of the NSFNET" from the Office of the Inspector General for the NSF, issued in March 1993, demonstrated the problems that occur when private entities are charged with oversight of a public network. It documented that conflicts of interest can develop. The thrust of privatizing the public backbone to the U.S. portion of the Internet creates a conflict of interest between private commercial entities and the further expansion of the Net for the public benefit.

The Net has grown up in a scientific and research environment. It flourished under the educational and cooperative principles embodied in the AUP. These principles placed the development of the Net into the hands of the public, educational, and scientific sectors of society. Instead, the NII Agenda for Action created a small committee in support of private and commercial interests to recommend how to turn the public Net over to the private sector, thereby subordinating the more advanced academic and public sectors involved with the Net to the private sector. The OIG report recommended that the AUP be strengthened, not removed.

The NII Agenda for Action proposed to subsume the scientific, research, and education network into a privately owned and operated "infrastructure" to serve business. The death of the Net has been predicted many times before. In the past, those who care about the Net have taken such challenges seriously, defending and protecting the Net and the cooperative resources and culture that are the "soul of the Net." The article "Computer Users Battle High-Tech Marketers Over Soul of the Internet" which appeared in the *Wall Street Journal* the day after the NII Agenda for Action was announced documented that the battle will continue.[7]

"Imminent death of the Net predicted. Film at 11:00." :-)[8]

NOTES

1. "Commercialization of the Internet: Summary Report," which was available via ftp from world.std.com. Quotes from the Summary Report are from this source. There is also an account of the same meeting by Brian Kahin in "RFC 1192: Commercialization of the Internet: Summary Report," November 1990.
2. "Commercialization of the Internet: Summary Report."
3. There was, however, an internal NSF policy restricting private entities with NSF funding (but not restricting the government) from gaining a commercial advantage from their NSF–supported work. Following is a description of this policy:

   NSF has a long-standing policy prohibiting NSF awardees from using NSF–supported facilities commercially in a manner that may have a material and deleterious effect on the success of private companies engaged in the provision of equivalent services (NSF Important Notice No. 91 [11 March 1983], quoted in "Review of the NSFNET," Office of the Inspector General, National Science Foundation, 23 March 1993, footnote on page 28).

4. "Revised Statement of Work/NSF Supplemental Proposal No. 8944037," April 20, 1990, quoted in "Review of the NSFNET," 11.
5. "The record is utterly barren of documentation of NSF's reasoning for allowing commercial use of the network. . . . Important program decisions, particularly those involving a program as large as NSFNET must be both well-reasoned and well-documented ("Review of the NSFNET," 27–28)."
6. *Ibid.*, 69–70.
7. Steve Stecklow, "Computer Users Battle High-Tech Marketers Over Soul of Internet," *Wall Street Journal,* September 16, 1993, 1.
8. For some of the history of the phrase "Imminent death of the Net predicted," see chapters 2 and 3 of this volume.

An earlier version of this chapter by Ronda Hauben appeared in the *Amateur Computerist* 5 (Summer/Fall 1993).

13

The Effect of the Net on the Professional News Media

The Usenet News Collective/ The Man–Computer News Symbiosis

The archdeacon contemplated the gigantic cathedral for a time in silence, then he sighed and stretched out his right hand towards the printed book lying open on his table and his left hand towards Notre-Dame, and he looked sadly from the book to the church:

"Alas," he said, "this will kill that". . . .

VICTOR HUGO, *NOTRE DAME DE PARIS*

MEDIA-CRITICISM

Will this kill that? Will the new online forms of discourse dethrone the professional news media? The French writer Victor Hugo observed that the printed book rose to replace the cathedral and the church as the conveyor of important ideas in the fifteenth century. Will Usenet and other young online discussion forums develop to replace the current news media? Various people throughout society are currently discussing this question.

The role of modern journalism is being reconsidered in a variety of ways. There are journalists and media critics, such as the late Professor Christopher Lasch, who have challenged the fundamental premises of professional journalism. There are other journalists, such as *Wall Street Journal* reporter Jared Sandberg, who cover an online beat and who are learning quickly about the growing online public forums. These two approaches are beginning to converge, making it possible to understand the changes in the role of the media in our society brought about by the development of the Internet and Usenet.

Media critics such as Christopher Lasch have established a theoretical foundation that makes it possible to critique the news media and to challenge the current practice of this media. In "Journalism, Publicity, and the Lost Art of Argument," Lasch argued:

> *What democracy requires is public debate, and not information. Of course, it needs information, too, but the kind of information it needs can be generated only by vigorous popular debate.*[1]

Applying his critique to the press, Lasch wrote:

> *From these considerations it follows the job of the press is to encourage debate, not to supply the public with information. But as things now stand the press generates information in abundance, and nobody pays any attention.*[2]

Lasch explained that more and more people are getting less and less interested in the press because, "Much of the press . . . now delivers an abundance of useless, indigestible information that nobody wants, most of which ends up as unread waste."[3]

Reporters such as Jared Sandberg of the *Wall Street Journal*, on the other hand, recognize that more and more of the information that the public is interested in is starting to come from people other than professional journalists. In an article about the April 1995 Oklahoma Federal building explosion, Sandberg wrote:

> *In times of crisis, the Internet has become the medium of choice for users to learn more about breaking news, often faster than many news organizations can deliver it.*[4]

People curious and concerned about relatives and others present on the scene turned to the Net to find timely information about survivors and to discuss the questions raised by the event. Soon after the explosion took place, it was reported and discussed live on Internet Relay Chat (IRC) and in newsgroups on Usenet (such as alt.current-events.amfb-explosion) and elsewhere online. Sandberg noted that many logged on to the Internet to get news from first-hand observers rather than turning on the television to CNN or comparable news sources.

Along with the broader strata of the population which has begun to report and discuss the news via the Internet and Usenet, a broader definition of who is a media critic is developing. Journalists and media critics like Martha

Fitzsimon and Lawrence T. McGill present such a definition when they write, "Everyone who watches television, listens to a radio or reads . . . passes judgment on what they see, hear or read."[5] Acknowledging the public's discontent with the traditional forms of the media, they note that, "the evaluations of the media put forward by the public are grim and getting worse."[6]

Other journalists have written about public criticism of the news media. In his article, "Encounters On-Line," Thomas Valovic recognizes some of the advantages inherent in the new online form of criticism. Unlike old criticism, the new type "fosters dialogue between reporters and readers."[7] He observes how this dialogue "can subject reporters to interrogations by experts that undermine journalists' claim to speak with authority."[8]

Changes are taking place in the field of journalism, and these changes are apparent to some, but not all, journalists and media critics. Tom Goldstein, then Dean of the University of California, Berkeley Journalism School, acknowledged that change is occurring, but that the results are not fully understood.[9]

EXAMINING THE ROLE OF INTERNET/USENET AND THE PRESS

There are discussions online about the role of the press and the role of online discussion forums. The debate is active, and there are those who believe the print press is here to stay, while others contend that interactive discussion forums are likely to replace the authority of the print news media. Those who argue for the dominance of the online media present impassioned and well-reasoned arguments. Their comments are much more persuasive than those who defend the traditional role of the print media as something that is handy to read over breakfast or on the train. In a newsgroup thread discussing the future of print journalism, Gloria Stern stated:

> *My experience is that I have garnered more information from the internet than I ever could from any newspaper. Topical or not, it has given me community that I never had before. I touch base with more informed kindred souls than any tonnage of paper could ever bring me.*[10]

Regularly, people online are commenting on how they have stopped reading newspapers. Even those who continue to read printed newspapers note that Usenet has become one of their important sources of news. For example, a user wrote:

> *I _do_ get the NYT every day, and the Post and the Washington Times and the Wall Street Journal (along with about 100 other hardcopy publications),*

and I _still_ find usenet a valuable source of in-depth news reporting.[11]

More and more people on Usenet have announced their discontent with the traditional one-way media, often leading to their refusal to seriously read newspapers again. In a discussion about a *Time* magazine article about the Internet and Usenet, Elizabeth Fischer wrote:

> *The point of the whole exercise is that for us, most of us, paper media is a dead issue (so to speak).*[12]

In the same thread, Jim Zoes stated the challenge posed for reporters by the online media:

> *This writer believes that you (the traditional press) face the same challenge that the monks in the monastery faced when Gutenberg started printing Bibles.*[13]

Describing why the new media represents such a formidable foe, Zoes continued:

> *Your top-down model of journalism allows traditional media to control the debate, and even if you provide opportunity for opposing views, the editor *always* had the last word. In the new paradigm, not only do you not necessarily have the last word, you no longer even control the flow of the debate.*[14]

He concludes with his understanding of the value of Usenet to society:

> *The growth and acceptance of email, coupled with discussion groups (Usenet) and mail lists provide for a "market place of ideas" hitherto not possible since perhaps the days of the classic Athenians.*[15]

Others present their views on a more personal level. One poster writes:

> *I will not purchase another issue of Newsweek. I won't even glance through their magazine if it's lying around now given what a shoddy job they did on that article.*[16]

Another writes:

> *My husband brought [an article] home. . .for me to read and [I] said, "Where is that damn followup key? ARGH!" I've pretty much quit reading mainstream media except when someone puts something in front of me or I'm riding the bus to work. . . .*[17]

These are just some recent examples of people voicing their discontent with the professional news media. The online forum provides a public way of sharing this discontent with others. It is in sharing ideas and understanding with others with similar views that grassroots efforts to change society begin.

While some of those online have stopped reading the professional news media, others are interested in influencing the media to more accurately portray the Net. Many are critical of the news media's reporting of the Internet and other events. Users of the Internet are interested in protecting the Internet. They do this by watch-dogging politicians and journalists. Concern with press coverage of the Internet comes from first-hand experience with the Internet. One netuser expressing such dissatisfaction writes:

> *The net is a special problem for reporters, because bad reporting in other areas is protected by distance. If someone reports to the Times from Croatia, you're not going to have a better source unless you've been there (imagine how many people in that part of the world could correct the reports we read). All points of Usenet are equidistant from the user and the reporter—we can check their accuracy at every move. And what do we notice? Not the parts that the reporter gets right, just the errors. And Usenet is such a complete culture that no reporter, absent some form of formal training or total immersion in the net, is going to get it all right.*[18]

Another online critic writes:

> *It's scary when you actually are familiar with what a journalist is writing about. Kinda punches a whole bunch of holes in the "facts." Unfortunately it's been going on for a looooooong time . . . we, the general viewing public, just aren't up to speed on the majority of issues. That whole "faith in media" thing. Yick. I can't even trust the damn AP wire anymore after reading an enormous amount of total crap on it during the first few hours of the Oklahoma bombing.*[19]

In Usenet's formation of a community, that community has developed the self-awareness to respond to and reject outside descriptions of the Net. If the Net were just the telephone line and computer infrastructure making up a machine, that very machine couldn't object and scold journalists for describing it as a pornography press or a bomb-production press. Wesley Howard believes that the critical online commentary is having a healthy effect on the press:

> *The coverage has become more accurate and less sloppy in its coverage of the Net because it (the Net) has become more defined itself from a cultural point of view. Partly because of growth and partly because of what the media was saying fed debates and caused a firmer definition within itself . . . This does not mean the print media was in any way responsible for the Net's self definition, but was one influence of many.*[20]

Another person, writing from Japan, believed that journalists should be more responsible, urging that "all journalists should be forced to have an e-mail address." He explained:

> *Journalists usually have a much bigger audience than their critics. I often feel a sense of helplessness in trying to counter the damage they cause when they abuse their privilege. Often it is impossible even to get the attention of the persons responsible for the lies and distortions.*[21]

Usenet newsgroups and mailing lists provide a media where people are in control. People who are online understand the value of this control and are trying to articulate their understandings. Some of this discussion is being carried on on Usenet. Having the ability to control a mass media also encourages people to try and affect other media. The proposal to require print journalists to make available an e-mail address is an example of how online users are trying to apply the lessons learned from the online media to change the print media.

PEOPLE AS CRITICS: THE ROLE THE NET IS PLAYING AND WILL PLAY IN THE FUTURE

People online are excited, and this is not an exaggeration. The various discussion forums connected to the Net are the prototype for a new public form of communication. This new form of human communication will either supplement the current forms of news or replace them. One person on a newsgroup succinctly stated: "The real news is right here. And it can't get any newer because I watch it as it happens."[22]

The very concept of news is being reinvented as people begin to realize that they can provide the news about the environment they live in and their real-life conditions and this information proves worthwhile for others. The post continued:

> *As other segments of society come online, we will have less and less need for some commercially driven entity that gathers the news for me, filters it, and then delivers it to me, hoping fervently that I'll find enough of interest to keep paying for it.*[23]

Such sentiment represents a fundamental challenge to the professional creation and dissemination of news. The online discussion forums allow open and free discourse. Individuals outside of the traditional power structures are finding a forum in which to contribute, where those contributions are welcomed. Describing the importance of the open forum available on the Net, Dolores Dege wrote:

> *The most important and eventually most powerful aspect of the net will be*

> *the effect(s) of having access to alternative viewpoints to the published and usually (although not always either intentionally or consciously) biased local news media. This access to differing "truths" is similar to the communication revolution which occurred when the first printing presses made knowledge available to the common populace, instead of held in the tight fists of the clergy and ruling classes.*[24]

This change in who makes the news is also apparent to Keith Cowing:

> *How one becomes a "provider" and "receiver" of information is being totally revamped. The status quo hasn't quite noticed—yet—THIS is what is so interesting.*[25]

While this openness also encourages different conspiracy theorists and crackpots to write messages, their contributions are scrutinized as much as any other posting. This uncensored environment leads to a sorting out of mistruths from thoughtful convictions. Many people online keep their wits about them, and seek to refute half-truths and lies. A post from Australia notes that it is common to post refutations of inaccurate posts:

> *One of the good things about USEnet is the propensity of people to post refutations of false information that others have posted.*[26]

Because the online media is in the control of many people, no one person can come online and drastically alter the flow or quality of discussion. The multiplicity of ideas and opinions make Usenet and mailing lists the opposite of a free-for-all.

QUALITIES OF THIS NEW MEDIUM

A common assumption of the ethic of individualism is that the individual is in control and is the prime mover of society. Others believe that it is not the individual who is in control, but that society is being controlled by people organized around the various large corporations that own so much of our society—whether those corporations are involved in the media, in manufacturing, or in other industries. The global computer communication networks currently allow uncensored expression from the individual at a bottom rung of society. The grassroots connection of people around the world and in local communities, based on common interests, is an important step in bringing people more control over their lives. Lisa Pease wrote in alt.journalism:

> *There is nothing like finding a group of people who share your same interests and background knowledge. Some of my interests I didn't know one person in a hundred that shared—and now I've met many. What makes it a community is ultimately in-person meetings.*[27]

She continued on in her message to state why such connections and discussions are important:

> *The net . . . requires no permissions, no groveling to authority, no editors to deal with—no one basically to say "no don't say that." As a result—far more has been said here publicly than has probably been said in a hundred years about issues that really matter—political prisoners, democratic uprisings, exposure of disinformation—THIS is what makes the net more valuable than any other news source.*[28]

Similar views are expressed by others about the power of the Internet to work in favor of people rather than commercial conglomerates:

> *The internet is our last hope for a medium that will enable individuals to combat the overpowering influence of the commercial media to shape public opinion, voter attitudes, select candidates, influence legislation, etc. . .*[29]

People are beginning to be empowered by the open communication that online media provide. This empowerment is beginning to lead to more active involvement by people in the societal issues they care about.

THE PENTIUM STORY

In discussions about the future of the online media, people have observed how Usenet makes it possible to challenge the privileges inherent in the traditional news media. For example, John Pike started a thread describing the challenge the Net presents to the former content providers:

> *To me this is the really exciting opportunity for usenet, namely that the professional content providers will be directly confronted with and by their audience. The prevailing infostructure privileges certain individuals by virtue of institutional affiliation. But cyberspace is a far more meritocratic environment—the free exchange of ideas can take place regardless of institutional affiliation.*[30]

Pike continues by arguing that online forums are becoming a place where "news" is both made and reported, and thus traditional sources are often scooped. He writes:

> *This has tremendously exciting possibilities for democratizing the infostructure, as the "official" hardcopy implementations are increasingly lagging cyberspace in breaking news.*[31]

An example of news being made online occurred when Intel, the computer chip manufacturer, was forced to recall faulty Pentium chips because of online pressure and the effect of that pressure on computer manufacturers such as IBM and Gateway. These companies put pressure on Intel because people using Usenet discovered problems with the Pentium chip. Online discussion led to people becoming active and getting the manufacturers of their computers and Intel to fix the problems.

In the article "On-Line Snits Fomenting Public Storms," *Wall Street Journal* reporters Bart Ziegler and Jared Sandberg commented:

> *Some industry insiders say that had the Pentium flub occurred five years ago, before the Internet got hot and the media caught on, Intel might have escaped a public flogging and avoided a costly recall.*[32]

Buried in the report is the acknowledgment that the traditional press would not have caught the defect in the Pentium chip, but that the online media forced the traditional media to respond. The original reporting about the problem was done in the Usenet newsgroup comp.sys.intel, and further online discussion took place in that newsgroup, in other newsgroups, and on Internet mailing lists. The *Wall Street Journal* reporters recognized their debt to online posts which came up with a story that dealt with a major computer company and with the real-world role played by Usenet.

In another *Wall Street Journal* article, reporter Fara Warner focused on the impact on Intel of the online news. "[Intel] offered consumers a promise of reliability and quality, and now that promise has been called into question," she writes, quoting the CEO of a consulting firm.[33] The people raising these questions were the users of computers with the faulty chips. By communicating about the problem online, these users were able to have an impact not otherwise possible. Ziegler and Sandberg noted that the discussions were online rather than in "traditional public forums like trade journals, newspapers, or the electronic media."[34] Online users were able to work together to deal with a problem, instead of depending on other forums traditionally associated with reporting dissatisfaction with consumer goods. After all of the criticisms, Intel had to replace faulty chips in order to keep their reputation viable. *The Wall Street Journal, New York Times,* and other newspapers and magazines played second fiddle to what was happening online. In their article, Ziegler and Sandberg quote Dean Goldstein: "It's absolutely changing how journalism is practiced in ways that aren't fully developed."[35] These journalists acknowledge that the field of journalism is changing as a result of the existence of such online complaints. The online connection of people is forming a large and important social force.

As a community where news is made, reported, and discussed, Usenet has been a hotbed of more than just technical developments. Other stories have included the Church of Scientology and the suppression of speech. An Australian reporter, John Hilvert, commented on the value of being online:

> *It [Usenet] can be a great source of leads about the mood of the Net. The recent GIF-Unisys-Compuserve row and the Intel Pentium bug are examples of USENET taking an activist and educative role.*[36]

Nevertheless, Hilvert warned about the authenticity of information available online:

> *However the risk is you can easily be spooked by stuff on the Net. Things have to be shaped, confirmed and tested off-line as well. One of the interesting side-effects of USENet is that we have to work even harder to get a good story because, there is not much value-added in just summarizing a USENet discussion.*[37]

With Usenet it is not necessary to rely on any single piece of information. Usenet is not about ideas in a vacuum. Usenet is about discussion and discourse. Tom Kimball, in a Usenet post, writes about the value of a public Usenet discussion:

> *I have great respect for the usenet ideal of everyone having the chance to respond to the ideas of others and the resulting exchanges of information and clashes of ideas I think is of some value (despite the flame-war garbage that gets in the way).*[38]

The great number and range of unedited posts on Usenet brings up the question of whether editors are needed to deal with the amount of information. Discussing the need to take time to deal with the growing amount of information, a post on alt.internet.media-coverage commented:

> *The difference being that for the first time in human history, the general populace has the ability to determine what it finds important, rather than relying on the whims of those who knew how to write, or controlled the printing presses. It means that we as individuals are going to have to deal with sifting through a lot of information on our own, but in the end I believe that we will all benefit from it.*[39]

Such posts lead to the question of what is meant by the general populace and a popular press. The point is important, as those who are on the Net make up but a small percentage of the total population of either the United States or the world. However, that online population of an estimated 27.5 million people[40] is a significant body of people connecting to each other online. The fast rate of growth also makes one take note of trends and developments. Defining general populace and a popular press, the post continues:

> *By general populace, I mean those who can actually afford a computer, and a connection to the 'net, or have access to a public terminal. As computer prices go down, the amount of people who fit this description will increase. At any rate, comparing the 5–10 million people with USENET access, to the handful who control the mass media shows that even in a nascent stage, USENET is far more the "people's voice" than any media conglomerate could ever be.*[41]

The comments from the last two people lead to asking whether or not the new technologies are helping the human species to evolve or to deal with the ever-increasing amount of information. Computer pioneers like Norbert Wiener, J. C. R. Licklider, and John Kemeny discussed the need for man–computer symbiosis to help humans deal with the growing problems of our times.[42] The online discussion forums provide a new form of man–computer symbiosis. They are helpful intellectual exercises. It is healthy for society if all members think and make active use of their brains—and Usenet is conducive to thinking. It is not the role of journalists to provide us with the answers. Even if people's lives are busy, what happens when they come to depend on the opinions and summaries of others as their own? Usenet is helping to create a mass community that works communally to aid the individual. Usenet works via the active involvement and thoughtful contributions of each user. Usenet software facilitates the creation of a community whose thought processes can accumulate and benefit the entire community. The creation of the book and the printed book helped to increase the speed of the accumulation of ideas. Usenet now speeds up that process further to help accumulate the thoughts of the moment. The resulting discussion seen on Usenet could not have been produced beforehand as the work of one individual. The bias or point of view of any one individual is no longer presented as the whole truth.

Karl Krueger describes some of the value of Usenet in a post:

> *Over time, USENETters get better at being parts of the USENET matrix—because their *own* condensations support USENET's, and this helps other users. In a way, USENET is a "meta-symbiont" with each user—the user is a part of USENET and benefits USENET (with a few exceptions. . .), and USENET includes the user and benefits him/her.*[43]

Krueger points out how experienced Usenet users contribute to the Usenet community. He writes:

> *As time increases normally, the experienced USENET user uses USENET to make himself more knowledgeable and successful. Experienced users also contribute back to USENET, primarily in the forms of conveying knowledge (answering questions, compiling FAQs), conveying experience (being part of*

> *the environment a newbie interacts with), and protecting USENET (upholding responsible and non-destructive use, canceling potentially damaging spam, fighting "newsgroup invasions," etc.).*[44]

As new users connect to Usenet, and learn from others, the Usenet collective grows and becomes one person richer. Krueger continues:

> *Provided that all users are willing to spend the minimal amount of effort to gain some basic USENET experience then they can be added to this loop. In USENET, old users gain their benefits from other old users, while simultaneously bringing new users into the old-users group to gain benefits.*[45]

The collective body of people, assisted by the Usenet software, has grown larger than any individual newspaper. As people continue to connect to Usenet and other discussion forums, the collective global population will contribute back to the human community in this new form of news.

JOURNALISTS AND THE INTERNET

Professional journalists are beginning to understand that the online discussion forums will change their field, although they may not fully understand what the changes will be. After my posing the question "What, if any, effect do Usenet News and mailing lists have on reporters and editors you are in contact with?" several journalists responded. Some stated that Usenet and mailing lists are valuable information and opinion gathering tools that also help them to get in touch with experts, while others are either timid about the new technology or do not want to bother with yet another reporting tool. Several of the reporters stated that they do not participate in any discussion forums *per se,* but rather lurk in these areas and contact posters who they feel will have valuable information for a story by e-mail. Their main concern was that they might waste time online trying to get information when there would only be a small amount of worthwhile material from a lot of waste. Lastly, one or two did not see any value in online discussion forums, and have stayed away from them after initial negative impressions.

These reporters were asked if they sensed any pressure to get Internet accounts or to connect to Usenet and mailing lists. Josh Quittner of *Time* said the pressure came from the publishing side, as publishers are looking for the development of new markets. John Verity of *Business Week* and Lorraine Goods of *Time Interactive* said editors are responding to interest about the Internet and want stories about it. Brock Meeks, an independent journalist, stated that the pressure comes from reporters such as himself who have been online for some time and have beaten other reporters to stories because of the power of online communications. Some reported that they understood that it was important to get online without knowing why. A few said that there is no push for them to go online.

Asked whether it is important to be online, some did not see it as necessary, given that they are already connected to those they consider to be experts in their respective fields without being online. Others felt the speed of e-mail helped them gather timely information for the stories they were working on. Farhon Memon of the *New York Post* compared today's online forums to conferences because they make contacting experts much easier both in terms of time and place.

When asked about the best forms of reader feedback, a number of journalists stated that letters to the editor and op-ed pages were helpful. One reporter noted that letters to the editor were not particularly heeded. E-mail was named as the next most important means for readers to send in commentary. Whether or not this commentary is listened to is another story. One reporter did suggest that the online criticism, correct or not, encourages journalists to do the best possible job.

When it came to the question of whether online discussion forums would ever replace newspapers, the journalists almost universally stated that each form has its own role to play. Quittner didn't think traditional journalists would evolve into online discussion leaders. Such a job might emerge, but not as an additional responsibility of the regular journalist. Maia Szalavitz responded:

> *The print media can't beat online stuff for interactivity; online stuff can't beat print journalism for organization, ease of portability and use at this point.*[46]

Goods offered a similar analysis:

> *An online news outfit can obviously do things that print cannot. However, there are certain things you can do with a newspaper that you can't do on a computer (like read it on the subway on the way to work, or in the bathroom). Just as tv did not replace radio, computers will not replace newspapers. I do think, however, that the introduction of new media will have an effect on traditional media. What those effects will be, however, I don't know.*[47]

There is a growing trend of journalists coming online for various reasons. Some use the Net as a new information source, and some look for people to interview. Lastly, there are those who are actually joining the community or responding to their reading audience. A growing number of journalists have participated in such newsgroups as alt.internet.media-coverage, alt.journalism.criticism, alt.news-media, in forums on some of the commercial online services and in online communities such as the Well, among other places.[48]

Reporters are entering the discussion and both asking for people's suggestions on how to improve their coverage of the Internet and for remarks on their stories.

Newspapers and magazines are developing online counterparts to their print editions (for example, the *San Jose Mercury News* and *Business Week*) on commercial online services such as Prodigy and America Online and are experimenting with new content differing from their print editions on the World Wide Web (WWW) (for example, *HotWired, Time On-Line, NandoNet*). These online offerings sometimes provide another interface between journalists and readers. Message areas or public discussion boards are offered along with e-mail addresses for particular journalists or for letters to the editor.[49]

CONCLUSION

Newspapers and magazines are a convenient form for dealing with information transfer. People have grown accustomed to reading them wherever and whenever they please. The growing dissatisfaction with the print media is more with the content than with the form. There is a significant criticism that the current print media does not allow for a dynamic response or follow-up to the articles in hand. One possible direction would be toward online distribution and home or on-site printing. This would allow the convenience of the traditional newspaper and magazine form to be connected to the dynamic conversation that online Netnews allows. The reader could choose how much of the discussion to make a part of the printed form. But this leaves out the element of interactivity. Still, it could be a temporary solution until the time when ubiquitous slate computers with mobile networks would allow the combination of a light, easy-to-handle screen with a continuous connection to the Internet from any location.

Newspapers could continue to provide entertainment in the form of cross-word puzzles, comics, classified ads, and entertainment sections (for example, entertainment, lifestyles, sports, fashion, gossip, reviews, coupons, and so on). However, the real challenge comes in what is traditionally known as news, or information and newly breaking events from around the world. Citizen, or now Netizen, reporters are challenging the premise that authoritative professional reporters are the only possible reporters of the news. The news of the day is biased and opinionated no matter how many claims for objectivity exist in the world of journalism. In addition, the choice of what becomes news is clearly subjective. Now that more people are gaining a voice on the open public electronic discussion forums, previously unheard "news" is being made available. The current professional news reporting is not really reporting the news, rather it is reporting the news as decided by a certain set of economic or political interests. Todd Masco contrasts the two contending forms of the news media:

> *Free communication is essential to the proper functioning of an open, free society such as ours. In recent years, the functioning of this society has been impaired by the monolithic control of our means of communication and news gathering (through television and conglomerate-owned newspapers). This monolithic control allows issues to be talked about only really in terms that only the people who control the media and access to same can frame . . . USENET, and News in general, changes this: it allows real debate on issues, allowing perspectives from all sides to be seen.*[50]

Journalists may survive, but they will be secondary to the symbiosis that the combination of the Usenet software, computers, and the Usenet community produces. Karl Krueger observes how the Usenet collective is evolving to join man and machine into a news gathering, sorting, and disseminating body. He writes:

> *There is no need for Official Summarizers (aka journalists) on USENET, because everyone does it—by crossposting, following-up, forwarding relevant articles to other places, maintaining FTP archives and WWW indexes of USENET articles (yes, FTP and WWW are Internet things, not USENET things—but if USENET articles are stored in them, the metaphor extends).*[51]

He continues:

> *Journalists will never replace software. The purpose of journalists is similar to scribes in medieval times: to provide an information service when there is insufficient technology or insufficient general skill at using it. I'm not insulting journalism; it is a respectable profession and useful. But you won't *need* a journalist when you have a good enough newsreader/browser and know how to use it.*[52]

These online commentators echo Victor Hugo's description of how the printed book grew up to replace the authority that the cathedral had represented in earlier times. Hugo wrote:

> *This was the presentiment that as human ideas changed their form they would change their mode of expression, that the crucial idea of each generation would no longer be written in the same material or in the same way, that the book of stone, so solid and durable, would give way to the book of paper, which was more solid and durable still.*[53]

Today, similarly, the need for a broader and more cooperative gathering and reporting of the news has helped create the new online media that is gradually supplanting traditional forms of journalism. Professional media critics writing in the Freedom Forum's *Media Studies Journal* acknowledge that online critics and news gatherers are presenting a challenge to the professional news media that can lead to their overthrow:

> *News organizations can weather the blasts of professional media critics, but their credibility cannot survive if they lose the trust of the multitude of citizen critics throughout the United States.*[54]

As more and more people come online and realize the grassroots power of becoming a Netizen reporter, the professional news media must evolve a new role or it will be increasingly marginalized.

NOTES

1. Christopher Lasch, "Journalism, Publicity, and the Lost Art of Argument," *Media Studies Journal* 9 (Winter 1995): 81.
2. *Ibid.*
3. *Ibid.*, 91.
4. Jared Sandberg, "Oklahoma City Blast Turns Users Onto Internet for Facts, Some Fiction," *Wall Street Journal*, April 20, 1995, A6.
5. Martha Fitzsimon and Lawrence T. McGill, "The Citizen as Media Critic," *Media Studies Journal* 9 (Spring 1995): 91.
6. *Ibid.*
7. Thomas S. Volovic, "Encounters On-Line," *Media Studies Journal* 9 (Spring 1995): 115.
8. *Ibid.*
9. Bart Ziegler and Jared Sandberg, "On-Line Snits Fomenting Public Storms," *Wall Street Journal*, December 23, 1994, B1.
10. From: Gloria Stern
    Date: 7 Apr 1995
    Subject: Re: Future of print journalism
    Newsgroups: alt.journalism
    Message-ID:<1995Apr7.214157.11293@lafn.org>
11. From: John Pike
    Date: 24 Apr 1995
    Subject: Re: Usenet's political power (was Re: Content Providers—Professionals versus Amateurs on Usenet)
    Newsgroups: alt.culture.usenet
    Message-ID: <3ngntr$giu@clarknet.clark.net>
12. From: Elizabeth Fischer
    Date: 20 July 1994
    Subject: Re: TIME Cover Story: pipeline to editors

Newsgroups: Alt.internet.media-coverage
Message-ID: <efischer-200794133211@pme16.pomo.wis.net>

13. From: Jim Zoes
Date: 22 July 1994
Subject: Re: TIME Cover Story: pipeline to editors
Newsgroups: alt.internet.media-coverage
Message-ID: <30nmf4$bgg@News1.mcs.com>
14. *Ibid.*
15. *Ibid.*
16. From: Catherine Stanton
Date: 21 July 1994
Subject: Re: TIME Cover Story: pipeline to editors
Newsgroups: alt.internet.media-coverage
Message-ID: <30ltmc$huu@rodan.UU.NET>
17. From: Abby Franquemont-Guillory
Date: 22 July 1994 13:45:19 -0500
Subject: Re: TIME Cover Story: pipeline to editors
Newsgroups: alt.internet.media-coverage
Message-ID: <30p43v$5o6@xochi.tezcat.com>
18. From: The Nutty Professor
Date: Mon 16 Jan 1995 13:35:34 GMT
Subject: Re: Reporter Seeking Net-Abuse Comments
Newsgroups: alt.internet.media-coverage
Message-ID: <D2I33A.MtC@dorsai.org>
19. From: Mikez
Date: Tue 25 Apr 95 03:58:55 GMT
Subject: Re: Mass media exploiting 'cyberspace' for ratings . . .
Newsgroups: alt.journalism.criticism
Message-ID: <3nhs1v$cds_002@news.cris.com>
20. From: Wesley Howard
Date: 8 Apr 1995 05:39:43 GMT
Subject: Re: Does Usenet have an effect on the print news media?
Newsgroups: alt.internet.media-coverage
Message-ID: <3m57iv$m90@ddi2.digital.net>
21. From: John DeHoog
Date: Fri 21 Apr 1995 20:01:24 +0900
Subject: Make journalists get an email address!
Newsgroups: alt.journalism
Message-ID: <ABBDBF94966820B78D@ppp017.st.rim.or.jp>
22. Message-Id: <elknox.35.00091823@bsu.idbsu.edu>
23. *Ibid.*
24. Delores Dege, "Re: Impact of the Net on Society," e-mail message, February 21, 1995.

25. From: Keith L. Cowing
Subject: Re: Content Providers—Professionals versus Amateurs on Usenet
Newsgroups: alt.culture.internet
Date: Mon 17 Apr 1995 12:33:23-0500
Message-ID: <kcowing-1704951233230001@168.143.0.239>
26. From: William Logan Lee
Subject: Re: Is hobby computing dead?
Newsgroups: alt.folklore.computers
Message-ID: <1993Apr6.121613.16236@ucc.su.OZ.AU>
27. From: Lisa Pease
Date: Wed 5 Apr 1995 23:17:24 GMT
Subject: Re: Future of print journalism
Newsgroups: alt.journalism
Message-ID: <lpeaseD6L4p0.2K0@netcom.com>
28. *Ibid.*
29. From: Norman
Date: 20 Mar 1995 21:05:54 -0500
Subject: Re: Impact of the Net on Society
Newsgroups: alt.culture.internet
Message-ID: <3klca2$ma1@newsbf02.news.aol.com>
30. From: John Pike
Date: 17 Apr 1995 12:21:49 GMT
Subject: Content Providers—Professionals versus Amateurs on Usenet
Message-ID: <3mtmgt$56a@clarknet.clark.net>
31. *Ibid.*
32. Ziegler and Sandberg.
33. Fara Warner, "Experts Surprised Intel Isn't Reaching Out To Consumers More," *Wall Street Journal*, December 14, 1994.
34. Ziegler and Sandberg.
35. *Ibid.*
36. From: John Hilvert
Date: Wed 5 Apr 1995 03:40:57 GMT
Subject: Re: Does Usenet have an effect on the print news media?
Newsgroups: alt.culture.usenet
Message-ID: <hilvertj.107.2F821149@ozemail.com.au>
37. *Ibid.*
38. From: Tom Kimball
Date: Thu 26 Aug 1993 02:25:28 GMT
Subject: Usenet impact upon reading habits and skills
Message-ID: <1993Aug26.022528.6376@europa.lonestar.org>
39. From: Miskatonic Gryn
Date: 17 Apr 1995 15:31:22 -0400
Subject: Re: Cliff Stoll

Newsgroups: alt.internet.media-coverage
Message-ID: <3mufmt$47n@iii1.iii.net>

40. The number of people accessible via e-mail was placed at 27.5 million as of October 1994, according to John Quarterman and MIDS at http://www.tic.com/mids/howbig.html
41. Miskatonic Gryn
42. See John Kemeny, *Man and the Computer*, J. C. R. Licklider, "Man–Computer Symbiosis," Norbert Wiener, *God & Golem, Inc.*
43. From: Karl A. Krueger
Date: Mon 27 Mar.1995 08:58:33 GMT
Subject: Re: Special Issue of TIME: Welcome to Cyberspace
Newsgroups: alt.internet.media-coverage
Message-ID: <D63CxL.DJv@plato.simons-rock.edu>
44. *Ibid.*
45. *Ibid.*
46. Maia Szalavitz, "Re: Questions about the effect of Usenet on journalism," e-mail message, April 18, 1995.
47. Lorraine Goods, "Questions about the effect of Usenet on journalism," e-mail message, April 23, 1995.
48. While I was writing this paper, there was a debate online over moving discussion from alt.internet.media-coverage into a new newsgroup tentatively called talk.media.net-coverage.
49. Jennifer Wolff wrote an interesting article entitled "Opening Up Online: What Happens When the Public Comes at You from Cyberspace," *Columbia Journalism Review* (Nov./Dec. 1994): 62–65.
50. From: L. Todd Masco
(No Subject Line)
Newsgroups: news.future,comp.society.futures,ny.general
51. Karl A. Krueger.
52. *Ibid.*
53. Victor Hugo, *Notre Dame of Paris*, John Sturrock, trans. (London: Penguin Books, 1978), 189.
54. Fitzsimon and McGill, 201.

An earlier version of this chapter by Michael Hauben was presented at INET '96 in Montreal, Quebec, in June 1996. It was printed in the *Amateur Computerist* 7 (Winter 1997).

14

The Net and the Future of Politics
The Ascendancy of the Commons

What democracy requires is public debate. . . . We do not know what we need to know until we ask the right questions, and we can identify the right questions only by subjecting our own ideas about the world to the test of public controversy.

CHRISTOPHER LASCH, "JOURNALISM, PUBLICITY, AND THE LOST ART OF ARGUMENT"

Throughout American history, the town meeting has been the premier, and often the only, example of "direct democracy". . . . The issue of whether the town meeting can be redesigned to empower ordinary citizens, as it was intended to do, is of vital concern for the future.

JEFFREY B. ABRAMSON, "ELECTRONIC TOWN MEETINGS: PROPOSALS FOR DEMOCRACY'S FUTURE"

INTRODUCTION

Democracy, or rule by the people, is by definition a popular form of government. Writers throughout the ages have thought about democracy and understood the limitations imposed by various factors. Today, computer communications networks, such as Usenet and the Internet, are technical innovations which make true participatory democracy more feasible.

James Mill, a political theorist of the early nineteenth century and the father of philosopher John Stuart Mill, wrote about democracy in his 1825 essay, "On Government" for that year's *Supplement for the Encyclopedia Britannica.* Mill argued that democracy is the only governmental form that is fair to society as a whole. Although he did not trust representative government, he ended up advocating it. But he warned of its dangers:

> *Whenever the powers of Government are placed in any hands other than those of the community, whether those of one man, of a few, or of several, those principles of human nature which imply that Government is at all necessary, imply that those persons will make use of them to defeat the very end for which Government exists.*[1]

Democracy is a desirable form of government, but Mill found it to be impossible to maintain. Mill listed two practical obstacles in his essay. First, he found it impossible for the whole people to assemble to perform the duties of government. Citizens would have to leave their normal jobs on a regular basis to help govern the community. Second, Mill argued that an assembled body of differing interests would find it impossible to come to any agreements. Mill spoke to this point in his essay:

> *In an assembly, every thing must be done by speaking and assenting. But where the assembly is numerous, so many persons desire to speak, and feelings, by mutual inflammation, become so violent, that calm and effectual deliberation is impossible.*[2]

In lieu of participatory democracies, republics have arisen as the actual form of government. Mill recognized that an elected body of representatives serves to facilitate the role of governing society in the interests of the body politic. However, the representative body needs to be overseen so as to not abuse its powers. Mill wrote:

> *. . . whether Government is intrusted to one or a few, they have not only motives opposite to those ends, but motives which will carry them, if unchecked, to inflict the greatest evils.*[3]

A more recent scholar, the late Professor Christopher Lasch of the University of Rochester, also had qualms about representative government. In his essay, "Journalism, Publicity, and the Lost Art of Argument,"[4] Lasch argued that any form of democracy requires discourse and debate to function properly. His article is critical of modern journalism. He points out that modern journalism is failing in its role as a public forum. That role is to help raise the needed questions of society. Lasch recommended the re-creation of direct democracy when he wrote:

> *Instead of dismissing direct democracy as irrelevant to modern conditions, we need to recreate it on a large scale. And from this point of view, the press serves as the equivalent of the town meeting.* [5]

But even the traditional town meeting had its limitations. For example, everyone should be allowed to speak, as long as they share an interest in the well-being of the whole community, rather than in any particular part. One scholar wrote that a

> *well-known study of a surviving small Vermont town meeting traces the breaking apart of the deliberative ideal once developers catering to tourism bought property in a farming community; the farmers and developers had such opposed interests about zoning ordinances that debate collapsed into angry shouting matches.*[6]

The development of the Internet and of Usenet is an investment in making direct democracy a reality. These new technologies present the chance to overcome the obstacles preventing the implementation of direct democracy. Online communication forums also make possible Lasch's desire to see the discussion necessary to identify today's fundamental questions. Mill could not foresee the successful assembly of the body politic in person at one time. The Net allows for a meeting which takes place on each person's own time, rather than all at one time.[7] Usenet newsgroups are discussion forums where questions are raised, and people can leave comments when convenient, rather than at a particular time and at a particular place. Individuals can connect from their own computers or from publicly accessible computers across the nation to participate in a particular debate. The real discussion takes place in one concrete time and place, although the discussants can be dispersed. Current Usenet newsgroups and mailing lists prove that citizens can do their daily jobs and still participate within their daily schedules in discussions that interest them.

Mill's second observation was that people would not be able to communicate peacefully after assembling. Online discussions do not have the same characteristics as in-person meetings. Since people connect to the discussion forum when they wish, and when they have time, they can be thoughtful in their responses to the discussion, whereas in a traditional meeting, participants have to think quickly to respond. In addition, online discussions allow everyone to have a say, whereas meetings of finite length allow only a certain number of people to have their say. Online meetings allow everyone to contribute his or her thoughts in a message, which is then accessible to whoever else is participating in the discussion.

These new communication technologies hold the potential for the implementation of direct democracy in a country as long as the necessary computer and communications infrastructure are installed. Advancement toward a more responsible government is possible with these new technologies. While the future is discussed and planned for, it will also be possible to use these technologies to support citizen participation in government. Netizens are watching various government institutions on various newsgroups and mailing lists throughout the global computer communications network. People's thoughts about and criticisms of their respective governments are being aired on the currently uncensored networks.

These networks can revitalize the concept of a democratic "town meeting" via online communication and discussion. Discussions involve people interacting with others. Voting involves the isolated thoughts of an individual on an issue, and then his or her acting on those thoughts in a private vote. In society where people live together, it is important for people to communicate with each other about their situations to understand the world from the broadest possible viewpoint.

Public and open discussions and debates are grassroots, bottom-up developments that enable people to participate in democracy with enthusiasm and interest more than the current system of secret ballots allows. Of course, at some point or other, votes might be taken, but only after time has been given to air an issue in the commons.

THE NTIA VIRTUAL CONFERENCE

A recent example and prototype of this public and open discussion was the Virtual Conference on Universal Service and Open Access to the Telecommunications Network in November 1994. The National Telecommunications and Information Administration (NTIA), under the U.S. Department of Commerce, sponsored this e-mail and newsgroup conference and encouraged public access sites to allow broad-based discussion. Several public libraries across the nation provided the most visible public sites for the conference. This NTIA conference is an example of an online "town meeting." The conference was a prototype of what the new technology facilitates. The NTIA conference was a new social form made possible by the Net. It was an example of citizen-government interaction through citizen debate over important public questions. It was a public forum held with the support of public institutions. It was a viable attempt to revitalize the democratic definition of government of and by the people. This particular two-week forum was a prototype for:

1. Public debate, making it possible for previously unheard voices to be part of the discussion
2. A new form of politics involving the people in the real questions of society

3. The clarification of a public question
4. The testing of new technological means to make more democracy possible

Following is a study of the archives of this prototype conference, along with a discussion of the implications for the future.[8]

David J. Barram, the Deputy Secretary of the U.S. Department of Commerce, closed the National Telecommunications and Information Administration's (NTIA) Virtual Conference on Universal and Service and Open Access by stating the conference was "... a tremendous example of how our information infrastructure can allow greater citizen participation in the development of government policies." To hear such a comment from a government representative is important. It came after many users of the Net had demonstrated to the U.S. government that they opposed the planned conversion of the communications-based Internet into the commerce-based National Information Infrastructure.

The goals of the two-week conference were stated in the Welcoming Statement,[9] which promised to replace the one-way top-down approach with a new form of dialogue both among citizens and between citizens and their government.

Open discussion is powerful. Such exchange makes it possible to examine difficult and controversial issues. In the NTIA online conference, participants in the forums on "Availability and Affordability" and "Redefining Universal Service and Open Access" documented that the "free market" cannot solve the problem of spreading network access to all. Usually unheard voices spoke out loud and clear that there is a strong need for government to assure that online access is equally available to urban, rural, disabled, and poor citizens and to everyone else. The government must ensure that Net access will be available in unprofitable situations that the "free market" will not touch. Non-governmental and non-profit organizations, community representatives, college students, and everyday people made this clear in their contributions to the discussion. Although the NTIA Virtual Conference was not advertised broadly, the organizers set up 80 public access points across the United States in places such as public libraries and community centers. This helped include the opinions of people who might not have been heard otherwise.

THE IMPORTANCE OF THE INTERNET TO SOCIETY

The Internet and Usenet represent important developments in technology which will have a profound effect on human society and intellectual development. We are in an early stage of the development and distribution of these technologies, and it is important to look towards the future. Some areas of human society that these new communications technologies are likely to affect include government, human communication and community formation. Democracy is government by the people, and both Usenet and mailing lists allow everyone to speak out without the fear that their voices will not be heard. Individuals can still be uncooperative, but these new communications technologies make it possible to have one's voice presented equally. These technologies could be integrated with other online information and communication technologies to make possible a true participatory democracy. This potential excited several of the participants.

Many participants in the NTIA virtual conference recognized the value inherent in these new communication technologies and discussed the need for universal access to the technology. The Internet was identified as a "public good" that needs to be accessible to all of the population throughout the land. This led to the understanding of the importance of making access equally available across all strata of society. Citizens living in rural areas, people with various handicaps or low income, should have equal opportunity with everyone else to access and utilize the Internet. Particular cases were described which would be unprofitable for businesses to provide as equal access for equal payment. Businesses make profits from the mass production of like goods or services. Members of society who cannot use the common product wind up paying extra. This was seen as discriminatory by various participants. The problems described included the high long-distance phone rates, which most rural inhabitants need to pay to communicate with the majority of other people. These rates would have to be paid to connect to the closest Internet access phone number. Rural access would be costly, as would access from territories such as the Virgin Islands. Another concern was the extra cost to those with handicaps. People with handicaps would need to purchase expensive input/output devices in order to compensate for their individual disadvantage. Access is expensive, but so are computers and training. Participants felt it important to make access to Internet accounts and computers more easily available.

The number of subscribers averaged about 400 people per conference. The conferences sponsored a debate on the issues, and people with different ideas contributed. However, there was a clear call by many participants that the U.S. government stay involved with the backbone of U.S. portion of the Internet to best provide equal access and service to all individuals throughout U.S. society. One of the arguments in favor of continued government involvement is that it is vital for people from all walks of life and all possible backgrounds to be using the Internet. Only if there is access for all can the Internet work as a medium of communication and discussion, including all the differences and diversity of the population. A network connecting only a few types of individuals would not benefit society. The question was raised by one participant as to whether we as a society can afford being split into two distinct societies—those online and those not.

Following are excerpts taken from the archives of the NTIA Virtual Conference about the importance of the Internet to society. Subsequent sections will focus on particular topics discussed during the conference.

The Benefits of the Net

FROM: RANDOLPH LANGLEY

I agree wholeheartedly—the Internet costs so little, and benefits so many. As with the interstate highway system, it is a proper and effective activity for the federal government. I believe most of the citizenry would not care to see the interstate system given over to a few large toll companies, and I believe the Internet will be on the scale of economic and cultural benefit as the interstate system.[10]

FROM: BOB SUMMERS

In order for the nation to access a common pool of information, such as the library of congress, an efficient system must be in place to handle the load of thousands of library's and other users to access the information. Yes, I believe that there will have to be an outlay of funds to provide such a system, not to mention the cost of putting the information online. These funds must come from the Federal government, since it is for the public.[11]

FROM: W. CURTISS PRIEST

Government should supply/support activities where there are public goods (public information) and when the benefits of this support exceeds the cost to we taxpayers.[12]

FROM: WAYNE COUNTY RESA

The Net is certainly not free, I agree. We all pay to a certain degree for it. I am a little concerned about the commercialism aspect of it, though. I think if it is privatized we will see more ads. Seems logical. Why would someone pay good money to be on the Net and not advertise their wares. I imagine it is inevitable but I would like the inevitable forestalled or better yet somehow modified so that information and the kinds of information is not compromised.[13]

FROM: BNN TELEVISION

Public access is a "public good", not only because it allows people from disadvantaged backgrounds the opportunity to use new technology, but also because it increases the collective pool of information from which even newer technology is born. Analyze this increase from a business perspective if you must-I'll keep on rooting for the future of my species.[14]

FROM: BRENT WALL

The draft financial plan for the Leon County Free-Net project, while proposing a number of different financial opportunities to make universal service a reality to the community, will emphasize an old notion practiced for years in this and other countries: cross-subsidies. Based on the view that citizen communication and education are public goods and should not be constrained by cost of service pricing mechanisms, the financial plan proposes that business uses and enhanced services shall be charged a fee that underwrites the first Amendment communication functions of the Net as well as its educational employment.

This entire argument hinges on defining communication and education (and I recognize that there are grey areas that would need to be ironed out) as PUBLIC GOODS. This is not, in my judgement simply a matter of determining whether Net communication is "divisible" etc. as the economic profession would tend to analyze the problem. It deals with fundamental philosophies of the social value of education and communication in a democracy. If, to email my County Commissioners on a topic that affects me, I have to pay a charge that I really can't afford, while Mr. Thickwallet has no such impediment, then this means something to democratic participation in an electronic world.

This is nothing new: witness C-Span, local access channels, and the like. If we adopt a concept and policy like the above, more and more citizens, over time, would be able to join the virtual community as a full member. To have this membership driven by one's personal income will surely result in two societies that are separate and unequal. Can we afford this future?[15]

FROM: STEPHEN BRENNER

We are dealing with a major paradigm shift when it comes to this lateral flow of communication and the kinds of community building processes and empowerment that this can catalyze. We need to put some thought into how a real democracy could function, given these new communication tools.[16]

FROM: LEW MCDANIEL

In my opinion, information access is sufficiently important to be a guaranteed right. By guaranteed information access, I mean for K-12, adult education, health services, and government access. Movies on demand, games, and electronic shopping (ala the shopping channels) should be charged at an additional rate.[17]

FROM: DAVE W. MITCHELL

I agree that the knowledge base of a society and the ability of its citizens to use it will determine the ultimate survival of free peoples.[18]

FROM: DANIEL LIEBERMAN

We are looking towards the future. Anyone who hopes to participate in the society will need to have access. Banking, schooling, books, its all coming very fast. Just think of the rate of change in the last five years or the last six months on the WWW. Voters handbooks, policy papers etc. How can one hope to be a knowledgeable citizen without access. The hardware will trickle down like automobiles. But the communication links must be available.[19]

FROM: SEAN CONNELL

*The Internet offers a chance for us to follow through on a promise of democracy that was betrayed over two hundred years ago. Our Constitution, clever as it may be, was written to *prevent* civic action. [Jefferson] was the first to recommend public education, because he knew that it was vital to a healthy democracy. We must all be informed and capable of contributing to the governing of our country. The public does not have the means to act in concert and it is not [in] the interest of the current power players to afford us those means. The Internet . . . is a means to create vocal, active, communities that transcend race, geography, and wealth. It is entirely necessary that we recognize this fact and make a stand now to maintain this highway to real Democracy.*[20]

FROM: COLETTE BROOKS

And many of us feel that the Infobahn is not primarily a private preserve but a national/world resource which should be extended to all, for reasons already explored in other posts this week.[21]

FROM: BILL RUSSELL

What SERVICES should be guaranteed to every citizen. The old definition of universal service has been called POTS: Plain Old Telephone Service. As I understand it, the NEED for this service was so great that it is public policy that every one (hence universal) should have it. It has been also called "life line service." . . . IMHO universal service needs to be defined as a set of SERVICES that are so important to our civilization that they should be made universally available. Foremost among them is POTS. Next is access to a network that provides at least an e-mail bridge to the worldwide Internet at an equitable price. It is just plain not fair for urban cybernauts to pay zero while rural cybernauts pay ten cents per minute for telephone connection to the net.[22]

The Cry for Equal Access and Universal Access

Following are some excerpts from the conference demonstrating concern that access to the Internet be available universally, with respect both to physical access and to price.

FROM: BRENT WALL

An early post to this group from an individual from the Anneberg NPR group suggested that, as a beginning, universal access, as defined from the consumer's and not the supplier's viewpoint, merely entails, at present, a phone line to every home. The implicit definition of availability in the Leon County Library Tallahassee Free-Net adds one important dimension on top of the phone line notion. It is the expansion to as many homes as possible of the communication and educational benefits of a community Net over the phone lines.[23]

FROM: HARVEY GOODSTEIN

. . . [T]aking into consideration the needs and rights of deaf and hard of hearing individuals in particular (and individuals with disabilities in general). . . . federal regulations on minimum standards are necessary to enhance equal access for all. . . . Thus, universal service provisions should not discriminate against individuals with disabilities (irrespective of their financial status) who invariably would have to pay abnormally high costs for technical connectivity.[24]

FROM: ELLEN DAVIS BURNHAM

*This whole segment of the conference is about "Availability and Affordability" to all NOT just some that live in a largely populated area. People in Mississippi NEED the Internet just like everyone, probably more so than people who live in large areas with ready access to libraries or any form of research. Should we teach just **SOME** of our children to read, maybe just a few should learn Algebra, and heaven knows no one needs to know grammar rules. We can't pick and choose who is allowed access. We live in a democratic society that says everyone is equal and should receive equal access to schooling among other inalienable rights.*

The rural area should be addressed first because we have such a hard time to find access (affordable access). If you could just go into a school one day and help students who are struggling to find the needed 12 sources for a research paper, students who know what they need is out there SOMEWHERE if only they had access to it.

*YES, WE MUST PROVIDE INTERNET ACCESS TO **EVERYONE**, not just to those who are easy to put online. . . .*

*The competition may be greater in larger cities BUT the need is not. I don't mean to berate anyone but if you could only see first-hand the great need in our schools you would understand. I teach in a school that has only 3700 books total in the library. Our situation is extreme because the school burned a couple of years ago. I try to help the students by hunting for needed items on the Internet. Until I began teaching there this year *ONLY* one student knew about the Superhighway. . . . [W]hat about . . . the children who have parents that have never heard of the Internet either. We have to start somewhere and I believe the population of America as a whole is as good a place to begin as any.*[25]

FROM: LUCY CO

Hearing the real-life experiences of people like Ellen Davis Burnham, who wrote of introducing school children in rural Mississippi to the Internet — is one of the best aspects of this conference. Helps ward off the tendency to discuss concepts such as "availability" as though they were theoretical only. Keep up the good work, Ellen—and don't apologize for your "preaching."[26]

GOVERNMENT AS PRODUCER AND DISSEMINATOR OF INFORMATION

The U.S. government is a major producer of information, most of which is public and printed on paper. The government would save money if it distributed that information electronically and let the user decide whether or not to print it. Having handed over the Internet backbone to commercial entities, the U.S. government can no longer distribute that information without the increased cost of contributing to some company's profit margins. A government-run backbone would have allowed the efficient distribution of governmental information without the increased cost profit requires. U.S. citizens will now have to pay a profit-making company overhead to access the very information we pay for with our taxes. In any case, if the U.S. government works towards providing governmental information and services online, even more incentive will exist for more of the U.S. population to get connected to the Internet.

FROM: CARL HAGE

*. . . [T]he government would be the main beneficiaries of an *information* infrastructure. The government is a major producer and consumer of information, most of which is inaccessible to the public in practice. . . . We need a new kind of freedom of information, a glasnost for the information age, in which the public at large can access any public information without charge (other than low network charges). That means every public library, school, government office, business or home could have access to everything.*[27]

FROM: CHLOE LEWIS

We might legislate that all public gov't information—stuff that The Public has already paid for and usually has a right to, if near enough a G-Doc depository—be made available to anyone with email. This will, if done with common sense, reduce the expenses of both the government agencies involved and of anyone who needs frequent access to government publications. This is an obvious reason for schools and libraries to have Internet access, and a reason for citizens and businesses to acquire it.

The US has been subsidizing access to paper information, for the sake of knowledge and self-government; we have found a more efficient way to provide this information; where possible, we should subsidize this more efficient way instead. It isn't as whizbang attractive as giving everyone realtime video, but it would be useful immediately.[28]

FROM: CARL HAGE

The largest single producer of information is the federal government, most of which is public. Although these days virtually all documents are produced in electronic form on a word processor, etc., very little of the information is available in electronic form. Nearly all information is distributed in paper form, typically obtained by calling over a telephone. A similar case can be made for state and local governments.[29]

FROM: SUSAN HADDEN

If the federal and state government would announce a policy of making their services available in electronic form there would be a package of stuff . . . that should make the net worthwhile to most people. (Examples: Renewing drivers' license, hunting licenses, finding the right official for your problem the first time, getting on-line help on your income tax where you didn't just talk to someone but showed them the calculations in real time, etc.)[30]

WHY IT IS IMPORTANT FOR ALL TO HAVE ACCESS

Early in the "redefining universal service" segment of the virtual conference, people started discussing how to determine access rates. One participant, Bob Johnson, proposed that the starting point be to figure out why it was important for people to have Internet access. His point is important, and others echoed it throughout the conference. It is necessary to understand why it is important for both individuals and organizations in our society to have access to the Internet for both its information and communication benefits. Another participant, Carly Henderson, raised a parallel question, asking why access to public libraries is important. Part of the debate taking place dealt with a difference in views. One view was that the United States is a democracy where everyone is equal and should receive equal opportunities. The other was that the United States is a nation of individuals, and access should only be for those who strive for it.

FROM: BOB JACOBSON

An appropriate question is not how much a particular individual or organization should pay for access to the Internet or its successors, but why they should have access, individually and collectively? Once you figure this out, and define access to suit, you can figure on pricing. Everything else is premature, unless people get out their basic premises on which they are operating.[31]

FROM: CARLY HENDERSON

I agree with Bob; this is a very important question that deserves a well thought out answer. Why should people have access to the Internet? In response, I pose the question, why should every community have a library and allow its citizens access to all that it contains?[32]

FROM: ROBERT J. BERRINGTON III

But what I'm willing to bet is that most of the people that we're talking about providing a service to haven't the slightest clue as to what the Internet is.[33]

FROM: MARTIN KESSEL

A final requirement for universal access is that people need to understand what the Information Highway can do for them—how it can benefit their lives.[34]

WHAT THE INTERNET CAN DO FOR PEOPLE

The significance of Internet access for all in society is not necessarily obvious because it is a new way to think about communication between people. Before the Internet and Usenet, most broadcast forms of communication were owned and operated by large companies. Other, more democratic, forms of broadcast, which provide one-to-many communication, exist for small segments of the population in particular regions: public access cable, various self-produced newsletters or 'zines, "pirate" radio, and so on. The Internet makes available an alternative to the corporate-owned mass media and allows grassroots communication from the many to the many. As it has taken a struggle for an individual to be seen as a information provider, it is not immediately obvious to all that it is possible to speak out and have your voice heard by many people. It is also important that people can express their views and be in contact with others around the world who are expressing their views.

Participants in the virtual conference were active in defining their interest in keeping the Internet protected from dominance by commercial interests. Commercial information and communication is vastly different from individual grassroots information and communication that the Net makes possible. Participants recognized this difference and voiced their opinions on the importance of keeping the Net an open channel for non-commercial voices.

The picture of the Internet painted by the U.S. government has been one of an "information superhighway" or "information infrastructure" to which people could connect, download some data or purchase some goods, and then disconnect. This image is very different from the current cooperative communications forums on Usenet where everyone can contribute. The transfer of information is secondary. The descriptions by much of the news media portraying people's contributions as being pornographic or otherwise illegal are in contrast to the reality that the Internet and Usenet provide a place where people can share ideas, observations, and questions. Those participating in the virtual conference debated whether and why people would want access to the Net.

FROM: R. M.

Overlooked in the current free market vs. regulated access debate is any argument convincing me why the average American will want access to the net. Apart from the "information elite" (most already on the net), I don't know too many people interested in communications capability not already available using existing infrastructures. How many people do you know, not associated with research or education, who care about access to government information repositories? Or virtual conferences?[35]

FROM: DR. ROBERT LAROSE

In response to Woody Dowling's comment that the average American is not interested in advanced communications infrastructure, at least not those who don't already have it.

Not so. We did a national survey a couple of years ago and asked about interest in videotex, ISDN, etc., found interest levels far beyond those of then-current penetration levels. Found the most intense interest among low income homes, in fact, suggesting that it is cost and not interest that holds them back. Want a killer application for low income households? Email. Many can't afford long distance rates, some move too often or have no home, can't keep a phone line . . . The applications already exist, but the people who need them most can't afford them—or don't constitute an attractive enough market.[36]

FROM: CURT HOWLAND

*While the inverse relation between cost and pervasiveness is certainly true, I must take issue with comparing the Net to TV. Such comparisons allow for the taking of information, but not for the tremendous possibilities involved with ease of *providing* info. There is no reason to think that a future Stephen Hawkings isn't sitting right now in front of a boob-tube sucking down Mighty Morphin Power Rangers because there is no way for his ideas to be expressed. Without the facility to put ideas out, with each person acting as a information provider assumed from the outset, we are doing ourselves a great disservice.*[37]

FROM: DON EVANS

A two way street for all Americans. not only should they be able to receive from the net, but they also must be able to provide their unique information.[38]

FROM: MICHAEL HAUBEN

I. Universal Access Basic Principles

In order for communications networks to be as useful as possible, it is necessary for [them] both to

A) Connect every possible resource and opinion,

B) Make this connection available to all who desire it.

A and B call for Universal Interconnection, rather than Universal Access. The usage of "interconnection" highlights the importance and role of every user also being an information provider. The term "access" stresses the status-quo understanding of one-way communication, the user accesses information that other "authorized" information providers make available. This is the old model. The new model is of interconnection of many different types of people, information, and ideas. The new model stresses the breakdown of old definitions of communication and information. Diversity allows for both the increasing speed in the formation of new ideas, and the ability for previously unauthorized ideas to have the airing and consideration they rightfully deserve.

II. Definition of "Services" to be available on this Universal Interconnection

The new era of interconnection and many-to-many communication afforded by Netnews and mailing lists (among other technologies) brings to the forefront a model of bottom-up rather than top-down communication and information. It is time to reexamine society and welcome the democratizing trends of many-to-many communication over the one-to-many models as represented by broadcast television, radio, newspapers and other media.

As such, I would say it would be important to highlight, discuss, and make available interactive modes of communication instead of the passive transfer of information. Thus I am suggesting emphasizing forms of multiple ways of communication and broadcasting. Forms currently defined by newsgroups, mailing lists, talk sessions, IRC sessions, MOO experiences, and other forms of sharing and collaboration. These types of forums are where this new technology excels. Plenty of media exist that facilitate the passive transfer of information and goods. (Such as mail-order, stores, telephone orders, etc.) It would be best to explore and develop the new forms of communication which this new media facilitates, and which were less possible and present in the past.[39]

FROM: B. HARRIS

Summary of the Affordability and Availability Conference

The Internet and the Global Computer Network are providing a very important means for the people of our society to have an ability to speak for themselves and to fight their own battles to better the society.[40]

FROM: ERIC REHM

. . . [C]onception of access, I would posit, demands a much more interactive use of the medium and perhaps the bandwidth needs are more balanced: This example can then be extended to any number of community organizations with members as avid information producers.

In other words, basic service based on enabling "many producers" might actually prompt a larger share to be allocated to bandwidth OUT of the home than that envisaged by the Baby Bells and cable companies.

It seems to me, in rural America, there would be even more fear of not having ample "basic" bandwidth to be a producer because the distance to such an "access point" might be enough to effectively deny community production.[41]

EFFICIENCY OF E-MAIL VERSUS VIDEO

In the discussion about universal and equal access to the Internet, access to live video and the problems it creates was introduced. Some participants argued that "video on demand" would be a resource hog. It would again introduce inequality into the online world based on who could pay and also create a different priority in use of network bandwidth. One participant contributed a message titled "Net Economics 101" which gave tables showing the relative sizes of different forms of data. Carl Hage made his comparisons clear by writing, "A single video movie is equivalent to 6 million people sending a one page email message." He concluded his message by writing, "Why should we provide subsidized video access to a few when we could use those resources to provide textual information to millions?"

Another participant disagreed, stating that providing video is important so that access can be offered to the percentage of the U.S. population which is illiterate. A couple of other participants stated that video has enormous educational and expressive potential. It was important that the virtual conference allowed for the presentation of different points of views, as that assists in figuring out the best way forward.

FROM: DEBBIE SINMAO

> What would a basic basket of services be in five years? In ten? And, by
> what process do we change our minds and expand our definition?

Whatever the basket will be in 5, 10, etc. years, it should not include Al Gore's idea of video on demand . . . unless it is for educational uses—if you want to see a movie, go to your nearest movie theater or rent a video from Blockbuster.[42]

FROM: ROBERT J. BERRINGTON III

I agree with Debbie. At the current date, we don't have the technology to support such things. It may be 50 years down the road before that technology is available. Why clutter up a system that can't handle such a load.[43]

FROM: REY BARRY

> Date: Thurs., 17 Nov. 1994 14:56:57 CDT
> From: gunzerat@vaxa.weeg.uiowa.edu
>
> 2) To debbie: I think it's shortsighted to equate "video on demand," or
> video in any form in the new age with what we can presently pick up at
> Blockbuster. For that matter, to think in terms of video as a passive,
> "something to watch" form seems to me to ignore its potential.
>
> That's why I don't think it's right at this point to dismiss Al Gore; video
> has the potential to allow for perhaps even greater educational and
> expressive possibilities than text. To limit ourselves at the outset could
> mean missing out on the greatest possibilities.

Creative video is a neat concept. Thanks for bringing that up. The fear that Gore is bursting with desire to sell out to commercial interests is the opposite of what comes through when you talk to him or look at the work he focused his life on.[44]

FROM: RON CHOURA

Advanced telecommunications services should not be legislatively mandated for inclusion in the definition of universal service. Universal service funding of such services is not appropriate unless and until a critical mass of demand develops. Inclusion of such services in the definition would yield anticompetitive results, since services typically included in universal service do not have all relevant costs allocated to them.[45]

FROM: CARL HAGE

One thing to keep in mind is that digital transmission of text, e.g. email is very efficient. For each user who sends email instead of fax or telephone call, hundreds of additional users can send email in the transmission resource saved.

Access of gopher or www text is similar to email in efficiency. Pictures, voice/audio and video are, of course, much more expensive.[46]

FROM: CARL HAGE

But according to the polls, the public is skeptical about the ways in which the industry is touting the NII and they see other more important uses. With the focus on video entertainment, my fear is that the less glitzy uses will be delayed and left out. Also, the focus towards high-end technology is a diversion of resources which could be used to provide low end data communications to all instead of video for a few.[47]

FROM: CARL HAGE

Here are some tables showing the relative sizes of data in different forms:

The following table gives a comparison of a page of text (obtained from an OTA report on the NII) in various forms, either in compressed or uncompressed ASCII text (averaged), as a page of fax, voice where the text was read aloud, or in video form where the speaker read the information aloud.

Relative Sizes for Multi-Media Information Text

Type	*Pages*	*MB*
Compressed Text	*1*	*0.0011*
Uncompressed Text	*3*	*0.003*
Fax Image	*40*	*0.04*
Fax Modem Transmission	*270*	*.27*
Compressed Voice (8:1)	*200*	*0.2*
Compressed Voice (2:1)	*800*	*0.8*
Voice Telephone (64Kb)	*1600*	*1.6*
Low Quality VideoPhone (H.320)	*3200*	*3.2*
Commercial VideoConf	*6400*	*6.4*
High Q VideoConf (H.120 1.5Mb/s)	*37000*	*37.5*

Compressed Broadcast Video	1670	167
Uncompressed Video (currently used)	1100000	1100

The last entry of about one million to one is the size as used in an actual NII-sponsored video classroom, <http://www.ncih.net/>. Access for schools costs $4000/mo for 1 video link or $8000/mo for 2, paid for by state grants.

An ordinary voice telephone call consumes more than 3000 times the data inside an email message (calls use 64Kb in two directions). Fax images are about 50 times more than the equivalent compressed text in disk storage space, but consume about 300 times the telecommunications resources when transmitted via modem, or 100 times if the text is not compressed.

Comparisons of 1GB of Digital Information

	Number/GB
1 page documents	1000000
100 page documents	10000
Kodak Photo-CD pictures	1000
JPEG Images (640x480 @ 10:1)	10000
Minutes of Voice Telephone	400
1.44MB Diskette	700
CD-ROM	1.5
2 Hour Movies	0.2
Purchase cost of hard disk	$500
Purchase cost of floppy disks	$250
Equivalent of a 2 Hour Digital Video Movie	
1 page documents	6000000
100 page documents	60000
Kodak Photo-CD pictures	6000
JPEG Images (640x480 @ 10:1)	60000
Minutes of Voice Telephone	2600
Hours of Voice Telephone	43
1.44MB Diskettes	4200
CD-ROMs	10
GigaBytes	6

A single video movie is equivalent to 6 million people sending a one page email message. . . .

Why should we provide subsidized video access to a few when we could use those resources to provide textual information to millions? For example, we could make the federal register and congressional record available to every-

one for free rather than have to pay $375 per person/year to access any part.[48]

LIBRARIES AS POINTS OF PUBLIC ACCESS

Libraries were proposed as a central public location where people could gain access to the Internet. This would be especially helpful to those who cannot currently afford to buy a computer. There was discussion about how the role of libraries might change from a location where information is stored, to one where information access is facilitated through training and individual help from librarians.

There were problems inherent in suggesting libraries be the public access point. First, library hours would limit when access would be available for those without computers and Internet accounts, and libraries might only be able to provide limited access to the Internet—if, for example, they could only afford the cheapest modems. One participant mentioned that his local library did not receive its latest funding because a bond was voted down. If libraries are to take on the role of Internet access provider, the issue of funding has to be raised. Another participant pointed out that since many communities do not have a local library, those communities would also not have any public access sites if libraries were to be the only public sites for access to the Net.

FOR: Libraries as universal points of access

FROM: KATHLEEN L. BLOOMBERG

Libraries are universal access points to information for school students, faculty at higher education institutions, and the general public. Not everyone will have a microcomputer and modem at home in the future just like everyone doesn't have plain old telephone service now. Librarians are trained in facilitating access to information and are an integral part of the emerging information superhighway.

According to a recent survey by the National Commission on Libraries and Information Science, 21% of the public libraries in the United States are accessing the Internet now. That number is growing monthly. Most academic libraries and many school and special libraries also are using the Internet regularly to meet their patrons' needs.[49]

FROM: SOLOMON PHILIP HILL

Until the time comes when everyone can afford a personal terminal of some sort, I think that the community center or library model of access works pretty well. This leaves open the question of training which seems to be the least talked about, but possibly most important aspect here.[50]

FROM: DAVE W. MITCHELL

It is indeed true that the public library model provides a philosophical and structural underpinning, yet the immense popularity of talk radio (for example) shows a strong underlying hunger for communication of individual reactivity and creativity. In its satisfaction may lie the tool wherein we redefine the compact with one another on which this society was founded.[51]

FROM: SUSAN G.

I agree—the public library is definitely a good place to start for public access. It isn't the only solution, but there is rarely just one good answer to a complex problem. Rather multiple good answers.[52]

FROM: CARL HAGE

Currently libraries pay substantial fees to obtain reference material in print or microfilm form. Actually, due to budget problems, many libraries, including my own, are cutting back on this material. If this material were available electronically, then purchases of microfilm, etc. could be discontinued and the money saved could be used for hardware and network access fees.

I believe that better dissemination of information could be used to provide more cost effective access for libraries, where the equipment, software, and methods of access can be tailored to the needs [of] libraries.[53]

FROM: LEW MCDANIEL

> I believe that better dissemination of information could be used
> to provide more cost effective access for libraries

The ideas which follow the above are good ones. To me, they show the concept of "library" evolving from common source of information and repository to "facilitator of access" in addition to today's functions. Particularly if all the have-nots are going to head for the library I-way access point.

I see libraries, K-12, and higher education all becoming significantly more competitive, more virtual, and less corporeal if the I-way reaches fruition. Even though each provides a great deal of value inappropriate to a telecommunications line—social interaction, community cohesiveness, etc.[54]

AGAINST: Libraries are not the solution to the access question

Others disagreed that libraries could solve the problem of universal access. They presented some of the problems libraries are having even as libraries and noted that many locations do not have libraries.

FROM: MTN

Much as I'd like to believe it, I do not feel that libraries solve the access problem. First, access is already limited by the hours of the library. In a world where success and (em)power(ment) may hinge upon immediate access to information, it's tough to assume that people who must schlep over to the library and wait in line for a 1200 baud (when I last checked) modem and terminal are on an equal footing.[55]

FROM: STEPHEN BRENNER

I like the library model as well. Unfortunately, our library bond went down to defeat in the last election and they aren't likely to take on this role without funding. In the meantime, providing free access to the Internet, including public access terminals, is part of Oregon Public Network's charter.[56]

FROM: CAROL DEERING

I just wanted to mention the large Indian reservation which surrounds our town. A great many people who live there have no telephones and some even no TV. I have seen mention in this conference of other rural situations, but I wanted to be sure to include this type of rural instance. There is no library service to this area, either.[57]

FROM: MARILYN LETITIA KORHONEN

I agree to the extent that schools and libraries will allow this. We do not have a library in my local phone exchange, so that wouldn't serve my area and many others. The schools would be an answer for some, but the school in my district is not interested, even if I'll write grants for them. They do not trust it, they can not see the usefulness in their day-to-day lives, and they are simply not interested.[58]

DEBATE OVER THE "FREE MARKET"

A strong debate took place in both conferences over how Internet access could be best deployed throughout society. Some people argued "the market" would provide the best quality service to most people, while others challenged the notion that "the market" could provide such access. Many said that it was important for government to play a strong role in making access available universally. Those encouraging a governmental role described why "the market" would not work toward providing access to those living in areas where access would be harder to provide, or for those with special needs.

On the Need for a Government Role

FROM: RON CHOURA

Now, however, there is near universal consensus that opening up these markets to competition will lead to enhanced benefit for most consumers. But, can we be sure that market forces alone will achieve the goal of widely available, affordable services for all Americans? Is action by state and federal governments needed? What should be done? . . . States must have the ability to ensure that high quality service is provided in markets that are less competitive or attractive for investment.[59]

FROM: FRANK WHITTLE

The term "economic development" has become prominent in state telecommunication policy during the last ten years as the states battle to retain and attract industry. It appears from the preliminary research that the issue of providing universal access (services) has become less prominent in policy documents.[60]

FROM: BRENT WALL

If one reads the testimony given at the hearings conducted on the NII and the global infrastructure by the Dept. of Commerce, one can detect two sense[s] of the terms "universal access" at work. The Motorolas, with their pleas for a wireless world, and cable companies with their arguments for phone service, and phone companies with their exhortations for delivering cable service, one comes away with a sense that universal access means: supply access—or the ability of service providers to access the NII (whatever infrastructure this may turn out to be) and sell their wares.

Yet, there is a second sense ascribed to these terms, one often advocated by community-based advocates, almost invisible in the national dialogues of service purveyors. And this is that universal access refers to access to the net by all, rich and poor.

Given the tenor of the NII discussions I have monitored, there is a threat that the latter meaning is being absorbed by the former.[61]

FROM: HENRY HUANG

The idea that the "free market" is going to solve all our problems is a MYTH. Go back and look over the history of most of the major on-line providers PRIOR to the recent big Internet expansion, and consider their current policies regarding Net access. No one who values their time, money, or access would seriously consider getting on the Internet through ANY of the major services, be it Compu$erve, Delphi, Prodigy (HA!), or America Online.

The reason for this is simple: each one of these services has either restricted the Net services available (hence restricting your access), and/or charges you way too much for it compared to some of the other access providers currently around.[62]

FROM: REY BARRY

Provide any sort of datahighway with near-universal access and people will spend money developing ways to make a living from it. The glory of the system. Tailor the highway to commercial interests from the start and you surely build in roadblocks to pro bono services, the danger of the system.[63]

FROM: PAUL WEISMANTEL

Dr. Priest's observation regarding the Advisory Council is clear. . . . Business in general is frightened by the very underpinnings of Universal Access, because it amounts to a mandate, which is usually a drain on profits.

Unless we can approach the discussion so as to fit into the business scheme (and that does not necessarily mean full recovery of investment in all cases), some members of the council will prevail in pushing off this issue by a lowest common denominator solution.[64]

FROM: MARTIN KESSEL

There was strong sentiment that the competitive market alone will not serve the nation's needs. As Steve Miller said, "The free market is like a ship with 100 sails blowing full blast and no rudder. Public policy provides the rudder."[65]

FROM: RICHARD M. KENSHALO

We can't be led to believe that market forces will eventually provide for the investments necessary for rural America, where loop costs remain extremely high. Without existing (and probably re-defined) price support structures, and an expanded definition of Universal Service to include guaranteed information access, we will truly develop a society of information "haves" and "have-nots".[66]

FROM: JEANNE GALLO

We would like to urge the administration and congress to pass legislation which mandates the setting up of community sites where citizens of all ages, etc. can have access provided. This will mean that funding will need to be available for setting up such centers with the technology that is needed to be on-line and that universal access will need to be built into any proposals, such as was done for universal access to the telephone. Subsidies may be a "dirty" word in D.C. at this moment, but they will be necessary if we are to include all of our citizens in the technology of the future.[67]

FROM: B. HARRIS

Summary of the Affordability and Availability Conference . . .

The territories are not naive in insisting that the information infrastructure must accommodate both access and low rates. Without both, the territories will receive no benefit and will in fact find their needs increasingly marginalized.

General summary:

Several people expressed concern that the development of the NII has focused on business interests and economic development rather than on ensuring access for all Americans. The theme [that] economic development will not by itself bring universal service to reality surfaced repeatedly.[68]

FROM: CARL HAGE

I certainly agree with your point, and I would use these examples as proof that a free market does not exist. I don't think most people fail to value their money, just that the big advertising machines, and the PC magazine-industrial complex have duped an uneducated public and an uneducated government. . . .

Yes, the free market will *not* provide equal access to rural areas, etc. However, the solutions for rural areas might be radically different. It is least likely that there will be much of any competitive market in rural areas, so co-ops, monopolies, etc. might be required.[69]

Opposition to Government Regulation

FROM: VIRAJ JHA

>> While "public access" is sometimes considered either a necessity or
>> a public good, what effects will the above choices make on a market
>> that is still in the early stages of development? Specifically, will
>> public access stunt market and technological development in the long
>> term[?]
>
. . .

>What does "stunt" mean in this case? . . .

By "stunt" I probably more accurately meant "distort"—in other words, would the rate of technological development be slowed by such a policy? Certainly industry leaders fear that strict regulation would hinder their profit-maximizing activities; in high competition technology markets these profits are often linked to innovation. Congressman Boucher in '92 agreed with Bell Atlantic that its deployment time for fiber optic lines could be halved absent stringent line of business regulation. Might similar regulations/subsidies for universal access not cause technological stagnation?[70]

FROM: CHRISTINE WEISS

Another viewpoint to add to the discussion comes from John Browning in an article from the Sept. '94 issue of WIRED:

". . . universal service is a 1930's solution to a 21st century problem. . . . the solution is Open Access."

In a nutshell, it seems that Open Access would ensure a competitive marketplace, that would in turn keep costs low.

Another option, for what its worth . . .[71]

FROM: CARL HAGE

I believe we can use the free market and competition to significantly lower the cost to access the net and provide a wide variety of options. There are a number of things that the government could do to enhance the competition and available services which would cost very little.[72]

FROM: STAN WITNOV

Dear Conferees,

. . .

Why are so many participants against unleashing American business (AND its stereotypical greed) in order to let the invisible hand lead us to the most efficient use of resources[?] I certainly trust that our government regulators and court system will move in at the appropriate time and correct some of the "wrongs" which are inevitable (whether we're under a government OR private enterprise umbrella).

I believe our great advantage here is to let venture capital risk itself for a profit but in so doing create and market services which increase user knowledge, accessibility, and the population of users.[73]

FROM: JAWAID BAZYAR

In response to ab368@virgin.uvi.edu (Bruce Potter):

> *>To the NTIA, we ask careful attention to the equity issues of access, and*
> *>a federal guarantee of access and availability.*

Oh my, it looks like the Socialists have grabbed onto the Internet as their next great crusade. . . .

If you choose to live on an island in the middle of the ocean with a small population, you can expect to pay a lot for high-tech services.[74]

FROM: CURT HOWLAND

There are left only the people making Universal Access in one form or another happen, and those that just talk, begging the Big Friendly Government to wait on them hand and foot.[75]

THE NTIA CONFERENCE AS A PROTOTYPE FOR FUTURE DEMOCRACY

Some participants understood that the conference could be seen as a model of citizen participation in government. They were thus thoughtful in considering the future and how these technologies could be used. A participant from Boston suggested that it was important that permanent public access sites be established in order for any policy decisions to be made with citizen input.

FROM: MARTIN KESSEL

Some participants questioned whether it will be truly feasible to put a computer terminal in every home. However, there was strong agreement that access should be available at public sites, such as libraries, schools, and other community places. This would be an extension of the model used by the NTIA in holding this Virtual Conference, noted Michelle Johnson, a reporter for the Boston Globe. Federal help is needed to provide libraries with resources and technical expertise.[76]

FROM: CARL HAGE

Thank you for the opportunity to participate in this discussion, and provide my input into the shaping of the future information age in America. I believe that using the Internet offers the potential to obtain high quality information needed for proper decision making, as well as improving the access of the government to the public.[77]

FROM: HUBERT JESSUP

Reading the discussion of the past two days about redefining universal access has confirmed our conviction that public access sites are not just important for this virtual conference but are needed as a permanent aspect of the development of the NII. Typically, only universities and certain businesses have Internet access. For the average American, these forms of access are far too limited. Consequently, citizens have little experience with the net and [little] understanding of what is at stake in its development. Also, basic computer skills—even as simple as logging on and typing a message—are lacking for most Americans.

What is needed in our opinion [are] on-going, institutionalized public access sites. We think these should be based in a variety of community based institutions, including the public libraries, public schools, and public access cable centers. These sites need equipment, Internet connection, staffing, and basic operating support. And, of course, these sites need funding. . . .

If we as a country do not develop a permanent, institutionalized and consistently supported system of public access sites, the NII will develop quickly among the current information "haves" but will totally leave behind the vast majority of Americans who are information "have nots". Facing this same situation concerning literacy in the early part of the 19th century, the response by public spirited Bostonians was the development of funding for the first public schools and public library in America. Soon, these institutions were quickly adopted by every city and town in America. Now, with a new technology and a new type of literacy, we as Americans should strive to expand our democracy by developing public access sites on the NII.[78]

THE IMPORTANCE OF TIME TO LEARN AT ONE'S OWN PACE

Paying for access per unit time or per kilobyte of data limits what most people will do online. First, it limits how much time an individual can spend learning, as the time spent will be costly; people with limited means will be selective in what they attempt to learn. Second, it is hard for people to take the time to be helpful to others when they are paying by the hour or by the kilobyte. The Internet and Usenet have grown to be such a cooperative community because there was no price tag on that cooperation. It will be a step backward to have to pay metered charges to access these communities. Individuals should be honored for their contributions to the Net and not expected to pay in proportion to their contributions.

FROM: A PUBLIC ACCESS SITE IN SEATTLE

Obviously, SCN (Seatle Community Network) has been wonderful, since it has allowed me to learn at my own (slow!) pace, without worrying about "wasting money". I am presently on NW Nexus, since I purchased the Internet Starter Kit which came with a coupon for 2 free weeks. I am continuing to pay for it, for a while, because it allows so much more opportunity to learn all the plusses of the Internet. . . . I am willing to pay the monthly fee for a short time, but unfortunately, I am not in a financial position to be able to continue at this rate for very long. It seems a shame that those of us who are not "well off" cannot reap the benefit of the whole Internet. I am grateful that SCN is there for us.[79]

FROM: HENRY HUANG

Hence, in limiting my time, you limit the quality of my posts, and hence the general quality of the discussion.

Many of the people who would want or NEED such free/cheap access are newbies—and hence EXACTLY the sort of people who WOULDN'T have the experience, knowledge, or time necessary to overcome the limits on their access. The less access you provide a person with, the more trouble that person has to go through JUST to get UP to a sufficiently useful level.[80]

FROM: SEAN CONNELL

An open communication infrastructure will allow children ample opportunity to explore and increase their knowledge at a pace with which they are comfortable.[81]

A NEED FOR OPENNESS

The Internet developed out of connecting networks together based on open and available standards. These protocols were developed by many people over the ARPANET and Internet. Commercial development is usually proprietary and closed. The Internet will develop much more slowly if pressure toward commercialism is allowed to overwhelm the open and cooperative culture of the Net.

FROM: HENRY HUANG

The NII is NOT a harbinger of change . . . the Internet WAS—hence this conference (run using list server software on a UNIX box, and sent mostly over Internet links).[82]

FROM: HENRY HUANG

Now look at the development of the Internet. Even with the astonishing growth of the World Wide Web and Mosaic (and perhaps soon Netscape), much of the Net is STILL ruled by text-based standards first set down perhaps a decade or more ago. The vast majority of E-mail is STILL text . . . E-mail and News are often cited as two of the most useful services offered by the Net, despite their clunkiness. As quirky and outdated as they are, they still WORK—more to the point, everyone HAS them. If everyone had a different format for E-mail messages, no one could communicate with anyone else—thus defeating the very purpose of E-mail! . . .

Even more important, many of the standards adopted by the Internet are OPEN standards, freely available to anyone who's interested in modifying or improving them. Compare this to companies which charge you an arm and a leg for their proprietary code. Now, which one do YOU think people will be more willing to work with, and improve? . . .

*What no one seems to realize is that the Net is anything BUT a commodity—it's a means to an end. And that end is not profit, but *GLOBAL COMMUNITY*.*

If we treat the Net as a commodity, then inevitably that's what it's bound to become—a balkanized, divided, proprietary collection of private networks which neither know nor care about the existence of the others. It would be like a giant version of Compu$erve, only many times worse. And in the end, by putting walls and barriers between the very users who need to communicate with each other, they will have eliminated the sole reason for their own existence—as a means to COMMUNICATE, quickly and efficiently. And when that happens, either they will die, or the future which they (and all of US) sought to promote will be relegated to obscurity.

And that would be an absolute shame.[83]

FROM: CARL HAGE

How can we devise incentives for investment in technologies for the "last mile" to the home?

The key to an investment in products needed and availability at a mass produced low price, is the establishment of standards and a detailed goal.

If there is an agreed upon standard and a large market, then a number of companies will build very low cost products designed for high volume sales. If the standard is not agreed upon, and/or deployment is uncertain, then there may not be cost effective products available.

The best way to establish standards and then insure there is a rich market of supporting products is to have open, public domain standards, with public domain reference implementations and test software.

The Internet standards established by the IETF are a good example. All the specifications are available electronically and free to the public. In order to be adopted, there must be a working implementation, and typically there was a public domain version available as a starting point and as a comparison.

Part of the research money for the NII could go toward producing some competing designs for these technologies, which could result in a public version of the specifications, and a sample reference design. Also, research money could go to produce testing software and an interoperability laboratory. Vendors who produce chipsets and boards can take the standards and reference implementation and use that as a basis for a specific product, and could then make use of the test suites and interoperability laboratory.

Public funding for the establishment of the standards, reference implementation, and test suite would eliminate many interoperability problems, and would yield low cost products very quickly, as each vendor would not need to duplicate this basic research. The money saved in lower cost product availability for the government's internal use would more than pay for the investment in a publicly available technology.[84]

CONCLUSION

Because the NTIA conference was held online, many more points of view were heard than is normal. Prominent debates included that of encouraging "economic development" versus mandating "universal service" and depending on the "free market" versus recognizing the need for government regulation to make access available to all. Another issue raised was, will the NII be an extension of the Internet or something completely new? If the former, then it is important to acknowledge the origin and significance of the Internet, and to properly study and understand the contribution the current global computer communications network makes to society. Many who participated in the online conference expressed the hope that the government would be helpful to society at large in providing access to these networks to all who desire access.

Despite the many objections to privatization of the NSFNet expressed during the NTIA conference in November 1994, the public NSFnet (National Science Foundation Network) was put to death quietly on May 1, 1995. Users heard about the shut-down indirectly. Universities and other providers who depended on the NSFnet might have reported service disruptions the week or two before while they re-established their network providers and routing tables. No announcements were made about the transfer from a publicly subsidized U.S. Internet backbone to a commercial backbone. The switch signaled a change in priorities of what the Internet will be used for. May 1, 1995 was also the opening date of a national electronic open meeting sponsored by the U.S. government on "People and their Governments in the Information Age." Apparently, the U.S. government was sponsoring this online meeting from various public access sites and paying commercial providers in the process. Something is deeply ironic in this government-mandated change to increase government expenses.

But also, on May 1, 1995, there was a presentation at a branch of the New York Public Library which focused on the value of the Internet and Usenet as a cooperative network. The Internet and Usenet have provided the means for new voices to be heard without being overwhelmed by the more established voices of society. May Day is traditionally a people's holiday around the world. On May Day 1995, the domain of the commons was opened up to the commercial world. But the commercial world already has a strong hold on all other broadcast media, and these media have become of little or no value. The Internet has been a social treasure for people in the United States and around the world. It is important to value this treasure and protect it from commercial interests. As such, this move by the U.S. government is disappointing, especially considering the testimony presented by many Internet and Usenet users who participated in the November 1994 NTIA Virtual Conference on Universal Service and Open Access to the Telecommunications Network.

In order to make any socially useful policy concerning the National Information Infrastructure (NII), it is necessary to bring the greatest possible number of people into the process of discussion and debate.[85] The NTIA online conference is a prototype of possible future online meetings leading to direct democracy. There are several steps that need to be taken for the online media to function to support direct democracy. First of all, it is necessary to make access easily available, including establishing permanent public Internet access computer locations throughout the country, along with local phone numbers to allow citizens to connect their personal computers to the Net. Second, it is wrong to encourage people to participate in online discussions about government policy and then ask them to pay for that participation. Rather, it is important to figure out some system for paying people who participate in their government. Payment for participation is not an easy issue to decide, but it is a necessary step forward in order to facilitate more participation by more people.

The online archives of the avail forum and the redefus forum provide important reading.[86] It would be useful if they were available in print form to those involved with NII policy decisions and for people around the United States and the world who are interested in the future of the Net. This online conference was an important event in the effort to examine how the NII will grow from the foundation established by the Internet. However, it should not only stand as a landmark. Rather, it should set a precedent for future conferences which will begin to provide the basis of a new social contract between people and their government.

NOTES

1. James Mill, *Essays on Government, Jurisprudence, Liberty of the Press and Law of Nations,* (New York: Augustus Kelley Publishers, 1986), 8. Reprint.
2. *Ibid.*, 6.
3. *Ibid.*, 13.
4. Christopher Lasch, "Journalism, Publicity, and the Lost Art of Argument," *Media Studies Journal* 9 (Winter 1995): 81–91.
5. *Ibid.*, 89.
6. Jeffrey B. Abramson, "Electronic Town Meetings: Proposals for Democracy's Future," prepared for the Aspen Institute Communications and Society Program.
7. The Net is the Internet, Usenet, mailing lists, and so on.
8. The NTIA virtual conference was sponsored by the National Telecommunications Information Administration (NTIA) and the Information Infrastructure Task Force (IITF), as part of the Administration's National Information Infrastructure initiative. This study draws on excerpts from the archives.
9. The goals of the NTIA Conference are listed in chapter 11.
10. From: Randolph Langley <langley@dirac.scri.fsu.edu>
    Date: Thu 17 Nov 1994 09:27:51 -0500
    Subject: [AVAIL:57] Re: my question
    Message-Id: <199411171427.AA91585@dirac.scri.fsu.edu>
11. From: Bob Summers <bsummers@vt.edu>
    Date: Thu 17 Nov 1994 17:27:09 -0500
    Subject: Re: [AVAIL:96] Re: my question
    Message-Id: <199411180135.RAA07684@virtconf.digex.net>
12. From: W. Curtiss Priest <BMSLIB@MITVMA.MIT.EDU>
    Date: Mon 21 Nov 94 09:10:21 EST
    Subject: Re: [REDEFUS:189] REDEFUS digest 29
    Message-Id: <199411211811.KAA17129@virtconf.digex.net>

13. From: wc_resa@server.greatlakes.k12.mi.us (Wayne County RESA)
    Date: Mon 14 Nov 1994 14:17:11 -0500
    Subject: Re: [REDEFUS:17] Re: Public Access
    Message-Id: <9411141918.AA07357@server.greatlakes.k12.mi.us>
14. From: BNN Television <bnn@world.std.com>
    Date: Thu 17 Nov 1994 18:20:01 +0001 EST
    Subject: Re: [REDEFUS:37] Re: Public Access
    Message-Id: <Pine.3.89.9411171753.A23713-0100000@world.std.com>
15. From: Brent Wall <brentw@freenet.scri.fsu.edu>
    Date: Sat 19 Nov 1994 11:22:46 -0500 EST
    Message-Id: <Pine.3.89.9411191130.C17368-0100000@freenet3.scri.fsu.edu>
16. From: Stephen Brenner <sbrenner@efn.org>
    Date: Wed 16 Nov 1994 05:07:24 -0800
    Subject: Re: [REDEFUS:31] Re: Public Access
    Message-Id: <9411161210.AA17284@efn.efn.org>
17. From: Lew McDaniel <MCDANIEL@wvuadmin3.csc.wvu.edu>
    Organization: WVU Computing Services
    Date: Mon 14 Nov 1994 14:55:34 EST
    Subject: Re: [REDEFUS:15] Pilot Projects
    Message-Id: <3A45E1049AE@wvuadmin3.csc.wvu.edu>
18. From: Dave W Mitchell <dmitchel@ednet1.osl.or.gov>
    Date: Mon 14 Nov 1994 14:12:54 -0800
    Subject: Re: [REDEFUS:22] Re: Pilot Projects
    Message-Id: <199411142212.AA12401@ednet1.osl.or.gov>
19. From: Daniel Lieberman <danlie@ix.netcom.com>
    Date: Thu 17 Nov 1994 14:11:03 -0800
    Subject: Competency and access
    Message-Id: <199411172211.OAA24888@ix.ix.netcom.com>
20. From: Sean <sconnell@silver.ucs.indiana.edu>
    Date: Thu 17 Nov 1994 23:00:28 -0500 EST
    Subject: A Plea
    Message-Id: <199411180708.XAA21950@virtconf.digex.net>
21. From: Colette Brooks <crb@well.sf.ca.us>
    Date: Sat., 19 Nov 1994 09:30:16 -0800
    Subject: my 2$
    Message-Id: <199411191730.JAA19829@well.sf.ca.us>
22. From: Bill Russell <RUSSELLB@ext23.oes.orst.edu>
    Message-Id: <2ed3a9cf.ext23@ext23.OES.ORST.EDU>
    Date: 23 Nov 94 12:45:00
    Subject: Re[2]: [REDEFUS:68] Re: NTIA Virtual Conference universal access.
23. From: Brent Wall <brentw@freenet.scri.fsu.edu>
    To: avail@virtconf.ntia.doc.gov
    Date: Sat 19 Nov 1994 11:00:24 -0500 EST
    Message-Id: <Pine.3.89.9411191018.A17368-0100000@freenet3.scri.fsu.edu>

24. From: HARVEY GOODSTEIN <HGOODSTEIN@gallua.gallaudet.edu>
Date: Thu 17 Nov 1994 14:18:52 -0500 EST
Subject: Universal Service definition
Message-id: <01HJL7LBBLQQ01ERLS@GALLUA.BITNET>
25. From: Ellen Davis Burnham<edb1@Ra.MsState.Edu>
Date: Sat 19 Nov 1994 22:09:22 -0600 CST
Subject: Re: [AVAIL:124] AVAIL digest 29
Message-ID: <Pine.SUN.3.91.941119212024.9892B-100000@Isis.MsState.Edu>
26. From: LucyCo@aol.com
Date: Sun 20 Nov 1994 15:09:31 -0500
Subject: Re: [AVAIL:137] AVAIL digest 37
Message-Id: <941120150557_3543309@aol.com>
27. From: Carl Hage <chage@rahul.net>
Date: Sun 20 Nov 94 18:52:16 PST
Subject: Glasnost for the Information Age
Message-Id: <9411210252.AA20328@slick.chage.com>
28. From: Chloe Lewis <chloel@microsoft.com>
Date: Tue 22 Nov 94 14:00:29 TZ
Subject: the Internet's other ancestor
Message-Id: <9411222159.AA07745@netmail2.microsoft.com>
29. From: Carl Hage <chage@rahul.net>
Date: Tue 15 Nov 94 05:21:42 PST
Subject: Redefining Universal Service and Open Access
Message-Id: <9411151321.AA18686@slick.chage.com>
30. From: Susan Hadden <shadden@mail.utexas.edu>
Date: Thu 17 Nov 1994 14:52:01 -0600
Subject: Re: [REDEFUS:128] REDEFUS digest 14
Message-Id: <199411172052.OAA23573@mail.utexas.edu>
31. From: Bob Jacobson <cyberoid@u.washington.edu>
Date: Mon 14 Nov 94 22:04:12 -0800
Subject: Re: [REDEFUS:19] Re: Public Access
Message-Id: <9411150604.AA25921@stein1.u.washington.edu>
32. From: Carly Henderson <cmh@lclark.edu>
Date: Thu 17 Nov 1994 13:36:33 -0800 PST
Message-Id: <Pine.OSF.3.91.941117131202.5097A-100000@sun>
33. From: Robert J. Berrington III <berringr@river.it.gvsu.edu>
Date: Fri18 Nov 1994 11:11:42 -0500 EST
Subject: Public awareness
Message-Id: <Pine.HPP.3.90.941118104318.23355A-100000@river.it.gvsu.edu>
34. From: Martin Kessel <mkessel@world.std.com>
Date: Wed 23 Nov 1994 15:29:57 -0500

Subject: BNN Cablecast on Universal Access
Message-Id: <199411232029.AA16911@world.std.com>

35. From: <MAADR007@SIVM.SI.EDU>
Date: Thu 17 Nov 94 14:00:16 EST
Subject: universal access but not ubiquitous use
Message-Id: <199411172209.OAA20275@virtconf.digex.net>
36. From: Dr. Robert LaRose <LAROSE@tc.msu.edu>
Date: Thu 17 Nov 1994 15:03:37 EST
Subject: Re: [REDEFUS:123] universal access but not ubiquitous use
Message-ID: <224FE632CC5@tc.msu.edu>
37. From: howland@nsipo.nasa.gov
Date: Wed 16 Nov 1994 19:19:23 -0800
Subject: Re: [REDEFUS:67] Re: Public Access
Message-Id: <199411170319.TAA11501@noc2.arc.nasa.gov>
38. From: Don Evans <don@dcez.com>
Date: Mon 14 Nov 1994 13:25:42 -500 EST
Subject: Universal Access...
Message-ID: <Pine.3.89.9411141352.G26106-0100000@dcez.dcez.com>
39. From: Michael Hauben <hauben@columbia.edu>
Date: Tue 22 Nov 1994 01:54:36 -0500
Subject: Need to stress concept of active communication and interconnection
Message-Id: <199411220654.AA28036@merhaba.cc.columbia.edu>
40. From: BHARRIS@ntia.doc.gov
Date: Mon 21 Nov 1994 16:04:59 -0500
Subject: Interim Summary for Availability List
41. From: rehm@zso.dec.com
Date: Mon 14 Nov 94 13:50:03 -0800
Subject: Re: [REDEFUS:22] Re: Pilot Projects
Message-Id: <9411142150.AA09999@slugbt.zso.dec.com>
42. From: Debbie Sinmao <debbie@harmony.cdinet.com>
Date: Thu 17 Nov 1994 13:17:18 -0500 EST
Subject: Re: [REDEFUS:40] Re: NTIA Virtual Conference KeyNote Address
Message-Id: <Pine.3.89.9411171341.A27812-0100000@harmony.cdinet.com>
43. From: Robert J. Berrington III <berringr@river.it.gvsu.edu>
Date: Thu 17 Nov 1994 13:30:11 -0500 EST
Subject: Re: [REDEFUS:115] Re: NTIA Virtual Conference KeyNote Address
Message-Id: <Pine.HPP.3.90.941117132629.13213C-100000@river.it.gvsu.edu>
44. From: Rey Barry <rbarry@hopper.itc.virginia.edu>
Date: Thu 17 Nov 1994 17:19:34 -0500 EST
Subject: Re: [REDEFUS:133] REDEFUS digest 15
Message-Id: <199411172219.RAA15419@Hopper.itc.Virginia.EDU>

45. From: Ron Choura 517-334-6240
    <CHOURA%A1@COMMERCE.STATE.MI.US>
    Posting-date: Mon 14 Nov 1994 15:37:00 -0400 EDT
    Subject: NARUC Comments D. J. Miller
46. From: Carl Hage <hage@netcom.com>
    Date: Wed 23 Nov 1994 14:41:39 -0800 PST
    Subject: What happens when usage expands?
    Message-ID: <Pine.3.89.9411231431.A11463-0100000@netcom13>
47. From: Carl Hage <hage@netcom.com>
    Date: Wed 23 Nov 1994 16:33:17 -0800
    Subject: Re: Comments to C. Hage concerns
    Message-Id: <199411240033.QAA24975@netcom13.netcom.com>
48. From: Carl Hage <chage@rahul.net>
    Date: Thu 17 Nov 94 19:31:52 PST
    Subject: Net Economics 101
    Message-Id: <9411180331.AA19584@slick.chage.com>
49. From: Kathleen L. Bloomberg <bloomber@eagle.sangamon.edu>
    Date: Tue 15 Nov 1994 13:03:22 -0600
    Subject: Universal access & libraries
50. From: Solomon Philip Hill <blast@leland.Stanford.EDU>
    Date: Mon 14 Nov 1994 13:51:04 -0800 PST
    Subject: Re: [REDEFUS:17] Re: Public Accesss
    Message-ID: <Pine.3.89.9411141310.A6158-
    0100000@elaine30.Stanford.EDU>
51. From: Dave W. Mitchell <dmitchel@ednet1.osl.or.gov>
    Date: Mon 14 Nov 1994 08:17:20 -0800
    Subject: Statement
    Message-Id: <199411141617.AA25971@ednet1.osl.or.gov>
52. From: msyssft!microsys!susang@uu6.psi.com
    Date: 16-Nov.-94 11:35
    Message-Id: E0E6C92E01B361E1
53. From: Carl Hage <chage@rahul.net>
    Date: Thu 17 Nov 94 14:14:54 PST
    Subject: Re: [REDEFUS:19] Re: Public Accesss
    Message-Id: <9411172214.AA19457@slick.chage.com>
54. From: Lew McDaniel <MCDANIEL@wvuadmin3.csc.wvu.edu>
    Date: Fri., 18 Nov 1994 08:40:12 EST
    Subject: Re: [REDEFUS:139] REDEFUS digest 16
    Message-ID: <3FE206E223A@wvuadmin3.csc.wvu.edu>
55. From: mtn@mtn.org (MTN)
    Date: Tue 15 Nov 1994 12:39:33 -0600
    Subject: Re: [REDEFUS:19] Re: Public Accesss
    Message-Id: <aaee6246010210049a8a@[198.174.235.202]>

56. From: Stephen Brenner <sbrenner@efn.org>
Date: Wed., 16 Nov 1994 05:07:24 -0800
Subject: Re: [REDEFUS:31] Re: Public Accesss
Message-Id: <9411161210.AA17284@efn.efn.org>
57. From: Carol Deering <deering@odi.cwc.whecn.edu>
Date: Fri., 18 Nov 1994 09:33:14 -700 MST
Subject: rural areas
Message-ID: <Pine.SCO.3.90.941118085624.725A-100000@odi.cwc.whecn.edu>
58. From: Marilyn Letitia Korhonen <korhonen@tenet.edu>
Date: Fri., 18 Nov 1994 07:52:32 -0600 CST
Subject: Re: [AVAIL:100] Re: Rural areas
Message-ID: <Pine.3.89.9411180704.C27478-0100000@Gayle-Gaston.tenet.edu>
59. From: Ron Choura 517-334-6240
<CHOURA%A1@COMMERCE.STATE.MI.US>
Posting-date: Mon., 14 Nov 1994 15:37:00 -0400 EDT
Subject: NARUC Comments D. J. Miller
60. From: Frank Whittle <WHITTLE@SMTPGATE.sunydutchess.edu>
Date: Mon Nov 14 21:53:09 1994
Message-Id: <9411150254.AA51246@admaix.sunydutchess.edu>
61. From: Brent Wall <brentw@freenet.scri.fsu.edu>
Date: Wed 16 Nov 1994 19:39:09 -0500 EST
Subject: Universal Access—an Equivocation
Message-Id: <Pine.3.89.9411161905.A19851-0100000@freenet3.scri.fsu.edu>
62. From: Henry Huang <hwh6k@fulton.seas.virginia.edu>
Date: Wed 23 Nov 1994 12:52:37 -0500
Subject: Some Thoughts on Public Access (and this Conference)
Message-Id: <199411231752.MAA45745@fulton.seas.Virginia.EDU>
63. From: Rey Barry <rbarry@hopper.itc.virginia.edu>
Date: Thu 17 Nov 1994 17:19:34 -0500 EST
Subject: Re: [REDEFUS:133] REDEFUS digest 15
Message-Id: <199411172219.RAA15419@Hopper.itc.Virginia.EDU>
64. From: Paul Weismantel <weismant@esd.dl.nec.com>
Organization: NEC America Inc
Date: Wed 16 Nov 94 13:31:46 -0600
Subject: Re: [REDEFUS:80] Re: NTIA Virt
Message-Id: <E15CCA2E011C0000@smtp.esd.dl.nec.com>
65. From: Martin Kessel <mkessel@world.std.com>
Date: Wed 23 Nov 1994 15:29:57 -0500
Subject: BNN Cablecast on Universal Access
Message-Id: <199411232029.AA16911@world.std.com>

66. From: RICHARD M. KENSHALO <PMRMK@tundra.alaska.edu>
    Date: Tue 15 Nov 1994 08:16:08 -0800
    Subject: Universal Service
    Message-id: <01HJI2DC28PIHSJAJE@UA.ORCA.ALASKA.EDU>
67. From: Jeanne Gallo (using BNN Television) <bnn@world.std.com>
    Date: Fri18 Nov 1994 12:22:53 +0001 EST
    Subject: Community Centers
    Message-Id: <Pine.3.89.9411181228.A2135-0100000@world.std.com>
68. From: BHARRIS@ntia.doc.gov
    Date: Mon 21 Nov 1994 16:04:59 -0500
    Subject: Interim Summary for Availability List
69. From: Carl Hage <hage@netcom.com>
    Date: Wed 23 Nov 1994 18:27:53 -0800
    Subject: Re: Some Thoughts on Public Access (and this Conference)
    Message-Id: <199411240227.SAA08168@netcom13.netcom.com>
70. From: Viraj Jha <jhav@bcvms.bc.edu>
    Date: Wed 16 Nov 1994 09:48:34 +0000
    Subject: Re: [REDEFUS:37] Re: Public Accesss
    Message-Id: <MailDrop1.0b13.941116094834@onra01p6.bc.edu.>
71. From: Christine Weiss <chrisw@muskox.alaska.edu>
    Date: Thu 17 Nov 1994 09:28:56 -0900 AST
    Subject: Who will fund?
    Message-Id: <Pine.HPP.3.90.941117091241.9833A-100000@muskox.alaska.edu>
72. From: Carl Hage <chage@rahul.net>
    Date: Thu 17 Nov 94 12:23:44 PST
    Subject: Re: Cheap Public Access
    Message-Id: <9411172023.AA19431@slick.chage.com>
73. From: Stan Witnov <74543.720@compuserve.com>
    Date: 18 Nov 94 02:33:42 EST
    Subject: FOUR DAY CONFERENCE THOTS
    Message-ID: <941118073341_74543.720_EHH62-2@CompuServe.COM>
74. From: Jawaid Bazyar <bazyar@netcom.com>
    Subject: Re: Need for Federal Oversight of Access and Availability
    Date: Fri 18 Nov 1994 18:34:41 GMT
    Message-ID: <bazyarCzH7Lu.HoE@netcom.com>
75. From: howland@nsipo.nasa.gov
    Date: Wed 23 Nov 1994 19:35:33 -0800
    Subject: Re: [REDEFUS:253] REDEFUS digest 56
    Message-Id: <199411240335.TAA13844@noc.arc.nasa.gov>
76. From: Martin Kessel <mkessel@world.std.com>
    Date: Wed 23 Nov 1994 15:29:57 -0500
    Subject: BNN Cablecast on Universal Access
    Message-Id: <199411232029.AA16911@world.std.com>

77. From: Carl Hage <chage@rahul.net>
Date: Tue 15 Nov 94 05:21:42 PST
Subject: Redefining Universal Service and Open Access
Message-Id: <9411151321.AA18686@slick.chage.com>
78. From: Hubert Jessup, General Manager at BNN Television <bnn@world.std.com>
Date: Thu 17 Nov 1994 11:20:11 +0001 EST
Subject: Need for on-going public access sites
Message-Id: <Pine.3.89.9411171052.A20944-0100000@world.std.com>
79. From: Public Access Site <vcavail@latte.spl.lib.wa.us>
Date: Wed 23 Nov 1994 12:46:30 -0800 PST
Subject: Affordability
Message-Id: <Pine.OSF.3.91.941121204346.1399A-100000@latte.spl.lib.wa.us>
80. From: Henry Huang <hwh6k@fulton.seas.virginia.edu>
Date: Wed 23 Nov 1994 12:52:37 -0500
Subject: Some Thoughts on Public Access (and this Conference)
Message-Id: <199411231752.MAA45745@fulton.seas.Virginia.EDU>
81. From: Sean <sconnell@silver.ucs.indiana.edu>
Date: Fri 18 Nov 1994 15:01:16 -0500 EST
Subject: Re: [REDEFUS:155] REDEFUS digest 20
Message-Id: <199411182309.PAA21212@virtconf.digex.net>
82. From: Henry Huang <hwh6k@fulton.seas.virginia.edu>
Date: Tue 15 Nov 1994 22:04:37 -0500
Subject: Re: [AVAIL:1] NTIA Virtual Conference KeyNote Address
Message-Id: <199411160304.WAA57037@fulton.seas.Virginia.EDU>
83. From: Henry Huang <hwh6k@fulton.seas.virginia.edu>
Date: Wed 23 Nov 1994 12:52:37 -0500
Subject: Some Thoughts on Public Access (and this Conference)
Message-Id: <199411231752.MAA45745@fulton.seas.Virginia.EDU>
84. From: Carl Hage <chage@rahul.net>
Date: Thu 17 Nov 94 23:00:22 PST
Subject: Comments on Susan G. Hadden Essay
Message-Id: <9411180700.AA19595@slick.chage.com>
85. See the opening speech by C. P. Snow in *Management and the Computer of the Future,* Martin Greenberger, ed. (Cambridge, Mass.: The MIT Press, 1962).
86. The NTIA Virtual Archives are available via the World Wide Web at http://www.ntia.doc./opadhome/virtual/

An early version of this chapter by Michael Hauben appeared in *Proceedings Telecommunities '95 August 19–23, 1995: Equity on the Internet.*

15

Exploring New York City's Online Community

A Snapshot of nyc.general

Something new is gradually sneaking into every part of our world. The agent of change is the global computer communications network, "the full map of [which] no one knows; it changes every day."[1] Not only is the change on a world scale, the Net is having local effects as well. Local social communities are being redefined more and more by the global online community. This is happening in New York City.

The topic of community is one of the themes that Sally Banes explores in her book, *Greenwich Village 1963*. Banes' study of this bohemian community at the beginning of the 1960s presents an interesting model with which to compare today's growing online community in the Big Apple. Community has traditionally been understood to mean a body of people who affiliate with one another based on family ties, location, shared religious practices, or common work places.[2] There are, of course, other definitions, such as that of historian Thomas Bender, who Banes says "prefers to reconceptualize community, suggesting that it is not a static social form that is disappearing, but rather that new, dynamic, overlapping forms of small-scale networks have arisen. . . ."[3]

Bender proposes that it is important to examine the technological structure behind a community. The technological structure upon which today's online communities exist is that of the Internet. The Internet is the interconnection of smaller networks. As such, the Internet provides the glue which connects other networks together. This means that by being on the New York State Education and Research Network (NYSERNET), I can send e-mail from New York City to someone on a different network (for example, Michnet in Michigan) because the networks automatically route my message from my network to the intended recipient's network through intermediate networks. The global computer communications network consists of small-scale networks of computers (and, in turn, of people) connected to each other.

Banes' initial definition of community translates into saying people living in New York City are part of the community of New York City. As everyone knows, New York City is a large place. Yet people are proud to say they are from New York City and to relate to things New York. New York can also be an isolating and alienating place, however. Thanks to developing technology, the contemporary concept of community in New York is evolving in ways similar to Bender's model, leading to less isolation.

The '60s had the soapbox, the '90s have computer networks. People are communicating with other people both locally and globally in public discussion forums, such as Usenet newsgroups and mailing lists, and through private e-mail, forming in the process new communities of common interests. Before these communities became a reality, their possible benefits were envisioned by J. C. R. Licklider and Robert Taylor in their paper, "The Computer as a Communication Device."[4] Bender's idea of ever-changing, overlapping social communities is similar to what Licklider and Taylor foresaw as a result of developments in computer communications. Already today, computer assisted networking allows groups to form to discuss an idea, focus in or broaden out, and reform to fit the new ideas that have resulted from the process.

In the new forms of communication technologies, the distinction between a stranger and a friend is becoming blurred. Strangers are no longer strange; rather they are people who might prove to be valuable resources. One example of the public discussion forums is a Usenet newsgroup called New York City General or nyc.general (see the chapter appendix for a partial listing of other New York City–related online resources). Following is only a little of what I found in one day's browsing, which represents about a week of discussion in this public space. Just a warning—you are about to witness a composite of life in New York City.

"My boss is going to fire me," begins the first of the discussions I decided to read. The subject line read "Getting Unemployment," but the message left that as a last recourse. The person continued in the request for help, "What can I do? I'm not a minority or member of a protected group so that rules out the labor board, EEOC, etc. . . . Could I find a lawyer to take the case on contingency? Else, how easy is it to get unemployment after being fired. No questions asked or do they give you the third degree? Thanks in advance!"[5]

A genuine problem was posted. As such, responses were likely to be sent by others, and indeed they were. The first public response went: "If you're being fired by your boss, and you've been on the job for a certain period of time (6 months possibly?), and you were being paid legally on the books, unemployment compensation is guaranteed. Just go to the unemployment office and do the bureaucracy dance."[6]

Probably neither the original poster nor the person who responded knew the other. The fact that these two are probably strangers and, before this point, totally unconnected, could be why the response was posted publicly. The time and effort that person put into publicly responding could be helpful to yet another person reading the discussion.

The next public response in sequence provided some clarification which could or could not be seen as being unfriendly. The poster added that unemployment insurance could not be collected if the person were "fired for cause, such as stealing."[7]

The last public response to the discussion that I saved brought up the right of the boss to contest the granting of unemployment insurance. The response ends with some support: "It is just another long, tedious hassle to get you to give up and forget about it. But if you feel you deserve the unemployment benefits because he/she did not fire you with just cause, fight till the very end . . . Good luck."[8]

All in all, these three public responses helped to define the previously tenuous concept of unemployment compensation held by the original poster. However, the picture is not complete. I am sure the person with the question, who could be reached via an e-address, probably received private e-mail with suggestions and comments that are not available as part of the public record of nyc.general.

What other issues are discussed? Concerns about public living conditions—such as discussions about the past, present, and future of the subway system—happen on a regular basis. Even an employee of the Metropolitan Transportation Authority, who claimed to be acting in an unofficial capacity, replied to questions and concerns about the subway. The open public forum of nyc.general allowed this person to talk about his job in a way he felt was helpful to many people. Apparently, such is not yet true for any New York politicians entrusted to represent their constituency. However, such attempts are happening. Former Governor Cuomo ran a gopher information server in his campaign for re-election, and New York State law and pending State Assembly bills are online, accessible by telnet at assembly.state.ny.us.

Some examples of questions by people on how to survive in Manhattan include where to get cheap checking accounts (Amalgamated Bank of New York with true no-fee checking), what dentist or doctor to visit for particular problems, what rights tenants have, how and when to approach the Department of Motor Vehicles, and what is the best slice of pizza in town (one person voted for Koronet, while another voted for Famous Famiglia).

Other issues raised were not so cut and dry. The pros and cons of rent control were discussed in the following exchange:

Well, having just moved from the West Coast, I can tell you this about New York in general: there is no such thing as a nice place for a reasonable rent. This place is absurdly expensive—God only knows how rents can be so high in a place where roughly 10 million people live.[9]

The first response was not much of a discussion, but would definitely start one. The person wrote in answer: "Two words: Rent control."[10]

A second answer about rent control went like this:

*Your solutions might be okay for the burbs, but this is New York you're talking about. These regulations were not the *cause* of high rents, they were enacted *because* of high rents. Removing them will harm the city in the short term and cause unpredictable results in the long term, as deregulation always does.*[11]

In these and other cases, the open quality of debate and discussion on nyc.general make it not only a helpful neighborhood, but a living newspaper that both criticizes current newspapers and provides features. My next brief example is a post about the quality of the *New York Times*. The subject of the message was "New York Times technology coverage." The poster argued: "No one should expect the NY Times . . . to cover underlying technology well—that's not their specialty. The Times is a general-interest paper."[12]

One of the responses was, "Sorry, they should do a better job. That they don't is an indication of the generally low level of scientific literacy in the US. Cutting them slack over stuff like this just reinforces this tendency."[13]

From this criticism of the *New York Times*, we go to an unusual experience that I could call a feature. The person wrote:

Reminds me when I was homeless and still had a valid VISA card which was maxed out. Apparently, between approximately 2:50AM and 4:25AM at night, Safeway stores would not check the validity of the transaction, and would just put it through. All the charges would show up on my VISA bill (which I never paid), and I would eat that day. It's funny because the bank decided that I needed a higher limit, and raised the limit twice, even after seven months of delinquency! My card wasn't canceled until one day I called and asked what the balance was —and a letter was promptly sent saying there was suspicious activity, and the card was thus canceled. Thank god I've since filled in the missing links between me and a job, and may even start making enough to pay past debts. Depends on a few factors. . . .[14]

These examples paint a picture of people today with a common interest, and only secondarily of a common location, making themselves available to be helpful to others with that interest. The obvious interest is life in New York City. These exchanges appear similar to both the Village community presented in *Greenwich Village 1963* and to Licklider and Taylor's observations on online communities in the 1960s. Greenwich Village in 1963 was made up partially of a community of artists and intellectuals who "formed a constructed network, based on work, school, and other interests."[15] Licklider and Taylor asked the question, "What will online interactive communities be like?"[16]. They answered by writing, "They will be communities not of common location, but of common interest."[17]

The community life made available in Greenwich Village gave residents "the warmth of face-to-face, 'authentic' experience in the midst of escalating metropolitan anonymity."[18]

Villagers also felt a part of the community because people were active politically to protect their community from large structural changes that other organizations wanted to make happen.[19] The online examples demonstrate a friendliness of a good neighborhood in the midst of an ever-growing city and show its active character. To be part of the online community one must become a part of the discussion. Otherwise, that which is discussed will be less helpful, and the online lurker will not be in touch with anyone else.

The examples of online activities are not provided to say there are no problems online, but to demonstrate that the advantages are more important and outweigh the disadvantages. I have attempted to present a snapshot of a fairly new entity which is both making New York a much more friendly place and providing a forum for people of disparate beliefs to meet on equal grounds. In the end, online communications can help to enrich local community and community relations rather than diminish them. Taking a serious look at the actual dynamic of the communication makes it possible to begin to understand the community of online New York City.

NOTES

1. Ithiel de Sola Pool, *Technologies Without Boundaries: On Telecommunications in a Global Age*, Eli Noam, ed. (Cambridge, Mass.: Harvard University Press, 1990), 56.
2. Sally Banes, *Greenwich Village 1963: Avant-Garde Performance and the Effervescent Body* (Durham, N.C.: Duke University Press, 1993), 37.
3. *Ibid.*
4. J. C. R. Licklider and Robert W. Taylor, "The Computer as a Communication Device," in *In Memoriam: J. C. R. Licklider 1915–1990* (Palo Alto, Calif.: Digital

Systems Research Center, 1990). Originally published in *Science and Technology*, April 1968.

5. nyc.general, Message-ID: <B6009I1.sorter@delphi.com>
6. nyc.general, Message-ID: <mbayerCzvypp.187@netcom.com>
7. nyc.general, Message-ID: <3bg5nb$bbu@titan.imsi.com>
8. nyc.general, Message-ID: <3beb21$461@dockmaster.phantom.com>
9. nyc.market.housing, Message-ID: <3bdkcr$fn5@syko.cosmic.com>
10. nyc.market.housing, Message-ID: <3be4jp$8eo@apakabar.cc.columbia.edu>
11. nyc.general, Message-ID: <39jbfr$3bo@cmcl2.NYU.EDU>
12. nyc.general, Message-ID: <D07EM1.3H3@world.std.com>
13. nyc.general, Message-ID: <3bq5hp$s0a@nntp.Stanford.EDU>
14. nyc.general, Message-ID: <3bjcvl$i9l@panix3.panix.com>
15. Banes, *Greenwich Village 1963*, 78.
16. Licklider and Taylor, "The Computer as a Communication Device," 37.
17. *Ibid.*, 38.
18. Banes, *Greenwich Village 1963*, 15.

An earlier version of this chapter by Michael Hauben appeared in *Computer-Mediated Communication Magazine* in May 1995.

Appendix

New York City Online Resources

Addresses for most sites listed available at http://www.columbia.edu/~hauben/nyc-guides.html.

I. PUBLIC DECENTRALIZED NEWSGROUPS

nyc hierarchy—nyc.general, nyc.food, nyc.market.housing, nyc.jobs.*, nyc.politics, nyc.announce, nyc.seminars, nyc.singles, nyc.personals, nyc.transit, etc.
ny hierarchy for state-wide issues—ny.general, ny.forsale, ny.wanted, ny.seminars, etc.
alt.sports hierarchy—such as alt.sports.baseball.ny-mets, alt.sports.football.pro.ny-giants, etc.
moderated newsfeed—clari.local.nyc, etc., clari.* groups

II. PUBLIC LISTSERVS AND MAILING LISTS

ebikes—Metro NYC bicycle discussion list
NYCOMNET—NY Community Networks list
NE-RAVES—electronic water cooler for ravers and others

III. LOCAL NEWSGROUP HIERARCHIES

Serving particular university communities e.g., nyu.general, columbia.general.bboard
Serving the community on a particular Internet provider's system, e.g., panix.*, dorsai.*, mindvox.*, etc.
Serving other particular communities

IV. INFORMATION SERVERS

Gopher

- Rutger's Net Person's Guide to NYC
- CUNY Graduate Center's Guide to NYC
- NYU's New York City and Greenwich Village Communities
- New York Book, Bike, and Art . . . from Panix

- Echo's Cool Stuff in NYC, contributed by members of ECHO
- Weather forecasts

FTP

- Lists of NYC bookstores
- Lists of NYC record stores
- NYC beer guide

WWW

- Lists of WWW web sites in NYC
- Theatre on Broadway: listings
- Dining information and menus
- Web sites for performance spaces (Kitchen, Knitting Factory)
- Mediabridge.com's NYC "tourist" info (previously Columbia CS Department)

PART 4

Contributions Toward Developing a Theoretical Framework

16

The Expanding Commonwealth of Learning

Printing and the Net

A revolution in human communications is happening. People around the world are connecting to each other via the new computer telecommunication networks now known as the Net. The Net, in a significant way, is a continuation of the important technological development of the printing press. The printing press might seem to be an unlikely choice for such a comparison considering the similarity that might be seen between the Net and, for example, television, the telephone, radio, or the news media. That is why it is important to compare the current networking developments with the history of printing to understand why the printing press should be seen as the forefather of the currently developing computer networks.

With the invention of the printing press in the second half of the fifteenth century, there arose print shops and printing trades. Printing and the distribution of printed works grew rapidly. In the last quarter of the twentieth century, a global computer network has emerged which gives users the ability to post and distribute their views and news broadly and inexpensively. Comparing the emergence of the printing press to the emergence of the global computer network will reveal some of the fascinating parallels which demonstrate how the Net is continuing the important social revolution that the printing press had begun.

The printing press developed out of a scribal culture surrounding the hand-copying of texts. This scribal culture could only go so far in furthering the distribution of information and ideas. Texts existed, but were largely unavailable for use by the common people. There were very few copies of books as each copy of a book had to be laboriously hand-copied from a previous copy. Relying on scribal culture for access to and distribution of knowledge caused many problems. Texts were often inaccurate as scribes made mistakes while copying them. Since a single scribe usually had access to only one copy of the text he was copying, he had no way to know if he was duplicating mistakes other scribes had made before him. The effect of copying mistakes or non-exact copies led to numerous "versions" of the same text. Also, scholars who wanted to use various texts had to travel in order to have a good variety of material to study. The majority of people could not afford, nor did they have the time, to undertake scholarly pursuits. In her book, *The Printing Revolution in Early Modern Europe*, Elizabeth Eisenstein writes:

> *[W]e need to recall the conditions that prevailed before texts could be set in type. No manuscript, however useful as a reference guide, could be preserved for long without undergoing corruption by copyists, and even this sort of "preservation" rested precariously on the shifting demands of local elites and a fluctuating incidence of trained scribal labor . . . wear and tear . . . moisture and vermin, theft or fire.*[1]

Under such conditions, scribal efforts did not preserve many valuable texts. Plenty did not survive.

Just as the printing press replaced the hand-copying of books in the Renaissance, people using computer networks are creating a new method of production and distribution of creative and intellectual written work today.

Around the same time that computer communications networks started to emerge from computer communications research communities in the early 1970s, the personal computer (PC) was developed by students, hobbyists, and proponents of the free-speech movement on the West Coast of the United States. The personal computer became widely available at prices many people could afford. The PC made the power of the multipurpose computer available to a wider cross section of people who otherwise would not have had access to time on the larger minicomputers or mainframe computers which were then owned by universities, businesses, and the government.

The personal computer movement made computers available to the mass of people in the United States. As computers are multipurpose, they can be used to accomplish many things. A PC can be made to duplicate the functions of a printing press, without the user having professional printing experience. In the past, a skilled printer combined movable type and engravings (woodcut, or otherwise) to mass produce copies of a page combining varied images (text and graphics). The personal computer brings this power from the master printer to the average individual—both in price and availability. The personal computer (for example, Apple II family, Commodore, Atari, TRS-80, etc. leading to the IBM PC family, the Apple Macintosh family, Amiga, etc.) linked to an electronic printer (first dot-matrix and daisy-wheel, later laser printers) and even more recently to scanners which convert images into usable data—make the production and reproduction of information processes available to all. Even if one does not own a PC, one can rent time on one in a store. Copy shops (in themselves part of the continual process that made publishing ubiquitous) have begun to have PCs available to rent time on. These advances make the act of publishing immensely easier. The personal computer, printers, and scanners, however, do not solve the problem of distribution.

The recent development, standardization, and interconnection of computers via computer communications networks help to solve the problem of distribution. Examples of online utilities include file transfer (ftp), remote login to other computers (telnet), remote execution of programs, electronic mail (e-mail), access to various information data bases (gopher, WWW), other information searching utilities (archie, veronica, Lycos), real-time chat (irc), and a distributed news service. These make it possible for people to share information publicly and become citizen reporters (Netnews). The two utilities most relevant to this revolution in human communication are e-mail and Netnews (or Usenet). E-mail allows for the private and semi-private distribution of information and communications through messages to a particular person or persons, or among a designated set of people via electronic mailing lists. Netnews allows for the public dissemination of information, opinions, and questions in an open forum. When a Netizen makes a contribution to any of the many defined subject areas (newsgroups), anyone from around the world who chooses to read that particular newsgroup will have a chance to read and respond to that message. Usenet's potential for inexpensive global distribution represents one major advance of Usenet beyond the printing press.

The printing press developed sometime in the 1460s and spread quickly throughout Europe. The broad distribution of presses ended the age of the scribal culture and ushered in the age of printing. "Unknown anywhere in Europe before the mid-fifteenth century," Eisenstein writes, "printers' workshops would be found in every important municipal center by 1500" (12).

Eisenstein points out that the printing press dramatically increased the total number of books, while at the same time decreasing the number of hours of labor necessary to create each book. She argues that this made the transition from hand-copied manuscripts to machine-produced books one of a revolutionary nature, and not evolutionary as claimed in much of the literature about this transformation (13). Understanding how the printing press unleashed a communications revolution provides a basis for assessing whether the establishment of worldwide computer communication networking is the next communications revolution.

New communications technologies facilitate new ways of organizing information and of thinking. The invention of the printing press changed the way texts were handled. From its outset, the men who controlled the presses, the printers, experimented with ways to use the printing press to change texts. Textual techniques such as "graduated types, running heads . . . footnotes . . . table of contents . . . superior figures, cross references. . . ." (22) are examples of the ways in which the press broke through some boundaries which had previously limited the production of books in scribal culture.

Moreover, the new technologies changed the way books were written. The establishment of printing shops in the major European cities formed a common meeting place for scholars and authors from across the continent. The great number of printing presses and printing shops enabled more people to write books and produce works that would be duplicated by the presses. When these new authors traveled they would gather in printing shops to meet other writers and scholars. Thus the printing press facilitated the meeting of minds following intellectual pursuits. The interconnection of people led to the quickening of the development of ideas and knowledge. These progenitors of the printing trade were in the forefront of the sweeping intellectual changes which the presses made possible (45). Similar connections among people are taking place on the Net today at a much faster rate. And, just as the printers were in the forefront of the printing revolution, so today the developers of computer communications software and hardware, and users are the first to experience the increased connectivity with other people around the world afforded by the computer networks.

As printing spread, publishers realized the value of utilizing input from readers to improve their product. Since the press could turn out multiple copies of a first edition quickly, many people would see the first edition and could send by letter their comments, corrections, and criticisms. Publishers and authors could then use this feedback to write and print second and third editions, and so on. Mistakes would be caught by careful readers, and printers thus "were also able to improve on themselves." Eisenstein explains that copied mistakes and mistakes in copying common with scribal copies now could be caught by the increasing number of readers. She writes, "the immemorial drift of scribal culture had been not merely arrested but actually reversed" (73).

The Net likewise provides a ready mechanism for the interaction between authors and readers. On the Net, people often keep track of knowledge, such as lists of a musician's records (discographies), or FAQ files of answers to Frequently Asked Questions. Authors of these works often act as both editor and compiler. People send further information, which the keeper of the file often adds. This makes for a communal base of information which is often available to anyone connected to the Net with at least electronic mail. The constant updating of information on the Net continues the tradition of revising intellectual work introduced by the printing press.

Eisenstein's description of how communal information was gathered is similar to how such procedures work on the Net. She writes:

> *But others created a vast network of correspondents and solicited criticism of each edition, sometimes publicly promising to mention the names of readers who sent in new information or who spotted the errors which would be weeded out (74).*

People who ask questions on the discussion sections of the Net (either Netnews or mailing lists) often summarize the answers they receive and post this summary back to the Net. When doing this, many compilers include acknowledgments of the people who supplied the information. Also, when people send in corrections to an FAQ, the keeper of the FAQ often makes a list at the end thanking these individuals.

Eisenstein details similar networks of correspondence in an example of a particular text titled the *Theatrum.*

> *By the simple expedient of being honest with his readers and inviting criticism and suggestions, Ortelius made his* Theatrum *a sort of cooperative enterprise on an international basis. He received helpful suggestions from far and wide, and cartographers stumbled over themselves to send him their latest maps of regions not covered in the* Theatrum *(74).*

On Usenet, too, making a contribution is an integral part of Netizen behavior. Netizens make a point of being helpful to others. Often the Net has made a positive difference in their lives, and they return the favor by making their own contribution, perhaps by answering the questions of others or developing an archive. These individual and, increasingly, group contributions are what have built the Net from a connection of computers and computing resources into a vast resource of people and knowledge. People who use the Net have access to Net resources and can contribute to them. Thus the culture of the Net has been shaped by people actively contributing to the growth and development of the Net. The example of the *Theatrum* shows there is a historical precedent in human nature for this "stumbling over oneself" in order to try to be helpful.[2]

The flow of information to the publishers of the *Theatrum* meant that at least 28 editions were published by the time of the publisher Ortelius' death in 1598.[3] In a similar way, Usenet is by its very nature constantly evolving. The basic element of Usenet is the post whose life is temporary. The Usenet software is designed to "expire" or delete messages after a certain time period. Without constant new contributions from people to Netnews, there would be no messages to read or discussions to take part in. So there is a constant evolution of Usenet. But, also the material in the more permanent information depositories is often updated so they evolve as well.

During the early days of the printing press, publishers' requests for information led to people starting their own research and work. "Thus a knowledge explosion was set off," Eisenstein exclaims (75). The Net follows in the tradition of the press, by having one set of people asking questions, leading to another set of people conducting research. In this sense the Net can serve the role of a think tank for the ordinary person. So the advanced possibilities the printing press made possible in the sixteenth century are being replicated many times more by the Net today. It is important to recognize and value Netnews for its contribution to human society and the advancement of knowledge.

Eisenstein observed that the art of printing opened people's eyes to their previous ignorance. She quotes the German historian, Johann Sleidan, in his *Address to the Estates of the Empire* of 1542, describing the impact printing had in Germany, "[T]he art of printing . . . [has] opened German eyes even as it is now bringing enlightenment to other countries. Each man became eager for knowledge, not without feeling a sense of amazement at his former blindness" (150).

This sentiment has been echoed by many Netizens on Usenet and in other online conversations. People have been amazed at what the Net made possible and how it has changed their lives.

Eisenstein comments in her book on the role of feedback to early authors and print publishers. She wrote that feedback helped to

> *define the difference between data collection before and after the communications shift. After printing, large-scale data collection did become subject to new forms of feedback which had not been possible in the age of the scribes (76).*

Computer networks likewise make possible very easy and natural feedback. Once one reads a message (either public or private), a simple keystroke allows the composition of an answer or response, and another keystroke is often all it takes to send the response. This takes less effort than writing a letter to a publishing house or calling a television station. Since responding to other messages is such a natural part of the online process, the procedure becomes almost automatic.

Many people who use Usenet find television dull rather than thought provoking. Doug Thompson, in a message he posted on Usenet, wrote "TV is so bloody tame and boring in comparison to Usenet." Others, too, have described how they have completely stopped watching television and reading the newspaper because of Usenet.

Eisenstein refers to the process of constant improvement which printing made possible, as observed by the Scottish philosopher David Hume: "The Power which Printing gives us of continually improving and correcting our Works in successive Editions appears to me the chief advantage of that art" (77–78). Eisenstein expands on this idea adding, "The future seem[ed] to hold more promise of enlightenment than the past" (78).

This promise of a better future is also seen by those on the Net. People online are being enlightened by the interconnection of peoples around the world. The Net helps people make social connections which were never before possible, or which were relatively hard to achieve. Geography and time no longer are boundaries. Social limitations and conventions no longer prevent potential friendships or partnerships. In this manner Netizens are meeting other Netizens from far-away and close by that they might never have met without the Net.

Eisenstein reports that the printing press also helped people interact with other people who they would not have met before its invention. "Vicarious participation in more distant events was enhanced," she writes, "and even while local ties were loosened, links to larger collective units were being forged" (95–96). Improvement of information about other parts of the world "by the output of more uniform maps containing more uniform boundaries and place names" helped people to know more of the facts of the world. "Similar developments affected local customs, laws, languages, and costumes" (56).

The Net similarly provides people with a broader view of the world by introducing them to other people's ideas and opinions. The Net makes it possible to access more and differing viewpoints than were normally available in a person's daily life.

Much as printers' houses in the sixteenth century served as places to stop when traveling, computers and phone lines connect people around the world in our times. Eisenstein describes how such print shops, "point to the formation of polyglot households in scattered urban centers upon the continent." She observes that during the sixteenth century,

> *such printing shops represented miniature "international houses." They provided wandering scholars with a meeting place, message center, sanctuary, and cultural center all in one. The new industry encouraged not only the formation of syndicates and far-flung trade networks, similar to those extended by merchants engaged in the cloth trade or in other large-scale enterprises during early modern times. It also encouraged the formation of an ethos which was specifically associated with the Commonwealth of Learning—ecumenical and tolerant without being secular, genuinely pious yet opposed to*

> *fanaticism, often combining outward conformity to diverse established churches with inner fidelity to heterodox creeds (101).*

The social networks made possible by Usenet and the emergence of the printing press are very similar. Even though Netnews has no official guiding body, Netizens have developed social rules which control and mediate the medium. For a forum to be democratic, it must be open. There may be people who have nothing intelligent to add, or only want to be disruptive or offensive. Others will often debate these troublemakers and through argumentation and the posting of opposite opinions help others to make up their own minds as to the value of the original postings.

The printing press facilitated new cross-cultural networks which "encouraged forms of combinatory activity which were social as well as intellectual" (45). Differing ideas were more easily set against one another. The theories of Arabists were set against the theories of Galenists and those of Aristotelians against Ptolemaists. Eisenstein writes:

> *Not only was confidence in old theories weakened, but an enriched reading matter also encouraged the development of new intellectual combinations and permutations. Combinatory intellectual activity . . . inspires many creative acts (44).*

The Net helps people communicate with each other who might not have communicated before. Strangers meet each other because of interest in each other's ideas, and this leads to new intellectual collaborations and combinations.

The connection of differing ideas and people meant the first century of printing is recognized for "intellectual ferment" and by what Eisenstein writes was a "'somewhat wide-angled, unfocused scholarship'" (45). The new availability of different theories or opinions about the same topics led Eisenstein to conclude that the contribution a scientist like Copernicus was able to make was not that he produced a new theory, but rather he was "confronting the next generation with a problem to be solved rather than a solution to be learned" (223). Eisenstein saw printing lead to the quickening of science toward a "cognitive breakthrough of an unprecedented kind" (225). The Net is continuing and accelerating that advance. The lure of being able to produce numerous copies of books cheaply was that an author's words could be spread around the world. This proved to be powerful. Eisenstein quotes Maurice Gravier on the power the press presented to the Protestant reformers:

> *The theses . . . were said to be known throughout Germany in a fortnight and throughout Europe in a month . . . Printing was recognized as a new power and publicity came into its own. In doing for Luther what copyists had done*

> *for Wycliffe, the printing press transformed the field of communications and fathered an international revolt. It was a revolution. The advent of printing was an important precondition for the Protestant Reformation taken as a whole; for without it one could not implement a "priesthood of all believers." At the same time, however, the new medium also acted as a precipitant. It provided the "stroke of magic" by which an obscure theologian in Wittenberg managed to shake Saint Peter's throne (153–154).*

This idea is repeated by the English writer Daniel Defoe (1660–1732), whom Eisenstein quotes: "The preaching of sermons is speaking to a few of mankind, printing books is talking to the whole world" (157). The Net has opened up a channel for "talking to the whole world" to an even wider set of people than did printed books. A social role which grew to be crucial in this new world of printing was that of the master printer. His was the business of running a print shop, and finding and promoting potential authors. In the course of this work his workshop became a center of intellectual excitement. Eisenstein explains that the master printer's "workshop became a veritable cultural center attracting local literati and celebrated foreigners, providing both a meeting place and message center for an expanding Commonwealth of Learning" (25).

This development of an intellectual family started to bring the world closer together. "In the late sixteenth century," Eisenstein maintains, "for the first time in the history of any civilization, the concept of a *Concordia Mundi* was being developed on a truly global scale and the 'family of man' was being extended to encompass all the peoples of the world" (182). The hospitality which the printers provided to travelers and intellectuals helped to make this happen.

The Net continues in this tradition of uniting the world. It is easy to hold conversations and develop relationships with others from around the world. The Net speeds this interaction as the conversation is brought from the print shop into a Netizen's home. A major advancement which the personal computer and the Net make possible is accessibility of publishing. Anyone who owns a personal computer can develop and print his or her own books, pamphlets, signs, and so forth. The Net comes in to help with distribution.

Eisenstein talks about one result that standardization of printing brought about. "[O]ne might consider," she writes, "the emergence of a new sense of individualism as a by-product of the new forms of standardization. The more standardized the type, indeed, the more compelling the sense of an idiosyncratic personal self" (56). Similarly, because Usenet and mailing lists only present people via their ideas and writing styles, people have to write the way they want themselves to be viewed. Thus people develop their own styles. Reading posts can therefore at times be an enjoyable experience. A famous cartoon printed in the *New Yorker* magazine in 1993 shows a dog at a computer. He says to another dog, "On the Internet, no one knows you're a dog." In fact, no one knows if you are white or black, yellow or purple, ugly or beautiful, short or tall. Discrimination based on appearance and visual impressions loses its basis. People can still be verbally harassed if they act stupid, or prove unhelpful to the Net. One problem, however, which has not yet been solved is harassment based on user name. For example, users with names that are clearly identifiable as women's names still receive unwanted attention and sometimes harassment.

The printing revolution affected both tool making and symbol manipulation, which led to new ways of thinking. As Eisenstein notes, "The decisions made by early printers, however, directly affected both tool making and symbol making. Their products reshaped powers to manipulate objects, to perceive and think about varied phenomena" (64). Computers, too, are in general directly affecting tool production and symbol manipulation. The tools on the Net are new tools—and thus lead to radical ways of thinking and dealing with information. People's thought processes can expand and develop in original ways. New ways of manipulating information, such as Unix tools, hypertext media, and search engines for searching distributed data sources foster new means of intellectual activity.

Printing made consultation of various texts much easier—no longer did someone have to be a "Wandering Scholar" to gain access to a variety of information. With the development of the Net, information access becomes much more varied and widespread.

The local public library, along with libraries around the world, other data banks, and knowledgeable people, are becoming accessible via the Net to many people online even from their homes. Only a few libraries currently offer electronic access to any of the actual texts of their holdings, but that is rapidly changing. Undertakings such as Project Gutenberg and various digital library initiatives are trying to make library resources available from any computer hooked into the Net.

Both the printing revolution and the Net revolution have been a catalyst for increased intellectual activity. Such activity tends to provide pressure for more democracy. When people have the chance and the means to start thinking, ideas of self-rule appear. Eisenstein describes how "Puritan tradesmen who had learned to talk to God in the presence of their apprentices, wives, and children were already on their way to self government" (167). Many social and political questions are being discussed on Usenet newsgroups especially questions which affect the Net directly, such as censorship and Net access. Based on these discussions, Netizens are exerting pressure on their governments to form new democratic structures like the NTIA on-line conference.[4]

Mass production via printing makes it possible to have sufficient books so that everyone who wants a copy can borrow one from a library or buy one. Eisenstein presents Thomas Jefferson's view of this "democratizing aspect of the preservative powers of print which secured precious documents not by putting them under lock and key but by removing them from chests and duplicating them for all to see." According to Eisenstein, "The notion that valuable data could be preserved best by being made public, rather than being kept secret, ran counter to tradition, led to clashes with new censors, and was central both to early modern science and to Enlightenment thought."[5] The democratizing power and effect of the printing revolution, Eisenstein contends, is overlooked in most historical writings.[6]

With the advent of printing, the law was affected by the onset of the ability to duplicate numerous copies of a single document cheaply. People saw that this capability would be helpful in making the law available for the common person to read and understand, and therefore the common person would be able to watch carefully if it was administered fairly. John Liburne, a person who lived in England during the Stuart Monarchy, felt that legal documents should be freed from the confines of Latin and old French so that "every Freeman may reade it as well as the lawyers." People like him also held that knowledge which had been esoteric, "rare, and difficult," should be transformed into a form where it could be useful to all. Eisenstein also quotes Florio, who made translations and dictionaries in English. He symbolized the democratic possibilities of the printing press saying, "Learning cannot be too common and the commoner the better . . . Why but the vulgar should not know all" (165).

Legal decisions are now being made available on the Net so that anyone with a computer, modem, and net connection will have access to them. There are legal newsgroups on Usenet such as misc.legal where various laws are examined and discussed. This provides a helpful perspective for understanding the value of the Net. The culture that is characteristic of the Net supports the principle that knowledge and communication should be available openly for the rest of the world to use. There is a collective, communal, and democratic aspect of it, too. The simple fact of the matter is that every single person who is connected to the Net and has Usenet access can make a post to Netnews and everyone online can send electronic mail to any other person who is on line.[7]

The scribal tradition restricted who made the choice of what was copied to the Church or those who had substantial property. "As long as texts could be duplicated only by hand, perpetuation of the classical heritage rested precariously on the shifting requirements of local elites."[8] With the spread of the printing press, the monopoly of these elites was broken. Netnews is a similar advance over other mass media. In the 'traditional' forms of mass media, the content is decided by the national 'elites'. However, on Netnews there is no control over the whole and the content is contributed to by every person who is active on the Net.

Eisenstein compares this control by elites over what manuscripts were copied to the role of the printer and publisher who have it in their interest to unleash all sorts of books. Eisenstein writes:

> *The politics of censorship made [the printers] the natural opponents not only of church officials but also of lay bureaucrats, regulations and red tape. As independent agents, they supplied organs of publicity and covert support to a "third force" that was not affiliated with any one church or one state. This third force was, however, obviously affiliated with the interests of early modern capitalists (178).*

These publishers were "the natural enemy of narrow minds," (177) and "encouraged the adoption of a new ethos which was cosmopolitan, ecumenical, and tolerant without being secular, incredulous or necessarily Protestant ...." (178). The Net has offered a parallel encouragement by providing a new kind of public space separate from either commercial purposes or religious or political limitations or ideas.

The printing press provided a new way for people to challenge the status quo. Eisenstein asks the question, "Did printing at first serve prelates and patricians as a 'divine art,' or should one think of it rather as the 'poor man's friend'?" She answers it might have served in both roles (31).

We can pose the same question about the Net. Should one think about the Net as a 'poor man's friend'? If we think of the Net as an alternative to the current media of television, radio, newspapers, and magazines—the answer is yes. A small number of wealthy people can afford to own a segment of the mass media described above and control the content of that media, whereas the Net is controlled by the mass of people connected to it, so it is "the poor man's" version of the mass media.

The printing revolution fostered the spread of education. Books were used by apprentices and students to learn more than was offered by their teachers. The Net similarly makes multiple resources available for people interested in learning. People can access more information resources and, even more important, other people. This increased accessibility of people to each other means we can all gain and learn from the interests and knowledge of others, more so than from any single teacher.

The impact of the new print technology on science was enormous. Collaboration and cooperation over longer distances were made possible by the power of print. In particular, Eisenstein refers to the impact on the science of Astronomy. The change she sees happened within Copernicus's lifetime.

"Copernicus was not supplied, as Tycho's successors would be, with precisely recorded fresh data," she notes. "But he was supplied, as Regiomontanus's successor and Aldus Manutius's contemporary, with guidance to technical literature carefully culled from the best Renaissance Greek manuscript collections, and for the first time, made available outside library walls" (209).

The progress of science can be even faster because of the speed of communication afforded by the Net. Articles to be published in scientific journals are often available as electronic preprints—and thus have wider distribution earlier than was the norm before the Net. An outstanding example of this increased speed of scientific activity occurred when researchers all over the world tried to reproduce the result of the two University of Utah researchers who had announced that they had achieved cold fusion. The newsgroup sci.physics.fusion was very quickly set up and researchers' questions, results and problems were posted regularly and feverishly. As a result, what might have taken years to retest and figure out was sorted out in a three- to four-month period. The physicists found the rapid exchange of data and results invigorating and encouraging and felt they were more productive and sharper in their work because of the Net. Also, they argued that the use of the Net saved much valuable research time that might have been wasted if the inaccurate claims had not been shown to have been faulty in such a short period of time and to such a wide body of scientists.

The invention of the printing press, which led to many developments not possible before the power of printing, "laid the basis for modern science . . . and remains indispensable for humanistic scholarship." Eisenstein poignantly claims that printing is responsible for "our museum without walls" (275). As a storehouse both of information, and of living information contained in other people, the Net could also be seen as a living "museum without walls." In her conclusion, Eisenstein states that "Cumulative processes were set in motion in the mid-fifteenth century, and they have not ceased to gather momentum in the age of the computer printout and the television guide" (276). We, too, are in an age of amazing changes in communications technologies, and it is important to realize how these changes are firmly based on the extension of the development of the printing press which took place in the fifteenth and sixteenth centuries.

NOTES

1. Elizabeth L. Eisenstein, *The Printing Revolution in Early Modern Europe* (Cambridge: Cambridge University Press, 1993), 78–79.
2. See Chapter 1 of this volume, "The Net and the Netizens."

3. Eisenstein, *Printing Revolution*, 74.
4. See Chapter 14 of this volume, "The Net and the Future of Politics."
5. Eisenstein, *Printing Revolution*, 81.
6. *Ibid.*, Chapter 1, "An Unacknowledged Revolution."
7. See Chapter 18 of this volume, "The Computer as a Democratizer."
8. Eisenstein, *Printing Revolution*, 125.

An earlier version of this chapter by Michael Hauben was posted to Usenet in Fall 1993.

17

"Arte": An Economic Perspective

The Role of "Arte" in the Production of Social Wealth

In communications, computing makes it possible to switch and route over 100 million long distance telephone calls per day.

NATIONAL RESEARCH COUNCIL, *COMPUTING THE FUTURE*

Can we expect, that a government will be well modelled by a people, who know not how to make a spinning-wheel, or to employ a loom to advantage?

DAVID HUME, "OF REFINEMENTS IN THE ARTS"

If computer-aided communication doubled the effectiveness of a man paid $16 per hour then, according to our estimate, it could be worth what it cost if it could be bought right now. Thus we have some basis for arguing that computer-aided communication is economically feasible.

J. C. R. LICKLIDER AND ROBERT TAYLOR
"THE COMPUTER AS A COMMUNICATION DEVICE"

Writing in the great French encyclopedia, Denis Diderot (1713–1784) pointed out the striking contradiction of modern society. Even though the wealth of society is produced by those who do the work of the society, they are the least respected, and the study of the mechanical arts, which is necessary to make work most productive, is treated with disdain and disrespect. Diderot describes this dilemma:

> *Place on one side of the balance the real benefits of the most exalted sciences and the most honored "arts" and on the other side those of the "mechanical arts," and you will find that the esteem granted to both has not been distributed in the correct proportion of these benefits; and that people praised much more highly those men who were engaged in making us believe that we were happy, than those men actually engaged in doing so. What odd judgments we make! We demand that people be usefully employed and we scorn useful men.*[1]

There is a similar tendency in our times, 250 years after Diderot wrote, to dismiss the study of the mechanical arts rather than encourage it. For example, in a study produced in 1992 by the National Research Council, the increasing importance of computers and computing in the daily life of our society was documented.[2] Yet the study noted how the ratio of funding for computer science and engineering research has dropped by more than 20 percent since 1985.[3] Voices defending the social benefits of technological developments such as the computer and the global computer network it makes possible need to be part of the public debate. Instead, there are numerous articles, books, and journals that claim such developments are mainly harmful to society.[4] The social implications of new technological developments such as the computer and telecommunications networks are important and should not be dismissed as harmful as this literature implies. To gain some perspective on the principles at stake in this controversy, it is helpful to look back to early economic writers and their studies about the value to a society of "arte."

The seventeenth and eighteenth centuries were a period of profound social and economic change in Europe. This period was one of great transformation in the ability to produce the necessities and conveniences of life for a growing population. Accompanying this social transformation was a growing attention to the role that the mechanical arts, often referred to as "arte," play in production.

Concern with the question of "arte" was not new. Philosophers such as Plato and Aristotle had identified this concept, considering it something important to be studied. For Plato, as he explains in his dialogue "Protagoras," the mechanical arts were akin to a gift from the gods, the sole advantage that humans had in their struggle for survival against the rest of the animal kingdom. They were the essential element that gave people the ability to survive in a hostile world.

Plato tells the story of how the gods Prometheus and Epimetheus were charged with populating the world with living creatures. They created a variety of life, giving to each species an advantage to help it survive. By the time they came to create humans, they had exhausted the traits they could provide, "Man alone was naked and shoeless, and had neither bed nor arms of defense."[5] Prometheus, Plato explains, not knowing how else to be helpful to humans, "stole the mechanical arts from Hephaestus and Athene, and fire with them (they could neither have been acquired nor used without fire), and gave them to man."[6] Using this parable, Plato shows how only the mechanical arts, which differentiated humans from the rest of the animal kingdom, have made human life sustainable.

Aristotle demonstrates a similar high regard for "arte" which is defined as "scientific knowledge and the corresponding skill of how to produce something in accordance with that knowledge."[7] In the "Nicomachean Ethics," Aristotle distinguishes art from nature and explains that "Every art is concerned with bringing something into existence and to think by art is to investigate how to generate something . . . of which the [moving] principle is in the producer and not in the thing produced."[8] He goes on to explain that "arte" is concerned with things which do not have this [moving] or regenerating principle in themselves. "Arte" describes the production of things that nature does not create on her own. Hence "arte" requires the human creator and makes possible the manifold inventions not provided by nature.

Several British writers of the seventeenth and eighteenth centuries examined the role that "arte" or the mechanical arts play in production. The mechanical arts were necessary for the production of the food, clothing, and shelter needed to provide for a population that was moving from the land under feudalism into the towns and cities that would characterize the industrial revolution. The annual production of such food, clothing, shelter, and other necessities and conveniences of life was seen as one of the pressing concerns in this time of change.

Sir William Petty (1623–1687), who has been called "The Father of Political Economy," isolated four economic categories as being crucial for the production of social wealth. They were labor, land (that is, nature), "arte," and stock. Petty maintained that the two essential categories were labor and land, and that labor was the active element and nature the passive element. He wrote "Labor is the Father and active principle of wealth, as Lands are the Mother."[9] Though human beings could survive without "arte," Petty believed that "arte" was an important component of life, making it possible to produce more with less labor. "Art," he explains is "equall to the labour & skill of many in producing commodityes."[10]

In order to increase production, Petty saw only two alternatives. "People must either work harder or introduce labor saving processes." These labor saving processes, according to Petty, save the labor of many hands and provide more riches for society. "One man by Art may do as much work, as many without it."[11] He gives several examples: "viz. one Man with a Mill can grind as much Corn as twenty can pound in a Mortar; one Printer can make as many Copies, as a Hundred Men can write by hand; one Horse can carry upon Wheels, as much as Five upon their Backs; and, in a Boat, or upon ice, as Twenty. . . ."[12] For Petty, the choice facing society was to have "hands . . . laboring harder, or by the introducing the Compendium, and Facilitations of Art," to have a few workers doing the work of many.[13]

Petty refers to the example of Holland, which had the advantage of being able to use windmills instead of hand labor and, thereby, the "advantage [of] the labor of many thousand Hands is saved, forasmuch as a Mill made by one Man in half a year, will do as much Labor, as four Men for five years together."[14] Petty reasoned that the use of "arte" to save human labor was a continuing benefit to society. He demonstrated the long-term social advantage gained from "arte" over simple labor by an illustration:

> *For if by such Simple Labor, I could dig and prepare for Seed a hundred acres in a thousand days; suppose then, I spend a hundred days in studying a more compendious way, and in contriving Tools for the same purpose; but in all the hundred days dig nothing. . . .*

If he now needs only the remaining nine hundred days to dig two hundred acres of ground, "then," Petty concludes, "I say, that the Art which cost but one hundred days Invention is worth one Mans labor for ever because the new Art, and one Man, perform'd as much as two Men could have done without it."[15]

The social advantage of "arte," according to Petty, is that a large portion of the population is freed from having to produce the goods needed by society and thus is available for other important work, especially for scientific pursuits. The remaining people, Petty writes "may safely and without possible prejudice to the Commonwealth, be employed in Arts and Exercises of pleasure and ornament; the greatest whereof is the Improvement of natural knowledge."[16]

Petty's work is part of a body of economic literature written during the seventeenth and eighteenth centuries which set out to scientifically define "arte." In "'Art' and 'Ingenious Labour'," E. A. J. Johnson gathers several descriptions of "arte" and looks at what Petty and other seventeenth and eighteenth century economic commentators considered as the role of "arte" and the effect it has had on the development of society.[17]

David Hume (1711–1776), one of the economists Johnson discusses, echoes Plato's emphasis on the importance of "arte" in distinguishing human beings from other animals. "There is one fundamental difference between man and other animals," Hume wrote, ". . . Nature has 'endowed the former with a sublime celestial spirit, and having given him an affinity with superior beings, she allows not such noble faculties to lie lethargic or idle, but urges him by necessity to employ, on every emergence, his utmost art and industry'."[18]

In this sense "Art" is, according to Johnson, "an ennobling faculty, implanted by Nature, which separates man from the rest of the zoological world by making greater production possible."[19] Writers such as Petty and Hume saw "arte" as the ability to utilize science and technology to abridge labor, and thus as a wondrous faculty peculiar to humans.

Other literary figures, such as Daniel Defoe (1660–1731) in *Plan of the English Commerce* and writers of economic tracts such as *The Advantages of the East India Trade to England Consider'd* (1707), provide examples of the environmental and economic benefits which accompany the increased use of tools and machines to lessen the labor necessary for production. In Russia, Defoe explains, where "Labor was not assisted by Art" there was "no other Way to cut out a large Plank, but by felling a great Tree and then with a multitude of Hands and Axes hew away all the Sides of the Timber, till they reduc'd the middle to one large Plank." The Swedes or Prussians, on the other hand, Defoe observes, could "cut three or four, or more Planks of the like Size from one Tree by the Help of Saws and Saw Mills: The Consequence must be that the miserable Russian labour'd ten times as much as the other [the Swede or the Prussian] did, for the Same Money."[20] Not only does "arte" make it possible for more goods to be produced by less labor, but "arte" also makes it possible to produce more planks of lumber from each tree. When "arte" is used, fewer trees need to be cut down. And higher wages can be paid to those using the most modern technology as they produce more goods with less labor than do those who use backward production techniques.

John Cary, in *An Essay on the State of England in Relation to its Trade* (1695), observes that because of "arte" the price of many manufactured wares such as glass bottles, silk stockings, and sugar went down even though the wages of the workers were not cut. "But then the question will be, how this is done?" he asks, and he answers, "It proceeds from the Ingenuity of the Manufacturer, and the Improvements he makes in his ways of working, thus the Refiner of Sugars goes thro' that operation in a Month, which our Forefathers required four Months to effect." And "the Distillers draw more Spirits, and in less time . . . than those formerly did who taught them the Art."[21]

Cary lists other examples of how improvements in "arte" have led to changes in production that have increased the goods available to the population, though they cost less labor and so are cheaper. He writes:

> *The Glassmaker hath found a quicker way of making it out of things which cost him little or nothing; Silk Stockings are wove instead of knit; Tobacco is cut by Engines instead of Knives; Books are printed instead of written; . . . Lead is smelted by Wind-Furnaces, instead of blowing with Bellows; all which save the labor of many Hands, so the Wages of those employed need not be lessened.*[22]

Cary also observes that the price of goods has come down, even though their desirability has improved.[23] After showing how a similar trend has occurred in the Navigation trades, Cary concludes, "New Projections are every day set on foot to render making our Manufactures easy, which are made cheap. . .not by falling the Price of poor People's Labor." He shows how these advances lead to a general environment of improved methods of production.[24] And, he notes, these improvements not only lessen the number of laborers needed to do the work, but also make possible the payment of higher wages. According to these early economists, government has a role to play to support the development of technology. "It should therefore," writes Johnson, "be the duty of the state to increase 'art'."[25]

Understanding "arte" as the means of mechanical or scientific abridgment of labor, it is useful to look at the effect it has had on the life and health of society. Several essays written by David Hume consider the role "arte" plays in determining whether a society flourishes or decays, and thus whether the society can produce the wealth needed to support its people. Hume observes the correlation between a society's support for the mechanical arts and its political and intellectual achievements. "The same age," writes Hume, "which produces great philosophers and politicians, renowned generals and poets, usually abounds with skillful weavers and ship-carpenters."[26]

Hume maintains that a vibrant intellectual environment is the product, not the cause, of social support for mechanical invention and the mastery of mechanical techniques. "Another advantage of industry and of refinements in the mechanical arts, is, that . . . minds . . . being once aroused from their lethargy, and put into a fermentation, turn themselves on all sides and carry improvements into every art and science."[27] Thus attention to the mechanical arts stimulates ferment in all other intellectual areas.

Not only does the ferment stimulated by mechanical activity and invention lead to a renaissance in intellectual development, but it also affects sociability. Hume writes:

> *The more these refined arts advance, the more sociable men become: nor is it possible, that, when enriched with science, and possessed of a fund of conversation, they should be contented to remain in solitude, or live with their fellow citizens in that distant manner, which is peculiar to ignorant and*

> *barbarous nations. They flock into cities; love to receive and communicate knowledge; to show their wit or their breeding; their taste in conversation or living, in clothes or furniture.*[28]

This ferment leads to the development of social organizations. Hume explains:

> *Particular clubs and societies are everywhere formed: Both sexes meet in an easy and sociable manner: and the tempers of men, as well as their behavior, refine apace. So that, beside the improvements which they receive from knowledge and the liberal arts, it is impossible but they must feel an encrease of humanity, from the very habit of conversing together and contribute to each other's pleasure and entertainment.*[29]

He summarizes, "Thus *industry, knowledge,* and *humanity,* are linked together by an indissoluble chain. . . ."[30]

People personally benefit from the development of technology and industry; more importantly, however, a public benefit is achieved. Hume writes:

> *Laws, order, police, discipline; these can never be carried to any degree of perfection, before human reason has refined itself by exercise, and by an application to the more vulgar arts, at least, of commerce and manufacture. Can we expect, that a government will be well modelled by a people, who know not how to make a spinning-wheel, or to employ a loom to advantage?*[31]

Similarly, Hume connects bad government with ignorance of the mechanical arts, "Not to mention that all ignorant ages are infested with superstition, which throws the government off its bias, and disturbs men in the pursuit of their interest and happiness."[32] Furthermore, he relates the development of political liberty to the development of technology. "The liberties of England," Hume writes, "so far from decaying since the improvements in the arts, have never flourished so much as during that period."[33]

He finds a symbiotic relationship between the progress of the mechanical arts in a society and the possibility of good government. In societies that encourage the mechanical arts to develop, larger sections of the population have the time and know-how to fashion a more democratic and responsive government. Where technological development is discouraged, a greater part of the population has to spend all of its time producing for subsistence and has no time to devote to the oversight of the government.

Hume traces the evolution of government in England, attributing changes to the level of technological development of the nation's industry. He describes how the House of Commons in England evolved from the growth and expansion of industry:

> *The lower house is the support of our popular government; and all the world acknowledges, that it owed its chief influence and consideration to the increase of commerce, which threw such a balance of property into the hands of the commons. How inconsistent then is it to blame so violently a refinement in the arts [mechanical arts], and to represent it as the bane of liberty and public spirit!*[34]

Hume's defense of technology against its detractors has a familiar ring. His writings provide a foundation for a critique of those who dismiss the benefits of the computer because of a supposed loss of privacy or supposed increase in the potential for government control over the lives of its citizens. Hume's writings provide a theoretical basis to challenge any efforts to blame the computer for such problems and instead point an arrow to the democratic achievements of the last part of the twentieth century that are the result of computer technology.

One of the most exciting of these achievements is the development of Usenet, the worldwide computer conferencing news network that makes possible democratic and uncensored debate and communication on thousands of subjects for computer users around the world. Hume's observation that "arte" leads to intellectual ferment and the possibility of a more democratic set of institutions is being demonstrated by the dramatic applications that have developed as a result of the widespread use of computer technology.

Writing in the eighteenth century, Hume described the intellectual ferment that accompanied the development of technology. Hume's observations provide a helpful perspective to use to view the phenomenal growth of technological achievements such as Usenet. This intellectual ferment is the needed support for the development of technology, and the development of technology makes possible political and social changes that are required to have the technology function. The study of economic writers of the seventeenth and eighteenth centuries who discuss the importance of "arte" provides a helpful theoretical foundation for assessing the significance of such practical developments for our times.

NOTES

1. "Art," in *The Encyclopedia: Selections*, Stephen J. Gendzier, ed. and trans, (New York: Harper and Row, 1967), 60. A modern example of such "arte" is provided by Carl Malamud. Describing a way of cutting logs in Finland, he writes: "The system takes raw timber and figures out the most efficient way to saw up the log to produce the most lumber. In an economy where 30 to 40 percent of GNP is

based on forestry, this system proved quite popular (*Exploring the Internet* (Englewood, N.J.: Prentice Hall, 1992), 100.)"The French title of the encyclopedia is *Encyclopedie ou Dictionnaire raisonne des sciences, des arts, et des metiers*. It was first published in France between 1751 and 1772.

2. *Computing the Future*, Juris Hartmanis and Herbert Lin, ed. (Washington, D.C.: National Academy Press, 1992): 13–16.
3. *Ibid.*, p. 3.
4. See, for example, Bob Ickes, "Die, Computer, Die," *New York Magazine*, July 24, 1995, 22–26. For references to some of this literature see "Questioning Technology,"*The Whole Earth Review* (Winter 1991).
5. "Protagoras," in *The Works of Plato*, Vol. I (Philadelphia, Penn.: The Franklin Library, 1979), 81.
6. *Ibid.*
7. *Aristotle: Selected Works*, Hippocrates G. Apostle and Lloyd P. Gerson, trans. (Grinnel, Iowa: Peripatetic Press, 1986), 676.
8. "Nicomachean Ethics," in *Aristotle, Selected Works*, 1140a lines 6–23.
9. "A Treatise of Taxes and Contributions," in *The Economic Writings of Sir William Petty*, Vol. 1, Charles Hull, ed. (Cambridge: C. J. Clay and Sons, 1899), 68.
10. "An Explication of Trade and Its Increase," in William Petty, *Petty Papers*, Vol. 1 (London: Constable & Company, Ltd., 1927), 211.
11. "Political Arithmetick," *Economic Writings*, Vol. 1, 249.
12. *Ibid.*, 249-250.
13. "Verbum Sapienti," *Economic Writings*, Vol. 1, 118.
14. "Political Arithmetick," *Economic Writings*, Vol. 1, 256.
15. "The Political Anatomy of Ireland," *Economic Writings*, Vol. 1, 182.
16. "Political Arithmetick," *Economic Writings*, Vol. 1, 270–271.
17. "'Art' and 'Ingenious Labour'" is a chapter in E.A.J. Johnson, *Predecessors of Adam Smith* (New York: Augustus Kelley, 1960). Reprint of 1937 edition.
18. *Predecessors of Adam Smith*, 264.
19. *Ibid.*
20. Daniel Defoe, *A Plan of the English Commerce Being a Compleat Prospect of the Trade of this Nation, as well the Home Trade as the Foreign*, 2d edition (New York: A. M. Kelley, 1967), 36. Reprint of 1730 edition.
21. John Cary, "An Essay on the State of England, in Relation to Its Trade, Its Poor and Its Taxes, for Carrying on the Present War Against France" (Bristoll: W. Bonny, 1695), 145–146.
22. *Ibid.*, 146.
23. *Ibid.* Cary writes:

    The variety of our Woollen Manufactures is so pretty, that Fashion makes a thing worth both at Home and Abroad twice the Price it is sold for. . . . Artificers by Tools and Laves fitted for different Uses make such things as would puzzle a Stander by to set a price on according to the worth of Men's Labor; the Plummer by new Inventions casts a Tun of Shott for Ten Shillings, which an indifferent Person could not guess worth less than Fifty.

24. *Ibid.*, 147–148. Cary writes:

    Pits are drained and Land made Healthy by Engines and Aquaeducts instead of Hands; the Husbandman turns up his Soil with the Sallow, not digs it with his Spade; Sowes his Grain, not plants it; covers it with the Harrow, not with the Rake; brings home his Harvest with Carts, not on Horseback; and many other easy Methods are used both for improving of Land and raising its Product, which are obvious to the Eyes of Men versed therein, though do not come within the Compass of my present Thoughts.

25. *Ibid.*, 266.
26. "Of Refinement in the Arts," *Writings on Economics*, 22. These essays are from *Political Discourses* (Edinburgh, 1752). Several of the essays have been reprinted in D. Hume, *Writings on Economics*, E. Rotwein, ed.. (Madison: University of Wisconsin Press, 1970). Reprint of 1955 edition.
27. *Ibid.*
28. *Ibid.*
29. *Ibid.*, 22–23.
30. *Ibid.*, 23.
31. *Ibid.*, 24.
32. *Ibid.*
33. *Ibid.*, 27. Hume explains

    If we consider the matter in a proper light, we shall find, that a progress in the arts is rather favourable to liberty, and has a natural tendency to preserve, if not produce a free government. In rude unpolished nations, where the arts are neglected, all labor is bestowed on the cultivation of the ground; and the whole society is divided into two classes, proprietors of land, and their vassals or tenants. The latter are necessarily dependent and fitted for slavery and subjection; especially where they possess no riches, and are not valued for their knowledge in agriculture; as must always be the case where the arts [mechanical arts] are neglected (page 28).

    He also observes that in a land based society, tyranny is the norm, writing,

    The former naturally erect themselves into petty tyrants; and must either submit to an absolute master, for the sake of peace and order; or if they will preserve their independency, like the ancient barons, they must fall into feuds and contests among themselves, and throw the whole society into such confusion, as is perhaps worse than the most despotic government.

34. *Ibid.*, 29.

An early version of this chapter by Ronda Hauben was posted on Usenet in Spring 1992. It was published in the *Amateur Computerist Supplement*, Fall 1992.

18

The Computer as a Democratizer

. . . only through diversity of opinion is there, in the existing state of human intellect, a chance of fair play to all sides of the truth.

JOHN STUART MILL, "ON LIBERTY"

In a very real sense, Usenet is a marketplace of ideas.

BART ANDERSON, BRYAN COSTALES, AND
HARRY HENDERSON, *UNIX COMMUNICATIONS*

Political thought has developed as writers presented the theoretical basis behind the various class structures from aristocracy to democracy. Plato wrote of the rule of the elite Guardians. Thomas Paine wrote about why people need to control their governments. The computer and the Net connect to this democratizing trend through facilitating wider communications from individual citizens to the whole body of citizens.

James Mill (1773–1836), the Scottish philosopher and father of John Stuart Mill, took a look at the principles of democratic government in his article "Liberty of the Press," in the *Supplement to the Encyclopedia Britannica* (1825). He wrote about the question of a government that works as it should—for the advantage and gain of the people instead of for the advantage and gain for those in control. Mill saw that government will be corrupted if the chance exists. Those in the position to rule would abuse their power for their own advantage. Mill felt, "If one man saw that he might promote misrule for his own advantage, so would another; so, of course would they all."[1] Mill believed that people needed a check on those in government. People need to keep watch on their government to make sure that it is working in the interest of the many. This led Mill to conclude that there is a crucial need for a press to watchdog over government. "There can be no adequate check without the freedom of the press," he wrote. "The evidence of this is irresistible."[2]

What Mill often phrased as freedom of the press, or liberty of the press, is more precisely defined as an uncensored press. An uncensored press provides for the dissemination of information that allows the reader or thinker to do two things. First, a person can size up an issue and honestly decide his or her own position. Second, as the press is uncensored, this person can make his or her distinctive contribution available for other people to consider and appreciate. Thus what Mill calls "freedom of the press" makes possible the free flow and exchange of different ideas.

Thomas Paine, in *The Rights of Man*, describes a fundamental principle of democracy. Paine writes, "that the right of altering the government was a national right, and not a right of the government."[3] Mill also expresses that active participation by the populace is a necessary principle of democracy.

> *Unless a door is left open to resistance of the government, in the largest sense of the word, the doctrine of passive obedience is adopted; and the consequence is, the universal prevalence of misgovernment, ensuring the misery and degradation of the people.* [4]

Another principle to which Mill links democracy is the right of the people to define who can responsibly represent their will. However, this right requires information to make a proper decision. Mill declares:

> *We may then ask, if there are any possible means by which the people can make a good choice, besides* liberty of the press? *The very foundation of a good choice is knowledge. The fuller and more perfect the knowledge, the better the chance, where all sinister interest is absent, of a good choice. How can the people receive the most perfect knowledge relative to the characters of those who present themselves to their choice, but by information conveyed freely, and without reserve, from one to another?*[5]

Without information being available to them, the people may elect candidates as bad as or worse than the incumbents. Therefore there is a need to prevent government from censoring the information available to people. Mill explains:

> *If it is in the power of their rulers to permit one person and forbid another, the people may be sure that a false report,—a report calculated to make them believe that they are well governed, when they are ill governed, will be often presented to them.*[6]

After electing their representatives, democracy gives the public the right to evaluate those in office. The public continually needs accurate information as to how their representatives are fulfilling their role. Once these representatives have abused their power, the principles established by Paine and Mill require that the public have the ability to replace those abusers. Mill also clarifies that free use of the means of communication is an extremely important principle in order for democratic government to exist:

> *That an accurate report of what is done by each of the representatives, a transcript of his speeches, and a statement of his propositions and votes, is necessary to be laid before the people, to enable them to judge of his conduct, nobody, we presume, will deny. This requires the use of the cheapest means of communication, and, we add, the free use of those means. Unless every man has the liberty of publishing the proceedings of the Legislative Assembly, the people can have no security that they are fairly published.*[7]

Paine calls ignorance the absence of knowledge and says that man with knowledge cannot be returned to a state of ignorance.[8] Mill shows how the knowledge man thirsts after leads to a communal feeling. General conformity of opinion seeds resistance against misgovernment. Both conformity of opinion and resistance require general information or knowledge. Mill explains:

> *In all countries people either have a power legally and peaceably of removing their governors, or they have not that power. If they have not that power, they can only obtain very considerable ameliorations of their governments by resistance, by applying physical force to their rulers, or, at least, by threats so likely to be followed by performance, as may frighten their rulers into compliance. But resistance, to have this effect, must be general. To be general, it must spring from a general conformity of opinion, and a general knowledge of that conformity. How is this effect to be produced, but by some means, fully enjoyed by the people of communicating their sentiments to one another? Unless the people can all meet in general assembly, there is no other means, known to the world, of attaining this object, to be compared with freedom of the press.*[9]

Mill champions freedom of the press as a realistic alternative to Rousseau's general assembly, which is not possible most of the time. Mill expands on the freedom of the press by establishing the criteria that an opinion cannot be well-founded until its converse is also present. Here he sets forth the importance of arriving at the truth from among the opinions that exist. Mill writes:

> *We have then arrived at the following important conclusions,—that there is no safety to the people in allowing anybody to choose opinions for them; that there are no marks by which it can be decided beforehand, what opinions are true and what are false; that there must, therefore, be equal freedom of declaring all opinions both true and false; and that, when all opinions, true and false, are equally declared, the assent of the greater number, when their*

> *interests are not opposed to them, may always be expected to be given to the true. These principles, the foundation of which appears to be impregnable, suffice for the speedy determination of every practical question.* [10]

The technology of the personal computer, of international computer networks, and of other recent contributions embodies and makes it feasible to implement James Mill's theory of liberty of the press. The personal computer makes it affordable for most people to have an information access and broadcast station in their very own home. The international computer networks that exist make it possible for people to have debates with others around the world, to search for data in various data banks, and to allow people to post an opinion or criticism for the whole world to see.

If a person is affiliated with a university community, works at a business which pays to connect to the Internet, is connected to a community network or Free-Net, or pays a fee to a commercial access provider, he or she can connect to an internetwork of computer networks around the world. A connection to this international network empowers a person by giving him or her access to e-mail, Usenet news, and perhaps ftp and telnet capabilities. E-mail makes it possible to send and receive messages electronically to and from anyone around the world who has an electronic mail box. Usenet is the public message and news posting system that allows its users to be part of worldwide debates and discussions.[11] These systems begin to make possible some of the activity James Mill saw as necessary for democracy to function.

The importance of Usenet also lies in that it is an improvement in communications technology from that of previous means of telecommunications. The predecessors to computer networks were the ham radio and Citizen Band radio (CB). The computer network is an advance in that it is easier to store, reproduce, and utilize the communications. It is easier to continue a prolonged question and answer session or debate. The newsgroups on Usenet have a distribution designation which allows them to be available to a variety of areas—local, city, national, or international. This allows for the person posting the message to determine how broadly or narrowly it will be available. The problem with the Internet is that, in a sense, it is only open to those who either have it provided to them by a university or company that they are affiliated with, or who pay for it. This limits part of the current development of the computer networks. Until free or very low cost access is universally available, the Net will fall short of its potential.

An example of a step toward universally available and affordable access is the community computing system called Free-Net in Cleveland, Ohio. Cleveland Free-Net is operated by Case Western Reserve University as a community service.[12] Anyone with a personal computer and a modem can call a local phone number to connect to the Free-Net without charge except for the phone call. If members of the public do not own computers, they can use the Free-Net at some branches of the Cleveland Public Library. Cleveland Free-Net provides free access to Usenet and a variety of community information and local discussion forums. Cleveland Free-Net is just one example of the community computer networks that are becoming much more readily available to broad sectors of society. As part of its newsgroups and discussion forums Cleveland Free-Net offers Supreme Court decisions, discussion of political issues and candidates, and debate over questions of law. Free-Nets like the one in Cleveland demonstrate that it is now possible to meet more of Mill's requirements for democracy, which include the "use of the cheapest means of communication, and, we add, the free use of those means."[13]

This is an exciting time because the democratic ideas of some great political thinkers are becoming practical. James Mill wrote that for government to serve the people, it must be watched over by the people utilizing an uncensored press. Freedom of the press also makes possible the debate necessary for people to form well founded opinions. Usenet and Cleveland Free-Net are contemporary examples of the uncensored accessible press required by Mill for good government to exist. These networks are also the result of hard work by many people aspiring for more democracy. However, to keep these forms developing and spreading requires constant work from those dedicated to the hard fight for democracy.

NOTES

1. James Mill, "Liberty of the Press," in *Essays on Government, Jurisprudence, Liberty of the Press, and Law of Nations* (New York: Augustus Kelley, New York, 1967), 20. Reprint.
2. *Ibid.*, 18.
3. Thomas Paine, "The Rights of Man" in *Two Classics of the French Revolution* (New York, Doubleday, 1989) 341.
4. Mill, "Liberty of the Press," 13–14.
5. *Ibid.*, 19.
6. *Ibid.*, 20.
7. *Ibid.*
8. Paine, "The Rights of Man," 357.
9. Mill, "Liberty of the Press," 18.
10. *Ibid.*, 23.
11. The Usenet newsgroup discussions are very active and provide a source of information that makes it possible to meet James Mill's criteria for both more oversight over government and a more informed population. In a sense, what was

once impossible is now possible: everyone's letter to the editor is published. What is important is that Usenet is conducted publicly and is mostly uncensored. This means that everyone can both contribute and gain from everyone else's opinion.

12. See for example, Beverly T. Watkins, "Freenet helps Case Western Fulfill Its Community-Service Mission," *Chronicle of Higher Education*, April 29, 1992, A21.
13. Mill, "Liberty of the Press," 20.

An early version of this chapter by Michael Hauben was posted in Usenet in Spring 1992. It was published in the *Amateur Computerist Supplement,* Fall 1992.

Glossary of Acronyms

AFIPS	American Federation of Information Processing Societies
ANS	Advanced Networks and Services
ARPA	Advanced Research Projects Agency
ARPANET	Advanced Research Projects Agency Network
AT&T	American Telephone and Telegraph Company
AUP	Acceptable Use Policy
BASIC	Beginners All Purpose Symbolic Instruction Code
BBN	Bolt Beranek and Newman
BBS	Bulletin Board System
Berknet	Berkeley Network
BESYS	Bell Operating System
BIS	Business Information Systems
BITnet	Because It's Time Network
BRL	Ballistics Research Laboratory
BSD	Berkeley Systems Distribution of Unix
BTL	Bell Telephone Laboratories
CBI	Charles Babbage Institute
CCC	Computer Chess Competition
CCR	Command and Control Research
CPU	Central Processing Unit
CS	Computer Science
CSnet	Computer Science Network (later Computer and Science Network)
CTSS	Compatible Time-Sharing System
DEC	Digital Equipment Corporation
DEL	Decode–Encode Language
DOD	United States Department of Defense
E-mail	Electronic Mail
EUUG	European Unix Users Group
FA	From ARPANET
FJCC	Fall Joint Computer Conference (AFIPS)
FIDOnet	FIDO Bulletin Board System Network
Free-Net	Free access community Network
ftp	File Transfer Protocol
GE	General Electric Corporation
GECOS	General Electric Comprehensive Operating System

honeydanber	Peter Honeyman, David A. Nowitz, and Brian E. Redman's version of uucp
IAB	Internet Activities Board
IBM	International Business Machines Corporation
IETF	Internet Engineering Task Force
IMP	Interface Message Processor
INWG	International Network Working Group
IPTO	Information Processing Technology Office
IRC	Internet Relay Chat
JCL	Job Control Language
K–12 Net	Kindergarten to Twelfth Grade Network
MAC	Machine-Aided Cognition, Multi-Access Computer
MC	Mathematisch Centrum (Amsterdam, the Netherlands)
MERIT	Michigan Education Research Instruction Triad
MILNET	Military Network
MIT	Massachusetts Institute of Technology
MOO	MUD, Object-Oriented
MUD	Multi-User Dungeon
MULTICS	Multiplexed Information and Computing Service
MUSH	Multi-User Shared Hallucinations
NAC	Network Analysis Corporation
NCP	Network Control Program *or* Network Control Protocol
Netiquette	Network users etiquette
Netnews	Network News
NII	National Information Infrastructure
NNTP	Network News Transfer Protocol
NREN	National Education and Research Network
NSF	National Science Foundation
NSFnet	National Science Foundation Network
NTIA	National Telecommunications Information Administration
NWG	Network Working Group
NYPSC	New York Public Service Commission
OIG	Office of the Inspector General
PWB	Programmer's Workbench
RFC	Request For Comment
RFP	Request For Proposal
RFQ	Request For Quotation
RJE	Remote Job Entry
RLE	Research Laboratory of Electronics
SDC	System Development Corporation

SJCC	Spring Joint Computer Conference (AFIPS)
SRI	Stanford Research Institute
TCP/IP	Transmission Control Protocol/Internet Protocol
TIP	Terminal IMP
UCB	University of California at Berkeley
UCLA	University of California at Los Angeles
UCSD	University of California at San Diego
UCSB	University of California at Santa Barbara
UNC	University of North Carolina
UNSW	University of New South Wales, Australia
Usenet	Users network
USG	Unix Support Group
uucp	Unix to Unix copy
V6	Version 6 (Unix)
V7	Version 7 (Unix)
VMSnet	Virtual Memory System Network
WWW	World Wide Web

References

Aboba, Bernard. *The Online User's Encyclopedia: Bulletin Boards and Beyond.* Reading, Mass. Addison-Wesley, 1993.

Abramson, Jeffrey B. "Electronic Town Meetings: Proposals for Democracy's Future." Paper presented at Aspen Institute Communications and Society Program, Washington, D.C.

Aizu, Izumi. *Cultural Impact on Network Evolution in Japan: Emergence Of Netizens.* Tokyo. Institute for HyperNetwork Society, 1995. http://www.glocom.ac.jp/Publications/Aizu/nete&c.html

Anderson, Bart, Bryan Costales, and Harry Henderson. *UNIX Communications.* 2d ed. Carmel, Ind. SAMS, 1991.

Anderson, Robert H., Tora K. Bikson, Sally Ann Law, and Bridger M. Mitchell. *Universal Access to E-mail: Feasibility and Societal Implications.* Santa Monica, Calif. Rand Corporation, 1995.

Aristotle. *Aristotle: Selected Works.* Translated by Hippocrates G. Apostle and Lloyd P. Gerson. Grinnel, Iowa. Peripatetic Press, 1982.

ARPANET Completion Report Draft. Unpublished manuscript. September 9, 1977.

Banes, Sally. *Greenwich Village 1963: Avant-Garde Performance and the Effervescent Body.* Durham, N.C. Duke University Press, 1993.

Baran, Paul. *On Distributed Communications Networks.* Santa Monica, Calif. Rand Corporation, 1962.

———, Sharla P. Boehm, and Joseph W. Smith. *On Distributed Communications.* Vols. I–XI. Memorandum. Santa Monica, Calif. Rand Corporation, 1964.

Bellovin, Steve M., and Mark Horton. "USENET—A Distributed Decentralized News System." Unpublished manuscript. 1985.

Bernstein, Alex, and M. de V. Roberts. "Computer versus Chess-Player." *Scientific American* 198 (June 1958): 96–105.

Brooks, Jr., Frederick P. *The Mythical Man-Month: Essays on Software Engineering.* Reading, Mass. Addison-Wesley, 1975.

———. "No Silver Bullets." *Unix Review* (November 1987): 39–48.

Bush, Vannevar. "As We May Think." *The Atlantic Monthly* 176 (July 1945): 101–108.

Cary, John. *An Essay on the State of England, in Relation to Its Trade, Its Poor and Its Taxes, for Carrying on the Present War Against France.* Bristoll, W. Bonny, 1695.

Cerf, Vinton G. "An Assessment of ARPANET Protocols." Palo Alto, Calif. Infotech Education Ltd. Stanford University, (nd).

———. "Requiem for the ARPANET." In Tracy L. LaQuey, *Users' Dictionary of Computer Networks*. Bedford, Mass. Digital Press, 1989.

Collyer, Geoff and Henry Spencer. "News Need Not Be Slow." *USENIX Conference Proceedings* (Winter 1987): 181–190.

Corbató, Fernando J. Interview by Arthur L. Norberg. 18 April 1989 and 14 November 1990. Tape recording. Charles Babbage Institute, Center for the History of Information Processing, University of Minnesota.

——— and Victor A. Vyssotsky. "Introduction and Overview of the Multics System." In *Proceedings–Fall Joint Computer Conference, AFIPS* 27. Part 1. 186–202. Washington, DC. Spartan Books, 1965.

———, Marjorie Merwin-Daggett, and Robert C. Daley. "An Experimental Time-Sharing System." In *Proceedings–Spring Joint Computer Conference, AFIPS* 21. 335–344. Palo Alto, Calif. National Press, 1962.

Crocker, Stephen. *RFC-3: Documentation Conventions.* April 3, 1968.

———. "The Origins of RFCs." In J. Reynolds and J. Postel. *RFC-1000: RFC Reference Guide.* 1987.

Daniel, Stephen, James Ellis, and Tom Truscott. "USENET—A General Access UNIX Network." Unpublished manuscript. Durham, N.C., Summer 1980.

Defoe, Daniel. *A Plan of the English Commerce Being a Compleat Prospect of the Trade of this Nation, as well the Home Trade as the Foreign.* 2d edition. New York. Augustus Kelly Publishers, 1967. Reprint of 1730 edition.

Diderot, Denis. *The Encyclopedia: Selections.* Edited and translated by Stephen J. Gendzier. New York. Harper & Row, 1967.

Dolotta, T. A., and J. R. Masey. "An Introduction to the Programmer's Workbench." In *Proceedings Second International Conference on Software Engineering.* 164–168. Long Beach, Calif. IEEE Computer Society Press, 1976.

———, R. C. Haight and J. R. Masey. "The Programmers Workbench." *Bell System Technical Journal* 57(6) Part 2 (July–August 1978): 2177–2200.

Eisenstein, Elizabeth L. *The Printing Revolution in Early Modern Europe.* Cambridge. Cambridge University Press, 1983.

Elias, Peter. "Twenty-Fifth Anniversary Project MAC Time Line." Chart. MIT Laboratory for Computer Science, 1988.

Fano, Robert M. *Transmission of Information.* Cambridge, Mass. and New York. The MIT Press and John Wiley & Sons, 1961.

———. Interview by Arthur L. Norberg. 20–21 April 1989. Tape recording. Charles Babbage Institute, Center for the History of Information Processing, University of Minnesota.

——— and Fernando Corbató . "Time-sharing on Computers." In *Information, A Scientific American Book*. San Francisco, Calif. W. H. Freeman, 1966. 76–95.

Federal Research Internet Coordinating Committee. "Program Plan for the National Research and Education Network." May 23, 1989.

Felton, William A., Gerald L. Miller and J. Michael Milner, "A Unix System Implementation for System/370." *AT&T Bell Laboratories Technical Journal* 63 (8) Part 2 (October 1984): 1751–1767.

Fitzsimon, Martha and Lawrence T. McGill. "The Citizen as Media Critic." *Media Studies Journal* 9 (Spring 1995): 91–101.

Geipel, Gary L., A. Tomasz Jarmoszko, and Seymour Goodman. "The Information Technologies and East European Societies." *East European Politics and Societies* 5 (Fall 1991): 394–438.

Glaser, E. L., J. F. Couleur, and G. A. Oliver. "System Design of a Computer for Time-Sharing Applications." In *Proceedings–Fall Joint Computer Conference, AFIPS* 27. Part 1. 197–202. Washington, D.C. Spartan Books, 1965.

Greenberger, Martin, ed. *Management and the Computer of the Future*. Cambridge, Mass. The MIT Press, 1962.

Haight, Dick. "Interview with Dick Haight" by Marc Rochkind. *Unix Review* (May 1986): 54–65.

Hall, Dennis E., Deborah K. Scherrer, and Joseph S. Sventek. "A Virtual Operating System." *Communications of the ACM* 23 (September 1980): 495–502.

Hauben, Michael. "Interview With Staff Member Michael Hauben on the Occasion of the 10th Anniversary of the Personal Computer." *Amateur Computerist* 4 (Winter/Spring 1992): 10–14.

———. "Common Sense: The Net and the Netizens." Parts 1, 2. *Amateur Computerist* 5 (Summer/Fall 1993): 11–13 and 6 (Fall/Winter 1994–1995): 22–35.

———, and Ronda Hauben. "The Netizens and the Wonderful World of the Net: On the History and the Impact of the Internet and Usenet News." Online manuscript. January 10, 1994. http://www.columbia.edu/~hauben/netbook/

Hauben, Ronda. "UNIX and Computer Science." *Amateur Computerist* 6 (Winter/Spring 1994–1995): 1–5. Unix issue.

Heart, Frank, Alexander A. McKenzie, John McQuillian, and David Walden. *ARPANET Completion Report*. Washington, D.C. DARPA and BBN, 1978.

Hugo, Victor. *Notre Dame of Paris*. Translated by John Sturrock. London. Penguin Books, 1978.

Hume, David. *Political Discourses*. Edinburgh. Printed by R. Fleming for A. Kinard and A. Donaldson, 1752.

———. *Writings on Economics*. Edited by Eugene Rotwein. Madison. University of Wisconsin Press, 1970.

Information, A Scientific American Book. San Francisco, Calif. W. H. Freeman, 1966.

Ingram, John Kelly. *A History of Political Economy*. 1888. Reprint. New York. Augustus Kelley Publishers, 1967.

In Memoriam: J. C. R. Licklider: 1915–1990. Palo Alto, Calif. Digital Systems Research Center, 1990. (URL http://memex.org/lick.html)

Internet Society. *Internet Society News* 2 (Spring 1993).

Ivie, Evan L. "The Programmer's Workbench—A Machine for Software Development." Unpublished report. AT&T Bell Laboratories, May 19, 1975.

———. "The Programmers Workbench—A Machine for Software Development." *Communications of the ACM* 20 (October 1977): 746–753.

Johnson, E. A. J. *Predecessors of Adam Smith: The Growth of British Economic Thought*. 1937. Reprint. New York. Augustus Kelley Publishers, 1960.

Johnson, Stephen C. "UNIX: The Language Forms." *USENIX Conference Proceedings*. (Winter 1987):16–20. El Cerrito, Calif. USENIX Association, 1987.

———, and Dennis. M. Ritchie. "Portability of C Programs and the UNIX System." *The Bell System Technical Journal* 57(6) Part 2 (July–August 1978): 2021–2048.

Johnstone, Ian, and Steve Rosenthal. "Unix on Big Iron." *UNIX Review* (October 1984): 22–26.

Kahin, Brian. "Commercialization of the Internet: Summary Report." November 1990. (Formerly online via ftp from world.std.com.)

Kemeny, John G. *Man and the Computer*. New York. Charles Scribner's Sons, 1972.

Kernighan, Brian W. "Program Design in the UNIX Environment." *AT&T Bell Laboratories Technical Journal* 63 (8) Part 2 (October 1984): 1595–1631.

———, and John R. Mashey. "The Unix Programming Environment." *Computer*. (April 1981): 12–24.

———, and Rob Pike. *The Unix Programming Environment*. Englewood Cliffs, N.J. Prentice-Hall, 1984.

———, and P. J. Plauger. *Software Tools*. Reading, Mass. Addison-Wesley, 1976.

Kleinrock, Leonard. "On Communications and Networks." *IEEE Transactions on Computers* C-25 (December 1976): 1320–1329.

Lasch, Christopher. "Journalism, Publicity, and the Lost Art of Argument." *Media Studies Journal* 9 (Winter 1995): 81–91.

———. *The Revolt of the Elites and the Betrayal of Democracy*. New York. W.W. Norton and Company, 1995.

Lee, John A. N., and Robert Rosin. "The Project MAC Interviews." *IEEE Annals of the History of Computing* 14 (2) (1992): 14–35.

———. "Claims to the Term Time-Sharing." *IEEE Annals of the History of Computing* 14 (1) (1992): 16–17.

Lesk, Michael. "Can UNIX Survive Secret Source Code?" *Computing Systems* 1 (Spring 1988): 189–199.

The Legacy of Norbert Wiener: A Centennial Symposium. Cambridge, Mass. MIT, 1994.

Licklider, J. C. R. Interview by William Aspray and Arthur L. Norberg. 28 October 1988. Tape recording. OH 150. Charles Babbage Institute, Center for the History of Information Processing, University of Minnesota.

———. "Man-Computer Symbiosis." *IRE Transactions on Human Factors in Electronics* HFE-1 (March 1960): 4–11. Reprinted in *In Memoriam: J. C. R. Licklider: 1915–1990*. 1–19. Palo Alto, Calif. Digital Systems Research Center, 1990. (URL http://memex.org/lick.html)

——— and Robert Taylor. "The Computer as a Communication Device." *Science and Technology: For the Technical Men in Management* 76 (April 1968): 21–31. Reprinted in *In Memoriam: J. C. R. Licklider: 1915–1990*. 21–41. Palo Alto, Calif. Digital Systems Research Center, 1990. (URL http://memex.org/lick.html)

——— and Albert Vezza. "Applications of Information Networks." *Proceedings of the IEEE* 66 (November 1978): 1330–1348.

Lions, John. *A Commentary on the UNIX Operating System*. Kensington: The University of New South Wales. (nd).

———. "Interview with John Lions" by Peter Ivanov. *UNIX Review* (October 1985): 50–58.

———. "Spreading UNIX around the World: An Interview with John Lions" by Ronda Hauben. *Amateur Computerist* 6 (Winter/Spring 1994–1995): 1, 5–7. Unix issue.

Malamud, Carl. *Exploring the Internet: A Technical Travelogue*. Englewood Cliffs, N.J. Prentice-Hall, 1992.

Marill, Thomas and Lawrence G. Roberts. "Toward a Cooperative Network of Time-Shared Computers." *Proceedings–Fall Joint Computer Conference, AFIPS* 29. 425–431. Washington, D.C. Spartan Books, 1966.

McCarthy, John. "Information." In *Information, A Scientific American Book.* 1–16. San Francisco, Calif. W. H. Freeman, 1966.

———. "John McCarthy's 1959 Memorandum." *IEEE Annals of the History of Computing* 14 (1)(1992): 20–23.

McIlroy, M. Doug. "A Research UNIX Reader: Annotated Excerpts from the Programmer's Manual, 1971–1986." *Computing Science Technical Report* No. 139, AT&T Bell Laboratories, Murray Hill, N.J. June 1987.

———. "Unix on My Mind." *Proc. Virginia Computer Users Conference (Blacksburgh)* 21. 1–6. 1991.

———, Elliot N. Pinson, and Berkley A. Tague. "Foreword." *Bell System Technical Journal* 57 (6) Part 2 (July–August 1978): 1899–1904.

McKenzie, Alexander A. and David C. Walden. "ARPANET, the Defense Data Network, and Internet." In *The Encyclopedia of Telecommunications.* Vol 1. Edited by Fritz E. Froehlich, Allen Kent and Carolyn M. Hall. 341–376. New York. Marcel Dekker, 1991.

McKusick, Marshall Kirk. "A Berkeley Odyssey: Ten Years of BSD History." *Unix Review* 3 (January 1985): 30–44, 108–114.

Mill, James. *Essays on Government, Jurisprudence, Liberty of the Press and Law of Nations.* Reprint. New York. Augustus Kelley Publishers, 1986.

Mohr, August. "The Genesis Story." *Unix Review* 3 (January 1985): 18–28, 117.

Morgan, Lewis Henry. *Ancient Society or Researches in the Lines of Human Progress from Savagery through Barbarism to Civilization.* Chicago. Charles H. Kerr, 1877.

National Research Council. *Computing the Future: A Broader Agenda for Computer Science and Engineering.* Edited by Juris Hartmanis and Herbert Lin. Washington, DC. National Academy Press, 1992.

Office of the Inspector General. "Review of NSFNET." Washington, DC. National Science Foundation, March 23, 1993.

Paine, Thomas, "The Rights of Man," In *Two Classics of the French Revolution,* New York. Anchor Books, 1989.

Perlis, Alan J. *Introduction to Computer Science.* New York. Harper and Row, 1972.

Petty, Sir William. *The Economic Writings of Sir William Petty.* Edited by Charles Hull. London. 1899. Reprint. New York. Augustus Kelley Publishers, 1986.

———. *The Petty Papers.* Edited by the Marquis of Lansdowne. Cheswick Press. London. 1927.

Pierce, John R. "Communication." *Scientific American* 227 (September 1972): 31–41.

Plato. *Works of Plato.* Vol I. Philadelphia. The Franklin Library, 1979.

Pool, Ithiel de Sola. *Technologies Without Boundaries: On Telecommunications in a Global Age*. Edited by Eli M. Noam. Cambridge, Mass. Harvard University Press, 1990.

"Proceedings of the NTIA Virtual Conference." URL: http://ntiaunix2.ntia.doc.gov:70/11s/virtual/ or http://www.ntia.doc.gov/opadhome/virtual/

Quarterman, John S. *The Matrix: Computer Networks and Conferencing Systems Worldwide*. Bedford, Mass. Digital Press, 1990.

Ritchie, Dennis M. "The Development of the C Language." Paper presented at the Second History of Programming Languages Conference, Cambridge, Mass. April, 1993.

———. "The Evolution of the UNIX Time-Sharing System." *AT&T Bell Laboratories Technical Journal* 63 (8) Part 2 (October 1984): 1577–1593.

———. "UNIX: A Retrospective." *The Bell System Technical Journal* 57 (6) Part 2 (July–August 1978): 1947–1969.

——— and Ken Thompson. "The UNIX Time-Sharing System." *Communications of the ACM* 17 (July 1974): 365–375.

Roberts, Lawrence G. "The Evolution of Packet Switching." *Proceedings of the IEEE* 66 (November 1978): 1307–1313.

———. "The ARPANET and Computer Networks." In *A History of Personal Workstations*. Edited by Adele Goldberg. ACM Press. New York. 1988. 143–167.

———. Interview by Arthur L. Norberg. 4 April 1989. Tape recording. Charles Babbage Institute, The Center for the History of Information Processing, University of Minnesota.

Shannon, Claude E. "A Chess-Playing Machine." *Scientific American* 182 (February 1950): 48–51.

———. "The Mathematical Theory of Communication." Parts 1, 2. *Bell System Technical Journal* 27 (July 1948): 379–423 and (October 1948): 623–656.

Snow, C.R. "The Software Tools Project." *Software—Practice and Experience* 8 (September–October 1978): 585–599.

Spafford, Eugene. "USENET Software: History and Sources." Usenet newsgroup news.admin.misc.

Spencer, Henry. "Interview with Henry Spencer: On Usenet News and C News" by Ronda Hauben. *Amateur Computerist* 5 (Winter/Spring 1993-1994): 1–10.

Stefferud, Einar et al. "Quotes from Some of the Players." Compiled by Daniel P. Dern. *ConneXions—The Interoperability Report* 3 (October 1989): 15–26. Foster City, Calif. Interop Company.

Stone, Alan. *Wrong Number: The Breakup of AT&T*. New York. Basic Books, 1989.

Stoneback, John. "The Collegiate Community." *Unix Review* (October 1985) 24–27, 46–48.

Strachey, Christopher. "Time-sharing in Large Fast Computers," *Proc. Int'l. Conf. on Infomation Processing*. 336–341. Paris. UNESCO, 1960.

Strandh, Sigvard. *The History of the Machine*. 1979. Reprint. New York. Dorset Press, 1989.

Tague, Berkley. "Automating Telephone Support Operations: An Interview with Berkley Tague" by Ronda Hauben. *Amateur Computerist* 6 (Winter/Spring 1994–1995): 7–13. Unix issue.

Taylor, Robert W. Interview by William Aspray. 28 February 1989. Tape recording. Charles Babbage Institute, The Center for the History of Information Processing, University of Minnesota.

Thompson, Ken. "Unix Implementation." *The Bell System Technical Journal* 57 (6) Part 2 (July–August 1978): 1931–1946.

"Time-Sharing and Interactive Computing at MIT—Part 1: CTSS." *IEEE Annals of the History of Computing* 14 (1) 1992. Special issue.

"Time-Sharing and Interactive Computing at MIT—Part 2: Project MAC." *IEEE Annals of the History of Computing* 14 (2) 1992. Special issue.

Truscott, Tom. "Invitation to a General Access Unix Network." Unpublished leaflet. Durham, N.C. 1980.

"The UNIX System." *AT&T Bell Laboratories Technical Journal* 63 (8) Part 2 (October 1984). Special issue.

"UNIX Time-Sharing System." *The Bell System Technical Journal* 57 (6) Part 2 (July–August 1978). Special issue

Usenet History Archives. http://www.duke.edu/~mg/usenet/usenet.hist/

Volovic, Thomas S. "Encounters On-Line." *Media Studies Journal* 9 (Spring 1995): 113–121.

Vyssotsky, Victor. "Putting UNIX in Perspective: An Interview with Victor Vyssotsky" by N. Peirce. *Unix Review* 3 (January, 1985): 58–70, 102–106.

Watkins, Beverly T. "Freenet Helps Case Western Fulfill Its Community-Service Mission." *Chronicle of Higher Education*. April 29, 1992. A 21.

Wiener, Norbert. *Cybernetics: Or Control and Communication in the Animal and the Machine*. New York. The Technology Press. John Wiley and Sons, 1948.

———. *I Am A Mathematician: The Later Life of a Prodigy*. Cambridge, Mass. The MIT Press. 1956.

———. *God & Golem, Inc.: A Comment on Certain Points where Cybernetics Impinges on Religion*. Cambridge, Mass. The MIT Press, 1964.

———. *Collected Works of Norbert Wiener with Commentaries.* Vol 4. Edited by P. Masani. Cambridge, Mass. The MIT Press, 1985.

Woodbury, Gregory G. "Net Cultural Assumptions." *Amateur Computerist* 6 (Fall/Winter 1994–1995). 6–9.

Acknowledgments

The idea for this book grew out of two independent events in 1992. Ronda was on Usenet and was also studying some seventeenth and eighteenth century economic works that helped her realize that the Internet was a important development and that it would be good to have a book documenting it. At the same time, Michael was corresponding via e-mail with Phil Fleisher, then in Ottawa, who had read some of the early pieces we had written about the democratic impact of the Net. Phil suggested that there was a need for a collection of articles from various perspectives describing the important new advance made by the participatory global network. We continued doing research, posting drafts and then the completed articles. The interesting and helpful comments and discussion the articles received either online or via e-mail made it clear that it would be good to plan a collected edition in book form. We began the search for a publisher. By August 1993 we had approached a few publishers, only to be told that such a book was not on their list of planned books. We decided to go ahead and put the book together anyway. On January 10, 1994 we held a reading at Henry Ford Community College in Michigan and announced the ftp site where the book was available online.

Throughout this period, there were several people who helped keep alive our determination to have both online and print editions of the book available. Ron Newman stands out for helping us and others online realize how important it was to have a book about the history and impact of the Net. He encouraged us to maintain the book online and to continue to seek a publisher for the print edition. Steve Samuel offered to print a small run to distribute to local book stores to make the book available to those not yet on the Net. Another offer came from Ireland to make a LaTex version of the book once we had a final manuscript. We continued revising and looking for a publisher. Rob Scott, Tom Truscott, and Cal Woods read through the whole book at various stages in its development and provided suggestions. Cal Woods also formatted the first html edition of the online book, maintained an online edition, and helped edit chapter 16. Over a long period of time, Tom Truscott continued his support for documenting Usenet's history and made available important research materials. In May 1996 the IEEE Computer Society Press indicated that they would publish a print edition. Shumpei Kumon recognized the importance of the concept of netizen and helped to spread it, most recently by publishing a book in Japanese on "The Age of Netizens." Hiroyuki Takahashi also helped spread the understanding of the importance of the Net in Japan and provided a mirror for the Netizens netbook so that it would be more readily available in Japan. Hiroki Inoue, Kozo Inoue, and Miwa Goto translated the book into Japanese so that it could be considered for a Japanese print edition. Takashi Miki's efforts to make the book available in a Japanese print edition also served as an important source of support for the English print edition. Tom Van Vleck and Deborah Scherrer provided encouragement and support at crucial stages.

We also thank Henry Spencer, Berkley Tague, John Lions, Fernando Corbató, Chris Maltby, Greg Rose, Robert Fano, Vint Cerf, Timothy Murphy, Robert Elz, Piers Lauder, Alex McKenzie, Doug McIlroy, Teus Hagen, Mike Blake-Knox, Jaap Akkerhuis, Dik Winter, Jim McKie, Mark Horton, David Nowitz, Gregory Woodbury, Steve Daniel, Art Nicholaysen, Dima Gromov, William Bohl and other Net pioneers who either made it possible to do in-person or e-mail interviews or provided helpful background online.

Thanks for support in doing the needed research go also to Brad Garton, Newcomb Greenleaf, Stephen Unger, Yechiam Yemini, Rob Scott, Al Aho, and Alan Westin at Columbia University, and to Jefferi Holland, Dennis Underwood, N. Naraimhamurthi, and Bernard Galler at the University of Michigan.

William Rohler and Norman O. Thompson, editors of the *Amateur Computerist,* provided constant support and encouragement toward solving the day-to-day problems that often seemed insurmountable. A special expression of appreciation goes to Jay Hauben. He helped with the research, editing, and checking of sources. He put together the list of references and continually contributed, doing whatever was needed at all stages in the process. His continued perseverance was an important factor which helped make the book possible.

We thank our editor, Bill Sanders, production editor Lisa O'Conner, copyeditor Lynne Bush, and indexer Joyce Teague for all their work to make the book possible. The most important help, however, came from the many Netizens whose participation online and responses via e-mail made possible the broad-ranging discussion and views that are the foundation of this book. Unfortunately, it is not possible to thank all by name.

We alone take responsibility for the shortcomings of the work and welcome comments from readers and others interested in these subjects. We hope the rich process that has helped give birth to this work will be further encouraged by this print publication. The book, along with related source materials, will continue to be available online at: http://computer.org/books/

Ronda Hauben
Michael Hauben
netizens@computer.org

Index

Proposed Declaration of the Rights of Netizens

We Netizens have begun to put together a Declaration of the Rights of Netizens and are requesting from other Netizens contributions, ideas, and suggestions of what rights should be included. Following are some beginning ideas.

The Declaration of the Rights of Netizens

In recognition that the Net represents a revolution in human communications that was built by a cooperative non-commercial process, the following Declaration of the Rights of the Netizen is presented for Netizen comment.

As Netizens are those who take responsibility and care for the Net, the following are proposed to be their rights:

- Universal access at no or low cost
- Freedom of Electronic Expression to promote the exchange of knowledge without fear of reprisal
- Uncensored Expression
- Access to Broad Distribution
- Universal and Equal access to knowledge and information
- Consideration of one's ideas on their merits
- No limitation to access to read, to post and to otherwise contribute
- Equal quality of connection
- Equal time of connection
- No Official Spokesperson
- Uphold the public grassroots purpose and participation
- Volunteer Contribution—no personal profit from the contribution freely given by others
- Protection of the public purpose from those who would use it for their private and money making purposes

The Net is not a Service, it is a Right. It is only valuable when it is collective and universal. Volunteer effort protects the intellectual and technological common-wealth that is being created. DO NOT UNDERESTIMATE THE POWER OF THE NET and NETIZENS.

Inspiration from: RFC 3 (1969), Thomas Paine, *Declaration of Independence* (1776), *Declaration of the Rights of Man and of the Citizen* (1789), NSF Acceptable Use Policy, Jean Jacques Rousseau, and the current cry for democracy worldwide.